Mozart
The golden years

H. C. ROBBINS LANDON

Mozart
The golden years
1781 – 1791

with 215 illustrations,
32 in colour

THAMES AND HUDSON

To Christopher Raeburn

IN FOND RECOLLECTION OF RESEARCH TRIPS TOGETHER TO
DONAUESCHINGEN (1957) AND PRAGUE (1959)

FRONTISPIECE *Wolfgang Amadeus Mozart, plaster medallion by L. Posch, 1788–9, displayed in Salzburg in the house in which the composer was born; height 8·2 cm.*

ABOVE *Vignette from the title page of Haydn's Piano Trio no. 23 in E flat (XV:10), published by Artaria & Co. in 1798 as 'Oeuvre 80'.*

© 1989 H. C. Robbins Landon
Reprinted, with minor revisions, 1990

Printed and bound in Spain by Artes Gráficas Toledo, S.A.
D.L.TO.: 265–1990

Contents

Introduction

*All art is at once surface and symbol. Those who go beneath the surface do so at
their peril. Those who read the symbol do so at their peril.*
Oscar Wilde, Preface to *Dorian Gray*

IT HAS BEEN many years since the two standard Mozart biographies were
published: (1) that by Hermann Abert (Leipzig 1919), which reached its
6th edition in 1922; and (2) that by T. de Wyzewa and G. de Saint-Foix, a five-
volume undertaking (Paris 1912–46), of which the last three were by Saint-
Foix alone. Abert was never translated into English or French, and Wyzewa/
Saint-Foix never into German or English. Since these massive publications
appeared, Mozart scholarship has advanced in all sorts of directions, but by
far the most important events since World War II have been: (1) the
publication, now nearly complete, of a new critical edition of all Mozart's
music, the *Neue Mozart-Ausgabe* (*NMA*), supplanting the old *Gesamtausgabe*
issued by Breitkopf & Härtel in Leipzig in the third quarter of the nineteenth
century; (2) the publication, as part of the *NMA*, of all the known letters
written by Mozart and his immediate family, their documents, together with a
volume of contemporary pictures – portraits, topographical views, etc. (O.E.
Deutsch, with collaborators, notably J.H. Eibl); and (3) the continuing
publication of the *Mozart-Jahrbuch* (together with the *Mitteilungen der
Internationalen Stiftung Mozarteum*, Salzburg), in which most of the important
scholarly articles on various aspects of Mozart research have appeared.

In recent years a greatly renewed interest in Mozart on the part of Anglo-
Saxon scholars has resulted in the publication of some important books and
articles on specialized aspects, such as chronology and watermarks (Alan
Tyson), textual problems (Tyson, Cliff Eisen, C.R.F. Maunder, etc.), operas
(Andrew Steptoe, B. Brophy, etc.), symphonies (Neal Zaslaw) – this list is very
selective. A summary of these developments will appear in a forthcoming
volume, *The Mozart Compendium* (with two dozen expert contributors). It must
be said, however, that it is astonishing how little of all this scholarly thinking
and research reaches the general reader. The *NMA*, which is an absolute
necessity if we are to perform Mozart correctly, is not always used, even in
cultural centres like Vienna.[1]

It will be some time before anyone dares to attempt a major biography on the scale of Abert or Wyzewa/Saint-Foix. We are constantly learning new and vital facts about Mozart; for instance, recently discovered ms. sources have rendered even the *NMA*'s edition of the 'Linz' symphony obsolete.[2] Undoubtedly the bicentenary of the composer's death in 1991 will yield a rich harvest of new Mozartiana.

There is also an ever-widening gap between the general reader and the specialist in matters concerning Mozart: in many cases the latter writes in a manner totally incomprehensible to the former, especially where detailed musical analysis is concerned. Possibly, with the great popularity that Mozart now enjoys worldwide, we need more books that try to explain complicated events and complex music to the general reader in terms he or she can understand. Some aspects of musical analysis require musical notation if they are to be understood at all; and some complexities can hardly be conveyed in simple terms by anyone.

However, I thought that such a procedure might be worth attempting; and in *1791: Mozart's Last Year* (1988), I tried to steer a middle course between a scholarly treatment and a more journalistic approach. The many letters I received, especially from practising musicians, would seem to indicate that the attempt was not without success; and thus I decided to essay a slightly larger task – an investigation into some aspects of what might be called Mozart's rise and fall in Vienna. The decade 1781–91, which was indeed a golden period for music history generally, was also a highly successful one for Mozart during the first five or six years. But even at the height of his creative and material success, there were demons in the man – it was May, as it were, for Mozart, and the eager world seemed to be opening her arms to him. 'And yet . . . it was different from the freshness of spring; the image and the gaiety of it were tinged with despair.'[3] Modern medical opinion attributes some of this despair to a manic-depressive state, which we shall discuss later.

I also believed that the Viennese archives would, if examined anew, help us in identifying some of the many colourful characters on the Mozartian stage – with results that may be seen here. We now have a fairly accurate idea of Mozart's Masonic world (and we include facsimile lists of his Lodge Brothers); of the audience at the first performance of *La clemenza di Tito* in Prague (1791); of the economic and social background to the Vienna of Mozart's time, as seen through the eyes of a fellow Mason, Johann Pezzl, extracts from whose *Skizze von Wien* ('Sketch of Vienna'; 1786–90) are cited here; we also have perhaps a greater understanding of the technical devices used by Mozart in forging a new kind of piano concerto and in constructing a deadly and calculating series of seduction scenes in Act II of *Così fan tutte*, where the succumbing of the women is plotted in a musical edifice of formidable intellectual power and effectiveness.

I thought, then, that such matters would interest the public at large, curious to know some of the background, and indeed foreground, of this extraordinary decade – which brought forth a new masterpiece by Haydn or Mozart twice a month on average. In case this claim be considered exaggerated, consider the following, very informal (and purposely not complete) list of indubitable masterpieces that emerged from Vienna or Eszterháza in the years 1781–91.

The combined total of Haydn's and Mozart's compositions listed below, 234 works, does not include any of either composer's dance music, Lieder, canons and other smaller pieces; nor does it include any of the music Haydn composed in London in 1791, even though two of his symphonies, nos. 95 and 96, reached Vienna by the late autumn of 1791. Even with the omissions, the total is a formidable one, hence the years 1781–91 truly merit the description 'golden years' for music.

Haydn	*no. of works*
STRING QUARTETS: opp.33 (six), 42 (one), 50 (six), 54/55 (six), 64 (six)	25
OPERA: *La fedeltà premiata* (1781, Vienna 1784)	1
ORATORIO: The Seven Words (1786–7)	1
MASS: *Missa Cellensis* ('Mariazellermesse', 1782)	1
SYMPHONIES: nos. 73 ('La Chasse'), 74, 76–81, 82–7 ('Paris'), 88–91, 92 ('Oxford')	19
PIANO WORKS: Sonatas nos. 58, 59; Fantasia in C (XVII:4); piano trios nos. 20–30 (XV:7–17)	14
CONCERTOS etc.: Concertos for lira organizzata (VIIh:1–5); Notturni for the King of Naples (II:25–32); Harpsichord (or Piano) Concerto in D (XVIII:11); Cello Concerto in D (VIIb:2)	15
TOTAL	76

Mozart	
OPERAS: *Die Entführung aus dem Serail; Le nozze di Figaro; Don Giovanni; Così fan tutte; Die Zauberflöte; La clemenza di Tito*	6
MASS IN C MINOR (K.427)	1
MOTET: 'Ave, verum corpus' (K.618)	1
REQUIEM (K.626)	1
PIANO CONCERTOS nos. 11–27 AND CONCERT RONDO (K.382)	18
HORN CONCERTOS (K.412, 417, 447, 495)	4
CLARINET CONCERTO (K.622)	1
SYMPHONIES (K.385, 425, 504, 543, 550, 551)	6
SERENADES: for wind band (K.361, 375, 388); for strings ('Eine kleine Nachtmusik', K.525)	4
STRING QUARTETS (K.387, 421, 428, 458, 464, 465, 499, 575, 589, 590)	10
QUINTETS (K.406, 407, 515, 516, 581, 593, 614)	7
ADAGIO AND FUGUE in C minor (K.546)	1
DUETS for violin and viola (K.423, 424)	2
TRIOS, QUARTETS AND QUINTETS for piano and glass harmonica (K.442, 452, 496, 498, 502, 542, 548, 564; 478, 493, 617)	11
PIANO SONATAS, FANTASIAS etc.	*c.* 43
CONCERT AND INSERTION ARIAS, vocal duets, trios and quartets	*c.* 42
TOTAL	*c.* 158

On a musical plane, the relationship between Haydn and Mozart is perhaps more complex than has been hitherto realized. This study will show that there is even a fairly direct link between the complex, multi-movement finales of *La fedeltà premiata* (Eszterháza 1781, Vienna 1784) – probably Haydn's finest opera – and Mozart's *Le nozze di Figaro*, and even more the second act of *Così fan tutte*, where Mozart's use of key relationships mirrors some of Haydn's most advanced structural thinking. The Haydn-Mozart friendship had greater depth and substance than merely a cultivated exchange between the two greatest musical minds in Europe at the period.

On the pictorial side, the present volume, though not intended to emulate the work of the late Professor O.E. Deutsch for the *NMA*, does, however, include a number of portraits etc. not reproduced in Deutsch; among those illustrated are the Russian Ambassador in Vienna, Prince Galitzin, Mozart's first love, Aloysia Lange (*née* Weber), and other individuals central to Mozart's career, e.g. several Counts Esterházy and Count Heinrich Franz Rottenhan. Specimens of Mozart's autograph scores, together with musical examples, are also included to illustrate points discussed in the text.

It goes without saying that my wife, Else Radant, was a collaborator from beginning to end, and she has contributed a section on *La clemenza di Tito* (Appendix 7), as has my kind colleague László Berényi (Appendix 3 and much material in Chapter VII). (Other persons and institutions who helped make this book possible are listed in the Acknowledgments.) We all hope that lovers of Mozart will find in this book aspects which are moving, amusing, surprising and perhaps even shocking – but most of all that they will be impressed by the sheer number of musical masterpieces created within this decade, the end of which witnessed the French Revolution and the advent of political and social changes presaging the modern world, in which Mozart's music remains a very real, living presence.

Château de Foncoussières,   H. C. R. L.
10 August 1988 (the 200th anniversary
of the completion of Mozart's
'Jupiter' Symphony)

NOTE ON AUSTRIAN CURRENCY

In Austria in the 1780s, the principal currency was Gulden/gulden, abbreviated as 'fl.' or 'F.' (Florins – a term used interchangeably with 'Gulden'). The system was based on the duodecimal principle (as in Great Britain before decimalization in 1971). The smaller denomination was Kreuzer (abbreviated as 'kr' or 'xr'), 60 Kreuzer making 1 Gulden. Another denomination widely used was 'ducat' (a silver or gold coin), 1 ducat being equivalent to $4\frac{1}{2}$ Gulden. In 1791, £500 sterling converted to 4,883 Gulden.

I

Prelude

———

Leopold Mozart, detail of anonymous portrait, c. 1765; see pl. III.

I N THEIR TIME, 'the two Mozart parents [Leopold and his wife, *née* Maria Anna Pertl] were the most handsome couple in Salzburg, and the daughter was considered a regular beauty when she was young. But the son *Wolfgang* was small, thin, pale of complexion, and devoid of any distinguishing characteristics . . .'[1] This statement, from an authentic source dating from the spring of 1792, gives us an endearing view of Mozart's parents, and from surviving portraits one can see that both were indeed good-looking, Leopold strikingly so. (Is there not a hint of arrogance in that face, which was transmitted to the son as well?) The ancestry of the Mozarts has been traced back as far as the fourteenth century. Leopold's forebears were solid citizens with an artistic bent, master-masons and sculptors; recent research has shown that his wife's family, Pertl, mostly from the Salzburg region, included ancestors with a flair for music. The son of a master bookbinder in Augsburg, Johann Georg Leopold Mozart was born on 14 November 1719; his name-day was 15 November, in honour of the princely patron of Klosterneuburg Abbey and Lower Austria.[2] His wife, Maria Anna Pertl, the daughter of a leading local official, was born on Christmas Day 1720 at St Gilgen, near Salzburg: the handsome house in which she lived still exists.

Leopold Mozart studied with the Jesuits at St Salvator in Augsburg and received his diploma on 4 August 1736; the next year, he moved to Salzburg where he matriculated at the Benedictine University. There, he studied philosophy and jurisprudence, but was obliged to leave two years later because of 'insufficient attendance'. That same year, 1739, his musical instincts won the day, and he secured a position with Johann Baptist, Count Thurn-Valsassina und Taxis, who was a prebendary of Salzburg Cathedral; in 1739, Leopold dedicated to him his first published music, *Sonate sei per chiesa e da camera a tre Due Violini e Basso*. On 4 October 1743, Leopold was engaged as fourth violinist in the orchestra of the Prince-Archbishop of Salzburg, Leopold A.E., *Freiherr* von Firmian, the first of five Salzburg Archbishops under whom he would serve. Firmian is notorious for having banished the Protestants from *Land* (province) Salzburg in 1731. Leopold now felt secure enough financially to be able to marry Maria Anna Pertl in Salzburg on 21 November: they were

Mozart's sister Maria Anna, usually referred to as Nannerl; detail of an anonymous portrait, c. 1785, painted after her marriage to Johann Baptist von Berchtold zu Sonnenburg.

a devoted and happy couple. In 1756, the year of Wolfgang's birth, Leopold published his *Versuch einer gründlichen Violinschule* with Lotter in Augsburg, which was translated into several languages and enjoyed several later editions, one (1770) revised by the author: this treatise on the violin was immediately recognized to be one of the most important theoretical and practical works of its kind, and is still essential reading for all students of eighteenth-century music. In 1763 Leopold became Vice Court Chapel Master.

Leopold was a prolific composer, writing sacred and secular music, works for the chamber and pieces for toy instruments (the famous 'Toy' Symphony, formerly attributed to Haydn, is actually part of a delightful, larger work by Leopold,[3] entitled 'Cassatio'). One of his most enchanting works is a 'Musical Sleigh-Ride', with the same kind of orchestration that his son would use in his famous German Dance No. 3 ('Sleigh-Ride'; K.605). Leopold Mozart could not be called a great composer even by his most fervent admirers, but his music is deftly fashioned and often displays a delightful sense of humour and fun. Now that all his surviving correspondence is available in the new edition of the family letters (Mozart, *Briefe*), it is possible to appreciate him as a highly educated man with a profound knowledge of ancient and modern literature, of plants and medicine, speaking several languages, cultivated, polite, and moreover an excellent teacher. Both Leopold and his wife were very devout and entertained an unshakable belief in the order of God's world – rather like Haydn in this respect. Hence one is infinitely touched to read Leopold's phrase concerning a freezing day in January 1756: 'the miracle which God caused to be born in Salzburg'.

The miracle was Johannes Chrysostomus Wolfgang Theophilus Mozart, born on 27 January and baptized next day in Salzburg Cathedral: his first two given names refer to St John Chrysostom, whose feast day falls on 27 January; Wolfgang was in honour of his maternal grandfather, Wolfgang Nikolaus Pertl, while Theophilus was the name of his godfather, Johann Theophilus Pergmayr. When Wolfgang was confirmed, probably in 1769, he was given an additional Christian name, Sigismundus, probably because the then Archbishop, Siegmund Christoph, Count von Schrattenbach, stood sponsor.[4] Today, we know Mozart as Wolfgang Amadeus because in later years he himself used the Latin (or French, or Italian) or German form of Theophilus, the last of his given names, i.e. 'Wolfgang Amadeo' or (after *c.* 1777) 'Wolfgang Amadè'.

By 1759 it was clear to Leopold that his son was a musical prodigy. In a book of music Leopold wrote: 'These previous eight minuets were learned by little Wolfgang in his fourth year.' And later; 'Little Wolfgang also learned this minuet in his fourth year.' Under a scherzo by G.C. Wagenseil, Leopold wrote: 'Little Wolfgang learned this piece on 24 January 1761, 3 days before his fifth birthday, at night between 9 and 9.30 o'clock.'[5]

Of seven children in the Mozart family only Maria Anna (Nannerl), born in 1751 (the fourth), and Wolfgang (the seventh) survived infancy. In fact, the sister was also a child prodigy, though she never composed; later she gave piano lessons to 'young ladies of the town of Salzburg, and even today [1792]

one recognizes Nannétte [*sic*] Mozart's pupils above all others because of their neatness, precision and true diligence of performance.'[6]

Recognizing that his children could be presented in public and earn a great deal of money, Leopold took them all over Europe – from the Imperial court in Vienna to Germany, France, England, Holland and Switzerland. Later, he accompanied Wolfgang alone on three trips to Italy, where it was hoped the boy would find a permanent position. In fact, Wolfgang was soon enrolled in Salzburg among the 'Concertmeister', being listed in 1770 together with Ferdinand Seidl and Joseph Haydn's younger brother, Johann Michael.[7] But through the composition of three operas in 1770, 1771, and 1772 for the court at Milan, then under Habsburg rule, Mozart hoped to secure an appointment there. Archduke Ferdinand, Governor and Captain-General of Lombardy, actually wanted to engage Wolfgang, but his mother, Empress Maria Theresa, in a letter dated 12 December 1771 warned her son against employing 'useless people' (*gens inutils*) like that; and Ferdinand dutifully followed her advice.

A very interesting description of the Mozarts, father and son, survives from the pen of the then celebrated composer, Johann Adolph Hasse, writing from Vienna on 30 September 1769 to a friend in Venice:

Mozart's birthplace in Salzburg (now Getreidegasse No. 9): the third floor of the five-storey house (left background) remained the family home until 1773. Lithograph by C. Czichna, 1837.

13

I have made the acquaintance here of a certain Mr Mozard [*sic*], *maestro di capella* of the [Arch]bishop of Salzburg, a man of spirit, astute, experienced; and I think he well knows his way in the world of music and also in other things as well. He has a daughter and a son. The former plays the harpsichord very well and the latter, who can't be more than twelve or thirteen, even at that age composes and is a *maestro di musica*. I've seen compositions which appear to be his, and certainly they are not bad and not such as I would expect to find in a boy of twelve . . . That same Mr Mozard [*sic*] is a very polite man, and civil; and his children are very well educated. Moreover the boy is good-looking, vivacious, gracious and very well mannered; when you make his acquaintance, it is difficult not to like him. Certainly he will become a prodigy if as he grows older he continues to make the necessary progress . . .[8]

It was, in any event, a closely knit family; and the relationship between father and son was close to the point of becoming (for Wolfgang) slightly overpowering in later years. When Wolfgang was scarcely five, Leopold and the court trumpeter J.A. Schachtner went one Thursday to play at mass and when they returned they found Wolfgang composing a harpsichord concerto. Leopold wanted to see it; 'But it's not finished,' said Wolfgang. 'Let's look,' said Papa, 'that must be quite something.' After being amused by the ink spots and smudges, Leopold began to examine the actual content of the music, 'and for a long time he remained, stiff as a ramrod, looking at the paper, and finally tears of joy and amazement came to his eyes. "Look at this, Herr Schachtner," he said, "how carefully and correctly everything is written down, only it can't be used because it's so difficult that no one will be able to play it." "That's why it's a concerto," Wolfgang broke in, "you have to practise till you master it."'[9] And years later, when visiting Wolfgang and Constanze in Vienna (1785), Leopold wrote, after listening to his son playing a piano concerto – probably no. 18 in B flat (K.456) – '[I] had the pleasure of hearing all the instrumental exchanges so clearly that tears of joy came to my eyes.'[10]

When it was decided to send Wolfgang to Paris in 1778, Leopold was obliged to remain in Salzburg to fulfil his duties with the Archbishop (now Hieronymus, Count von Colloredo) and sent his wife to act as chaperone. The results of the Paris trip may be summarized thus: Mozart went first to Mannheim, fell in love with a young singer, Aloysia Weber, then continued to Paris (where his mother died) and failed to find an appointment in the French capital; on returning, he found Aloysia Weber had moved with the Electoral orchestra from Mannheim to Munich, and was no longer interested in him. Hitherto, Mozart's failure in Paris has been ascribed to factors outside his control, including the Philistine character of French musicians and audiences. But the distinguished Mozart scholar Rudolph Angermüller has a different and much less flattering explanation; 'The reason for Mozart's failure may be sought principally in his overweening self-confidence. He has not a good word for the French, makes negative remarks to the point of insulting them: he is against the prevailing musical taste in Paris, against French singers, doubts that the French understand anything about music, and finds himself – as far as music is concerned – among animals and beasts; . . . His arrogance can be measured in the sentence, "I don't care about the Parisians' applause." . . . If

one adds to this the musical scene in Paris, which was unfavourable to Mozart, one understands more readily the mistake of the whole venture, encouraged by Leopold.'[11]

Meanwhile, Leopold Mozart had been active in Salzburg, persuading the Archbishop to offer Wolfgang better terms; instead of being simply a violinist, Mozart would, while retaining the title of *Conzertmeister*, become court organist, with increased salary and opportunities to obtain leave. Dragging his heels, Wolfgang lingered a month in Mannheim and finally arrived in Munich on Christmas Day, 1778, still attired in French mourning garb (the colour of which was, curiously, not black but red). He was rebuffed by Aloysia, but her younger sister Constanze felt sorry for him and a friendship began. When he returned to Salzburg, in the middle of January 1779, he had been away for sixteen months and the trip had brought nothing but a considerable financial loss. Wolfgang now submitted his application for the position of court organist – the petition is, typically, all in Leopold's hand – and was granted it, at a salary of 450 gulden.

Mozart had left Salzburg as a young man of immense talents, with some extraordinarily prophetic compositions to his credit – works like the beautiful 'Haffner' Serenade (K.250), with its massively symphonic outer movements, and the forward-looking Piano Concerto no. 9 in E flat (K.271), as well as some striking church music. When he returned to Salzburg and began composing in 1779 and 1780, however, he acquired the mantle of greatness. During these two years, Mozart developed a new and special musical language which touched many forms – symphony, mass, vespers, serenade,

The Parade Ground and the palace known as the Pfälzer Hof in Mannheim. Mozart stayed briefly in the town in 1777 and 1778 on his way to and from Paris. Engraving by J.A. Riedel, 1779.

concerto, and finally, dramatic music. The three symphonies of this period are all uniquely beautiful works of quite differing kinds. The first is no. 32, the terse three-movement 'Overture' in G (K.318), in which the first movement leads directly to the second and the second to the third; it is the most scintillating overture that Mozart had yet composed, full of brilliance and (in the slow movement) that tenderness and nostalgia which had characterized the slow movements in the 'Haffner' Serenade. The next work, the lyrical B flat Symphony no. 33 (K.319), is in that Austrian tradition of chamber symphony perfected by Haydn (and by his followers, such as J.B. Vanhal). In keeping with the general tradition, the orchestration omits trumpets and drums and the entire score is of a feathery lightness. The third symphony, no. 34 (K.338), is, again, totally different – a grand work in C major with trumpets and drums, in the key associated with spiritual and temporal power. We notice that Mozart has made something of a speciality of this incisive and brilliant use of C major: one of the characteristics of his music in general, but especially of this pageantry in C, is the use of the dotted rhythm in 4/4 time ♩ ♫♩♩ . This particularly Mozartian marching motif pervades the first movement in a quite extraordinary way, announcing itself in the horns and trumpets in bar 3, but proceeding to the whole orchestra in bars 7, 11, 13, and so forth, thus making us almost continuously aware of its presence, sometimes for bars on end. Haydn had made a great speciality of such C major pageantry, and had composed a dozen symphonies with trumpets and drums and (an Eszterháza speciality) horns in C *alto*, an octave above normal, culminating in his Symphony no. 56 of 1774, a work widely diffused in manuscript copies and several printed editions and hence probably well known to Mozart. Mozart, as was his wont, assimilated this C major style of Haydn's and made it even more brilliant and penetrating. There is an unprecedented tension in the coda of the first movement of K.338, where – with the exception of nine bars – that dotted rhythm or a derivative thereof features throughout, from bar 233 to bar 264. It is one of the means that Mozart uses to increase the tension.

Furthermore, in a cathedral context, C major is the key of no less than four major church works composed at Salzburg in 1779–80 – all with that brass-heavy type of orchestration (at its biggest with three trombones, two horns and two trumpets) which had a long tradition there. Two of these are grand settings of the Vespers, the *Vesperae de Dominica* (K.321) and the more celebrated *Vesperae solennes de confessore* (K.339). Both are magnificent examples of Wolfgang's newly found majesty and power in the key of C, but both contain movements of striking and moving contrast, particularly the 'Laudate pueri' (in the ancient D minor *a cappella* tradition) of K.339, and the justly famous 'Laudate Dominum' which follows, with its soaring soprano solo written for Michael Haydn's wife, Maria Magdalena (*née* Lipp), clearly a remarkable singer, for whom Mozart always composed music of ravishing beauty. One feature strikes every listener: the extraordinary purity and simplicity of the Doxology in both Vespers settings ('as it was in the beginning, is now, and ever shall be') – evidence, direct and immensely moving, of Wolfgang's deep religious feelings.

I *Wolfgang Amadeus Mozart, detail of the unfinished portrait painted c. 1789–90 by the composer's brother-in-law, Joseph Lange. This, the last important painted likeness of Mozart, was considered by his wife Constanze to be the best.*

V   *Aloysia Lange, née Weber, was Mozart's first love. She was a soprano*
with the Court Opera in Vienna from 1779, and married the actor and
amateur painter Joseph Lange in 1780. She is seen here, in the title role, as
Zémire in a German translation of Grétry's opera Zémire et Azor, *in a*
painting by J.B. von Lampi, 1784.

VI   *Constanze Mozart, née Weber, who was Aloysia's younger sister,
married Mozart in St Stephen's Cathedral, Vienna, on 4 August 1782. This
portrait was painted not long after the wedding by her brother-in-law, Joseph
Lange, whose unfinished portrait of Mozart (see pl. I) dates from c. 1789–90.*

VII   *The only two of Wolfgang and Constanze's children to survive infancy were Karl Thomas (right), born in 1784, and Franz Xaver, born in 1791. This painting, which dates from c. 1798, is by Hans Hansen, who also executed a portrait of Constanze in 1802, commissioned by her future husband, Georg Nikolaus Nissen, whom she married in Preßburg in 1809.*

The other two works in this glorious C major tradition are settings of the mass – the 'Coronation' Mass (K.317)[12] and the less well-known but austerely beautiful K.337, whose opening slow Kyrie is in a tradition which will culminate in the slow beginnings of the Mass in C minor (K.427), the (misdated) Kyrie in D minor (K.341) and, finally, in the Requiem itself. The 'Coronation' Mass is Mozart's most popular work in the genre, in turn powerfully symphonic (with the famous dotted rhythm positively dominating the Credo in a compulsive way) and movingly tender (as in the Agnus Dei, with another great solo for Maria Magdalena Lipp-Haydn, anticipating in a quite uncanny way 'Porgi amor' in *Le nozze di Figaro*). There is yet another C major church work of miniature greatness: in Salzburg it was the tradition to have a sonata with organ and orchestra instead of the Epistle; hence these works are called 'Epistle Sonatas'. Each of the masses includes such a sonata: that for K.337 is a delightful miniature organ concerto (K.336); while that for the 'Coronation' Mass is a real surprise, a hugely powerful Allegro with trumpets and drums (K.329), which contains in its three minutes' duration a highly condensed outline of this new C major language, even to the omnipresent dotted rhythm, especially towards the end.

The last serenade composed for Salzburg is also a large-scale work having (in its main sections) massive symphonic proportions; this was the 'Posthorn' Serenade in D (K.320), which Mozart later turned into a three-movement symphony by omitting four of the movements. This is yet another work whose heroic language and powerful thematic concentration look forward to the great D major symphonies of the Vienna period, no. 35, the 'Haffner' (K.385), and no. 38, the 'Prague' (K.504). It transcends everything that had gone before it, even the 'Haffner' Serenade (K.250) of 1776, its immediate stylistic precursor. Its boldness and, in one of its slow movements (that in D minor), its sombre overtones recur in Mozart's last work in concerto form of the Salzburg years, the *sinfonia concertante* in E flat for violin, viola and orchestra (K.364), one of the most original compositions of this glorious galaxy.

Mozart always yearned to compose full-length Italian operas. There was no real opportunity to do so within the confines of the Salzburg court, but in 1779 and 1780 he completed the final version of a stage work which has only recently come to be recognized for the masterpiece that Mozart (and his father) knew it to be – the incidental music to *Thamos, König in Ägypten* (K.345). It is thought that the work existed in three versions, of which the final one is definitive. While both the instrumental sections and the choral pieces are of soul-enhancing strength, the one part which is positively terrifying and looks forward directly to the world of *Don Giovanni* is the scene with the High Priest, 'Ihr Kinder des Staubes', in D minor. No such portrayal of fear had ever appeared in Haydn's or indeed Mozart's previous music: its effect is like a curtain opening to reveal a whole realm of stark, creeping fears that are archetypal for a coming musical world. There is an earlier D minor number for orchestra, to be performed after the fourth act, which also unleashes the demons; it is soon to be the world of the new opera *Idomeneo*, and ultimately of the Piano Concerto no. 20 in D minor (K.466).

When he had been in Mannheim and Munich, Wolfgang had hoped to receive a commission for a large-scale Italian *opera seria*, but the Electoral court had remained unforthcoming. Then, in the summer of 1780, came the long-awaited commission: *Idomeneo*, Mozart's first great opera, first performed with success in the (still extant) Court Theatre in Munich on 29 January 1781. Now, after the great Salzburg music of 1779–80, we have come to expect the dark-hued Overture with its ability to make D major sound grandly disturbing; we might have expected the power and magnetic quality of the choruses, especially the uncanny 'O voto tremendo' featuring muted trumpets (the mutes had to be imported especially from Salzburg) and covered drums; and after *Thamos* we might, just possibly, have imagined the tortured, flaming drama of Elettra's music, especially her final 'exit' aria (having to cut this at the last minute must have been agonizing for Mozart). But there is absolutely nothing in the whole range of Mozart's (or anyone else's) music to suggest the muted power of the great Act III quartet, wherein Mozart displays the conflicting emotions of his principal characters; it is the highpoint of a work during the course of which Mozart strove to create real flesh-and-blood figures on stage – where has raging jealousy ever been more horrifyingly portrayed, as Elettra becomes unhinged, and the music with it? She, and we, see the serpents that writhe in her crazed and fathomless ravings. But what was the result of this magnificent expenditure of effort on Mozart's part? A few performances in Munich, and in 1786 one private performance in Vienna which Mozart supervised. Otherwise, this supremely original work was never repeated in the composer's lifetime: it was not published until 1797 and thus its original production was a purely local success of no influence on the course of musical drama for the next fifteen years; in fact, *Idomeneo* achieved real, international success only after World War II.[13].

One of the problems for all of Mozart's magnificent music written in 1779 and 1780 was a lack of dissemination at the time: a small coterie in Salzburg knew the symphonies and serenades; a slightly larger, and certainly more varied, congregation heard the church music performed in Salzburg Cathedral; but it was not until Mozart reached Vienna that he began to exploit this rich vein consisting of works composed in Salzburg. He began to have many of these works sent to Vienna, and one such volume, containing a group of nine Salzburg symphonies of the 1770s (among them the lovely no. 29 in A major, K.201), was, apparently, to be used during Mozart's subscription concerts in Vienna in the 1780s: this is the reason why he carefully obliterated the original dates on these autographs, so that Viennese copyists would not know they were preparing works that were already up to ten years old. In 1987 this volume was sold at Sotheby's in London and set a new world record price for any collection of music sold at auction: £2,935,000.[14]

All this lay in the future, however. Mozart considered the time he spent composing *Idomeneo* the happiest of his life (as Constanze Mozart later told the English couple, Vincent and Mary Novello, in 1829).[15] But this happiness was to be short-lived. Archbishop Colloredo had granted Mozart permission to go to Munich to finish the opera and conduct the first performances, but the

IDOMENEO *(1781)*
The virtuoso tenor Anton Raaff (c. 1711–1797) who, at the end of his career, sang the title role in Mozart's opera when it was first produced in Munich; he is portrayed, in an anonymous watercolour (left) of 1781, in a heroic role.

The opening of the copy of the bravura aria for Raaff 'Fuor del mare' (ABOVE), in which later pages bear corrections in Mozart's own hand; the composer's autograph title (TOP) is also part of the original performance material.

composer overstayed his leave; in March 1781, he was summoned to Vienna, where the Archbishop and his retinue, including the musicians, were established. He arrived in the Imperial capital on 16 March 'all by myself in a post chaise' at 9 a.m. He and most of the other members of the archiepiscopal court were lodged in the Palace of the Teutonic Knights near St Stephen's Cathedral, and at once Mozart was plunged into a whirl of activity. The Archbishop was putting on concerts almost daily. 'We had a concert at 4 o'clock – there were present at least 20 persons of the highest nobility – Ceccarelli [a castrato in the Archbishop's service] had to sing at Balfi's [Count Pálffy's] yesterday – today we have to go to Prince Gallizin's [Galitzin, the Russian Ambassador], who was present yesterday . . . Now I must close, for when leaving I will mail the letter and then I must go at once to Prince Gallizin's . . .'[16]

Mozart would spend most of the next ten years in Vienna, where he was destined to contribute a new chapter of untold brilliance in the history of European music.

27

II

The Musical Scene in Vienna,
1781–82

The Opera – organization and repertoire

When Mozart arrived in Vienna, there were two official (Imperial) theatre-cum-opera houses, the Kärntnerthortheater and the Burgtheater. Although German-language plays and operas were in the repertoire of both houses, the most popular European opera – that by the Italian composers and of course in their language – officially did not exist in the Austrian capital. The reasons for this extraordinary state of affairs lie in the history of opera in Vienna in the 1770s.

Throughout the years of Mozart's youth, Italian opera had flourished in Vienna, including works by Italian masters and by local composers, such as Gluck and *maestro di cappella* Florian Leopold Gassmann, the teacher of Antonio Salieri; Emperor Joseph II greatly mourned Gassmann's death in 1774. The position of *maestro di cappella* was then given to Salieri, whose Italian operas were applauded both in Vienna and abroad; each year from 1770 Salieri wrote a new work, serious or comic, for the Vienna Opera up to (and including) 1776, which proved to be a highly significant year for the theatrical life of Vienna.

By the end of 1775, the standard of French and Italian operas and of the ballet had reached so low a point that Joseph II – co-regent with his mother, Empress Maria Theresa since 1765 – was prompted to suggest that urgent improvements were needed (he even advocated the cancellation of all ballets at the Kärntnerthortheater). He also wanted to have an interesting German-language spoken theatre. The theatrical management was, however, nearly bankrupt. On 16 March 1776, Joseph II took drastic action: the contracts for the *opera buffa* and the ballet were terminated. (The opera company proceeded to set up on its own, and managed to keep going until the end of 1777). Shortly afterwards, Joseph decided that the Burgtheater should henceforth be called the 'German National Theatre', financed by the court, and soon supported by an enthusiastic public as well. Joseph could – later in the same year – see a number of German-language plays and a dozen *Singspiele* (usually foreign) and particularly French *opéras comiques* (in German translation) playing in the

28

Kärntnerthortheater. But he also hoped to persuade local playwrights and composers to provide the theatres with original works; and Vienna eagerly awaited the first production of this kind on 17 February 1778, Ignaz Umlauf's *Die Bergknappen*, with the soprano Caterina Cavalieri making her theatrical debut as Sophie, the leading female role. The performance was well received by Joseph II and by the public; Cavalieri's performance and her music were very successful. Indeed, as evidence of the work's impact, engravings of some scenes were issued – a very unusual event. The success of this *Singspiel* persuaded the Emperor to include German operas (and a German-speaking opera company) as part of his 'German National Theatre', and Umlauf, who had been a viola player in the orchestra of the Burgtheater, was now promoted to *Kapellmeister* with a salary of 600 gulden (later as assistant and substitute to Salieri). The author of the work's libretto was Joseph Weidmann, who also collaborated in the production of Mozart's *Der Schauspieldirektor* (1786).

The German National Theatre continued to exist, then, until the end of 1782, although Italian operas were occasionally given (notably Gluck's *Orfeo* and *Alceste* in 1781, repeated in 1782, in which year two other Italian operas, by Antonio Sacchini and Antonio Salieri respectively, were also staged). Thereafter, despite the marked success of Mozart's contribution to the *Singspiel* (*Die Entführung aus dem Serail*), Italian opera returned to the Imperial

The Kärnterthortheater, one of the two official court theatres in Vienna in the 1780s, with the Bürgerspitalskirche. Engraving by J. Hyrtl after Carl Pfeffel.
(INSET, ABOVE) Antonio Salieri (1750–1825), the court Kapellmeister and composer of popular Italian operas; engraving by Johann Gottfried Scheffner.

29

Christoph Willibald von Gluck; anonymous portrait, chalk on paper.

Johann Baptist von Alxinger (1755–97); engraving by F. John.

Tobias Philipp, Freiherr von Gebler (1726–86); engraving by J.G. Mansfeld.

capital, to the joy of the city's inhabitants.[1] The theatrical season for the year 1781 in Vienna, with a complete list of the plays and operas given, as well as all the personnel, is contained in a publication entitled *Allgemeiner Theater Almanach vom Jahr 1782*.[2] The casts of all the plays and operas are given in this *Almanach*, as well as those of previous years, or since the inaugural production of the German National Theatre in 1778.

Apart from the German-language plays and *Singspiele*, French plays, operas and ballets were also given, put on (in 1780) by a special company under the direction of 'Messieurs Dalainville and Beaubourg' who, however, later 'found it expedient to leave secretly on 8 September 1781.' Some of the French company banded together to keep alive the enterprise, which, noted the 1782 *Almanach*, 'still exists'. This French company played in the Kärntnerthortheater, as did a group of strolling players from Preßburg under the direction of Herr Kuhn, starting in August 1781. Their repertoire included plays as well as a *Singspiel* and ballets. The *Almanach* also notes that the Marinelli Company was playing regularly in the Leopoldstadt Theatre (mostly farces and the like), with Imperial approval.

Among the theatrical writers listed in the 1782 *Almanach* are many with whom Mozart would be directly or indirectly associated, e.g. Johann von Alxinger (a fellow Mason), a successful author; *Freiherr* Philipp von Gebler (also a Mason), councillor of state and the author of *Thamos*, for which Mozart had composed the music (K.345); Christian Gottlob Stephanie, the author of many successful plays, and his son, Gottlieb, who supplied Mozart with the word-book of *Die Entführung* in July 1781 and was director of opera productions at the Burgtheater. Works from the 1780 season still in the repertoire and new productions for the 1781 season included operas by, among others, Gluck, Grétry, Gassmann, Paisiello and Salieri.[3] A new ballet, *Phyrrus und Polyxene* (with music by Peter Winter), was staged on 17 October at the end of *Der Barbier von Sevilien*, a German translation of the play by Beaumarchais, and was repeated six times. There were also 'melodramas' (music with spoken words), a genre which interested Mozart and which he had used in *Thamos* (final version 1779–80): Georg Benda's *Ariadne auf Naxos* (7 May) and *Medea* (19 December). Zimmermann's melodrama entitled *Andromeda und Perseus* featured a terrifying dragon which spouted steam from a cleverly constructed machine.[4] There were 101 nights reserved for opera performances (as distinct from plays, ballets, melodramas, etc.); German composers secured 44 evenings, Italians 35 and French 22. Gluck dominates the season's proceedings with 32 performances.[5] Four operas new to the repertoire were failures and were removed soon after their respective premieres.[6] It must be recalled that, unlike other theatres such as Naples, where each opera received a set number of performances regardless of its reception, in Vienna an opera survived only if it was well received. (The same applied to Haydn's opera productions at Eszterháza.)

In 1781, there were two great successes, the Paisiello opera *Die eingebildeten Philosophen* (originally *I filosofi immaginari*) and Salieri's *Der Rauchfangkehrer* (not a translation). Originally a successful composer of Italian operas, Salieri

shrewdly noted that Joseph favoured German-language *Singspiele*; therefore, as soon as the composer returned from a leave-of-absence in early April 1780, he procured a commission from Joseph II to write an opera for the German National Theatre. The death of Empress Maria Theresa at the end of November meant that, since the theatres were closed during the period of official mourning, Salieri could rehearse his new opera and cause the singers to give of their best. 'Mlle Cavalieri's action improves daily...' wrote one paper.[7]

Among the personnel, Mozart would have been, naturally, particularly interested in the orchestra (see Appendix 4), which consisted of its *maestro di cappella* (Antonio Salieri), his substitute (Ignaz Umlauf), six first violins and six second violins, four violas, three cellos, three double basses, pairs of flutes, oboes, clarinets, bassoons, horns, trumpets, and a timpani player – thirty-five players, a sizable orchestra in those days. (Haydn's at Eszterháza usually consisted of twenty-four players and for most of its existence lacked a second flute, clarinets and trumpets.)

The soprano Caterina Cavalieri in Scene 6 of Ignaz Umlauf's Die Bergknappen *at the Burgtheater. Engraving by J. Adam after Carl Schütz.*

'Maria Theresa's Last Day', a commemorative engraving by Hieronymus Löschenkohl issued in February 1781. According to Johann Pezzl, the artist/engraver sold some 7,000 copies of this, one of his first successful prints.

The 'Harmonie' (wind band)

One of the special characteristics of Bohemian musicians had been their aptitude for, and cultivation of, the wind band (German: *Harmonie*). At first, the standard form had been a sextet consisting of two oboes (or cors anglais), two bassoons and two horns; and it was this combination which had flourished in Prague and on the estates of the nobility, and for which Joseph Haydn had composed extensively *c.* 1760. There were also many wind-band divertimenti of that period by Bohemian composers such as Mozart's later friend, Franz Xaver Duschek, whose wife was a celebrated singer for whom Mozart composed arias: the collection of the Counts Pachta in Prague contains a large number of pieces, some dated 1762–64, by Duschek scored for wind sextet (or quintet, with just one bassoon).[8] The sound of this Bohemian combination is beguiling, especially when the oboes are replaced by cors anglais, as in some

Haydn works; there is a curiously subdued, melancholy quality about the slow movements – it must be said that composing for wind bands requires exceptional understanding of the medium and is a very specialized skill. Pieces for wind band seem rather *gauche* when transcribed, say, for string quartet (as happened in the case of some of Haydn's wind-band divertimenti transcribed for Austrian monasteries). Brevity is a prerequisite for wind-band writing, but produces an odd result when the music is rewritten for strings.

Johann Vent's arrangement for wind band of Die Entführung aus dem Serail: *title page and statement of account including (as item 4) work on this opera, both in the Schwarzenberg Archives, Český Krumlov (Krumau).*

Soon, when clarinets became more common – Haydn had written the occasional wind-band sextet in the early 1760s, but the writing is not much different from that for oboes – the Austro-Bohemian *Harmonie* became an octet, generally pairs of oboes, clarinets, horns and bassoons, though some groups, such as Prince Schwarzenberg's, combined oboes, cors anglais, horns and bassoons.[9] It seems that such wind octets began to become fashionable by *c.* 1780: one of the earliest was that of Cardinal Joseph, Prince Batthyány in Preßburg (Bratislava). But what set the seal on the success of this more elaborate grouping was the fact that Joseph II extrapolated from his Court Opera orchestra an official *Harmonie* intended primarily, for some extraordinary reason, to play wind-band arrangements of operas in the Imperial repertoire. Preparing such arrangements became a lucrative business; and one of the earliest and most successful arrangers was the second oboist of the Opera orchestra, Johann Nepomuk Vent (or Went), whose charming and clever adaptations of Mozart's operas have recently been performed and recorded. In the 1780s, they were primarily marketed by means of the local copyists. Originally, the function of such a wind band was also linked to military duties,[10] but in Vienna, the Imperial wind band was used, as was also the case with others in the provinces, to provide the household with *Tafelmusik*, i.e. pleasant music at mealtimes. Since operas were always the most fashionable form of music in society, the wind-band arrangements provided a particularly delightful way of recalling operatic melodies. This tradition of arranging operatic scores for wind band – and indeed maintaining a *Harmonie* created almost exclusively to perform them – remained a Viennese speciality for some time, though by 1787 Count Zinzendorf reported hearing Mozart's *Figaro* arranged (certainly in at least one case and probably in another) for wind band. On 21 September 1787 Zinzendorf was visiting the Schwarzenberg Castle at Krumau (Český Krumlov) and noted in his Diary: 'L'opera *de figaro* avec les instruments de Vent, joué, je ne l'écoutais pas. Ces messieurs souperent ici . . .' And on 25 September at Frauenberg: 'Après le diner musique de *figaro* . . .' Earlier in the year, on 2 March, he records attending an entire evening in Vienna when the Imperial *Harmonie* played *Una cosa rara* (Martin y Soler): 'le soir au concert ou les musiciens de l'Empereur jouerent toute la Cosa rara, dont la musique fit un effet charmant'.[11] It is not clear exactly when the Imperial *Harmonie* was formed – certainly by 24 April 1782, at which date a document in the Court Archives refers to eight known individuals as members of the Imperial *Harmonie*, involving duties for which they are to receive 50 gulden p.a. in addition to their usual salary as members of the orchestra.[12]

The effect of this wind-band combination on Mozart can be described as little short of sensational: not only did it revolutionize his orchestral scoring, but it provided an immediate impetus to compose wind-band serenades, one of the earliest of which was also the greatest – the Serenade for Thirteen Instruments in B flat (K.361), which used to be described as for 'thirteen wind instruments', although it is actually for twelve (2 oboes, 2 clarinets, 2 basset horns, 4 horns, 2 bassoons) plus double bass, as the autograph manuscript[13] clearly shows.

It has been realized for some time that this work was misdated – it was previously thought to have been composed in Munich, but there is no evidence whatever for this. The watermarks of the paper indicate that the work was composed in the early Viennese period, and a leading expert on the subject, Roger Hellyer, now considers that the Serenade was in fact (as had been occasionally mooted) Mozart's wedding present[14] to Constanze, in 1782. (This, like Wagner's *Siegfried Idyll*, must constitute one of the greatest gifts of music ever made by a composer to his wife.) In it – and of course in the other notable wind-band serenades, those in E flat (K.375) and C minor (K.388), of approximately the same period – Mozart shows that he has assimilated perfectly the language and mastered the special problems of writing for wind band. This is especially true of the brooding slow movements of K.361, with their undulating inner lines, showing an extraordinary sense of what groups of wind instruments can create in the way of a smooth, legato sound. But there is more to the assimilation of the wind-band language into Mozart's music than just serenades. The whole Court Opera orchestra must have been of an exceptional quality, as Mozart's (and later Beethoven's early) orchestral writing for it shows; yet curiously it is not in Mozart's symphonies that we find the boldest music for wind band, but in the piano concertos; and this aspect of their orchestration is one of their most striking innovative features. In the most spectacular examples we find whole miniature wind-band serenades in the concertos, such as in the middle of the slow movement of no. 22 (K.482), where the piano – and indeed the strings as well – remains totally silent for 28 bars, allowing the wind band to monopolize the listener's attention.

There are such instances in other piano concertos; more than that, however, Mozart allowed the excellence of this *Harmonie* to pervade the piano concertos in a host of new and subtle ways. To take one example: in his Vienna scores, when Mozart writes in B flat he almost invariably uses the horns in B flat *alto*, where their diatonic scale begins at sounding B flat' (in other words above middle C). This creates fiercely difficult technical problems, because even on an eighteenth-century valveless horn pitched in B flat *alto*, the range is dangerously high (Haydn's C *alto* horn writing at Eszterháza, an octave above normal, is equally difficult). The omnipresent and beneficial presence of the Josephinian *Harmonie* makes an equally spectacular appearance in Act II of *Così fan tutte*. And just as in the piano concertos, the Imperial wind band pervades the great Viennese opera scores of the 1780s: it revolutionizes the structure of Mozart's operatic orchestration, creating considerable technical (and hence musical) problems when the operas were exported to German theatres with less skilled wind players – and indeed, inferior orchestras altogether. 'The orchestra was also miserable,' wrote Count Ludwig von Bentheim-Steinfurt in his Diary,[15] after a performance of *Die Entführung* in Cologne on 24 October 1784, 'and the first violinist [leader], a brutish individual, worked so hard that he was covered in sweat and cursed and swore at so many mistakes, especially in the wind instruments . . .' German audiences – at least those of the 1780s – probably had a very curious impression of Mozart's breathtakingly new orchestration.[16]

The Singers in the Opera

Mozart was certainly interested in the actors and actresses of the German National Theatre, but it was naturally the singers who concerned him more personally and directly; he would work with many of them in *Die Entführung* and other works in German (*Der Schauspieldirektor*). In the 1782 *Almanach*[17] they are listed as follows:

GENTLEMEN OF THE OPERA LISTED ACCORDING TO THE DATES WHEN THEY WERE ENGAGED

1   Herr Joseph Ruprecht, made his début in the opera as Friz [*sic*] in Weidmann's *Bergknappen* [music by Umlauf], 1778. He sings lovers and comic servants.
2   Herr Joseph Souter, came from Brünn [Brno] with the Böhm Troupe Theatre. He made his début as Blunk in Schmidt's opera *Diesmal hat der Mann den Willen* [music by Carlos d'Ordoñez]. He sings tenor and his speciality is young lovers.

3 Herr Johann Baptist Hofman [Hoffmann]. He sings bass; his speciality is old men. He conducts the chorus in the Opera.

4 Herr Frankenburger, born in Vienna, made his début in 1779 as Jermis in the opera *Dorfjahrmarkt* [Georg Benda's *Der Jahrmarkt*]; sings low-comic roles.

5 Herr Gottfried Heinrich Schmidt, born in *Land* Dessau in 1744, entered the theatre in 1766, made his Vienna début in 1779. Sings comic roles, and on account of his wide knowledge of music is one of the directors of the Opera.

6 Herr Joseph Dauer, appeared in the Opera for the first time in 1779 as Alexis in [Monsigny's] *Le déserteur*; sings young lovers and character parts.

7 Herr Joseph Walther; born in Bohemia, made his début at the National Theatre in 1780 as Ernst in [J. Barta's] *Der adelige Taglöhner*. He sings tenor, and plays first and second lovers.

8 Herr Friedrich Günther. He sings bass, his roles are first comic old men, pedants and other caricature parts.

9 Herr Carl Ludewig [*recte*: Johann Ignaz Ludwig] Fischer, born in Dresden in 1743, came to the theatre in 1769, made his Vienna début in 1780 as Sander in [Grétry's] *Zemir und Azor*. He sings bass, his parts are leading comic roles and tender fathers, also caricature roles.

10 Herr Joseph [*recte* Johann Valentin] Adamberger, born in Munich, was engaged, while in Italy, to join the Vienna Opera, and made his début in 1780 as Astrubal in [a German translation of Anfossi's *L'incognita perseguitata* entitled] *Die verfolgte Unbekannte*. He sings tenor; leading young lovers, gentle and ardent, are his roles.

Mozart's favourite tenor, Johann Valentin Adamberger; anonymous miniature, c. 1785.

LADIES OF THE OPERA LISTED ACCORDING TO THE DATES WHEN THEY WERE ENGAGED

1 Demoiselle Katharine Cavallieri [*sic*], born in Vienna, made her début in the National Theatre in 1778 as Sophie in [Umlauf's] *Bergknappen*, plays young lovers and girls' roles.

2 Demoiselle Teiber, born in Vienna, made her début in the National Theatre in 1778 as Fiamette in [Maximilian Ulbrich's] *Frühling und Liebe*. She plays young lovers and naive girls.

3 Madame Haselbek, *née* Schindler, made her début in the National Theatre in 1778. She plays lovers, girls, coquettes and low-comic roles.

4 Demoiselle Brenner sang in the Opera for the first time as Louise in *Frühling und Liebe*. Her roles are young and naughty girls.

5 Madame Maria Anna Weiß, born in Vienna, made her début in 1779 at Laxenburg [Castle, near Vienna] in [Umlauf's] *Die schöne Schusterin*.

6 Mad[ame] Lang[e], *née* Weber, born in the Palatinate, was engaged by the Vienna Opera in 1779 and made her début in that year as Hanchen in [Philidor and Blaise's *La rosière de Salency* translated as] *Das Rosenfest von Salenci*. She plays leading gentle, quiet lovers, also naive parts.

7 Madame Maria Anna Fischer, *née* Strasser, born at Karlsruhe in 1756, made her début in the National Theatre in 1780 as Frau von Bieder in [Grétry's *La fausse magie*, translated as] *Die abgeredete Zauberei*. She plays gentle mothers and character parts.

8 Madame Antonia Barnaskoni [Bernasconi], *née* Risler, was engaged in 1780 from Italy for the National Theatre, made her début as Hanchen in *Die verfolgte Unbekannte*. She plays tragic and gentle lovers, young ladies and heroines. [She had created the title role in Gluck's *Alceste* in Vienna in 1768 and had gone to sing in Italy].

The chorus consists of thirty persons of both sexes.

When Mozart arrived in the Austrian capital, two of the principal music publishers there were, respectively, of Swiss and Italian origin; the third, soon to fade out of existence, was a once celebrated Frenchman.

The eldest of the three, Christoph Torricella, was born *c.* 1715 in Switzerland; he established himself as an engraver in Prince Liechtenstein's house in the Herrengasse in Vienna in the 1770s. On 31 January 1781, a few weeks before Mozart's arrival, Torricella opened a musical establishment and soon had the good fortune to attract Joseph Haydn, who in 1782 published his new Symphony no. 73 ('La Chasse') with Torricella, followed two years later by a particularly magnificent engraving of Symphonies nos. 76–78, dedicated to Prince Nicolaus Esterházy. It was also in 1784 that Mozart issued his Opus VII, *Trois Sonates dédiées a Son Excellence Madame La Comtesse Terese de Kobenzl*, two piano sonatas and one violin sonata (K.333, 284, 454), with the firm. Meanwhile, a rival music publisher had established itself in the Kohlmarkt – Artaria & Co.; like Torricella, it had begun life as engravers and art-dealers. The Artaria family were apparently more astute businessmen than Torricella, and by 1784 the latter was in serious financial difficulties; Haydn entrusted his Symphonies nos. 80, 79 and 81 to Torricella, who announced them in

Scene in the Kohlmarkt, detail of an engraving by Carl Schütz, 1786, showing the premises of Artaria & Co. (right) with a throng of passers-by outside the entrance.

February 1785, but was obliged to sell the plates to Artaria, who then issued the works. By 1786 Torricella was forced into bankruptcy, and in August of that year he held a public auction of his plates, all of which were bought by Artaria, by then the leading and to all intents the sole music publishers in the Austrian capital.[18]

The Artaria family came from Blevio on Lake Como. Five members of the family left Blevio in 1759 and attended fairs in Frankfurt, Leipzig and Würzburg. Two of them subsequently returned to Italy, while the other three formed a company in Mainz. Two of the three, the cousins Carlo and Francesco, then went on to Vienna where, in 1770, they established a business in engravings, optical goods and barometers. They soon imported music themselves. Late in 1779, the firm entered into a long-term association with Haydn – a business arrangement which was to prove highly profitable to both.

A few months after Mozart had moved to Vienna in 1781, his six Violin Sonatas (K.376, 296, 377–380) were announced by Artaria & Co. in the *Wiener Zeitung* (8 December). Mozart was to publish with many other houses, but Artaria was to remain his most important contact; and it was with that house that he issued, for example, his Symphonies nos. 33 (K.319) and 35 (K.385, 'Haffner'), as well as his six quartets dedicated to Haydn (K.387, 421, 428, 458, 464, 465).

Antoine Huberty had founded a publishing house in Paris *c.* 1756, and his first 'privilège' dates from 2 April 1757. Among his many distinguished French publications, we might single out Pergolesi's *Salve Regina*, symphonies by Johann Stamitz, Anton Filtz and J.C. Bach (no fewer than twelve works) and various works by Haydn, including the first edition of Symphony no. 6 ('Le

Matin') and, as early as 1764, some of the first quartets ('Opus 0', Hoboken II:6). By 1777 he had decided to leave Paris for Vienna, a move which proved disastrous; at the beginning, he seemed to be successful, but he was apparently too old to be a serious rival to Torricella and Artaria. He began to engrave for Artaria (e.g. Haydn's 'Ah, come il core' from *La fedeltà premiata*) and to allow his works to be sold through Christoph Torricella; so that by 1781, when Mozart arrived, Huberty's business was definitely on the decline (except as an engraver for other publishers, especially Artaria). Huberty died in utter poverty in Vienna – a fate that befell many musicians – on 13 January 1791, aged 69, most of his assets being pewter and copper plates.

The new fortepiano (Hammerklavier)

The piano was invented independently by several persons in different countries, but the best of these pioneers, and the one to whom credit for the invention is generally given, was Bartolommeo Cristofori (1655–1731), instrument-maker and curator to the Grand Dukes of Tuscany in Florence. Fortunately, enough of Cristofori's instruments have survived to show how beautiful in tone and excellent in technique they were: his escapement action, as may be seen from an instrument preserved in the Metropolitan Museum in New York, is brilliantly constructed. The fact that this instrument was able very clearly to produce a *piano* or a *forte* strictly from touch gave rise to the name 'fortepiano' which in the early nineteenth century gradually came to be turned round to 'pianoforte'. But in the early days Cristofori's instruments were not entirely accepted by musicians (Domenico Scarlatti's patron in Spain was actually converting fortepianos back into harpsichords);[19] later in the century, the reverse would happen, and many eighteenth-century decorated pianos survive which were in fact converted from harpsichords.

Cristofori's invention spread rapidly, and by the early 1760s British (or rather German) makers in London were turning out a different kind of piano. Whereas Cristofori's instruments had been long and shaped like a harpsichord, the cabinet- and instrument-makers in London and, only slightly later, in Paris, needed to save space, and so they produced a spinet-like instrument, the later Victorian version of which is known as a 'square piano'. The English variety, which had an elaborate system of hand pedals, was a compact and mechanically efficient instrument. Like the 'grand' fortepianos of Cristofori, they generally had a range of five octaves from ⟨music⟩ to ⟨music⟩ , in other words an F-oriented instrument. Although some of these instruments, and possibly a few of Cristofori's, penetrated to Austria, it may be confidently asserted that before *c.* 1765 or 1770 hardly any pianos were known in the Austro-Hungarian Empire.[20] In Germany, however, the situation was different. Always interested in new technical devices, the Germans immediately understood the importance of Cristofori's invention and began making their own instruments. We know that the great Gottfried Silbermann (1683–1753), primarily known as an organ-builder, also experimented with pianos and that J.S. Bach heard one when he visited the court of Frederick the Great in Berlin. Bach did not like the new instrument, or at least that is what tradition tells us; but there was no doubt that in Germany the fortepiano had come to stay. By the middle of the 1770s, several makers, foremost among them Franz Jakob Späth (1714–86) in Regensburg and Johann Andreas Stein (1720–92) in Augsburg, were making excellent instruments with elaborate pedals, which were operated by the knees. The Stein instruments were undoubtedly the finest being made in Europe, and it is interesting to think that the Stein manufactory later transferred to Vienna (where the name was changed to Streicher) and was patronized by Beethoven as early as 1796.

It is not recorded whether any pianos were known in Salzburg when Mozart was a boy – probably not. On his various travels throughout Europe, he undoubtedly saw many pianos at first hand, particularly when in England in 1765. Our first evidence that he was beginning to view the piano with newly opened eyes comes during his ill-fated trip through Germany to Paris in 1777. He went via Augsburg, where he visited Stein's shop incognito, introducing himself as Trazom (his name spelt backwards – the Mozarts were always corresponding with this kind of cryptogram to ensure secrecy, since in those days letters were often opened by the authorities). A few days later, on 17 October, he wrote to his father about Stein's pianos:

This time I shall begin at once with Stein's pianofortes. Before I had seen any of his make, Späth's claviers had always been my favourites; but now I prefer Stein's, for they damp much better than the Regensburg instruments. When I strike hard, I can keep my finger on the note or lift it, but the sound ceases the moment I have made it. In whatever way I touch the keys, the tone will always remain even. It never grates, it is never stronger or weaker or entirely missing; in a word, it's always even. . . . His instruments have this special advantage over others, that they are made with escape action. Only one maker in a hundred bothers about that. But without an escapement it is impossible to avoid rattling and vibration. When you touch the keys, his hammers fall back again the moment after they have struck the strings, whether you hold down the keys or release them. He himself told me that when he has finished making one of these pianos, he sits down at it and tries all kinds of passages, runs and jumps, and he shaves and works away until it is capable of anything. . . .

And his pianos really do last: he guarantees that the sounding-board will neither break nor split. When he has finished making a sounding-board for a piano he places it in the open air, exposing it to rain, snow, the heat of the sun and all devils in order to make it crack. Then he inserts wedges and glues them in to make the instrument very strong and firm. He is quite delighted when it [the board] cracks, for then he can be sure that nothing more can happen to it. Indeed he often cuts into it himself and then glues it together again and strengthens it. He has finished three pianofortes of this kind. Today I played on one again.

. . . The last one [Sonata, K.284 (205b)] in D sounds exquisite on *Stein's* pianforte [*sic*]. The device which you work with your knee is also better on his than on other instruments. I have only to touch it and it works; and when you shift your knee the slightest bit, you do not hear the least reverberation.[21]

VIII *St Stephen's Cathedral, Vienna, seen in an engraving by Carl Schütz, 1792 (cf. pl. XI). Mozart was married in the Cathedral in 1782 and his funeral also took place here in December 1791 before he was buried in an unmarked grave in the suburban St Marx cemetery.*

IX   *The Lindenallee in the Augarten; this park – like the Prater
(opposite) – was one of the favourite places among the Viennese for outdoor
recreation. There was a pavilion in the Augarten where concerts were given;
Mozart made his first appearance in one of these concerts on 26 May 1782.*

X   The Lusthaus in the Prater, with (left foreground) the carriage in
which Emperor Joseph II, who was favourably disposed towards Mozart, is
seen riding with the Director of the Court Opera, Count Orsini-Rosenberg;
detail of an engraving by Johann Ziegler, 1783.

XI   *View of Vienna seen from the Upper Belvedere, with the towering spire (140 m. high) of St Stephen's Cathedral as the central feature of the landscape. This is one of a series of views of the Imperial capital painted by Bernardo Bellotto c. 1760, shortly before Mozart first came to Vienna as a child prodigy in the autumn of 1762, when he played before the Empress Maria Theresa at Schönbrunn (see pl. XXIV).*

XII   *The Viennese suburb of Landstraße showing the broad main street leading to the parish church; engraving by Joseph Ziegler. Wolfgang and Constanze moved to this suburb for several months in 1787 when the cost of their lavish quarters in the Domgaße put too great a strain on their resources.*

XIII   *The Neuer Markt (Mehlmarkt), Vienna, seen from the south; in this square stood the city casino building known as the Mehlgrube (see p. 79), where concerts were given; detail of a painting by Bernardo Bellotto, c. 1759.*

XIV-XVI   *Men of influence in Mozart's Vienna of the 1780s included:*
(ABOVE) Antonio Salieri, Court Kapellmeister and a prolific composer of
Italian opera: anonymous portrait in oils.
(RIGHT, above) Prince Galitzin, the Russian Ambassador, who was a
major patron of Mozart in Vienna and of music in general. Portrait in oils
by Adam J. Braun. (RIGHT) Carlo Artaria, doyen of the famous publishing
firm of Artaria & Co., which began issuing works by Mozart in 1781;
portrait in oils by J. Kreutzinger, c. 1780

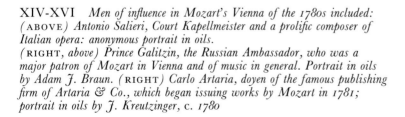

Today, there are a good many Steins available for examination in museums, among them an interesting instrument with a pedal attachment, now in the Metropolitan Museum of Art, New York. The pedal attachment, which was copied from the pedal harpsichord (such as J.S. Bach used), meant that one could have an independent part for the pedal, such as was used in organ writing. Later, Mozart would own such a pedal attachment for his Walter instrument.

The Stein pianos are eminently suitable for a delicate and rather staccato technique such as we know Mozart favoured. (Later, Beethoven used to complain that Mozart's piano playing was too choppy; he [Beethoven] preferred to treat the piano in a very legato fashion, almost like the organ.)[22] The slightly metallic sound rendered this instrument very satisfactory for chamber music, i.e. with other instruments, and for piano concertos; unlike modern instruments, the eighteenth-century piano blends well with wind instruments. The principal technical difficulty of these wooden-framed instruments was their lack of sustaining power, particularly in the treble range. Although techniques varied from maker to maker, most of these pianos had two strings in the bottom register and three in the top, to give more power to the upper *tessitura*, but soon makers began to construct pianos with three strings from top to bottom – the present writer used to own a Viennese instrument by Johann Heichele, *c.* 1795, strung with three strings throughout. The pedals of British (not Viennese or German) instruments included an effective device: the *sopra una corda*. By depressing this pedal, the player shifted the action so that the hammers played on only one string, the resulting sound being, as it were, muted. This beautiful and silvery effect was not imported into Vienna until after Mozart's death, but it came to be used frequently by composers of the period and was later immortalized by Beethoven in his 'Moonlight' Sonata, op. 27, no. 2.[23] All these characteristics may be heard on many recent recordings (including some produced by the Kunsthistorisches Museum, Vienna, and performed on instruments in the museum's collection),[24] where it will be seen that the old myth, no doubt propounded by our well-meaning but misguided Victorian forebears, that the modern piano is simply a technical improvement on the eighteenth-century variety, is certainly open to grave doubts. Nowadays, we tend to say that the modern piano is structurally and, particularly with reference to the frame, more solidly constructed than its eighteenth-century ancestor; but in the process much of the fortepiano's delicacy, subtlety and poetry have been sacrificed for loudness, vulgarity and pure brute strength. The most striking difference is in the bass. A passage such as the beginning of Beethoven's Waldstein Sonata, op. 53, simply does not work on a modern piano.[25]

When Mozart went to Vienna, he found a flourishing school of piano manufacturers, foremost among them Johann and Wenzel Schantz and Anton Walter. Walter supplied instruments to the castles of Prince Esterházy, but Haydn thought his instruments expensive and rather heavy to the touch; Haydn preferred Schantz's and several extant pianos by Johann Schantz have now been located.[26] Walter's instruments have survived in even greater numbers. The Mozarteum in Salzburg owns Mozart's instrument by Walter, unfortunately without the pedal attachment and inexpertly restored. The Haydn Museum in Eisenstadt owns one of the Esterházy instruments which has been competently restored, but which has a rather ineffectual upper *tessitura*. By contrast, the two magnificent Walter pianos in the Kunsthistorisches Museum have been beautifully restored and are in excellent playing condition. To hear Mozart or Haydn or early Beethoven played on such instruments is a complete revelation.[27]

When Mozart died in 1791, the piano was beginning to change. It was not only Beethoven who was responsible for this, but also the English school, led by Muzio Clementi, that highly individual composer, and soon joined by John

Anton Walter, the leading Viennese fortepiano builder, whose instruments were favoured by Mozart; anonymous portrait in oils. The composer's fortepiano, built in 1780 and acquired by him in 1784, is now displayed in the Mozarteum in Salzburg.

Cramer, whom Beethoven considered the finest pianist of his day. Mozart, obviously, did not live to see the outcome of this gradual but far-reaching metamorphosis, and thus it is particularly important to remember that the modern concert grand piano has only a nodding acquaintance with Mozart's delicate and beautiful instrument.

Concert Life in Vienna, 1781

The *Almanach* of 1782 contains (p. 162) a short note on what it terms 'Musical Academies', given in Lent either by the Society of Musicians (Tonkünstler-Societät) or by travelling virtuosi. Most of the programmes of these (benefit) concerts given in the Burgtheater and the Kärntnerthortheater – indeed, even reports of their actual existence – have not survived, since such events were generally not announced in the *Wiener Zeitung*. During Lent, the orchestras did not play in the opera houses and their members could be engaged, together with the actual houses themselves, for other performances (musicians had, however, to apply to the officials for permission). Thus, the number of public concerts given in Vienna was strictly limited. But in 1781 there were still several private orchestras, mostly belonging to very rich members of the aristocracy such as Prince Nicolaus Esterházy, which gave concerts in their owners' palaces, usually by invitation. Archbishop Colloredo's orchestra and some of the singers not only gave concerts in the House of the Order of Teutonic Knights – where most of them including Colloredo were actually staying – but gave guest appearances, for example, at the residence of the Russian Ambassador, Prince Galitzin.

Johann Georg Albrechtsberger (1736–1809), the noted composer and organist, who was Kapellmeister of St Stephen's Cathedral, Vienna; anonymous portrait in oils.

The one official organization which gave pairs of concerts at Christmas and in Lent – the Tonkünstler-Societät – was founded in 1771 to assist the widows and orphans of musicians. They gave these concerts with a very large orchestra, up to 180 strong, often with a chorus and soloists from the Opera as well, using all the best musicians of Vienna. Whether as a composer or as a working musician, it was a matter of prestige to provide one's services *gratis*. The concerts were patronized and attended by the Court and the nobility; usually an oratorio was performed, with a concerto or another instrumental piece in the interval. Mozart was very anxious to participate in these celebrated concerts, and the Archbishop's initial refusal to let him do so was a prime factor in the ensuing battle of wills, which resulted in Wolfgang's dismissal in May.

The concerts in 1781 consisted of *three* pairs: the reason for the additional (third) pair was that in 1780 the Society had been obliged to cancel its Christmas concerts because of the period of official mourning following Empress Maria Theresa's death. The first pair of concerts took place on 11 and 13 March, and the second pair on 1 and 3 April. On the two latter evenings J.G. Albrechtsberger's *Die Pilgrime auf Golgotha* was performed. Then came a sensation – Mozart's first public appearance in Vienna since he had been there as a boy. Wolfgang had related in letters to his father how much he had wished to appear in such a concert, because he considered it the best way to win not only the public's approval but also, perhaps more important, the Emperor's. He intended to play his Variations on 'Je suis Lindor' ['Son Lindoro'] from Paisiello's *Il barbiere di Siviglia* (K.354), improvise a fugue beforehand, and play a piano concerto (something of a novelty for Vienna). Mozart thought that he would borrow 'Countess Thun's beautiful Stein pianoforte', and remarked that 'whenever I've played this programme in public [e.g. in Viennese salons], I have always received the greatest applause – because the pieces contrast with one another so well and everyone has something to his taste.'[28]

The Archbishop, on whom Mozart and all his well-wishers put considerable pressure, relented, and in a postscript to the letter of 28 March 1781, Wolfgang tells his father that he will participate in a concert after all. For the second concert of the April series, given in the Kärntnerthortheater, the placard stated that the programme would begin with 'A symphony composed by *Herr Ritter* Wolfgang Amadi [*sic*] Mozart, . . . Then *Herr Ritter* Mozart will play quite alone on a pianoforte. He was here as a boy of seven years, and even then he gained the general applause of the public partly because of his abilities as a composer, but also on account of his reputation in the art altogether, and the particular brilliance and delicacy of his keyboard playing.'

It used to be thought that the Mozart symphony played on this occasion was no. 34 (K.338), the grandest of the Salzburg symphonies of 1779–80, with trumpets and drums, but now it is believed that the work was no. 31 (K.297), the 'Paris', with its large wind scoring. When the Symphony was rehearsed, relates Mozart in his letter of 11 April to his father, it was 'magnificent and had the greatest success. There were 40 violins – all the wind instruments were doubled – 10 violas – 10 Contre Bassi, 8 violoncelli, and 6 bassoons.'[29] After playing in the concert he wrote (on 4 April) that he had to admit that he was well satisfied with the Viennese public. 'I had to start all over again, because there was no end to the applause.' Emperor Joseph II was present.

Mozart was now launched on his spectacular career in Vienna.

Church Music in Vienna and the Josephinian Reforms

For hundreds of years there had existed in Vienna a great tradition of church music and compositions for the church. When Mozart arrived, Joseph II had been on the throne alone for scarcely three-and-a-half months, and was just beginning to implement his series of wide-ranging reforms. Among the matters to which he was soon to turn his attention was the power of the Church in the Monarchy as a whole, and also the kind of music being performed in churches. Charles Burney, when he was in Vienna in 1772, had noted that there was hardly a church or monastery where there was not a daily mass performed with singers, an organ, three or four violins, viola and double bass; and since the churches in Vienna were well attended, people's taste was conditioned by hearing this *figuraliter* church music, even if it was not always of the best quality. It was, therefore, in church and dance hall that the majority of the Viennese populace heard most of their music; and despite what Burney says,[30] music in both these categories in Vienna was of an extremely high standard (more conservative in church, of course).

In Salzburg, Mozart had been among the forefront of 'modern' church composers, but not being attached to any church in Vienna, he could hardly continue to write church music there. In fact, as we shall see, he was able to contribute one 'freelance' mass of epic proportions to the genre, a work which he began in 1782 of his own volition, showing that he was much attracted to music for the Church. In the event, church music in the Austrian crown lands was soon to suffer a serious setback because of the reforms which Joseph II was about to institute. The Emperor considered that music in church should be vastly simplified and that the congregation should participate; that German-language hymns should be preferred to the opera-like masses, with their 'arias' and seductive instrumental solos. By 1783, this series of reforms was fully effective, and hundreds of Viennese church musicians found themselves without a job.[31]

Dr Charles Burney, the English composer and music historian; pencil drawing by George Dance, 1794.

Mozart was soon to make the personal acquaintance of Joseph II, and he became an admirer of this brilliant, headstrong and violently controversial emperor who would guide Austria's fortunes for the next nine years. Even today, the controversy about Joseph II remains a live issue. No one, it seems, can be impartial about his reign. The following summary, by Karl A. Roider, Jr, seems to sum up Joseph's career in a fair and objective fashion:

Upon her death, Maria Theresa was succeeded by her son, Joseph II, who immediately implemented the sweeping reforms he had tried to persuade his mother to accept. Within a year after her death, he issued both an Edict of Toleration, allowing Protestants and Greek Orthodox a measure of religious freedom, and a Patent to Abolish Serfdom, guaranteeing freedom of person to every peasant. Joseph then instituted a thorough centralization of the monarchy by obliterating all traditional and provincial divisions, introduced extensive changes in law and judicial procedure, abolished all monasteries and convents that failed to serve social needs, and decreed equal taxation for all citizens. During the ten years of his reign, he issued over 6,000 edicts, covering virtually every matter of concern to himself and his subjects. To Joseph II, the state existed to ensure 'the greatest good for the greatest number,' and no customs, institutions, or sentiments were going to prevent him from achieving that goal.

Emperor Joseph II; detail of an anonymous portrait in oils, c. 1790.

Unfortunately for Joseph, however, his wholesale changes did not create a state of satisfied citizens but elicited instead an outburst of protest against him. Upon embarking on a war with the Ottoman Empire in 1788, Joseph found himself confronted by threatened revolution in Hungary and open rebellion in Belgium. Stunned by these outbursts and warned of seething discontent elsewhere in the monarchy, Joseph revoked many of his reforms. In February, 1790, he died, convinced that he had utterly failed.[32]

As for Mozart, his career during the reign of Joseph II is like the musical sign for a crescendo and decrescendo < > with (if the conceit be permitted to continue) *Le nozze di Figaro* perhaps in the middle. But in the midst of all Mozart's worries and, ultimately, miseries, he remained decently, indeed touchingly, attached to the ideas, and the person, of his Emperor.

III

Vienna: The Social Scene

T HE MOST INTERESTING and original chronicler of contemporary events and
the general ambience of Vienna during the years Mozart spent in the city
was Johann Pezzl (1756–1823). His *Skizze von Wien* ('Sketch of Vienna'),
covering the years 1786–90, first appeared in instalments and subsequently in
two volumes.

Pezzl was a perceptive and often witty observer of life in Josephinian
Vienna. He was, like Mozart, a follower of Joseph II's reform policies. He
approved of the Emperor's attempt to curtail the powers of the nobility and
the Church, to reform the judicial (and particularly penal) system; and of
Joseph's expressed desire to be a true representative of his subjects, which he
expressed in, for example, his simple dress, and his unaffected way of mingling
with the people.

Pezzl chronicles the whole spectrum of daily life in the city: how people
dressed, what food cost for a bachelor, how the prostitutes operated, how
ladies behaved in society. Everything interested him: why the Viennese like
beer as well as wine (Austria being a wine-producing country), how the ice-
floes on the Danube originated, how appalling were the public spectacles of
bear-baiting. Pezzl thought it disgusting that the Viennese should flock to see a
criminal branded and then, shrieking, broken on the wheel. He loved the
theatre and regularly attended performances of opera as well as spoken
theatre. He followed the amazing history of Vienna's first freedom of the Press
– one of Joseph's most daring innovations – and the severe curtailment
(although not abolition) of censorship. Pezzl thus brings the Vienna of the
1780s to life, and of course his great advantage is that he was Mozart's exact
contemporary; viewed from a modern perspective, therefore, it is almost as if
we too are looking at scenes of everyday life in the Imperial capital through
Mozart's own eyes.

Selected paragraphs from Pezzl's descriptions are included here as
accompaniments to a variety of contemporary and near-contemporary
engravings depicting life and places in the city as Mozart would have known
them.

OPPOSITE *View of the
Graben, looking towards the
Kohlmarkt. Pezzl compares
the popularity of the Graben
to that of St Mark's Square
in Venice: 'Anyone with half
an hour to spare or who
wants some exercise walks
up and down the Graben a
few times.' On the opposite
side of the square stood the
Trattnerhof, where Mozart
lived in 1784 (see p. 121).
Detail from an engraving by
Carl Schütz, 1781.*

EVERYDAY LIVING: STREETS AND SQUARES

PEZZL:

Assuming that you have no family, that you are not employed in a public office, that you are not a gambler, and that you do not keep a regular mistress, . . . you can live fairly comfortably in Vienna on the following annual outlay, which will enable you to move in respectable middle-class circles . . . 464 fl.

It is considerably cheaper to live in the suburbs. An apartment that will cost you 200 gulden [p.a.] in town can be had outside for 120. . . .

The Graben is to Vienna as St Mark's [Square] is to Venice, and is never without a crowd of people . . . As soon as darkness falls, there appear those girls of the oldest profession who are too poor to dress sufficiently attractively to show themselves at noon. The usual haunts of these birds of passage are the Graben, the Kohlmarkt and the Hof. . . .

If there is a new opera or play, the racket of the carriages, the stamping of the horses' hooves and the barkings of the coachmen as they cross the Graben and the Kohlmarkt combine to make a hellish concert. You cross St Michael's Square at your peril, for carriages come from all four sides. . . .

OPPOSITE *The entrance to St Michael's, the church generally favoured by the* beau monde, *and (below) fabrics and fashion accessories displayed for sale in the square known as the Stock am Eisen. Details from engravings by Carl Schütz, 1788 and 1779 respectively.*

ABOVE *View of the Neuer Markt (Mehlmarkt), one of Vienna's most imposing squares; in the background stands the palace of Johann Joseph Nepomuk, Prince Schwarzenberg, where semi-private concerts were given. Detail of an engraving by Carl Schütz, 1798.*

RIGHT *Aspects of the daily life of a young woman of easy virtue displaying her charms on two of Vienna's squares; engravings from the* Taschenbuch für Grabennymphen auf das Jahr 1787, *mentioned by Pezzl.*

LEISURE AND ENTERTAINMENT

PEZZL:

The Viennese love banquets, dancing, shows, distractions. On holidays they love to walk in the Prater and the Augarten, to attend animal baitings and firework displays, to go into the country with their families and sit down to a well-appointed table. . . .

The name of this pleasure garden [the Prater] derives presumably from the Spanish 'Prado'. . . . You enter it from an alley of chestnut trees . . . and find yourself in a wide semicircle, from which five alleys fan out to the woods and gardens. In the central part are a number of taverns, summer-houses . . .

This theatre [the Theater auf der Wieden, soon to be taken over by Emanuel Schikaneder] is now regularly visited because it is new. Various groups of strolling players arrive during market hours and perform in wooden buildings erected for them on the main squares. You had better take some tobacco with you or you will not be able to stand the smell of the lamps, of spilled beer, of the sweating public. On stage there is very rough play, and vulgar exchanges frequently occur between the public and actors.

ABOVE, LEFT *The Prater, with coffee-houses on the left and in the centre background, the Casino; detail of an engraving by Johann Ziegler after Lorenz Janscha, c. 1794.*

ABOVE, RIGHT *A private ball, with a small orchestra consisting of two oboes, two first violins, two second violins and a double bass; engraving by Clemens Kohl after a drawing by Sollerer.*

LEFT *Frontispiece from the* Almanach für Theaterfreunde *(1791), showing a performance of the opera* Der Stein der Weisen *at the* Theater auf der Wieden *(Freihaus Theater), where Mozart's* Die Zauberflöte *received its première.*

RIGHT *Popular street entertainment in Vienna in 1785; etching by F.A. Maulbertsch.*

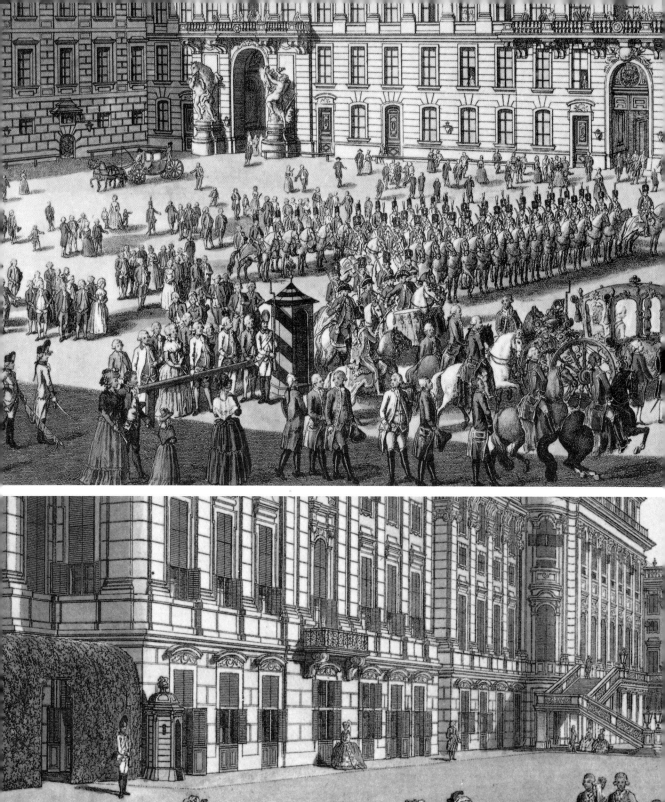

COURT AND CEREMONIAL

PEZZL:

The principal building in the city is the Imperial Castle which, as one knows, has an undistinguished exterior, but inside is worthy of a great monarch. The joke of a pamphleteer who wrote that 'the Emperor's horses are better housed than the man himself' is literally true.

Today [1786] the outward appearance of the [Imperial] Court has totally changed: its motto is economy . . . Except for Corpus Christi [the Thursday following Trinity Sunday] and the Feast of St Stephen [26 December], when the Emperor . . . shows himself in public in a kind of state procession, one would hardly be aware of his presence in Vienna at all, were it not for his occasional appearance, in a two-horse chaise painted green, driving in the Augarten.

[The Turkish War had dragged on since February 1788, and there had been no cause for celebrations until] In the following year . . . Prince Koburg won a victory at Foczan that was worthy of being celebrated, and was: on 22 September he was again victorious . . . in Wallachia . . .

On 12 October . . . General Kleebeck arrived . . . with the news that Belgrade had been taken. Now there were celebrations lasting three days . . . On 14 October there was a grand Te Deum in St Stephen's Cathedral, attended by the Emperor in full gala with his entire official retinue and the Noble Guards. . . .

ABOVE *Ceremonial procession of the Emperor and Empress leaving the inner courtyard of the Hofburg for St Stephen's Cathedral. The Imperial coach is preceded by pages of honour and escorted by members of the German Noble Bodyguard. Detail of an engraving by J.G. Mansfeld, after a drawing by Carl Schütz, 1792.*

LEFT *Emperor Joseph II (centre) with a group of distinguished visitors – Grand Duke Paul of Russia and his suite – in the grounds of Schönbrunn. Detail of an engraving by Carl Schütz, 1782.*

IV

The Two Constanzes

––––––––––

The actor and amateur artist Joseph Lange and his wife Aloysia; engraving by Daniel Berger, 1785, after an original drawing by Joseph Lange.

Since Mozart's visit to Munich in December 1778 and January 1779, the Weber family had moved to Vienna, where Aloysia had married the actor and excellent amateur painter, Joseph Lange. Madame Cäcilia Weber and her two unmarried daughters were living on the second floor of a house in St Peter's Square, 'Zum Auge Gottes' ('The Eye of God'), now No. 11. Although he was careful not to mention the fact to his father, Wolfgang obviously visited the Webers soon after his arrival in Vienna. Mozart was incensed at having to lunch, like other musicians, with liveried servants and kitchen personnel of the Archbishop's retinue: he relates to his father that he ate in icy silence as crude jokes passed across the table. Each member of the retinue received 3 ducats *per diem* to eat where they pleased in the evening. The orchestra and the castrato Ceccarelli gave concerts in the Archbishop's apartment in the house of the Order of Teutonic Knights, also at the house of one of the Counts Pálffy and at the home of the Russian Ambassador at Krugerstraße 1046. It was characteristic of Mozart as he entered the Embassy to storm past the flunkeys and go straight to Prince Galitzin (by whom the Mozarts had been received in 1768 when Wolfgang was still a child prodigy).

. . . I went there alone, because I'm ashamed to go anywhere with [those crude-mannered musicians from the Salzburg orchestra]; – when I got there and went upstairs, I found [the Archbishop's valet] H[err] Angelbauer waiting to instruct the lackeys to show me in – but I paid no attention to either the valet or the lackeys, and walked straight through to the music rooms, for all the doors were open. – And straight to the Prince to attend on him; – I had quite forgotten my Ceccarelli and [the violinist] Brunetti, who were nowhere to be seen – they were stuck behind the orchestra, leaning against the wall and didn't dare to advance a single step . . . Today Prince gallizin [*sic*] wanted to hear Ceccarelli sing – next time it will surely be my turn. . . .[1]

Mozart was already paying regular calls on members of Viennese society. 'I've lunched twice already at Countess Thun's, and go there almost every day – that's the most charming, dearest lady I ever saw in my life; and she holds a high opinion of me too.' Her husband, Count Franz Joseph Thun-Hohenstein (1734–1800), was a follower of Dr Mesmer – the doctor with the 'magnetic cures' – and a member of the Vienna Lodge 'Zur wahren Eintracht'. The Countess, *née* Maria Wilhelmine, Countess Ulfeld (1747–1800), seems to have been a genuine admirer of Mozart's. She was also the liberal and free-thinking mother of the three most celebrated and beautiful debutantes in Viennese society at the time – the 'Three Graces', as they were known: Elisabeth (born 1764), married in 1788 to Count Andreas Razumovsky (Beethoven's patron and later Russian Ambassador in Vienna); Christiane (born 1765), married in 1788 to Prince Carl von Lichnowsky (with whom Mozart travelled to Germany in 1789 and who was to be Beethoven's protector); and Maria Carolina (born 1769), married in 1793 to the British Attaché in Vienna, Richard Meade, Earl of Clanwilliam. Mozart had many ties to the Thun family; he wrote the 'Linz' Symphony (no. 36, K.425) in 1783 when a guest of the 'old' Count (Johann Joseph; 1711–88) in the Upper Austrian town, and stayed with the family in Prague in 1787.[2]

Elisabeth was scandalized by the events of her wedding night, and related the whole in gruesome detail to Christiane, who in turn was so appalled that she forthwith broke off her engagement to Prince Lichnowsky. She relented, however, and married him on 25 November 1788, only twelve days after Razumovsky had told Count Zinzendorf at dinner that the couple were no longer on speaking terms.[3] The Lichnowsky marriage, as might be expected, was not a success.

Another patron was Count Johann Philipp von Cobenzl, whom Mozart had known since 1763; Cobenzl was Court and State Chancellor in Vienna and had a pretty summer estate on the Reisenberg, above Grinzing (it is now a favourite excursion for the Viennese). Of his visits there in July 1781, Mozart noted: 'It's an hour away from Vienna, . . and is called Reisenberg. – I've spent

the night here once already; and now I am staying for several days. – The little house is nothing; but the countryside; – the forest [the famous 'Vienna Woods'] – where there is a grotto which they've constructed as if it were fashioned by Nature itself. That is all magnificent and extremely pleasant.'[4] Mozart's first piano pupil in Vienna was a young cousin of Count Cobenzl's, Maria Carolina, Countess Thiennes de Rumbeke (born 1755). Giving lessons was as yet a slender source of income, but one that would soon grow.

Mozart was proud and headstrong, and it was perhaps inevitable that he would soon clash with the arrogant Archbishop Colloredo, who strove to keep his young employee on a tight rein. The first serious argument was over the forthcoming concert (3 April 1781) of the Tonkünstler-Societät. There were other difficulties too, as he explained to his father on 4 April:

I've already written to you that the Archbishop is a great hindrance to me here, for he has done me out of at least 100 ducats, which I could quite certainly have earned from an academy at the theatre – for the ladies *themselves* offered to distribute tickets. . . . P.S. I assure you that this is a splendid place – and for *my métier* the best in the world – everybody will tell you that. – And I am happy to make as much money as possible; for that's the best, after good health. – Think no more of my follies, which I have long since regretted from the bottom of my heart – misfortune brings wisdom. . . .'[5]

In that postscript, Mozart seems to be referring obliquely to his failed Paris trip and the blighted affair with Aloysia Weber; but he was soon to plunge his father into despair as the tension between him and Colloredo mounted. On 11 April, referring to a concert for the Archbishop, Mozart angrily complains, 'what drives me half mad is that I had been invited to Countess Thun's, and therefore couldn't go, and who was there? *The Emperor*.'[6] Still, Wolfgang held back from a complete break because, as he wrote on 28 April, '*the whole world should and must know that the Archbishop of Salzburg has only you, my best of fathers, to thank for the fact that he didn't lose me forever (I mean by that, for his own person) . . .*' The letter is written *en clair*, i.e. not in cipher (the Mozarts thought that the censor in Salzburg was opening and reading their correspondence, which was entirely possible, even likely). Wolfgang intended to ask his father's permission to give concerts during next Lent (1782) in Vienna, and if his employer the Archbishop (who would have to be petitioned, of course) should refuse 'I shall go all the same'. Only on that condition would he consider returning to Salzburg at all. One can imagine Leopold's dismay, even if he could also read that 'yesterday the ladies kept me a whole hour at the piano after the academy – but I think I would still be there, if I hadn't slunk away – I thought I'd played enough *gratis* . . .'.

But there was worse to come in his son's next missive (9 May):

I am still full of anger . . . – My patience was sorely tried for a long time, but at last it is exhausted. I am no longer so unfortunate as to be in the Salzburg service – today was the happiest day for me; now listen – Twice already that – I don't know what I should call him – addressed me with the greatest insults and impertinences, which I have not wanted to repeat to you, so as to spare your feelings; – He called me a brat, a nasty rascal – said I should be off – and I – endured it all – but I felt that not only my but also your honour had been attacked – but I remained silent – now listen; – eight days ago the footman came upstairs and said I must leave immediately; – all the others had been told when they would depart, but not I; – so I quickly shoved everything into my trunk, and – old Madame Weber was kind enough to offer me her house – now I have my own pretty room; I am with obliging people who give me a helping hand with all these things that one often needs quickly and (if one is living alone) not in a position to have. [There was difficulty in finding a place on the next stagecoach] and when I came to attend upon him, the first thing I heard was

Archbishop: 'Well, brat, when is he leaving?'[7]
I: 'I wanted to leave tonight, but all the seats are reserved.'
Then all hell broke loose. – I was the nastiest brat he knows – no-one serves him as badly as I – he advises me to leave at once, today, otherwise he will write home to have my salary stopped – one couldn't get a word in edgeways, – finally my blood started to boil and so I said – 'well then, your archiepiscopal grace is not satisfied with me?'

'What?' he threatens me. 'Idiot, idiot! – There is the door, out he goes, I don't want to have anything more to do with such a miserable brat.' 'Well, at last', said I – 'and I want to have nothing to do with you either.' 'Be off, then.' – And I, in leaving: 'This is final; tomorrow you shall have it in writing.' Tell me, then, dearest father, did I not act too late rather than too soon? . . .

Write to me in cipher that you are pleased; . . . if . . . the Archbishop should be the least bit impertinent to you, come at once with my sister to Vienna – all 3 can live here on what I earn . . . – I never want to hear anything more about Salzburg . . .[8]

It must be said that Leopold's reaction was largely justified: Wolfgang's debacle with the Archbishop was scandalous. In 1781, one simply did not address a Prince-Archbishop in the way he did. If Mozart had been incensed enough to lay a hand on Colloredo's Master of the Kitchen, Count Arco, who shortly after the final interview physically booted Wolfgang out of the room and down the stairs, the result might have been similar to the fate of a young man in Innsbruck who struck a nobleman and was sentenced to fifty strokes of the cane – 'it was all over in two hours,' wrote Mozart to his father. 'After the fifth lash his breeches split . . he was carried away unconscious . . .' (letter of 8 August).[9]

Mozart was quite right about Vienna and the opportunities it offered and by 1784 he was the toast of the town, earning large sums of money; however, he had not only acted rashly with Colloredo, but – as far as his father was concerned – had also perpetrated a second folly by moving in with the Webers.

Die Entführung aus dem Serail

Before Mozart left the service of Archbishop Colloredo, he had been in contact with the well-known actor and playwright, Gottlieb Stephanie, Jr, who – as Wolfgang relates in his letter of 18 April 1781, the first to contain any reference to the subject – 'will give me a new and, as he says, good book'[10] to set to music. The book was to be *Die Entführung aus dem Serail* (*Il Seraglio*), Mozart's first great international success, and the first stage work in which the full flower of his genius reached a wider public.

Grand Duke Paul of Russia (later Tsar Paul I; 1754–1801), whose planned visit to Vienna provided a spur for Mozart to proceed quickly with the composition of Die Entführung aus dem Serail, *which was performed for the royal visitor under the composer's direction. Engraving by Hieronymus Löschenkohl.*

[26 May 1781] . . . I don't know why I should hold back with the opera. Count Rosenberg [Orsini-Rosenberg; Intendant of the Vienna Court Opera], on the two occasions I paid my respects to him, received me in the politest fashion, and he heard my opera [*Idomeneo*, performed privately] at Countess Thun's, together with van Suiten [Baron Gottfried van Swieten, head of the Court Censorship Commission and Prefect of the Imperial Library] and H[err] v[on] Sonnenfels [reformer of the Court Opera under Maria Theresa] – and since Stephani[e] is my good friend, all will be well . . . [9 June 1781] The Emperor [Joseph II] is away, . . . [Orsini-Rosenberg] commissioned Schröder (the actor) to look around for a good opera book and to give it to me to compose . . .[11]

[16 June 1781] Now I must explain to you why we were suspicious of Stephani[e]. This person, I am very sorry to say, has the worst possible reputation in the whole of Vienna . . . but I didn't want to involve myself in all that. It might be true, since everybody denigrates him – however, he is in great favour with the Emperor; and the very first time we met he was very friendly to me; and he said, we're already old friends, and he would be very pleased if he were to be in a position to serve me. – I've seen 2 new pieces by him which are really rather good; the first is *Das Loch in der Thüre* and the second *Der Oberamtman[n] und die Soldaten* . . . but even if I really do receive the libretto, I won't set a line, since Count Rosenberg isn't here – and if in the end he doesn't approve of it, I should have had the privilege of having worked for nothing. And that's something I simply won't do. – Do you think, then, that I shall write an opéra comique like an opera seria? – Just as there should be as little as possible of the trivial and as much of the learned and solid in an opera seria, there ought, in an opera buffa, to be as little as possible of the learned and all the more of the trivial and merry.

The fact that people want to have comic music also in an opera seria is something I can do nothing about; – but here [in Vienna], they make a very fine distinction between the two genres.[12]

On 4 July, Wolfgang wrote to his sister saying that his only amusement was the theatre. He continues: 'I wish you could see a tragedy here: I know of no other theatre where all genres are *excellently* performed; but here it is the case with every role, the lowliest and poorest role is well done, and the cast doubled [in case of illness] . . .'[13]

At the end of July, Mozart received from Stephanie the libretto for the opera *Die Entführung*. On 1 August he informed his father:

The book is quite good, the subject is Turkish and is called 'Bellmont & Konstanze' or 'Die Verführung [*sic*] aus dem Serail' [The Seduction from the Seraglio] – I will include Turkish music [with supplementary percussion instruments, triangle, bass drum, etc.] in the Overture, the Chorus in the first act and the final chorus. Mad^selle Cavalieri, Mad^selle Teyber, Mr Fischer, Mr Adamberger, Mr Dauer and Mr Walter will be the singers. I am so pleased to compose the libretto that I have already completed the first aria for Cavalieri, that for Adamberger and the concluding trio of the first act. It's true that there isn't much time, for it's supposed to be finished by the middle of September. . . . Grand Duke [Paul] of Russia is to come here, and so Stephani[e] asked me if it were possible to finish the opera in this short time. For the Emperor and Count Rosenberg will arrive soon and will ask right away if anything is ready? – and then he [Stephanie] will be pleased to be able to say that Umlauf will be ready with his opera (he's had it for a long time) and that I am writing one specially for the occasion – he will certainly consider it a credit to me that I have undertaken to

compose it for this purpose so quickly. No one except Adamberger and Fischer knows anything about it, for Stephani[e] begged us not to say a word, since Count Rosenberg is not here yet, and all kinds of gossip can arise – Stephani[e] doesn't want it thought that he is too great a friend of mine, but that rather he is doing all this because Count Rosenberg so wished it, and before he left he did in fact tell him to seek out a book for me. . . .[14]

It is not clear from this letter whether Mozart was aware that the opera book was not an original libretto by Stephanie but an adaptation of a play by Christoph Friedrich Bretzner (1748–1807); presumably, however, Mozart must have realized the opera's origins, especially since the printed word-book would state 'freely adapted from Bretzner . . .' But in those days it was not thought necessary to seek an author's permission (Bretzner lived in Germany), and this lack of courtesy was to have a curious sequel.

On 22 August, Mozart wrote to his father telling him that the first act of *Die Entführung* was finished; then, about 20 September, he writes: 'Excuse me if you have to pay a little more postage this time [on delivery] of the letter, but I wanted to give you at least some idea of the first act so that you could see what the whole thing will be like; and I couldn't do this with less.' On the reverse side of the paper is, in Constanze Weber's hand, Constanze's aria 'Ach, ich liebte' from *Die Entführung*, and on another sheet the proposed cast was included.[15] And thus it happened that Constanze Weber's handwriting reached her 'adversary' without his knowing it.

About a week later, Wolfgang expands his description:

[26 September] . . . The opera was supposed to begin with a monologue, but I asked H[err] Stephani[e] to turn it into a small arietta – and that, instead of the dialogue which the two have after Osmin's little song, there should be a duet. Since we intended H[err] Fischer to sing the part of Osmin, and indeed he has an excellent bass voice (notwithstanding the Archbishop's comment to me that he sings too low for a bass and my assurance to him that he will sing higher the next time): one has to make good use of such a man, especially since he has the public here totally on his side. – In the original libretto, however, Osmin had just that one single aria to sing, otherwise nothing except the trio and the finale. Now he's been given an aria in the first act, and will have another in the 2nd. I told H[err] Stephani[e] just how the aria should go, and most of the music was finished before Stephani[e] had even set the text for it. You have only the beginning and the end, which must create a good effect. Osmin's rage is transported into the comic through it, because the Turkish music is added. In the execution of the aria I allowed his fine, low notes (despite the Salzburg Midas) to shine through. His words, 'drum beym Barte des Propheten' etc. are in the same tempo but with quick notes, and since his rage increases steadily, one thinks the aria is already at an end, but the allegro assai – in quite another metre and in another key – will certainly be most effective; for a man who is in such a rage completely loses control and breaks all the rules, not being himself – and thus the music mustn't know what it's doing either. But since the passions, violent or not, must never be expressed in an offensive manner; and music, even in the most appalling situations, must never offend the ear and hence must always remain music; the key I have chosen is not foreign to F (the key of the aria) but related to it, though not the nearest, D minor, but the next one away, A minor. – Now, to Belmonte's aria in A major, 'O wie ängstlich, O wie feurig', do you know how that is expressed? Here, the heart, beating with love, is at once indicated – the two violin sections in octaves – this is the favourite aria with everyone who has heard it, also mine, and it's entirely tailored to Adamberger's voice; one sees the trembling – shaking –, one sees how his bursting breast swells, which is expressed by a crescendo; one hears his stuttering and sighing, which is expressed by the first violins using mutes and a flute in unison.

The Janissaries Chorus has everything one expects from a Janissaries Chorus – short and merry, and written specially for the Viennese. – I have slightly sacrificed the aria for Konstanze, 'Trennung war mein banges Loos, und nun schwimmt mein Aug' in Thränen', in favour of Mad^{selle} Cavallieri's [*sic*] agile throat, but as far as an Italianate bravura aria allows, I have tried to express the thought.

Now the trio at the end of the first act. Pedrillo has put it about that his master is an architect, to enable him to meet his Konstanze in the garden; the Bassa has taken him into his service. Osmin, as overseer, doesn't know any of this, is a rough lout, and, as the sworn enemy of all foreigners, impertinent; he does not want to allow them into the garden. The first piece that appears is very short, and because the text allows it, I wrote it rather nicely in three parts, for the whole thing starts in the major, *pianissimo*, and it must move very quickly, and the end will make quite a racket – and there is everything that the end of an act ought to have, the more noise the better, and the shorter the better, so that the audience won't be dissuaded from applauding.

Of the overture you have only fourteen bars. It is quite short, and switches from *forte* to *piano* all the time, whereby in the *forte* there is always Turkish music. – It modulates continually through various keys and I think they won't fall asleep over it even if they haven't slept for a whole night. – Now I am sitting here in a quandary: the first act has been ready for three weeks, also an aria in the 2nd act and the drinking duet (per le Sig^{ri} vieneri [for the Viennese]) which only consists of my Turkish tattoo. But I can't do any more, because the whole plot is being turned upside down, and at my instigation. At the beginning of the third act there is a charming quintet or rather a finale, and I would rather have that as the ending of the 2nd act; to do this, there has to be a big change, even a large new intrigue – and since Stephani[e] has his hands full with other work, one has to be patient. – Everyone grumbles about Stephani[e], and it may be that he is so friendly only to my face; but he does arrange the libretto just as I want it, down to the last detail, and by God; I can't ask more of him. . . .[16]

By 6 October, Wolfgang admits to his father

. . . I am gradually losing my patience at being unable to proceed with the opera. – Of course, I am composing other things – but the passion is there . . . I've composed Adamberger's aria in A, that for Cavallieri [*sic*] in B flat, and the trio in a single day, and wrote it down in one-and-one-half days. But it wouldn't help even if the whole opera were finished already, for it would have to wait until after Gluck's two [revived] operas are staged – and a good deal of preparation is needed for both. . . .[17]

Leopold Mozart appears to have made criticisms of the libretto, for on 13 October Wolfgang responds:

. . . you are quite right – but the poetry is quite suited to the character of the stupid, coarse and nasty Osmin. And I quite realize that the quality of the verse is not of the best; but it nicely fits my musical ideas (which have been swimming about in my head beforehand), so I have to agree with them. – And I will wager that nothing will be missing when they are performed. As far as the actual poetry contained in the book itself is concerned, I really couldn't dislike it. Belmonte's aria, 'O wie ängstlich' etc., could hardly be better written for the music. And except for 'hui' and 'Kummer ruht in meinem schoos' [Trouble rests in my lap] – for trouble can't rest – the aria is not bad, especially the first part. I don't know, in an opera poetry must of necessity be the handmaiden of the music. Why are Italian comic operas everywhere so successful? With all the misery of their libretti! Even in Paris, where I personally witnessed them. Because in them the music dominates completely, and one forgets everything else. The more pleasure, therefore, must an opera give where the plan of the piece has been well worked out; but the words must be written just for the music, and not just put down to enjoy, here and there, some miserable rhyme which, by God!, contributes absolutely nothing to a theatrical representation, whatever it may be, but on the contrary, harms it. There are whole strophes which ruin a composer's entire idea: verses are probably music's most urgent requirement, but rhyming just for its own sake is the most harmful. Those gentlemen who approach their work so pedantically will go under along with the music.

It is thus best if a good composer who understands the theatre and is capable of putting his own ideas into action collaborates with a clever poet, a real Phoenix. . . .[18]

On 17 November, Wolfgang was able to report having been given 'something more of my opera to compose . . .',[19] and on 30 January 1782 that the work had been held back partly because of the two Gluck works being revived and partly on account of the many changes required in the libretto, but 'it will be given right after Easter.'[20] It was not until 29 May that he could inform his father that the first rehearsal would take place 'this coming Monday'. The letter in which Wolfgang described the favourable reception of the première on 16 July, is alas, lost. On 20 July, however, following the second performance, he writes:

Johann Valentin Adamberger and Caterina Cavalieri, respectively the first Belmonte and Constanze in Die Entführung aus dem Serail *in 1782; silhouettes by Hieronymus Löschenkohl.*

Yesterday it was given for the 2nd time; can you believe it, there was yesterday an even stronger cabal than on the first evening? The whole first act was hissed – but they couldn't prevent the loud 'Bravo' calls after the arias. I placed my hopes on the final trio, but as luck would have it, that Fischer missed [an entrance], which caused Dauer (Pedrillo) to miss too, and Adamberger all by himself couldn't make up for all that, hence the whole effect was lost and this time *it [the trio] wasn't repeated*. I was so enraged that I could hardly contain myself, and likewise Adamberger, – and I said right away that I wouldn't give the opera again without having a little rehearsal (for the singers) beforehand. – In the 2nd act the two duets were repeated, as they had been at the first performance, and also Belmonte's Rondeau 'Wenn der Freude Thränen fließen'. The theatre was perhaps even fuller than the first time. The day before, one couldn't obtain any locked seats [at the Burgtheater, subscribers had their own seats which could be locked] either in the parterre noble or on the 3rd floor; and also there were no more boxes; the opera took 1,200 fl. [gulden] in two days.

I enclose herewith the original [score] and two word-books. You will find much that has been cancelled, this is because I knew that the score would be copied here at once, so I allowed my fancy to roam free before I gave it to be copied, here and there I made my changes and cancellations; you will receive it just as it was given. – Here and there the [parts for] trumpets and drums, flutes, clarinets and the Turkish music are missing, because I couldn't find paper with that many music staves – they [the parts] are written on extra sheets; the copyist has apparently lost them, for he couldn't find them. The first act, when I was taking it somewhere or other – I can't remember where –, fell in the mud; that's why it is so dirty.

Now I have no small work cut out for me; by Sunday week I must set out the whole opera for *Harmonie*, otherwise someone else will beat me to it and will collect the profit instead of me . . .[21]

It used to be assumed that Mozart's arrangement of the opera for wind band was never completed or, if completed, lost. However, a Dutch scholar, Bastiaan Blomhert, has re-examined a set of contemporary parts of a wind-band arrangement of *Die Entführung* in the castle of the Princes Fürstenberg in Donaueschingen, and considers it to be the long-lost Mozartian arrangement.[22] A similar mystery is connected with Mozart's statement to his father on 28 December 1782: '... Now I am also finishing the piano score of my opera, which will be engraved . . .'[23] Meanwhile, Mozart became more and more occupied with other matters; work on the piano transcription of the opera proceeded slowly. The work was sold to Torricella, but by the time Mozart had finished one act, and possibly more, Schott in Mainz had issued an engraved score (August 1785 in instalments). It is thought that poor Torricella had engraved the entire first act, though all that has survived is the overture (which is discussed in Blomhert's book).[24]

The Russian party did come to Vienna and heard the opera. On 19 October, Mozart reports: 'Recently, when they gave the opera for it [the Russian party], I thought it advisable to go to the clavier again and to conduct, partly to awaken the orchestra, which had become rather sleepy, and partly to show myself (since I happen to be here) as the father of my child . . .'[25] The most revealing part of the note is that Mozart conducted his opera, and presumably all the others in the future, from the keyboard, in the old *Kapellmeister* tradition.

Archbishop Colloredo – and Michael Haydn – heard the opera as it began to be played generally, even in Salzburg. On 19 November 1784, Leopold Mozart writes to his daughter Maria Anna in St Gilgen: '*Die Entführung aus dem Serail* was performed to great applause on the 17th and three pieces were encored . . . The Archbishop had the great grace to say "it really isn't bad" . . .'[26]

In a fuller letter, about 22 November, Leopold Mozart tells his daughter:

On Sunday the opera was performed again with the greatest success, and this opera is so much loved that the whole town is full of its praises. H[err] [Michael] Haydn sat behind the piano in the orchestra, naturally everybody asked his opinion, and he said 'all this opera needs is an orchestra of 60–70 persons and the necessary instruments now lacking, that is clarinet and cors anglais [the Salzburg orchestra had no clarinets], which parts had out of necessity to be played on the violas – then you would hear what a magnificent work it is. . . .'[27]

*   *   *

And so *Entführung* made its triumphant progress across German-speaking Europe. In Prague people admired in particular the beautiful wind-band writing. In much of Germany the opera was found to be very difficult, but it was revered and loved everywhere. Its youthful enthusiasm, the matchless beauty of the music, the comic scenes with Osmin, and above all the humanity of the ending (wherein, as under Joseph II, the spirit of the Enlightenment soars) – all this had an immediate appeal for audiences. Perhaps there were two features which may have particularly astonished contemporary listeners; the richness of the orchestration and the complexity and subtlety of the finales. But in the fabric of the plot – and of course nobly supported by the music – there is one other feature which was to become of supreme importance in several of Mozart's later operas: a magnanimous act of forgiveness. Here it is Bassa Selim's forgiveness of his old adversary, Belmonte's father, and hence Selim's freeing of Constanze, the girl he had hoped would grace his harem. It is a moment not, perhaps, as touchingly beautiful as the Countess's act of forgiveness at the end of *Figaro*, or as unexpected as the dénouement of *Così fan tutte*, but in its way it was equally a tribute to all that was good and decent in eighteenth-century Vienna. It has a message of serenity and confidence which was to rise to even greater heights in *Figaro*, but which does not, perhaps, figure to the same radiant extent in the later operas.

The incongruous postlude to the opera's success was that Bretzner, the author of the play on which the story is based, caused the following notice to be published:

A certain person by the name of *Mozart* in Vienna has had the impertinence to misuse my drama 'Belmonte and Constanze' as an opera text. I protest herewith formally against this abuse of my rights and reserve further action.

Christoph Friedrich *Bretzner*[28]

According to Mozart's later biographer, Georg Nikolaus Nissen (who had married the composer's widow in 1809), 'Mozart's friends used to refer to *Die Entführung aus dem Serail* also as "Die Entführung aus dem Auge Gottes"'[29] – a pointed allusion to the 'abduction' of Constanze Weber from her mother's home. After Mozart was obliged to leave the house of the Order of Teutonic Knights, his father was informed of the new address (that of the Weber family's flat) in a postscript to Wolfgang's letter of 9 May 1781.[30] The contents of Leopold's reply can now only be imagined from Wolfgang's reaction in a letter dated 16 May:

What you write about the Webers is not true, I can assure you. – I was mad about [the present Madame Aloysia] Lange, that's true, but what doesn't one do when one is in love! – I really loved her, and she is still not a matter of indifference to me – so it's a good thing for me that her husband is madly jealous and doesn't allow her to circulate, so I only rarely see her. – Believe, me, old Mad:me Weber is really a very obliging woman, and for my part I am not able to repay her kindness, because I haven't the time to do so. – [31]

At this juncture, Aloysia was about to give birth to a daughter, Maria Anna Sabina, on 31 May; since their marriage in St Stephen's Cathedral on 31 October 1780, Joseph and Aloysia Lange lived at Himmelpfortgasse No. 997. Before the marriage, Lange had been obliged to sign a document guaranteeing Frau Cäcilia Weber, the widowed mother, an annual income for life of 700 gulden and obliging him to repay the advance on salary which Aloysia had received from the Vienna Court Theatre in 1779. This extraordinary financial settlement was probably forced on Joseph Lange simply because he had got Aloysia pregnant before their marriage. Leopold's worst fears about the machinations of Cäcilia Weber were thus fully justified. The same blackmailing pressure was soon to be applied to Wolfgang. Leopold was evidently hearing all sorts of second-hand reports and was, altogether, worried about the state of his son's morals; Leopold's paternal concern gave rise to a situation which elicited one of Wolfgang's most characteristic and interesting answers (letter 13 June 1781):

Concerning the welfare of my soul, do not be anxious, best father! – I am a young man in every sense of the word like every other, and for my own consolation I could wish that all were as sensible as I. – You perhaps think things of me that are not true; ... – I attend Mass every Sunday and Feast-Day, and if possible on weekdays too; you know that, my father. – My only contact with that person of ill-repute was at the ball. – And that was arranged long before I know that she enjoyed a bad reputation – and only because I wanted to be sure of having a partner of the contredanse. – For, without explaining why, I could hardly abandon her all at once – and who wants to say such a thing to a person's face? – And did I not in the end frequently leave her, to dance with others? – And for that reason I was really very glad when Carnival came to an end. – Moreover, only a liar could say that I saw her anywhere else, or at her house. – Moreover [*sic*], rest assured that I surely keep my religion – and should I have the misfortune – which God forbid – to take the wrong road, I hereby absolve you, my dear and best father, from all responsibility . . .[32]

sepha Mayer gnn~hmn
Rnbnv. Schwrsta nr Mozn A

Leopold's informant seems to have been Wenzel Andreas Gilowsky von Urazowa (1716–99), Court surgeon and *Antecamerakammerdiener* (something like a 'valet of the antechamber'); his family had been friends of the Mozarts for years, and his son Franz Xaver Wenzel (1757–1816) would be Wolfgang's witness at his marriage. Years later, when Leopold was visiting Vienna, he wrote to Nannerl mentioning the '*disgustingly stupid letter* which he [Gilowsky] wrote at that time about your brother's falling in love, which shows that he [Gilowsky] too is capable of an act of madness . . .'[33]

In 1781, however, any act of madness seemed – in far-away Salzburg – to be entirely Wolfgang's, despite his attempts to defend himself. In a letter of 25 July 1781 to his father, Wolfgang repeats that he is thinking of moving from the Weber household, simply because people are gossiping: ' – because I am living with them, I am going to marry the daughter . . .'

At pains to convince his father, Wolfgang continues:

No talk about being in love, they've given that stage the miss . . . We went to the Prater a few times, but her mother was there, too; since I was at home, I couldn't refuse to accompany them. – And at that time I hadn't heard any such ridiculous tittle-tattle, moreover I must say that I only had to pay *my share*. – And when the mother learned about this chit-chat, and heard it from me too, I have to say that she too doesn't want us to go out together, and so as to avoid further unpleasantness she advised me to move somewhere else; for she said she didn't want to be the innocent cause of any misfortune to me . . . I am not in love with [Constanze]; I fool about and have fun with her, when I have time (which is only in the evening when I dine at home – for in the morning I write in my room and in the afternoon I am seldom at home) . . . If I were obliged to marry all the girls with whom I've had a little fun, I should already have at least 200 wives . . .[34]

On 29 August, Wolfgang writes, rather disingenuously, that he has found 'a rather prettily furnished room on the Graben',[35] and, a few days later, he identifies the address as No. 1175, 3rd floor: it was, as might be expected, round the corner from the Webers; and indeed, the whole thing may have been a smokescreen to allay Leopold's fears. In the event, Leopold was becoming steadily more frantic, as we may deduce from the tone of Wolfgang's answer: 'From the way you've taken my last letter, I see, alas, that you have relied more on the gossip and scribblings of other people than on me (as if I were the arch-villain or a clot, or both), and hence you have no trust in me at all . . .'

As the autumn advanced, Wolfgang reported on his name-day (31 October) celebrations with his sympathetic patroness, Martha Elisabeth, Baroness Waldstätten (*recte*), who lived apart from her husband. In a letter of 3 November to his father he wrote:

In the morning I performed my devotions and – just as I was wanting to write a letter to you, a crowd of congratulating friends descended on me – at 12 o'clock I went to Baroness Waldstädten's in the Leopoldstadt – where I spent my name-day. At 11 o'clock at night I was serenaded with a Night Music for two clarinets, two horns and two bassoons – and of my own composition. – I wrote this music on St Theresa's Day

[15 October] – for the sister of Fr[au] v[on] Hickl [*sic*], or the sister-in-law of H[err] v[on] Hickel (the court painter), at whose house it was actually first performed. – The six gentlemen who perform such things are poor as church-mice, but play rather nicely together; especially the first clarinettist and the two horn players – the main reason why I wrote it was so that H[err] v[on] Strack (who goes there daily) should be able to hear something by me. And that is why I wrote it rather nicely [*'vernünftig'*]. – It was applauded by all, too. – On St Theresa's night it was performed in three different places. – As soon as the players were finished in one place, they were taken away to another and paid to play it. – The gentlemen thus caused the street door to be opened and after placing themselves in the courtyard, they surprised me, just as I was getting ready to undress, in the most pleasant fashion . . . with the first E flat chord . . .[36]

This, then, was the origin of the sextet (and original) version of the Serenade in E flat (K.375), of which there is a better known, later version (that for eight wind instruments, including oboes). The practice of serenading people in Vienna is a charming tradition, also cultivated by the young Haydn in the 1750s.

Interestingly, the autograph of K.375 is especially neat, which may explain Mozart's remark (or, of course, he may be referring to the quality of the composition: his word 'vernünftig' can mean 'sensible' or 'careful'; or indeed, simply 'neat'). It is his first known work to exploit the great tradition of wind-band music in Vienna, and was intended to impress Johann Kilian Strack, valet-de-chambre and musical confidant of Joseph II. Strack is said to have caused the music of Haydn (and to a certain extent Mozart) to be regarded with some disfavour at court. For his part, however, Mozart continually refers to Strack as 'my good friend', evidence that Wolfgang always believed the best of people. Joseph Hickel (1736–1807), a competent portrait-painter, worked not only in Vienna but in Germany, Denmark and, in the 1790s, England; in 1786, he portrayed Joseph Lange as Hamlet.

Mozart's friends in Vienna included the Auernhammer family. The daughter, Josepha, took piano lessons from him, and he thought her a great bore ('*seccatrice*'); although apparently extremely ugly, she was an excellent pianist and in 1786 married a civil servant named Johann Bessenig. In 1781, Mozart dedicated to her his first Viennese publication, the six Violin Sonatas, op.2, and composed the Sonata in D for two pianos (K.448) for himself and her. The concert at which this work and the Concerto no. 10 for two pianos in E flat (K.365) – perhaps in the revised version with clarinets, trumpets and drums? – which Wolfgang had ordered to be sent from Salzburg,[37] took place in her family's house. On 24 November, Wolfgang writes:

Yesterday was the academy concert at Auernhammer's . . . to this academy came Countess Thun (whom I invited), Baron van Suiten [*sic*], Baron [Johann B.] Gudenus, the wealthy converted Jew, Wetzlar [Baron Carl Abraham Wetzlar (1716–99) or his son Raimund Wetzlar von Plankenstern (1752–1810), Mozart's landlord in 1782–83 and godfather to the Mozart's first child, Raimund Leopold], Count Firmian [a member of the illustrious family who had befriended Mozart *inter alia* when they were in the Austrian part of Italy], and H[err] v[on] Daubrawaick and his son [Johann Baptist Anton Daubrawa von Daubrawaick and his son Franz Anton,

75

members of a distinguished old Bohemian family; the father was in the Archbishop's service in Salzburg, and often travelled to Vienna on archiepiscopal business]. – We played the concerto à Due, and a Sonata for four hands which I composed expressly for the occasion, and which was a great success; I shall send this Sonata to you through H: v: Daubrawaick, who said he would be proud to have it lying in his luggage; the son said that, and *nota bene* he a Salzburgian; but the father, as he left, said in a loud voice to me, 'I am proud to be your countryman – you are a great credit to Salzburg – I hope that the times will change so that we can have you – and then we certainly won't let you leave.' – thereupon I said, – 'My fatherland will always have the first claim upon me . . .'[38]

Mozart was slowly but surely gaining a reputation in Vienna. Not everything was easy, of course. He had hoped to become the (temporary) piano teacher of Princess Elisabeth of Württemberg, visiting the city with the grand ducal party from Russia (Elisabeth was the sister of the Grand Duke's consort, Maria Feodorovna); but, said Wolfgang wrily in a letter dated 15 December, 'the Emperor Joseph II has spoiled everything for me, because he recognizes nothing except Salieri.'[39] This is the first, as it were, official mention by Mozart of Antonio Salieri, the director of the Court Opera, who was to be a thorn in Mozart's flesh – and vice versa – during the next decade. But the real 'meat' in this letter comes a few lines later: it was the nightmare situation which Leopold had dreaded – his son had decided to marry. 'You are shocked at this thought?', writes Wolfgang,

But dearest, best father, listen to me! I have been obliged to reveal my plans to you, now please permit me to explain my reasons, very well grounded reasons. Nature speaks in me as loudly as in any other man, and perhaps more loudly than in many another big, strong brute. I cannot possibly live the way most young men do nowadays. – First, I am too religious; secondly, I entertain too high a regard for my neighbour, and have too honourable intentions, to allow me to seduce an innocent girl; and thirdly, too much horror and disgust, too much dread and fear of diseases, and too much regard for my health, to fool about with whores; therefore I can swear to you that I've never had anything to do with women of this kind . . .

Mozart then goes on to say that his inclination is towards a quiet, domestic life; he has never had to look after his own linen, clothes, and so on; a wife would be able to manage all these things better. He has considered the matter carefully and is not going to change his mind. '. . . Now who is the object of my love? – Again, don't be shocked, I beg you; not one of the Webers? Yes, a Weber – not Josepha – not Sophie – but Costanza [*sic*], the middle one . . .' Mozart then proceeds to demolish the characters of the two sisters – possibly all true, but certainly designed to put Constanze (the usual spelling) in the best possible light.[40]

But it was no good. Leopold had been hearing appalling tales – not least from the German composer Peter von Winter, a pupil of Salieri in Vienna in this period, who seems to have kept Leopold informed of what was apparently common knowledge in Vienna: the fact that the Webers had managed to force Wolfgang to sign a contract (similar to that between Lange and Aloysia), in

which he 'bound himself to marry Mlle Constance [*sic*] Weber within the period of three years',[41] but should he fail to do so, he agreed to pay her 300 gulden p.a. Constanze tore up the document, but the damage was already done.

Of course, Mozart was young and foolish, and Madame Cäcilia Weber a calculating mother; Constanze was torn between the two, especially since she was by no means violently in love, for she later said of Wolfgang that she had been 'perhaps more attracted by his talents than by his person'.[42] But these events came as a shock to the family; and it would seem Nannerl, too, never overcame their suspicions concerning Constanze's character – unjustified though they may have been.

This same letter from Wolfgang (22–26 December) mentions the contest between himself and the Italian composer and pianist Muzio Clementi (1752–1832), arranged by Joseph II (Mozart added that at dinner the Emperor had said of him, 'C'est un talent décidé'), who sent Mozart 50 ducats afterwards. In a later letter (12 January 1782), Wolfgang writes to his father '. . . Clementi plays well, as far as execution in the right hand is concerned – his strength lies in passages in thirds – otherwise he has not a penny's worth of feeling or taste: in a word he is just a mechanic.'[43]

This famous contest – Count Zinzendorf noted in his Diary, nearly a year later, on 5 December 1782, that the Emperor 'talked endlessly about music, about the contest between Mozhardt [*sic*] and Clementi'[44] – brought Wolfgang much closer to the ultimate source of Austrian power. On 9 January 1782, he writes: '. . . Moreover I have it on good authority that he was most satisfied. The Emperor was very gracious to me, and spoke privately of many things. – He also spoke of my marriage. – Who knows? – perhaps – what do you think? – One can always try.'[45]

Obviously Mozart was casting his net wide – but an Imperial appointment, though hinted at, was not yet forthcoming. The composer had his eye on three possible appointments, which he set out in detail to his father in the next letter (23 January 1782):[46] the first was that the young Prince Alois Joseph Liechtenstein (1759–1805), son of the late reigning Prince Franz Joseph (1726–81), was in the process of establishing a 'Harmonie Musick' (wind band), for which Mozart was destined to compose – 'not much to be expected from that quarter' adds Wolfgang, but at least something definite, since he would not accept anything except a permanent contract. The second was, of course, a position with Joseph II; the third, one with Archduke Maximilian, who thought highly of Mozart (at least so Wolfgang believed). 'Dearest, best father! – if I could only get a written statement from our Heavenly Father that I shall remain healthy, and not be ill – Oh, I would marry my dear, faithful girl today. – I've three lady pupils – that brings 18 ducats a month – for I don't teach [a series of] 12 lessons any more, but on a monthly basis. – I have learned the hard way that they often skip whole weeks – now, whether they learn or not, each must pay me 6 ducats . . .' Mozart thought that he could write an opera, and give a benefit concert, every year; he could publish music, issue works by subscription, participate in other musicians' academy concerts, 'especially when one has been long in a place and enjoys some credit'. Mozart concluded these thoughts with the prediction, which was to prove (at least at the outset) entirely correct, that 'it can't go worse with me – on the contrary, things are bound to get better.' His haste was due to his need for Constanze: 'I must save her as soon as possible,' he exclaims.

Leopold still had doubts about his son's intended bride, for on 30 January we find Wolfgang writing, 'Don't suspect my dear Konstanze of such an evil way of thinking – believe me, I could certainly not love her if she entertained such thoughts. – She and I – both of us have long observed her mother's designs . . .'[47] Madame Weber expected the young couple to live with her after they were married. Wolfgang intended to frustrate this plan, but meanwhile he reported that when he went to visit Constanze at 9 p.m. 'the pleasure of seeing each other is thoroughly marred by the bitter remarks of her mother.'[48]

The great event of that spring in Vienna was the academy concert which Mozart gave at the Burgtheater on 3 March. It included extracts from *Idomeneo*, an improvised piano 'fantasy' and the Salzburg Piano Concerto no. 5 in D (K.175) with a new Rondo finale (K.382), which Mozart described as 'creating a big stir'.[49] This Rondo was to become his greatest success of the period: with its catchy tune and the brilliantly conceived soft orchestration (like toy trumpets and drums) with which the piece opens, its rhapsodic slow section for the piano, and its concluding panache, it entirely dwarfs the rest of the rather formal, Mannheim-like concerto to which it was attached. The traces of Haydn's popular, folk-like style are a clear indication that Wolfgang had learned very quickly what the Viennese liked and appreciated.

Mozart was beginning to participate in a number of concert ventures. On 8 May he writes to his father that

This summer there will be a concert every Sunday in the Augarten. A certain [Philipp Jakob] Martin established a series of dilettanti concerts this last winter, which took place every Friday at the Mehlgrube. – you know of course that there are many dilettanti here, and very good ones too, ladies as well as gentlemen. – Only with me things didn't work out very well. – This Martin has now received a decree from the Emperor, allowing 12 concerts to be given in the Augarten, ... Also four large evening concerts in all the finest squares in town. – The subscription price for the whole summer is 2 ducats. Now you can easily imagine that we shall find enough subscribers – the more so since I am now associated with the project and will busy myself with it ... Baron van Suiten [*sic*] and Countess Thun are being very helpful. – The orchestra consists entirely of dilettanti – with the exception of the bassoons, the trumpets and the drums . . .'[50]

*The Mehlgrube (*LEFT*) and the Schwarzenberg palace in the Neuer Markt (Mehlmarkt). The city casino in the Mehlgrube was the venue for winter concerts promoted by Philipp Jakob Martin. Mozart gave concerts here, notably in February and March 1785. Anonymous coloured engraving, c. 1825.*

Meanwhile, Leopold had requested a new symphony from his son for the festivities in Salzburg to celebrate the ennoblement of the Haffner family. Although desperately busy, Wolfgang complied with his father's wish, and on 27 July he wrote 'You will be astonished when you see just the opening Allegro [of the new 'Haffner' Symphony, no. 35, K.385]; but – I couldn't manage more – I had to write a Nacht Musique very quickly, but just for wind band (otherwise I could have used the piece for *you* too) – on Wednesday the 31st I shall send the two minuets, the Andante and the Finale – if I can – I shall also send a march [in other words, the whole piece was originally more of a large-

The opening of the autograph of the 'Haffner' Symphony, no. 35 (K.385) in D, showing the flute and clarinet parts added later in the top and bottom staves respectively.

scale serenade, though only four movements survive as K.385] . . . I wrote it in D because you prefer it . . .'[51]

The new 'Nacht Musique' is generally considered to have been the octet version of the Serenade in E flat (K.375); in the same letter we now witness the opening of the finale, as it were, of Mozart's courtship of Constanze Weber. He writes

Dearest, best father! – I must ask you by all you hold dear in this world: give your permission that I may marry my dear love Konstanze. – Don't think that it is just because of the marriage alone – for that I could gladly wait – but I see that it is urgently necessary because of my honour, the honour of my girl, and my health and state of mind. – My heart is restless, my mind confused – how can one think or work properly in such circumstances? – Where does this come from? Most people think we are already married – the mother is incensed about it – and the poor girl and I are being harried to death. – But this situation is so easily remedied. – Believe me, one can [manage to] live in expensive Vienna as easily as in another place, it depends on economy and order. – This is never the case with a bachelor, especially when he is in love. – Whoever receives a woman such as I am to receive can surely count himself fortunate. – We shall live a very quiet and retiring life – and we will be happy nonetheless. – And don't worry – for if, God forbid, I should become ill today (especially when married), I should wager that the leading families of the nobility would provide a great shelter for me. That I can state with confidence. – I know what Prince Kaunitz [the Austrian Chancellor] said about me to the Emperor and Arch [duke] Maximilian. – I await your permission, my best of fathers, with longing – I await it confidently – my honour and peace of mind depend upon it – Don't allow yourself to wait too long to have the pleasure in the near future of embracing your son with his wife. . . .

Mozart was evidently beginning to think that Viennese society would somehow come to his aid if anything should befall him. On the other hand, his father wrote that society too held quite a different opinion of their darling. Again, the gist of the argument must be reconstructed from Wolfgang's furious answer on 31 July:

the whole world, then, declares that by my boasting and criticizing I have made enemies of the music professors and also others as well! – Which world? – Presumably the Salzburg world; for whoever is here will be able easily enough to see and hear the contrary; – and that shall be my answer. Meanwhile you will have received my last letter; – and I don't doubt whatever that in your next letter I shall receive permission for my marriage; – you can't have anything against it – and you really don't have either! – your letters make that clear – for she is a decent, good girl of good parents, – I am capable of earning her *bread* – we love each other – and want each other . . .[52]

Matters soon came to a head. Shortly before 4 August, Mozart wrote to Baroness von Waldstätten, who had been acting as a kind of protector to the young couple (Constanze went to live with her to escape her mother's clutches), as follows:

Mad^me Weber's maid . . . told me something in confidence which, although I do not believe it could happen, since it would be a prostitution for the whole family, yet

Wenzel Anton, Prince Kaunitz (1711–94), the Austrian Chancellor. In July 1782, Mozart was invited by Count Zichy to drive with him to Laxenburg (BELOW) to be presented to Kaunitz. Engravings by J.G. Haid, 1774, and S. Kleiner, c. 1724.

seems possible considering the stupidity of Mad^{me} Weber; and which consequently worries me.

Sophie [Constanze's sister] came out in tears – and when the maid asked her why, she said – 'go and tell Mozart in secret to see that Constanz [*sic*] goes home, for – my mother is quite determined to have her fetched by the police!' – Can the police here enter any house without further ado? – Perhaps it's only a trap to make her go home. – But if that is really going to happen, I can think of no better solution than to marry Constance [*sic*] tomorrow morning – or even today if possible. – For I should not like to expose my darling to this scandal – and [with her] as my wife it can't happen. – One more thing: – [Constanze's guardian] Thorwath [Thorwart] has been asked to come [to the Webers] today. – I ask Your Grace for your friendly advice – and to give a helping hand to us poor creatures. – I shall be at home all the time. – I kiss your hands 1,000 times and am . . .

in the greatest haste. Constanze doesn't know anything as yet. Has H[err] v[on] Thorwath been to see Your Grace? –

Is it necessary for the two of us to go to him after lunch today?[253]

There was, then, reason enough to proceed with the marriage as speedily as possible; and this is precisely what Wolfgang and Constanze intended to do. The events are movingly related in two letters to Leopold, of 7 and 17 August 1782:

Mon très cher Père!

You are very much mistaken in your son if you can believe that he is capable of acting dishonestly –

My dear Konstanze, now (thank God) at last my wife, knew my circumstances and has for a long time known exactly what I can expect from you. – But her friendship and love for me were so great that she willingly – and with the greatest joy sacrificed her whole future to share – my fate. – I kiss your hands and thank you, with all the tenderness which a son has ever felt for a father, for your kind permission and paternal blessing: – But indeed, I knew I could rely on it . . . At the marriage only the mother and the youngest sister were present – no one else. – H[er] v[on] Thorwart as guardian and witness for both of us; H[er] v[on] Zetto [Johann Carl Cetto von Kronstorff] (district councillor), who gave away the bride; and Franz Gilowsky as my best man. – When we had been joined together, both my wife and I began to weep. – All those present were touched, even the priest. – And all wept to see how much our hearts were moved. – Our whole wedding feast consisted of a *souper* offered to us by Baroness v[on] Waldstädten [*sic*] – which was in truth more princely than baronial. – Now my dear Konstanze is a hundred times more anxious to go to Salzburg! – And I wager – I wager – that when you get to know her you will all rejoice in my good fortune . . .; Tomorrow I lunch with [Gluck, the celebrated composer]. . . .[54]

[17 August] I forgot to tell you last time that on the Day of Portiuncula [2 August] my wife and I performed our devotions together at the Theatines – even if our faith had not actually moved us to do so, we should have had to do it on account of the banns, without which we couldn't have been married. – But for some time before we were married we had always attended Holy Mass and gone to confession and received Communion together – and I discovered that I had never prayed so ardently or confessed and received communion so devoutly as by her side; – and she felt likewise. – In short, we are made for each other – and God who orders all things and hence this too, will not forsake us . . .[55]

82

The day afterwards, 18 August, the two Constanzes were united (as it were) at an evening serenade performance on the the Neumarkt, put on by Mozart's colleague P.J. Martin: the music was the new wind-band arrangement of *Die Entführung aus dem Serail*, and tickets could be had 'before the serenade begins... next to the Lemonade Stand...'[56] Here Constanze Weber, now Mozart, could enjoy listening to the warm-hearted and inspiring music written for her stage namesake.

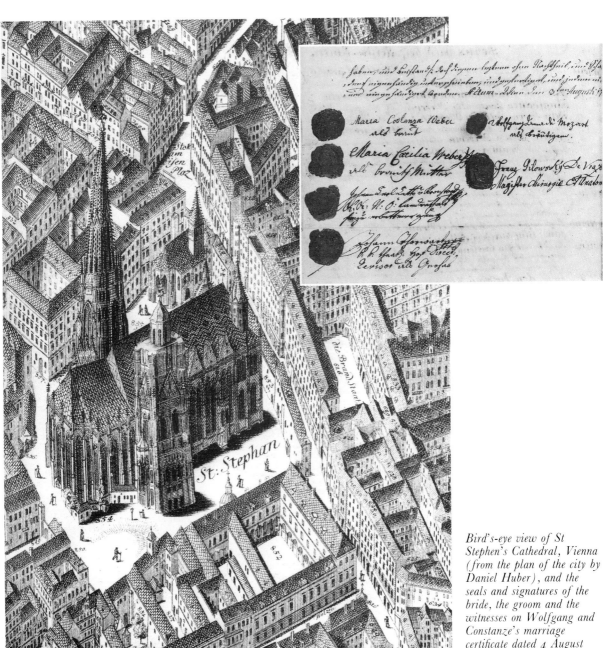

Bird's-eye view of St Stephen's Cathedral, Vienna (from the plan of the city by Daniel Huber), and the seals and signatures of the bride, the groom and the witnesses on Wolfgang and Constanze's marriage certificate dated 4 August 1782.

V

Concerts in Vienna
Interlude in Salzburg, 1783

Following their marriage, Wolfgang and Constanze intended to pay a visit to Salzburg as soon as possible, but two factors caused the trip to be postponed: one was the rumoured arrival in the Austrian capital of the Grand Duke Paul of Russia and his suite (Mozart obviously hoped to gain some kind of appointment or recognition from one or the other of the company); and the second was that Constanze soon found herself pregnant, and in November 1782, when the weather turned particularly nasty – the mail coach with eight horses setting out westwards from Vienna had to turn back before the first stage was reached – it was thought inadvisable for the young woman to travel. A final worry was Archbishop Colloredo's attitude: would he try to have Wolfgang arrested? (There had never been an official termination of his contract with the Salzburg court.)[1] It was even suggested that the family should meet on neutral ground; but Leopold was able to persuade his son that he had nothing to fear.

Wolfgang describes his busy life in a letter of 28 December 1782:

Altogether I have so much to do that I often don't know where to start; – the whole morning until 2 o'clock is devoted to lessons; – then we eat; – after lunch I must give my poor stomach at least a short hour to recover; then – it is only in the evening when I can compose – and even that is not certain, because I am often requested to play in academy concerts; – 2 concertos are still missing from the series of subscription concertos. – The concertos are in fact something intermediate between too difficult and too easy – they are very brilliant – fall pleasantly on the ear – without of course becoming vapid – here and there only connoisseurs can derive satisfaction – but in such a way that the non-connoisseur will be pleased without knowing why. I am distributing the subscription tickets – 6 ducats in cash . . .[2]

This is the famous description of the three Piano Concertos (nos. 11, 12 and 13, K.413–15), first offered for sale on 15 January 1783 in the *Wiener Zeitung*:

Musical News
Herr Kapellmeister Mozart announces herewith to the highly respected public the issuance of three newly completed piano concertos. These 3 concertos, which can be

84

performed with a large orchestra including wind instruments, or only *a quattro*, that is with 2 violins, 1 viola and violoncello, will be available at the beginning of April to those who have subscribed for them (they will be beautifully copied and revised by him personally). From the 20th inst. to the end of March, it is hereby further announced that subscription tickets are available at 4 ducats. His apartment is on the High Bridge in the small Herberstein House No, 437, on the third floor.

This announcement was printed twice more. It will be noted that Mozart's original price of 6 ducats (as stated in his letter) has now been reduced, possibly at the instigation of Leopold, who was (rightly as events proved) worried at the very high price proposed. Wolfgang writes on 22 January 1783: 'Concerning the 3 concertos, you mustn't worry that they are too dear; – after all I think I should earn a ducat for each concerto – and then – I would like to see how anyone can have them copied for a ducat! – They can't be copied [by others] because I won't issue them until I have a whole group of subscribers ... I will shortly be sending the cadenzas and *Eingänge* [short cadenzas] to my dear sister; – I haven't produced the *Eingänge* in the rondo [K.382] for when I play that concerto, I do whatever enters my head ...'[3] Mozart seems to be referring to the cadenzas etc. for the Concerto no. 12 in A (K.414), apparently the first to be written (and the first in Artaria's first edition).

It used to be thought that there were no extant copies of this subscription issue of 1783, but my belief is that parts of the set do exist: when in Czechoslovakia in the spring of 1959, I discovered a series of Mozart piano concertos in manuscript parts. They were in the town library of Cheb (formerly Eger in the Sudetenland), and the most interesting thing about them was that they were in part copied and signed by a careful and reliable copyist living in Vienna, whom Joseph Haydn used a great deal at this period: Johann Radnitzky. (Haydn's Symphonies nos. 76–79, composed in 1782, were copied by Radnitzky at the end of 1783 and the beginning of 1784 and sent, corrected and signed by Haydn, to Forster in London for publication: the copies are signed 'Radnitzky' or 'Rky'.)[4] The Mozart copies in Cheb include the Concerto no. 5 in D (K.175) with the later Rondo finale (K.382), both by Radnitzky, but not signed, and two of the concertos in the subscription trio: no. 11 in F (K.413) and no. 13 in C (K.415), both copied by Radnitzky, the latter signed 'Rky'.[5] There is another copyist involved in K.413. That is because composers generally obliged the copyists to come to them and do their work under personal supervision; and usually one copyist never prepared *all* the parts of any one work (to prevent it being pirated). In a letter dated 15 May 1784, Wolfgang asks his father for the four piano concertos to be copied at home, 'for the copyists in Salzburg are no more to be trusted than those in Vienna; – I know for certain that Hofstetter copies [Michael] Haydn's music twice – I *really* have his 3 latest symphonies ...'[6] And Joseph Haydn – although it was not *his* symphonies that Wolfgang caused to be copied for his new subscription concerts – states that even if 'you have everything copied on your own premises, you may be cheated all the same, because the rascals put a piece of paper *a parte* under the music, and thus by degrees they secretly copy the part they have before them ...'[7]

Johann Thomas von Trattner (1717–98), proprietor of the so-called Trattnerhof in the Graben (see p. 121), whose wife was a pupil of Mozart. He was a friend of the Mozarts and was godfather to three of their sons, none of whom survived infancy. Engraving by J.G. Mansfeld, 1781, after a portrait by Joseph Hickel.

It seems that Wolfgang's subscription plan was not a great success. We can see this from an ominous letter which he addressed to his patroness, Baroness Waldstätten in the middle of February 1783.[8] In it, Wolfgang discusses a debt he owes to the husband of one of his pupils, Theresia von Trattner (Mozart misspelled the name 'Tranner'), which had now been called in, 'and if I do not pay between today and tomorrow, he will *sue*; – Your Grace can imagine what an unpleasant situation that would create for me! – I cannot pay now, not even half of it! – If I could have imagined that it would take such a long time to secure the subscriptions to my concertos, I would have taken the money on a longer term! – I pray Your Grace, for Heaven's sake, help me so that I don't lose my honour and my good name! – . . . .'

Already in debt, Mozart was proceeding along the worst possible path: borrowing from one source to pay off an existing debt. It is, indeed, probable that the Mozarts were living not as modestly as Wolfgang had promised himself (and his father). Scarcely three weeks earlier, he had been asking his father to send a Harlequin fancy-dress from Salzburg.[9] Constanze and he wanted to attend the famous masked balls in the Redoutensaal, Wolfgang as Harlequin, but he notes, 'we prefer house balls.' He continues:

Last week I gave a ball in my flat. Naturally the beaux had to pay 2 gulden for it. – We started in the evening at 6 o'clock and stopped at 7 o'clock; – what, only an hour? – No, no – in the morning at 7 o'clock; – you won't understand how I had the necessary space? – Well – it occurs to me that I keep forgetting to tell you that for the last month and a half I have had a new apartment – also on the High Bridge – and a few houses further along; – we are living, then, in the small Herberstein House No. 412, on the 3rd floor – at H[err] v[on] Wezlar [Wetzlar von Plankenstern], a wealthy Jew. – Now here I have a room – 1,000 feet long [i.e. extremely large] . . . and a bedroom – plus a hall – and a fine great kitchen; – also two other large rooms next to ours which are still empty – and these are the ones we used for this house ball – Baron Wezlar and she [his wife] – were also present – as were Baroness Waldstätten – H[err] v[on] Edelbach [Benedikt S., son of the Salzburg teacher of jurisprudence, Franz Joseph] – Gilowsky [Mozart's witness at the wedding], that wind-bag – the young Stephani[e] and wife – Adamberger [the tenor] and she [his wife] – Lange and Mrs L. – etc., etc., – I can hardly write down *all* the names. . . .

Even if the guests contributed to the expenses, this still sounds like high living. In February, Mozart was obliged to move to temporary quarters on the Kohlmarkt, the rent for which Baron Wetzlar paid (also the removal expenses); the Baron had rented his flat (so perhaps the Mozarts had been living there for nothing). Mozart did not mention that the flat into which he moved had been owned (until 1780) by Frau Cäcilia Weber, through whom he probably received the address.

On 12 March, relates Mozart to his father,

. . . our masquerade company performed at the Redout [in the Hofburg] – it consisted of a pantomime which just filled the half-hour when there is a pause in dancing, – My sister-in-law was Columbine, I was Harlequin, my brother-in-law was Pierrot, an old dancing-master (Merk) was Pantaloon, a painter (Grassi) was the doctor. – Both the plot and the music of the pantomime were mine. – The dancing-master Merk was kind

enough to teach us the steps; and I can tell you, we played very nicely. – I include herewith the announcement which was handed out by a mask, dressed as a postillion . . .[10]

Ball scene in the large Redoutensaal (cf. pl. XXII), where many important social events took place; coloured engraving by Carl Schütz, c. 1800. Mozart attended fancy-dress balls held here in 1783 and 1786.

Mozart's debts hardly worried him as yet. He was beginning to be an essential part of almost every grand concert in Vienna. On 11 March, he participated in Aloysia Lange's benefit concert at the Burgtheater, in which, as he wrote to Salzburg,

I also played a concerto [unidentified]. – The theatre was very full, and I was again received by the Viennese public in such a warm fashion that I really felt I should be very pleased. – I had already gone off-stage. – But they wouldn't stop clapping – and I had to repeat the Rondeau [K.382, the new finale for Concerto no. 5, K.175]; – there was a real torrent of applause. – That's a good omen for my academy concert which I'm going to give on Sunday, 23 March. – I also gave my Symphony for the Concert Spirituel ['Paris' Symphony, no. 31, K.297]. – My sister-in-law sang the Aria 'Non sò d'onde viene' [K.294, which Wolfgang had written for her in 1778] – *Gluck* had the box next to the Lange family's, in which my wife also sat. – He could not praise the symphony and the aria enough, and invited all four of us to dine next Sunday . . .[11]

The event of the musical season in Vienna was Wolfgang's own benefit concert at the Burgtheater. The theatre was filled to bursting-point; Emperor Joseph II came and applauded vigorously (he had sent 25 ducats in advance). The programme, set out in a letter to Leopold of 29 March,[12] was as follows:

1 Symphony in D [no. 35, K.385 ('Haffner')], first three movements.
2 'Se il padre perdei' from *Idomeneo* (Madame Lange).
3 'I played the third of my subscription concertos', i.e. no. 13 in C (K.415), for which occasion, possibly, the trumpets and drums (missing in the autograph's original version) were added.
4 Johann Valentin Adamberger sang the Scena for Countess Paumgarten, K.369 ('Misera, dove son', originally for soprano). Adamberger was, of course, Mozart's star tenor.
5 The concertante movements (Nos. 3 and 4) from the Serenade in D, K.320 ('Posthorn').
6 'I played my Concerto in D, which is so popular here, of which I sent you the Rondeau with variations' (K.175 and K.382).
7 Therese Teyber sang 'Parto, m'affretto' from *Lucio Silla*, 'my last Milan opera' of 1772.
8 'I played a short fugue solo (because the Emperor was present) and then variations on an aria from an opera called *The Philosophers* [later written down as 'Salve tu, Domine' from Giovanni Paisiello's *I filosofi immaginari*, K.398] – had to play it again. Variations on the Aria 'Unser dummer Pöbel meint' from [Gluck's] *Die Pilgrimme von Mekka* [K.455].'
9 'Madame Lange sang my new Rondeau' [Recitative and Rondo 'Mia speranza adorata' and 'Ah, non sai', K.416, which she had first sung in an academy concert at the Mehlgrube on 11 January 1783].
10 The last movement of the opening symphony.

This was a tremendous achievement and the high-point of Mozart's career in Vienna to date. But with all this success, why was Mozart not able to sell his three concertos as he has wished to? Their lack of success is particularly baffling in view of the fact that when these works were finally sold to Artaria, demand for prints was exceptionally heavy, necessitating the replacement of several worn plates.[13] The Artaria edition came out at the end of 1784 and early in 1785, and by the end of the century 'well over 500 copies' had been sold. Then why was Mozart unable even to approach this figure, especially since he had taken great care to write the works so that they could readily be performed as chamber music, in the home (on British models such as Samuel Schroeter's *Six Concertos for the Harpsichord, or Piano Forte: With an Accompanyment for two Violins and a Bass . . . op.* III, 1774)? Or was Artaria, quite simply, in a better position to market Mozart's music than the composer himself? (Curiously, Artaria did not include the trumpet and timpani parts for no. 13, K.415.)

The biggest news for Mozart was the re-establishment of the Italian Opera in Vienna. He reports to his father on 7 May that 'the Italian *opera buffa* has begun again; and pleases greatly. – The *buffo* is especially good. His name is Francesco Benucci . . .'[14] We also learn of the presence of Lorenzo Da Ponte, whose collaboration with Mozart would be a major force in the composer's operatic career.

Mozart had become a father on 17 June. The boy's name was Raimund Leopold: his godfather was Raimund von Wetzlar, the oldest son of the Baron, who (to Mozart's great regret) had just died. Wetzlar was unable to attend and Wolfgang's musical colleague, Philipp Jakob Martin, stood proxy at the ceremony in the Kirche am Hof. In a letter to Leopold the day after, Wolfgang described his son as a 'fine, sturdy boy, round as a ball'.[15] The way was now open for the Mozarts to travel to Salzburg. (It never seems to have occurred to them that it might be considered odd to leave the infant in the care of a wet nurse, and when Wolfgang and Constanze returned to Vienna, they found the child had died.)

*   *   *

The visit to Salzburg was to be Mozart's last. The Archbishop proved to be benevolent, and Mozart was overjoyed at being with his father and sister again. As for Constanze, it would seem that neither Leopold nor Nannerl really took to her. A year after her brother's death, Nannerl must have summed up her family's feelings about Constanze when she wrote that Wolfgang had 'married, against his father's will, a girl not at all suitable for him . . .'[16] The present writer has attempted, in another context, to provide a 'vindication' of Constanze Mozart.[17] To summarize the argument, one may state: (1) except for the letter quoted above (from a prejudiced source), there are no eighteenth-century documents that present Constanze in an unfavourable light; (2) Mozart adored her and considered that she was the right wife for him; (3) Constanze saved all Mozart's letters in which he criticized her, mostly for flirting (this she would hardly have done if she had thought them really damaging – obviously they were not).

Johann Michael Haydn, younger brother of Joseph, who was in the service of Archbishop Colloredo of Salzburg; anonymous silhouette published in 1808.

Wolfgang and Constanze seem to have arrived in Salzburg about 28 July; on the 29th they and Nannerl made the rounds of their Salzburg friends. Nannerl's Diary – written in telegraphic style – gives the bare bones of her brother's and sister-in-law's activities: '29th [July] to Mass at 7 a.m. with my brother and sister-in-law, to Hagenauer, Schidenhofen and Barisany for visits. Afternoon we went to Catherl, afterwards made music. Sandmayer, with his Hanserl, Bologna, Schachtner, Ceccarelli, Biber, Reitter, Catherl came to us: Hr. and Frau von Schidenhofen to us. Afterwards for a walk with Bologna, a fine day, thunderstorm in the evening. Thunder in the night.' There was a trip to the pilgrimage church of Maria Plain ('in two carriages'), a walk on the pretty Capuciner-Berg, an excursion to the castle of Leopoldskron ('saw everything out there'); one day, Wolfgang 'offered me an ice in the afternoon and punch in the evening'. On 4 September 'at 11.30 a.m. we all, my brother and his wife the first time, went bathing. Played cards, heavy rain.' Twice Michael Haydn is mentioned: on 12 September he came with 'mr. fiala' and played quartets, and he came again two days later.[18]

Constanze remembered several events, long afterwards, which she caused to be entered into the Nissen biography:[19] 'Unfavourable circumstances prevented him [Wolfgang] from undertaking this trip for several months, and even as he left [Vienna] he was in a sad frame of mind: a creditor did not want to let him leave without receiving the 30 fl. owed to him. Mozart could ill afford to do without them . . . He . . . wrote two beautiful Duets for violin and viola for Michael Haydn . . .'

There follows an account of how these works came to be written:

Michael Haydn was supposed to compose duets for violin and viola on the highest orders [i.e. for the Archbishop]. But he was unable to deliver them on time, because he fell ill and was incapable of working for a longer period than he had expected. Because of this delay, he was threatened with cancellation of his salary, for his patron was presumably unaware of Haydn's state of health or had been misinformed. Mozart, who visited Haydn every day, learned of this, sat down and wrote for his distressed friend with such uninterrupted speed that the duets were finished in a matter of days and could be delivered a few days later under Michael Haydn's name.

Constanze took this particular quotation verbatim from a biography of Michael Haydn published by two friends of his in 1808.[20]

Composing these two works for his Salzburg colleague was at once a kind deed and an act of homage. Mozart thought highly of Michael Haydn's music (which is only now beginning to receive its due); when he left Salzburg to go to Linz, Mozart took with him a new Symphony in G (formerly known as Mozart's no. 37) by Michael Haydn, adding a slow introduction (K.444) and performing the work there in this guise.

Michael Haydn had apparently intended to compose a series of six violin and viola duets for the Archbishop; the Berlin Library owns copies of four such duets (in C, D, E and F major). When we examine these four works, it becomes quite obvious that Mozart's two, in G and B flat (K.423, 424), were carefully designed – by the choice of two keys not employed in the four already composed by Michael Haydn – to complete the set. Mozart also took great pains to compose in Michael Haydn's style, since he did not want to compromise Haydn by possible detection. The Archbishop was, after all, a great connoisseur, and although he had dismissed Mozart from his service, he was well acquainted with his former employee's music and continued to have it played at the Salzburg court. However, he never suspected that Mozart was behind two of the six duets Haydn delivered. (Michael Haydn 'kept [Mozart's] original manuscripts as a sacred relic', and they still exist today, in private possession. The works were not published in Mozart's lifetime, for obvious reasons, and were first issued in 1793 by J. André in Offenbach.)

Among the devices Mozart uses to camouflage his authorship are the chirping grace notes and trills in the opening movement of K.424 and the popular tunes in the finale of K.423. It is worth bearing in mind, when studying these charming pastiches, that one of Mozart's specialties was an ability to imitate other composers perfectly. Five years before writing these duets he had remarked, in a letter to his father, 'As you know, I can more or less adopt or imitate any kind and any style of composition.'[21] But it must also be added that Mozart became interested, indeed involved, in these little duets and ended up writing two miniature masterpieces.

*   *   *

Nearly half a century later, Constanze was to recall an incident in Salzburg. We may establish the setting with a quotation from Nannerl's Diary:

The month of October 1783

On the 1st morning Bologna and Bullinger to us, afternoon Robiny, Ceccarelj [*sic*], Bulinger [*sic*], Tomasellj, Fiala, Feiner and others to us. A symphony, the quartet from the opera, a Concerto in C for piano, Henry a fiddle concerto, Bologna sang an aria. Afterwards to the theatre. A fine day.[22]

Vincent Novello, who with his wife Mary visited Constanze Nissen in 1829; both kept diaries that record their conversations in which Constanze recalled aspects of her life with Mozart. Engraving by William Humphreys after a painting by Edward Peter Novello, Vincent's son.

After Vincent and Mary Novello visited Constanze in 1829, Mary – they both kept diaries – reported: 'She told us that after their marriage they paid a visit to Salzburg and were singing the Quartet of 'Andrò ramingo' when he was so overcome that he burst into tears and quitted the chamber and it was some time before she could console him.' They were, of course, performing the profound and darkly troubled Quartet from Act III of *Idomeneo*, 'in which,' says Rosemary Hughes, the sympathetic editor of the Novello diaries, 'the young Idamante faces exile and disaster . . . [and their performance] had brought upon [Wolfgang] a wave of overwhelming and unaccountable emotion, like a presage of woe.'

The C minor Mass (K.427)

One of the principal reasons for the Mozarts' visit to Salzburg was connected with one of his greatest religious compositions – a votive Mass for Constanze. The exact circumstances are shrouded in mystery: in a letter quoted below, Mozart refers to some illness of Constanze's, her recovery from which provided the reason for composing the Mass, whereas in the Nissen biography the work is said to have celebrated the safe delivery of their first child. Perhaps the Mass was to mark their marriage, contracted and fulfilled despite all the difficulties. As early as 4 January 1783, Mozart wrote to his father,

Concerning the vow, it is quite true; – it did not flow from my pen without premeditation – I have really promised it in my innermost heart, and hope to be able to keep it. – My wife was not yet married when I made it – since I was firmly persuaded that I would marry her soon after her recovery, I could make the promise easily – the time and circumstances prevented our trip, as you yourself know; – as witness, however, that I fully intend to keep my promise, there is the score of half a mass, which is lying on my desk in the best of hopes.[23]

Because of his involvement with Baron Gottfried van Swieten's Sunday Concerts, Mozart had become particularly concerned with fugues, and Constanze's interest in works in this genre by Handel and J.S. Bach inspired Wolfgang to write some splendid preludes and fugues. Speaking of the Fantasia and Fugue in C (K.394) for piano, Wolfgang writes, in a letter to his sister on 20 April 1782,

. . . this fugue came into the world really because of my dear Konstanze. – Baron van Suiten [*sic*], to whom I go every Sunday, gave me all the works of Handel and

Sebastian Bach to take home (after I had played them to him). – When Konstanze heard the fugues, she quite fell in love with them; . . . – since she often heard me improvise . . . she asked me if I had ever written any of them down. – And when I told her no – she scolded me thoroughly . . . and she never stopped entreating me until I wrote down a fugue for her, and that is the work's origin. – I've written the tempo 'Andante Maestoso' on purpose, so that it won't be played too quickly. I intend – with time and if I find the right opportunity – to write another five and then present them to Baron van Suiten . . .'[24]

In this letter we have the most obvious explanation for the fugues which close the Gloria ('Cum Sancto Spiritu') and Sanctus ('Osanna in excelsis') movements of the Mass. Opening in a lofty and noble C minor, the slow Kyrie then modulates to the relative major (E flat) and the central 'Christe' section, which proves to be a long and rapturous soprano solo – destined for Constanze (who in fact sang it at the first performance). When they were engaged, and in the early years of their marriage, Mozart wrote vocal exercises for Constanze, one of which (K.393, no. 2), supposedly written for her in August 1782, contains the essence of this soaring 'Christe', surely the most beautiful of wedding presents (to which, as noted above, we may add the Serenade for Thirteen Instruments).

Not being confined to writing the kind of Mass which Archbishop Colloredo would have expected – the principal requirements of which were brevity and an absence of fugues – Mozart allowed his imagination to take flight. He obviously intended to compose a kind of gigantic 'compendium', in which all sorts of different styles could be combined in a single large work – hence the amazing juxtaposition of Saxon fugues with Italian-like arias ('Laudamus Te'). Perhaps the most inspired and unconventional movement is the 'Qui tollis', where suddenly a double choir (eight parts) appears (it will be used again in the Sanctus): in this Largo, supported *inter alia* by three trombones, we have the kind of sequential, double-dotted ostinato-like movement well known in the Baroque tradition, wherein Mozart presents us with a mighty pageant – like an endless procession of desperate penitents before the Cross, as the great Mozart scholar Hermann Abert said many years ago.[25] Mozart had very definite ideas about church music and the fact that it ought by its very nature to be conservative. Here we can hear in solid form the essence of Mozartian church music, which was not to be repeated until 1791, with the magical 'Ave, verum corpus' and the composition of the Requiem.

It is not known what condition the Mass was in when Mozart took it to Salzburg to have it performed. It was probably, as he wrote, half finished: perhaps the Kyrie and the Gloria. The Credo was destined never to be completed, and the Agnus was never composed at all. Obviously the Mass could not be performed in the Cathedral, where Archbishop Colloredo reigned; but there was another place, equally grand, with which the Mozarts had long maintained friendly relations – the Benedictine Abbey of St Peter's. Information about the Mass's first performance comes exclusively from Nannerl's Diary: 'the 23 [of October 1783] to Mass. Then to the *Capellhaus* [Nannerl writes 'capelHaus', a building for the choir-boys in what is now the

Dominicus Hagenauer, O.S.B., of St Peter's Abbey, Salzburg, a friend and supporter of Mozart who in 1801 became Abbot of St Peter's. Engraving by C. Kohl after an original drawing, 1801.

The opening of the Gloria from the organ part (ABOVE) of the original performance material of Mozart's Mass in C Minor (K.427) with corrections in the composer's own hand.

The first performance of the Mass took place on 26 October 1783 in St Peter's Abbey, Salzburg (BELOW), rather than in the Cathedral (ABOVE), the preserve of Mozart's former employer, Archbishop Colloredo; both buildings are seen in engravings by Kurt Remshard after drawings by Anton Danreiter.

Siegmund-Haffner-Gasse] for the rehearsal of my brother's Mass, in which my sister-in-law sings the [soprano] solo . . . on the [26] to St Peter's where my brother's Mass was performed, the entire *Hofmusik* was present. . . .'[26]

Fortunately, fragments of the original performance material survive, and from these we can see: (1) that the Kyrie, Gloria, Sanctus and Benedictus were performed; (2) that the extant parts – organ, trombone I, II and III – are transposed down from C minor to the initially difficult key of B flat minor (easier to perform when the music changes to C major = B flat major). It has been suggested that this curious change was to make the solo soprano part (Constanze's), which is extremely high and difficult, somewhat less 'exposed'. Or possibly there was another, technical reason, of which we now have no knowledge.

Now it happens that each year, on 26 October, St Peter's in Salzburg celebrated the Feast of St Amand, Bishop of Maastricht, the second patron saint of the Abbey. The occasion was celebrated with especial pomp and ceremony, and one of its peculiar features was that usually the entire Credo was omitted – *just that portion of the Mass in C minor which Mozart had not completed* (and which contained, in the unperformed but rather fully sketched 'Et incarnatus est', the most difficult soprano solo of the entire work). As we have seen, there was no Credo in the original parts. There is, however, one catch, for when the Feast of St Amand fell on a Sunday – which was the case in 1783 – the Credo was included. We shall never know precisely what occurred, but it may

The Hannibal Platz (now Makart Platz), Salzburg, with the so-called Tanzmeisterhaus (Dancing Master's House), the home of Leopold Mozart from 1773 until his death in 1787; Wolfgang stayed here in 1783 when he first introduced Constanze to his father and sister. Engraving after Georg Pezolt, c. 1830.

be that the Credo was either omitted or simply sung in Gregorian Chant (like, perhaps, the missing Agnus?).

The choir of St Peter's Abbey consisted of about ten boys and men and perhaps the same number of instruments. The ensemble did not contain bassoons or trombones, which the Mozarts would have engaged either from the court orchestra, or from the Stadtthurnermeister (town tower master) and his apprentices. Nannerl tells us that the entire *Hofmusik* participated, which meant that the second solo soprano part, almost as difficult as the first, could have been sung by one of the castrati who were friends of the family, Francesco Ceccarelli or Michelangelo Bologna, the tenor part by another family friend mentioned in Nannerl's Diary, Giuseppe Tomaselli (1756–1837). The only (modest) bass solo, in the Benedictus, could have been sung by any competent member of the bass section in the choir. Presumably Mozart either played the organ or conducted (from a violin?).[27]

* * *

The next day, at 9.30 a.m., Constanze and Wolfgang left Salzburg. They proceeded to Linz, via Lambach Abbey, arriving there just in time for Wolfgang to take over the organ part in the Agnus Dei. ('The Prelate was most overjoyed to see me again . . .'). On Tuesday, 4 November, Mozart gave an academy concert at the Linz theatre, '. . . and since I didn't have a single symphony with me, I'm writing a new one at great speed'. This was to be the much-loved 'Linz' Symphony (K.425), written in five days at the most, and containing a quiet, but for musicians highly dramatic, innovation – the introduction of trumpets and drums into the slow movement. This gives a note of solemn splendour to the quietly radiant Andante.

As the Mozarts entered the Upper Austrian capital, a servant of the 'old' Count Thun was waiting: 'the young Count Thun (brother of the Thun in Vienna) came to me right away and said that his father had been expecting me for the last two weeks, and I should drive straight there, for I was to be his guest . . . – I can't say strongly enough how extremely politely I am treated in this house . . .'[28]

*   *   *

On 22 and 23 December 1783 the annual Christmas concerts given by the Tonkünstler-Societät took place in Vienna. Works by Haydn were performed, singers from the newly-established Italian Opera in Vienna participated, and Mozart supplied a new 'Rondo' (Recitative and Aria, 'Misero! o sogno!', K.431) which was sung by his friend, the tenor Johann Valentin Adamberger. Wolfgang also played a piano concerto, possibly the new 'enlarged' version of no. 13 (K.415). The programmes were as follows:[29]

Symphony [Overture] and Chorus – Haydn [possibly the Overture and opening Chorus from his oratorio of 1775, *Il ritorno di Tobia*].
Arias by Antonio M.G. Sacchini (Sig. Mandini & Mlle. Cavalieri).
Concerto for Forte-Piano & Orchestra, composed and played by Mozart [only on 22 December; in the second concert a violin concerto was played instead by Schlesinger].
Symphony by Koželuch [presumably Leopold].
A new Rondo by Mozart (Adamberger).
Terzetto by Giuseppe Sarti (Cavalieri, Adamberger, Mandini).
Choruses by J.A. Hasse, Sacchini and Carl Ditters von Dittersdorf.
Conductor: Joseph Starzer.

On 24 December, Mozart wrote to his father about the concerts, saying that the first one was full and the second one empty. Can these concerts have been the occasion when Mozart met Joseph Haydn for the first time? Haydn had been able to leave Eszterháza earlier then usual that year, the opera season there having closed at the end of November. It is likely that he was at the Tonkünstler-Societät, not least because it was soon decided to repeat *Il ritorno di Tobia* in the forthcoming concerts (Lent 1784) of the Society. If in fact both men were there, Haydn will have heard one of Mozart's greatest vocal pieces, in which the intensity, passion and personal involvement with the text clearly distinguish his treatment of a libretto, as compared to Haydn's more objective and sometimes more cynical approach. 'Misero! o sogno!' must have been a revelation not only for Haydn but for the other composers in the hall – a clear foretaste of what Mozart was soon to demonstrate in the field of Italian opera.

XVII
(OPPOSITE) *Emperor Joseph II making music with two of his sisters, the Archduchesses Anna and Elisabeth. A keen amateur musician, the Emperor made the acquaintance of Mozart soon after his arrival in Vienna in 1781. The score shown open on the piano is a duet by Salieri. Oil painting by Joseph Hauzinger, before 1780.*

XVIII, XIX SALZBURG

*Hieronymus, Count Colloredo, Prince-Archbishop of Salzburg from 1772,
under whom both Leopold and Wolfgang Mozart served; following his break
with the Archbishop in Vienna in 1781, which occurred while the Salzburg
archiepiscopal court was in temporary residence there, Wolfgang returned only
once to his birthplace, in 1783, to introduce his wife Constanze to his family
and friends. Anonymous portrait in oils.*

*A contemporary view of the Residenzplatz showing (left) the late sixteenth-
century New Building with the Glockenspiel, (centre) the Cathedral and
(right) the Archbishop's Palace; coloured engraving by F. Müller after
Franz von Naumann.*

XX *The Michaelerplatz, one of Vienna's principal squares, showing
(left) the entrance to St Michael's church, the domed Riding School and (far
right) the old Burgtheater, the interior of which is shown overleaf; engraving
by Carl Schütz, 1783.*

XXI   *The interior of the old Burgtheater, Vienna; concerts were also given in this auditorium, including Mozart's own benefit concert on 23 March 1783 (the programme for which is given in detail on p. 88); anonymous coloured engraving, c. 1830.*

XXII   *A lavish entertainment in the Redoutensaal consisting of a performance of J.A. Hasse's* Alcide in Bivio *and Gluck's* Tétide, *staged in celebration of the marriage in 1760 of Archduke Joseph (later Emperor Joseph II) to Isabella of Parma; detail of a painting by Martin van Meytens and studio. The Redoutensaal was a focal point of social activity in Vienna, including the regular masked balls such as the one Mozart attended in January 1783.*

VI

Patronage and the subscription concerts of 1784 Mozart joins the Freemasons

---

O N 9 FEBRUARY 1784, Mozart began to keep a kind of musical diary of his new compositions – a running thematic 'Catalogue of all my Works'.[1] This document is of immense importance, establishing authenticity and confirming chronology (although many surviving autographs are dated, too). Unfortunately, it is not complete: not only are a considerable number of genuine works not included, but sometimes Mozart made 'block' entries, listing several works under one date. Such a case occurs on 26 June 1788, under which date are listed the E flat Symphony no. 39 (K.543), a 'Small March' (K.544), the Piano Sonata in C (K.545), and the Adagio and Fugue for strings (K.546); obviously all four works were not composed, or even completed, on 26 June. But the catalogue is also valuable because it gives complete casts of operas (assisting us in such dubious cases of identification as the original performers of *La clemenza di Tito*) and also lists the orchestration. For the Piano Concerto no. 19 in F (K.459), the entry lists trumpets and drums, which parts have not survived (they are missing on the autograph and were perhaps added on separate sheets, a practice which Mozart and Haydn followed when the number of staves on the page was insufficient for all instruments or voices).

Why did Mozart begin the catalogue? Perhaps because he felt it necessary to introduce some order into his compositional life; perhaps, too, he realized that his career was now embarked on a sharply 'upwards' curve and he needed the catalogue as a reference 'tool'. After all, Haydn kept a similar (though less well-organized) catalogue – known as the *Entwurf-Katalog* (Draft Catalogue) – but without dates, orchestration, or lists of singers.

The first catalogue entry is the Piano Concerto no. 14 in E flat (K.449), composed for Wolfgang's pupil, Barbara ('Babette') von Ployer, daughter of Court Councillor Gottfried Ignaz von Ployer, who in the winter months lived in town ('am Lugeck') and in summer in the pretty suburb of Döbling. Mozart wrote for her not only this lively and transparently scored concerto, but the great G major Concerto no. 17 (K.453). Barbara kept a commonplace book,

ABOVE *Ticket to a concert given by Mozart in Vienna in the 1780s; one of only two known examples of its kind.*

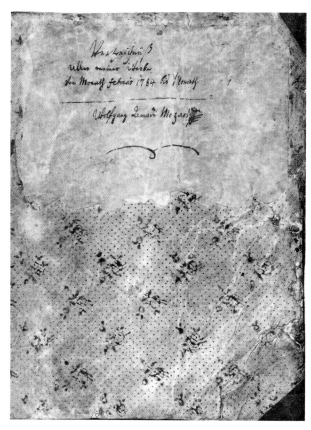

RIGHT *The cover of Mozart's autograph catalogue of his works composed between February 1784 and 1791, with* (OPPOSITE) *the first entries which include four Piano Concertos (nos. 14–17, K.449, 450, 451 and 453) and (second from bottom) the Quintet for piano, oboe, clarinet, horn and bassoon (K.452). See also p. 215.*

with entries by her friends, including Haydn (a canon), Mozart ('Marche funebre del sigʳ: Maestro Contrapunto' for piano, K.453a) and Constanze Mozart, who after her husband's death dedicated a watercolour portrait of Wolfgang to his former pupil.[2] She played the first of her new concertos at a concert in her family home on 23 March 1784. Count Zinzendorf thought she played marvellously.[3]

The tremendous upsurge in Mozart's musical activity in Vienna is revealed with dramatic suddenness in a letter to his father of 3 March 1784.

On the last 3 Wednesdays of Lent starting with the 17th inst., I shall give 3 subscription concerts in Trattner's Rooms, for which I already have 100 subscribers, and shall have another 30 easily by the time they start. – The price for all 3 concerts is 6 fl., – I shall probably give 2 academy concerts in the theatre this year – so you can easily imagine that I am obliged to play new things – hence I must compose. – The whole of the morning is devoted to pupils. – And in the evening I must play [in public] almost every day. – Below you will read a list of all the academy concerts in which it is *certain* I must appear. – Now I must relate to you quickly how it happened that I shall be giving private academy concerts at this very moment. – *Claviermeister* Richter gives 6 Saturday concerts in the above-named rooms. – The nobility let it be known that they were not interested unless I played in them. H[err] Richter asked me to do so – I promised him I would play 3 times. – And then I issued subscriptions for 3 of my own concerts, to which everybody subscribed. . . .[4]

In the list that follows, Mozart notes 22 concert appearances, including five at the house of the Russian Ambassador, Prince Galitzin, nine at that of Johann Baptist, Count Esterházy, and three engagements at Richter's academies; in addition, there were the three private academies and two public performances in the theatre.

Several days later, on 20 March, Wolfgang sent his father a list of his personal subscribers.[5] The names it contains read like a cross-section of those appearing in the *Almanach de Gotha*, including the cream of Viennese society. It is an extraordinary testimony to his popularity. Referring to the list (see Appendix 1), he notes:

I have about 30 subscribers more than Richter and Fischer together. – The first academy concert, on the 17th inst., went very well – the hall was full to bursting. – And the new Concerto [for piano, no. 15, K.450] which I played was an extraordinary success. – Wherever one goes, one hears praises of this concert. – Tomorrow should have been my first academy concert in the theatre – Prince Louis Lichtenstein [*sic*] is, however, putting on an opera in his palace – and will attract not only the core of the nobility, but will lure away all the best members of the [Court] orchestra. – So by means of a printed announcement I've postponed it until 1st April. – Now I must close, because I must attend Count Zitchi's [Carl, Count Zichy von Vasonykö, Hungarian nobleman] academy concert. – Until Lent is over, you will have to be patient with me. . . .

The grand concert Mozart gave in the Burgtheater consisted, according to the *Wienerblättchen* of 1 April,[6] of the following programme:

1 A grand symphony with trumpets and drums [no. 35, 'Haffner,' K.385, or no. 31, 'Paris,' K.297? – probably only the first three movements]
2 An aria, sung by Herr Adamberger.
3 Herr Kapellmeister Mozart will play an entirely new concerto on the forte piano [no. 16, K.451, completed on 22 March].
4 An entirely new grand symphony [no. 36, 'Linz', K.425?].
5 An aria, sung by Mlle. Cavalieri.
6 Herr Kapellmeister Mozart will play an entirely new grand quintet [for piano and wind instruments, K.452, completed on 30 March].
7 An aria, sung by Herr [Antonio] Marchesi, Sr.
8 Herr Kapellmeister Mozart will improvise alone on the forte piano.
9 At the end a symphony [finale of item 1]. Except for the three arias, everything will be the composition of Herr Kapellmeister Mozart.

Ten days later, Wolfgang apologizes again to his father for not writing,[7]

but you know how much I have to do at present! – I have reaped a great deal of honour through my 3 subscription academy concerts. – Also my academy concert in the theatre went very well. – I have written 2 grand concertos [K.450, 451], plus a quintet [K.452] which has been exceptionally well received; – I myself consider it the best thing I have ever written in my life. – It is for *1 oboe, 1 clarinet, 1 horn, 1 bassoon* and the *piano forte*; I would have wished you could hear it! – and how beautifully it was performed! – Otherwise I am (to tell truth) tired of late – with all that playing – And it is no little compliment to me that my listeners were *never* tired . . . Now today I've completed another concerto for Miss Ployer [K.453, entered in Mozart's catalogue two days later]; – and now I am half dressed to go to Prince Kaunitz's. – Yesterday I played at Leopold Palfy's [Count Pálffy, married to a Countess Waldstein]. – Tomorrow at the academy concert that will be given by Mad:^elle [Nanette] Bayer [the daughter of a retired court trumpeter, Johann Ernst Bayer; as it was Easter Sunday, when public concerts were not allowed, this must have been a private affair]. . . .[8]

*   *   *

Among the names of Mozart's patrons of this Lenten season in 1784, we may single out three of particular importance to the composer: Gottfried, Baron van Swieten; Dimitri Mikhailovich, Prince Galitzin; and the Esterházy family in general, with particular reference to Johann Baptist, Count Esterházy. All three proved to be long-lasting patrons of Mozart.

Baron van Swieten

The son of Empress Maria Theresa's personal physician, Gerhard van Swieten, Gottfried (1733–1803) was born in Holland and, at the age of eleven, went with his father to Vienna, where he entered the Austrian diplomatic service. He was sent to Brussels and Paris, was in England in 1769, and at the end of the next year received his most important posting – as Ambassador to

the Court of Frederick the Great in Berlin. There he spent seven years, studying and being strongly influenced by the works of Johann Sebastian Bach and Handel – at that time still major influences in Prussian musical life. Swieten was also impressed with the music of two of Bach's sons, Carl Philipp Emanuel and the dissolute, but perhaps most talented of them all, Wilhelm Friedemann. When Swieten returned to Vienna, he became Prefect of the Imperial Royal Library; a few years later – in 1781, just as Mozart was arriving in Vienna – he was made President of the Court Commission for Education. Shortly after receiving this prestigious appointment, with a salary of 7,000 gulden and 1,000 gulden lodging money, Swieten was given the added task of supervising the censorship of all printed material in the kingdom – an awesome responsibility. A devoted civil servant, Swieten was very much *en rapport* with the reforming ideas and ideals of Emperor Joseph II.

The Baron, a confirmed bachelor, had been following Mozart's career off and on since 1768, when – in a typical Viennese intrigue – *La finta semplice* had been forced off the boards before it could be performed. When Mozart arrived in Vienna in 1781, he naturally gravitated to the National Library on the Josephsplatz, where concerts were given in the great hall and volumes of Bach and Handel were available to be studied in the Baron's apartment in the same building. We learn of the Swieten circle from Wolfgang's letter to his father:

[Vienna, 10 April 1782] . . . I wanted to ask you when you return the Rondo [K.382] to me, would you please also send the 6 fugues by Handel, and the Toccatas and Fugues by Eberlin. – Every Sunday at 12 noon I go to Baron von Suiten [*sic*] – and there nothing but Handel and Bach is played.

I am making a collection of Bach fugues – not only Sebastian's but Emanuel and Friedeman [*sic*] Bach's – Also Handel's, and these I don't have. – I also want to have the Baron hear Eberlin's. . . .[9]

The Josephsplatz in Vienna, with the Imperial Royal Library and, on the right, the Assembly Rooms (Redoutensäle); engraving by Carl Schütz, 1780. The library building included a grand hall in which concerts were given under the aegis of the Prefect of the I.R. Library, Baron Gottfried van Swieten, portrayed (ABOVE) in an engraving by J.G. Mansfeld.

Mozart asked his father to send some of his music to Vienna to be played at Swieten's concerts, but apparently Leopold modestly demurred, to which Wolfgang replied on 12 April 1783:

When it gets warmer, please go up to the attic and send us something of your own church music; – you don't need to be embarrassed about it. – Baron van Suiten and Starzer know as well as you and I that taste constantly changes – and also – that this change in taste extends, alas, even to church music, which shouldn't be the case – and that is why it also happens that true church music is found – in the attic – and almost consumed by worms. . . .[10]

In the course of the 1780s, Swieten found time to organize a group of the nobility for the purposes of performing 'old' music at private concerts held in the Vienna palaces of the families concerned; it adopted the name Gesellschaft der Associirten ('Society of Associates') and undertook to perform works by C.P.E. Bach and oratorios by Handel, usually arranged (and adapted to suit the availability of, say, trumpet players) by Mozart. As we shall see, some of these Handel performances took place in the quarters of Johann Baptist, Count Esterházy. During Mozart's 'lean' years, these Handel arrangements were to be one of his few sources of regular income.

After Mozart's death, Haydn moved closer to van Swieten, partly because the composer was no longer absent in Hungary for months at a time and their proximity in the capital enabled the two men to collaborate on the last three oratorios Haydn composed, the vocal version of *The Seven Words*, *The Creation* and *The Seasons*. Beethoven was also a protégé of Swieten's, playing Bach's *Well Tempered Clavier* to the old Baron and dedicating to him the First Symphony in 1800.

The Baron had a reputation for being stiff, difficult and tight-fisted. He was not – despite many references to the contrary – a member of any known Masonic Lodge in Vienna, but he had probably earlier joined a Berlin Lodge and his ideas and principles were of the kind generally propagated by Freemasons of the period – enlightened and reformist. Much of *The Creation* contains distinctly Masonic ideas, though how many of them were Swieten's and how many derived from the original English libretto must remain a matter for speculation. As far as Mozart was concerned, Swieten was a major patron and a loyal supporter in bad times – he was the only subscriber for Mozart's proposed concert series in 1789.[11]

Some years ago, Else Radant discovered an unpublished Austrian diary, in which Swieten plays a major role in 1791, the last year of Mozart's life. The story is that of Franz (later Ritter von) Heintl,[12] son of a poor mountain farmer from the border country of Moravia; not least thanks to Swieten, this young man became a prominent and wealthy lawyer. His story puts Swieten into perspective as being a decent and generous man of the Enlightenment.

[p. 55] On 24 August 1789 I arrived in Vienna . . . My entire capital consisted of 12 gulden. My first quarters were in the rooms of a master tailor . . . for which I had to pay 2F in advance monthly. My shoes and boots had to be put in good order and that cost

6F 30x, thus I had only 3F 30x for the rest of life's necessities . . . [p. 56] I never had any breakfast, for lunch I went with several other students to a *Traiteur* . . . where the portions were small – a small bowl of soup, a tiny piece of beef with vegetables and a $\frac{1}{4}$ loaf of bread costing 1 Groschen. That cost 6x daily . . . My evening meal was dry bread. In those days a loaf of bread at 6x weighed 1 ₦ 17 Loth. A third of that was my evening meal.

He finds children to tutor, two hours daily, providing an income of 4F 30x in the month. But since Latin is not his forte, he loses the job, but finds other pupils. They live so far apart that he has to run between jobs in order to arrive on time; he now teaches nine hours daily and that gives him a monthly income of 24F. With this he supports his two brothers in college in Olmütz, while he studies at night. In 1791 he is very ill, hopes for a scholarship but is not awarded one. He turns to Baron Gottfried van Swieten, for help. The account continues:

[pp. 75ff.] Feeling scared, I went to Hr. Baron van Swieten's quarters, which were in the I.R. Castle on the Josephsplatz [2 April 1791, 4 p.m.]. At this unusual hour of the day, I was let into the antechamber, announced and at once admitted to His Excellency's study. He was holding my petition in his hand and had written my name on the outside in red ink; he addressed me in the following words, which I shall never forget: 'I have read your petition. I have found it good and I was touched by it. Take this as the first sign of my sympathy towards you' (and he handed me a banknote for 5 Fl); 'there is not very much that I can do to help, but come and pick up the money every month.' That was quite beyond my wildest hopes. . . . I bent down to kiss the benefactor's green silk dressing gown adorned with the Knight Commander's Cross of the Order of St Stephen, in which he had received me. . . . [p. 77] After the first month had passed, I found it difficult to go to him to get the 5 F: I was afraid he wouldn't remember me, and since I was no longer in an emergency, I found it hard to remind him of his promise. On the other hand, it would be unseemly, indeed ungrateful, not to accept such a philanthropic invitation. And the noble Swieten had not forgotten me: he recognized me as soon as I entered, asked me how I fared, and pressed the 5 F into my hand; he had them ready without [my] having to mention them specifically . . .

Swieten continued to help Heintl and, when the young man became a doctor of law, visited him in his quarters in the Stoss in Himmel and even entrusted the affairs of his niece, Countess Rosetti, to him.

We shall see that, partly as a result of Swieten's supposed connection with the Freemasons' conspiracy of 1791, he was dismissed from his post on the day of Mozart's death, 5 December 1791. The fates of the two men were curiously intertwined.

Dimitri Mikhailovich, Prince Galitzin

First a word as to the actual name. It is generally listed under 'Dimitri', and among the various spellings of 'Galitzin' (Golozin, Gallizin, etc. – the stress should be on the second part, Galítzin), I have chosen the form most

The pavilion in the Prater owned by the Russian Ambassador, Prince Galitzin; engraving by Kilian Ponheimer the Elder, after a drawing by A. Braun, c. 1775.

commonly used in Vienna at the period, and the one by which most of Mozart's contemporaries would have recognized the distinguished Russian diplomat.

In the 1789 *Schematismus* for Vienna, he is listed among the foreign ambassadors, under the heading 'Russia', as 'Ambassador Extraordinary and Minister Plenipotentiary to the Imp. Roy. Court, Knight of the Orders of St Andrew and St Alexander Nmosky [Nevsky], Grand Cross of the Order of St Vladimir, the Knight of the Order of St Anne. Lives at Krugerstraße [No.] 1046.'[13]

For thirty years, from 1762 to 1792, Galitzin was Ambassador in Vienna, where he had the ear of Joseph II and was instrumental in shaping Austro-Russian foreign policy. He was born on 15 May 1721 in Åbo (Turku), now Finland, a member of a numerous and famous family of Boyars. The family can be traced back to Rurik, founder of the Russian Empire (reigned 862–79). The founder of the Galitzin family was a military captain under Ivan III. Because he used to put strong leather gloves ('golitsa') over his woollen gloves, he was called Golizün or Galitzin. He died as a monk with the name Jonas in 1558. His descendants included diplomats, ministers, scientists, but were mostly military men; some were revolutionaries who ended their days in prison or in Siberia.

The prince's father, Mikhail Mikhailovich Galitzin, was a guards officer, and distinguished himself in the service of Peter the Great, who appointed him governor-general in occupied Finland. Despite the severe Russian domination, the Finns loved and revered Galitzin, calling him 'Finski bog' (God of the Finns). Later, the prince was in charge of troops in the Ukraine, where he amassed a large fortune. He died in Moscow on 21 December 1730 as General Field-Marshal and President of the College of War, aged fifty-five.

Dimitri Mikhailovich was one of seventeen children; he entered the diplomatic corps and was sent to Paris as Ambassador to the Court of Louis xv. It was there in 1761 that he lost his wife, Princess Catherine Dimitrovna; he never married again. On 12 January 1762, he was appointed Ambassador to the Court in Vienna. In those days, ambassadors could expect to stay many years in the same posting. Sir William Hamilton and, later, his wife Lady Emma, became celebrated ornaments in the Naples firmament. In Vienna, Prince Galitzin soon acquired his first property situated in the Prater, which Joseph II ceded to the public on 7 April 1766; there the Prince purchased a piece of land where the old forester's house stood, and there – between the present-day Hauptallee and the Feuerwerksallee (Ausstellungsstraße) – he erected a pavilion.

The palace in the Krugerstraße where Prince Galitzin resided contained some eleven principal rooms with smaller chambers. The head of the household was a major domo; there was also a secretary, a clerk, three valets-de-chambre, a lackey, a house-attendant, two cooks, a translator, a pastry-cook, a gate-keeper, a stoker, a purchaser (of household necessities), two gardeners, a table-setter and a baker, plus twenty-three male and female servants (for the stable, as scullery maids, and so on). His walls were covered with paintings, etchings, drawings etc. – 254 are listed in his will, as are his elegant clothes, fourteen carriages, eleven horses and 552 bottles of rare wines.

His summer house, on what is even now referred to as the 'Galitzinberg' in the Viennese suburb of Ottakring, was built on a splendid site surrounded by woods, gardens and fields, and included a separate pavilion (which still exists). There, Galitzin created an eighteenth-century paradise with grottos, streams, fountains, mock Roman ruins and Grecian temples. The Prince supported the poor and needy of Ottakring, and he in turn was much loved by them.

In the winter of 1781–2, during the visit to Vienna of Grand Duke Paul of Russia with his wife (travelling under the name of Count and Countess of the North) with their entourage, the Russian Embassy will have been a centre of social activity. Later, in October 1782, on their return from Italy, the Russian visitors, accompanied by Joseph II, Archduke Maxmilian and a group of the local nobility, went to inspect Galitzin's estate in Dornbach at the so-called Predigstuhl, 'to enjoy the particularly beautiful view and to visit the improvements which the Imperial Russian Ambasador Prince von Galitzin has been making on this property, which he has recently acquired . . .'[14]

By 1790, Galitzin was nearly seventy; he was joined by Count A. K. Razumovsky. Razumovsky was to be for Beethoven that which Galitzin had been for Mozart. When Galitzin died of a blocked urinary tract on 30 September 1793, he was universally mourned. He made generous bequests to his family, friends and servants, but two musicians – Franz Schuppanzigh and his colleague Peter Polasovsky together put in a claim for 6,500 gulden. Such a sum owed to the distinguished violinist and founder of a great string quartet in the Haydn-Beethoven tradition must have represented countless concerts – chamber music, no doubt, but perhaps even for orchestras – which had not been paid for. This failure casts a doubt over this diplomat's seemingly blameless life.[15]

Mozart not only played twice a week at the Galitzin salon in 1784, but even before that he mentions the prince frequently. On 21 December 1782, he names him twice in a letter to Leopold: 'I'm engaged for all his [Galitzin's] concerts; every time I am fetched with equipages and taken home afterwards, and when there I am treated in the noblest fashion . . .; Count Rosenberg himself talked to me at Gallitzin's [sic], and said I really ought to write an Italian opera . . .'[16] The Galitzin salon was, then, a useful place not only for participating in 'academy concerts' but for meeting influential members of Viennese society. It is probable that Mozart played there regularly throughout the seasons of 1782–3 and 1783–4 and possibly thereafter as well, though there is no more documentary evidence after 1784. However, Galitzin had without question a decisive influence in boosting Wolfgang's career in Vienna in the early 1780s.

The Esterházy family and Count Johann Baptist

This great Hungarian noble family is usually associated with Joseph Haydn, but, as we shall see, it has every right to be associated as well – and proudly so, too – with Mozart.

In the 1780s there were two principal lines of the family – the princely side and that of the counts, who were numerous and subdivided into various branches, identified by the name of a certain estate (thus the 'senior Frakno' branch, the 'cadet Frakno' branch, and so on). When Mozart arrived in Vienna, the princely line was headed by Nicolaus I (1714–90), known as 'the Magnificent', whose chief monument is Eszterháza Castle, on the Neusiedlersee in Hungary. The princely branch had immense wealth and power, owning enormous landed estates stretching from the far north of Hungary as far as present-day Yugoslavia. In 1780, the princely bursar reported total income of nearly 800,000 gulden.[17]

Until 1783 the hereditary title of Prince (Prinz) was reserved to the senior male member of the princely branch of the family, and the estates and title normally passed (under the law of primogeniture) to the eldest son; the sons and daughters of a prince bore the title of Count or Countess. In 1783, however, Joseph II extended the hereditary title of 'Prince (Princess) of the Holy Roman Empire' to all members of this branch, and henceforth the senior (reigning) male member of the family was styled 'Fürst' – a title which has no English equivalent – from the date of his succession.[18] This development has an important bearing on the identification of at least one of the most notable members of Mozart's Masonic Lodge in Vienna in 1790 and 1792.

Mozart's first known contact with the Esterházy household is recorded in a letter to his father in Salzburg. On 15 February 1783, he writes: 'Please send

Prince Nicolaus Esterházy (1714–90), known as 'the Magnificent'; anonymous portrait.

me as soon as you can the music book in which is the Oboe Concerto [original version of the Flute Concerto (K.314)] for [the Mannheim oboist Friedrich] Ramm or rather for [the Bergamo oboist Giuseppe] Ferlendi [Ferlendis, from 1775 to 1778 a member of the Salzburg orchestra]; – the oboist of Prince Esterhazi [*sic*] will pay me 3 ducats for it; – and if I write a new one for him, 6 [ducats] . . .'[19] The first oboist of the Eszterháza orchestra, from 1781 to 1790, was Anton Mayer, but I suggest that Mozart may have been referring to an ex-member of the orchestra, Vittorino Colombazzo, who had been engaged by Haydn in September 1768. Colombazzo left the orchestra at the end of December 1768, but was back again in October 1779, until Prince Nicolaus dismissed him on 15 March 1780. Afterwards, he appeared many times in Vienna, as a soloist, and – most interesting of all – became a member of Mozart's Lodge 'New Crowned Hope' and was thus closely associated with the composer, though not as early as 1783. Whereas nothing is known of Anton Mayer's concert activity outside the princely *Capelle*, it would seem that Colombazzo was constantly in evidence in Vienna in the 1780s, where he is listed as a member of the princely Thurn und Taxis orchestra. In any event, the contact with the Esterházy orchestra was established by Mozart in 1783.[20]

A second, more direct contact was with Prince Nicolaus Esterházy himself. Some years ago, the present writer identified Prince Nicolaus as Master of Ceremonies in a group picture of a meeting of Mozart's Lodge 'New Crowned Hope', painted *c*. 1790; this became possible because a previously unpublished ms. Lodge list of that year lists Prince Nicolaus among the officers as Master of Ceremonies, and the central figure depicted in the painting bears an extraordinary resemblance to other known portraits of Nicolaus the Magnificent.[21] We have since located in Melk Abbey a printed Lodge list of 'New Crowned Hope' for 1790 – with some small but significant details in which it differs from the ms.; the printed list (see Appendix 2) dates from later in the year. Nicolaus Esterházy died in September 1790, hence – if our analysis is correct – the painting will have been executed between January and September 1790 (or possibly later, as a 'memento').

Recently, Joachim Hurwitz discovered in the files of the Provincial Grand Lodge (Landesloge) in Vienna a printed list of 'New Crowned Hope' for 1792, and as No. 18 among 'Brothers present' we find 'Esterházy, Nikolaus Fürst', his profession being given as 'Imperial Royal Chamberlain' ('k.k. Kämmerer'). Here the title 'Fürst' is used erroneously, as often happens, for this entry can only refer to the second son of Nicolaus the Magnificent,[22] also named Nicolaus, who lived from 1741 to 1809 and who was styled 'Count' until 1783 and thereafter 'Prince'. It was for his marriage in August 1777 to Maria Anna Franzisca Ungnad, Countess von Weissenwolf, that Haydn composed his festive opera *Il mondo della luna*. But, it may be asked, could the younger Nicolaus and not his father have been Master of Ceremonies in 1790? That question can be resolved thanks to the survival of a pair of oil paintings that I discovered some years ago, in a damaged state, in a castle – Steyeregg in Upper Austria – owned by one of the Weissenwolf descendants, Altgraf Salm: they are portraits of Count Nicolaus and his wife, each identified on the reverse

Johann Nepomuk, Count Esterházy de Galántha; lithograph by F. Lütgendorff, 1827.

and both dated 1783.[23] In 1790, this younger Prince Nicolaus, then aged 49, was still relatively robust and 'in his best years', whereas the Master of Ceremonies in the group portrait is clearly an older man with features closely resembling – as noted above – known portraits of Nicolaus the Magnificent. It should be noted that in 1790 the latter's grandson, Fürst Nicolaus II (1765–1833), was (a) only twenty-five and (b) unlikely to join a Brotherhood which was becoming out-of-fashion and indeed dangerous to be associated with by 1790 or 1792.

In case the reader is hoping to be provided with an easier history with regard to the Counts Esterházy, it must be stated at the outset that:

1   One of Mozart's principal patrons, from 1783 until 1789, was a Count Johann Esterházy.

2   Throughout the period in question, there were two Counts Esterházy named Johann: Johann Baptist and Johann Nepomuk.

3   Mozart scholarship has to date not only confused the two but has – except for P.A. Autexier – opted for the wrong one (Johann Nepomuk).

In order to unravel the complicated threads of the Esterházy family's genealogy, we turned first to a direct descendant, Countess Monika Esterházy; she referred us to her cousin, László Berényi, who generously made available for the purpose of this book the entire known histories of the princes and counts of the period in question. Without this extraordinary fund of information, we would still be in the same unenlightened position as hitherto. Relevant details of this genealogy are included here, by courtesy of László Berényi, as Appendix 3. One is now able to conclude that it was Count *Johann Baptist* who was Mozart's patron in Vienna, since the other Count, *Johann Nepomuk*, was largely absent from the city during this critical period as he held official appointments in Transylvania (now part of Romania).

In addition to the information provided by the place and date of birth of four of the Count's children, corroborative evidence exists from the lists of the Lodge 'Crowned Hope' (of which Count Johann Nepomuk was Master in 1781) and 'New Crowned Hope'. On 27 March 1782 he became a member of the Governing Council for Transylvania. 'This was,' László Berényi says in his report, 'apparently followed by the vital appointment as President of the School Commission in 1785 and by the Lord Lieutenancy of the Transylvanian Counties Hunyad and Zaránd in 1789.' Thus, in the crucial years 1783–4, when Mozart played regularly at the house of Count 'Jean' or 'Johann' Esterházy, and also in 1789, when the same patron had Mozart's arrangements of Handel's *Messiah* performed, Count Johann Nepomuk was far away in Transylvania.[24] For this reason, when the Lodge meeting was painted in or after 1790, Count Johann Nepomuk is shown on the left-hand side of the picture, wearing a travelling cloak, apparently observing, rather than participating in, the ceremony – he was, literally, absent.

As further confirmation, Mozart is known to have played at Count Johann Esterházy's academy concerts in Vienna on 26 and 27 March 1784, and on 30 March 1784 Count Johann Nepomuk was listed among 'Brothers absent' from his Viennese Lodge. Thus, the 'Johann' Esterházy, Mozart's patron, could

only have been the other living candidate, Count Johann Baptist (1748–1800).

Johann Baptist, known in the family as 'Roter Johann' ('Red John') on account of the colour of his hair when young, became Imperial Royal Chamberlain in 1771 and next year married Maria Anna, Countess Pálffy (1747–99). He was a scion of the cadet Frakno branch of the family, members of which, László Berényi relates, 'throughout the eighteenth century maintained at their town palace in Pozsony (Preßburg) a regular orchestra which usually followed them to their castles Cseklész (Lanschütz), Tata (Totis) and Csákvar. Alas, only a fraction of the music survived the ravages of the two World Wars, and particularly the aftermath of the second, but even so the remaining material runs to several hundred works, including several dozen by Mozart.'[25]

It is worth mentioning that among the members of the 'Crowned Hope' Lodge in 1784 was Paul Wranizky, who was 'Music Director of the worthy Br[other] Esterházy' (by which is meant Count Johann Baptist). Wranizky (1756–1808), born in the same year as Mozart, was a prolific composer, violinist and orchestra leader – e.g. at the first public performance of *The Creation* in 1799.

It is curious that the *Jahrbuch der Tonkunst von Wien und Prag*, 1796, states: 'Esterházy, Johann Count von, an estimable friend of music, who himself plays the oboe with feeling and delicacy' (p. 16). This cultivated man who became one of Mozart's first patrons in Vienna in the 1780s, was clearly an interesting and unusual figure in his own right.

When Mozart joined the Masons, he became acquainted with several other Esterházys. Franz, Count Esterházy de Galántha (known as 'Quin-Quin'), Royal Hungarian Court Chancellor, was a member of the Lodge 'Crowned

*Paul Wranizky, Music
Director to Count Johann
Baptist Esterházy;
engraving by Heinrich
Philipp Boßler.*

The two deceased fellow Masons, in honour of whose memory Mozart wrote the Masonic Funeral Music (K.477) in 1785: Georg August, Duke of Mecklenburg-Strelitz, seen in an anonymous oil painting, c.1769 (detail); and Franz, Count Esterházy, portrayed in a mezzotint by Franz Balko after J.G. Haid, 1769.

Hope'. He died in 1785, and in honour of his memory, and that of another deceased Brother, Georg August, Duke of Mecklenburg-Strelitz (honorary member of the 'Three Eagles' Lodge), Mozart composed his greatest piece of Masonic music, the Masonic Funeral Music (K.477), to be played at a Lodge of Sorrows. When he joined the 'New Crowned Hope' Lodge early in 1786, Mozart found no fewer than four Counts Esterházy as members – three present and one absent:

1 Johann Baptist, his friend and patron;
2 Franz (1746–1811), of the cadet Frakno branch, who was lord of Tata, older brother of Johann Baptist and Ambassador to the Court of Naples and the Two Sicilies, Chamberlain, Privy Councillor and Knight of the Golden Fleece.
3 Franz Seraph(im) (1758–1815), son of Count Franz ('Quin-Quin'), Chamberlain (1780) and Privy Councillor.
4 Johann Nepomuk, Count Esterházy de Galántha (1754–1840) of the Csesznek branch, was Chamberlain (1775), Privy Councillor and member of the Governing Council for Transylvania.

In the former secret archives of Vienna is a series of printed lists of a Parisian Lodge,[26] 'Les Amis-réunis', for the years 1784–6. In them we find some familiar names, such as Baron (later Count) d'Ogny, who was responsible for commissioning Haydn's 'Paris' symphonies. In a section 'Associés libres correspondans' we note that on 8 December 1784 three Austrians (Hungarians) joined: the Counts Pálf(f)y, Zapary (Szapáry) and Esterházy, who could in 1786 enjoy the fraternal company of 'M. le Baron de Tall[e]yrand, Ambass. du Roi de Naples' and 'M. Mgr de Montesquieu'. The Esterházy who could have been involved was – according to László Berényi – Count Franz, son of Count Nicolaus (1711–64), the Ambassador to St Petersburg, and his wife, Princess Anna Maria Lubomirska – the very Count Franz whom Mozart came to know in the Lodge 'New Crowned Hope' – No. 2 noted above. The Count was a notorious womanizer, and while he was attached to the Austrian Embassy in Paris under Count Mercy, his name was linked to a series of cuckolded husbands and duels. His name also features in correspondence between Empress Maria Theresa and her daughter Marie Antoinette, who thought that persons of Esterházy's habits (here there is some confusion between Count Franz and his distant cousin Count Valentine, of the French branch of the family) had no place in the retinue of the Queen of France.

*   *   *

In Vienna, at this time, Mozart's name was on every tongue. A wind-band concert put on by his friend, the clarinettist Anton Stadler, in the Burgtheater on 23 March 1784 included the first public performance of sections from the great Serenade for Thirteen Instruments (K.361). A critic, one J.F. Schink, who was present, described precisely the scoring, adding: 'A master sat at every instrument – and oh, what an effect! – magnificent and grand . . . *Mozart*. That's a life here, like the land of the blessed, the land of music . . .'[27] Anyone with ears to hear could only be astonished by the new wind-band writing of which Mozart was now the leading exponent.

A month later – on 29 April – Mozart was playing in a concert at the Burgtheater attended by the Emperor; it featured a superb violinist from Mantua, Regina Strinasacchi (1764–1823),[28] for whom Wolfgang wrote the Violin Sonata in B flat (K.454). They played it together and he also performed a piano concerto. Mozart was late in finishing the sonata, and it had to be performed without rehearsal; he wrote out the violin part for Signorina Strinasacchi, but is said to have played the piano part from memory, using a kind of shorthand notation on the autograph. Joseph II could hardly believe

Giovanni Paisiello (1740–1816), the well-known operatic composer. Engraving by Vincent Alloga after Élisabeth Vigée-Lebrun.

his eyes and ears. And when, nearly two hundred years later, the autograph was located in a Swedish private collection, it became clear that the violin part had been written first, in a (now) paler ink, and the piano part squeezed in later.[29] A few months later, Christoph Torricella (a Freemason) published the new Sonata, together with two others (K.333 and 284 for piano alone); the handsome print was dedicated to Countess Theresa Cobenzl, and contained unmistakable Masonic emblems – a foreshadowing of Mozart's own allegiance to the Craft.

'Paesiello [*sic*] is here now, returned again from Russia, – he is to compose a new opera here', Wolfgang wrote to his father in May.[30] On 8 May, Paisiello himself writes that he had arrived on the 1st, was received by the Emperor and had an hour's conversation with him, and had been commissioned to compose a new opera, which would turn out to be the immensely successful *Il rè Teodoro in Venezia*. On 9 June, Wolfgang writes to his father:

Tomorrow there is to be an academy concert at the country place in Döbling of the Agent Ployer, where Miss Babette will play her new Concerto in G [K.453] – I the Quintet [for piano and wind instruments (K.452)] – and then both of us the grand Sonata for 2 pianos [K.448]. I shall fetch Paesello [*sic*] with the carriage, to give him a chance to hear my compositions and my pupil's playing: – if Maestro [Giuseppe] Sarti had not been obliged to leave today [for Russia] I would have taken him out there too. – Sarti is a thoroughly honest, decent man! – I played a great deal for him . . .[31]

It was a heady success, also financially, and the Mozarts urgently required a new and much larger apartment, where they could accommodate the constant presence of copyists, pupils and the complicated organization needed to deal with academy concerts, subscription invitations, and so on. On 18 June, Mozart paid off the rest of his rent for the quarters in the Trattnerhof and a few days later gave notice to his landlord. The note in the Trattnerhof's books reads, 'This party gave official and legal notice on 23 June [1]784 to leave at Michaelmas. In future he will live at No. 816 [*recte* 846], the Camesina House in town, in the Große Schulerstraße.' The move was to be made on 29 September to splendid, very expensive, and spacious quarters, for which the rent was 460 gulden p.a. (compared with the 150 gulden for his previous flat).

When Paisiello's new opera was first performed on 13 August, Wolfgang attended. What happened is known to us only from the account in Leopold Mozart's letter to his daughter of 14 September 1784:

My son in Vienna was very ill, – all his clothes were soaked with perspiration during the new opera by Paesiello [*sic*] . . . Then he contracted a rheumatic fever which, if not treated at once, can become septic. He writes: 'I had a dreadful attack of colic for 4 days in a row, which have always ended in vomiting; now I must be extremely careful. My doctor is H[err] Sigmund Barisani [younger son of Dr Silvester Barisani, personal physician to the Archbishop of Salzburg], who has been to see me almost every day since he arrived; he is much esteemed here; and he's very clever . . .'[32]

OPPOSITE *The Graben with, in the right foreground, the large building known as the Trattnerhof where the Mozarts lived before moving to more spacious quarters in September 1784. Detail of an engraving by Carl Schütz, 1781.*

On 23 August 1784 in St Gilgen (her mother's birthplace), Mozart's sister Maria Anna married Johann Baptist von Berchtold zu Sonnenburg, a local magistrate. He was a widower with five children and she would outlive him by

many years (he died in 1801). After she moved to St Gilgen, Leopold Mozart wrote to her regularly, and these letters often contain precious information originally in lost letters sent to Leopold from Wolfgang in Vienna. On 21 September, Mozart's second child, Carl Thomas, was born; he lived until 1858 and became an Austrian official in Italy.

* * *

Throughout his stay in Vienna, Mozart had come into contact with Freemasons. Their ideals – humanity, tolerance, brotherhood – were very much Mozart's and it was natural that he should gravitate towards the Craft. In the secret files of the Vienna State Archives, we find the following document which was circulated on 5 December 1784 by the Freemasons' Lodge 'Zur Wohlthätigkeit' ('Beneficence') to its sister Lodges in Vienna:[33]

Prosposed Kapellmeister Mozart. – Our former Sec'y Bro. Hoffman forgot to register this proposed member at the most honourable sister ⬜⬜. He was already proposed four weeks ago at the honourable district ⬜ and we should like therefore in the coming week to take steps for his admission if the most honourable sister ⬜ ⬜ have no objections to him.

    In the Orient of Vienna

5
―――――
57 XII 84

                                  Schwanckhardt: Secr:

    On 14 December, Mozart was duly initiated as an Entered Apprentice. In Freemasonry, to which Mozart became devoted, the composer seems to have found a congenial group of men with ideas and aspirations similar to his own. He was to compose a considerable amount of music for his Lodges. The Masons had a profound influence on Mozart's life and thinking. It was probably at a Lodge meeting in November 1791, during which Mozart's last completed work – *Eine kleine Freymaurer-Kantate* (Little Masonic Cantata; K.623) – was performed, that the composer caught the infection which would lead, via a chain of medical complications, to his early death from kidney failure some three weeks later.[34]

Seals of the Viennese Masonic Lodges, of which Mozart was a member: 'Zur Wohlthätigkeit' ('Beneficence') and, after the reorganization of 1785, 'Zur neugekrönten Hoffnung' ('New Crowned Hope', from which the word 'New' was later dropped).

VII

Leopold Mozart's Visit to Vienna The Haydn–Mozart Friendship

———

FOLLOWING THE VISIT to Salzburg in 1783, when Wolfgang introduced Constanze to his father and sister, Leopold Mozart made a return visit to his son and daughter-in-law in Vienna in 1785. Wolfgang had been urging him to come and there is no doubt that his father was looking forward to making the visit (his first trip to Vienna for some years), especially – as he put it sarcastically to his daughter in St Gilgen on 14 January 1785 – since he 'could travel [there] not at my expense, so as to admire your brother's magnificent way of life'.[1] Actually, he was taking to Vienna the young Heinrich Marchand, then some fifteen years old and destined to become a good violinist, who with his sister Margarete (a year younger and soon to become a singer) had been staying with Leopold to study music. Their father, the theatrical manager in Munich, Theobald Marchand (1741–1800), provided a carriage (chaise).

Obviously, Leopold was sceptical about the ability of his son and Constanze to manage their affairs – wrongly, as he was soon the first to admit. He knew that Wolfgang was about to launch an important series of subscription concerts:

This very moment [writes Leopold to his daughter on 22 January] I have received 10 lines from your brother, in which he writes that his first subscription concert will take place on 11 Feb. and [the series will] continue every Friday; that he will certainly have time in the third week of Lent to find a day for Heinrich's [Marchand] concert in the theatre; that I should come soon, – that last Saturday [15 January] he performed his 6 quartets, which he has sold to Artaria for 100 ducats, before his dear friend Haydn and other good friends. He ends by saying: 'Now I must sit down again to the concerto I have just begun [no. 20, K.466, completed 10 February]'. Adieu![2]

This short but historic letter-within-a-letter is the first mention of (1) the six string quartets (K.387 etc.) later to be dedicated to Haydn and published as Op. X by Artaria, and (2) the epochal D minor Piano Concerto. The subscription concerts took place in the city casino in the Mehlgrube on the Neuer Markt (New Market) on 11, 13 and 25 February and 4, 11, 18 March,

123

Johann Anton, Count Pergen, who was required by Joseph II to ensure that any adaptation of the play Le Mariage de Figaro *be censored if necessary to render its content and sentiments acceptable. Engraving by F. John after Schmid.*

whereas Heinrich Marchand's concert was to occur on 2 March 1785 at the Burgtheater.

On 28 January Leopold left Salzburg for Munich, where he would see Marchand *père* and pick up the carriage. He thought he would leave on the first Sunday of Carnival, but in fact it was a day later. Leopold informed his daughter on 2 February, 'the Marchands weren't expecting me until Saturday evening, but I arrived unannounced after 1 o'clock and went into the dining room crying, "I want to have something to eat too", you can easily imagine how they all rushed out, jumped upon me and almost overwhelmed me with joy and kisses . . .'[3]

Meanwhile, in Vienna, Emperor Joseph II wrote a letter to Johann Anton, Count Pergen, President of the Government of Lower Austria; which was to be of crucial importance in Mozart's life: [31 January 1785] 'I understand that the well-known play *Le Mariage de Figaro* has been proposed for the Kärntnerthortheater in a German translation; since, however, this piece contains much that is reprehensible, I am obliged to state that the censor must either forbid it completely or undertake to make such changes in it as to be able to vouch for the piece's performance and the impression it might make . . .'[4] The performance was planned by the troupe of Hubert Kumpf and Emanuel Schikaneder – whom Mozart had known from his appearance in Salzburg a few years earlier – in the translation by Johann Rautenstrauch, which was printed in Vienna in this same year, and of which Mozart owned a copy. (In the foreword to the printed libretto, Rautenstrauch dedicated the translation to 'the memory of two hundred [lost] ducats' caused by the non-performance.)

On 11 February 1785 several significant events took place in Vienna:

1   Mozart applied to join the Tonkünstler-Societät, membership of which would qualify his widow and children for a comfortable pension in the event of his death. In his petition Mozart 'regretted that he could not at the moment produce his baptismal certificate', but promised to have it sent for. In the middle of March, Mozart wrote another petition, reminding the Society that he had 'several times been of considerable service to it and is minded to do so in the future.' The records of the Society thereupon noted (24 August 1785), 'when the baptismal certificate is produced, further decision will be made.' Mozart never produced the document, and the formalities were never completed. Hence, Constanze in her bitter need in 1792 could count on no assistance from the organization.

2   At 1 p.m., Leopold Mozart (and young Marchand) arrived in the city. Leopold was to remain with his son and family until 25 April, and the letters he wrote to his daughter and son-in-law in St Gilgen provide the most vivid and accurate description of Mozart's way of life and his concerts.

3   Joseph Haydn became an Entered Apprentice in the Freemasons' Lodge 'Zur wahren Eintracht' ('True Concord'), but subsequently failed to attend any further meetings.[5] Haydn's initiation had been postponed from 28 January (because he had been in Hungary). Mozart had appeared on the previous date, but this time he was prevented from attending because he was

giving the first performance of his D minor Piano Concerto at his first subscription concert in the Mehlgrube.

Leopold had travelled in the worst sort of winter weather – snow, ice and slippery roads – which was to continue while he was in Vienna. In his first letter to St Gilgen, completed on 16 February, he writes:

That your brother has fine quarters *with all the necessary decorations* [probably furniture, curtains, screens, etc.] you may gather from the fact that he pays 480 fl. [*recte*, 460 fl.] rent [p.a.]. That same Friday [11 February] we drove at 6 o'clock to his first subscription concert, where there was a vast concourse of people of rank. Each person pays one souverain d'or [13½ gulden] or 3 ducats for the 6 Lenten concerts. It is in the Mehlgrube; for the use of the room he pays only *one half a souverain d'or*. The concert was incomparable, the orchestra excellent, apart from the symphonies there was a singer from the Italian theatre who sang 2 arias. Then came a *new, superb piano concerto by Wolfgang*, which the copyist was still writing out when we arrived, and your brother had not even found time to play through the Rondeau because he had to supervise the copying. Saturday evening [12 February] H[err] *Joseph Haydn* and the 2 Barons Tindi [Anton and Bartholomäus, Freiherrn von Tinti; Anton was resident Salzburg minister in Vienna; both were members of Haydn's Lodge] were with us, the new quartets [K.458, 464, 465] were performed, but only the *3 new ones* which he has added to the other 3 we already have; they are perhaps a little easier, but excellently composed. H: Haydn said to me: '*I tell you before God, and as an honest man, that your son is the greatest composer I know, either personally or by reputation: he has taste and moreover the greatest possible knowledge of the science of composing.*' On Sunday evening in the theatre [Burgtheater] there was the academy concert of the Italian singer [Luisa or Aloysia] Laschi [Mozart's Countess in *Figaro* of 1786], who is leaving for Italy. She sang 2 arias, there was a violoncello concerto; a tenor and a bass each sang an aria, and *your brother played the marvellous Concerto which he wrote for Paradis and sent to Paris* [possibly no. 18 in B flat (K.456), written for the blind pianist Maria Theresia von Paradies, who had been in Salzburg in the summer of 1783]. I was only 2 boxes away from the rather pretty Princess [Elisabeth] of Württemberg [later married to Archduke Francis] and had the pleasure of hearing all the exchanges of the instruments so clearly that tears of joy came in my eyes.

When your brother left the stage, the Emperor, with hat in hand, paid his compliments and, leaning over, called out 'bravo, Mozart!' – When he came out to play, he was welcomed with applause. – Yesterday we didn't go the theatre – for there is an academy concert every day. Just now I began to feel the effects of the cold during the trip. Even on Sunday evening I drank elder-flower tea before the academy concert and dressed very warmly: on Monday I had tea again in bed, stayed in bed until 10 o'clock, drank tea again in the afternoon and this morning as well: – then a doctor came, secretly arranged by your sister-in-law, to my bedside, took my pulse and said it was good, and then proceeded to prescribe what I was taking anyway. This evening there is another concert in the theatre, – your brother will again play a concerto. I am now feeling much better, and will drink another good portion of elder-flower tea. I shall bring with me several new pieces by your brother. The *little* [son] *Carl* is rather like your brother. I found him in very good health – but children have teething problems from time to time – and yesterday he wasn't so well – today he's better again. The child is otherwise very pleasant; for he is most friendly, and laughs as soon as you address him: I only saw him cry once, but he began to laugh right away afterwards. – Now he has teething troubles again. – Yesterday, the 15th [the letter was composed over a period of several days] there was another concert in the theatre, for a girl [Elisabeth Distler, a teenage soprano in the Italian opera ensemble] who sang charmingly, your brother played the grand new [piano] Concerto in D [probably no. 16, K.451]. Magnificent, etc. Today we shall go to a private academy concert of the Salzburg agent *v[on] Ployer.* . . .[6]

On Monday, 21 February, Leopold continues his account of life in the Domgasse (Große Schulerstraße):

You will have received my first letter. – I thought I had managed to shake off that cold I caught on the trip: but yesterday evening I noticed that I had pains in my left thigh and before I went to bed I found that I really had rheumatism. So this morning I had to have burr root [burdock] tea in bed and didn't get up until 1:30 p.m. to have lunch, at which I had the company of your sister-in-law's youngest sister M:^lle Sophia; and she is still with me this evening at 8 o'clock because your brother, his wife and Heinrich [Marchand] ate luncheon at H[err] v[on] Trattner's, an invitation I had to refuse, alas; and this evening your brother is at a grand concert given by Count Cizi [one of the members of the Zichy family], where H[err] Lebrun and his wife [the oboist Ludwig August Lebrun and his wife, Franziska Dorothea, *née* Danzi, members of the Mannheim court orchestra] will perform for the first time here; your sister-in-law and Marchand are, however, at the concert given by H[err] v[on] Ployer, our agent. Today we probably won't go to bed before 1 o'clock a.m. as usual. *On the 17th, Thursday*, we lunched with your brother's mother-in-law, Frau Weber, just the 4 of us, she and her daughter Sophie, for the eldest daughter [Aloysia] is in Graz. I must tell you that the meal was not too much and not too little, but superbly cooked; the roast was a fine plump pheasant – altogether everything excellently prepared. *Friday the 18th* lunch at the younger Stephani[e]'s where again there were only the 4 of us, plus H[err] Le brun [*sic*], his wife, [the composer from Mannheim] Carl Cannabich [1764–1806] and a *cleric*. Now let me say at once that here no one observes fast-days [Friday was of course – apart from Lent – a regular fast-day, on which fish rather than meat was served]. Nothing but meat dishes were served, the pheasant was in addition to the cabbage, the rest was fit for a prince, they served *oysters* at the end, then delicious *petits fours* [*Confect*] not to mention many bottles of champagne. Coffee is *de rigueur*, that goes without saying. From there we drove to your brother's 2nd academy concert in the Mehlgrube at 7 o'clock, which was again wonderful. Henry [Heinrich Marchand] played a violin concerto. H[err] Stephani[e] asked about you right away, and we couldn't stop talking about the good old days. Up to now we haven't had any Lenten [fast] dishes served to us here. The 20th *yesterday* we were at lunch for 21 persons given by the actor H[err] Miller [Johann Heinrich Friedrich Müller]. It too was magnificent, but not so overdone. He has to have large quarters because he has 8 children, and pays 700 f annual rent. H[err] Stephani[e] has a small flat – but he has to pay 500 f rent for it because it is on St Michael's Square next to the theatre [Burgtheater]. On *Wednesday the 23rd* and *Monday the 28th* there are the two academy concerts given by H[err] Lebrun and his wife in the theatre. By the 18th not a single box was to be had for the first concert, these people are going to take in amazingly much money. – . . . *Tuesday the 22nd.* This morning I again took burr root tea and didn't get up until 10:30. H[err] and Mad: Lebrun were with us until 1:30 p.m., at 2 o'clock we went to lunch, as usual. As I write this it is already 5 in the afternoon; it is snowing heavily . . . I've not yet gone anywhere outside on foot except to go to Mass at St Stephen's [Cathedral], which is very near. I am so worried about the cold wind that I will certainly not travel home until milder weather arrives . . . I've met various acquaintances at the academies, for example *Baron van Swieten*, to whose quarters I've also been invited, the 2 sisters *Countesses Thun* and *Wallenstein* [Maria Wilhelmine, Countess Thun, *née* Countess Ulfeld, and her sister Marie Elisabeth, Countess Waldstein (*recte*)], a *Baron Freyberg*, *Baron Nagl* [Joseph Anton von Nagl, father of Theresia von Trattner, who was in turn Mozart's piano pupil, very shortly to be the dedicatee of the great Fantasia (K.475) and Sonata (K.457), both in C minor] the Prussian Ambassador H[err] [Freiherr Konstans P.W.] v[on] Jacobi [Freemason and a friend of Haydn and Mozart], *Benedict Edelbach* [son of a Salzburg lawyer], *H[err] von Sonnenfels and his wife*, [the composers] *H[err] Starzer & H[err] Aspelmayr*, *Prince Baar* [Wenzl Johann, Prince Paar (1719–92), an old family friend, now Mozart's Lodge Brother], *Prince* [Carl] *Auersperg* [Field Marshal and Mozart's patron]; and various others whose names I can't recall . . .'[7]

On 10 March, another academy concert was given by Mozart in the Burgtheater. The announcement stated that 'he will play not only a *new, just completed concerto for forte piano* [no. 21 in C, K.467], but will also use a special, *large forte piano pedal* when he improvises.'[8] This pedal board, like that of an organ, is also referred to in Leopold Mozart's next letter (12 March):

Lebrun and his wife have had 3 astonishing concerts: at the first they made, 1,100 f., at the 2nd 900 f. and at the 3rd 500 f. Your brother made 559 f. in his academy concert, better than expected, for his subscription [list] to the 6 concerts in the Mehlgrube consists of more than 150 persons, – everybody pays 1 souverain for the 6 concerts: and apart from that he plays so often as a favour in other academies at the theatre. . . . We never get to bed before 1 o'clock in the morning, never rise before 9 a.m. and go to table at 2 or 2:30 p.m. Disgusting weather! Concerts every day, always teaching, music, copying, etc. Where can I escape to? – if only the academies were finished already: I am quite unable to describe all the bustle and disturbance: your brother's grand fortepiano has been taken to the theatre or to some other house at least 12 times while I have been here. He has had a large *Forte piano pedal* made, which stands under the piano and is two feet [*3 spann*] longer [than the piano] and astonishingly heavy, and which was also taken to Count Cziczi's [Zichy] and Prince Kaunitz's. . . . Tomorrow the academy concert for the widows [Tonkünstler-Societät] takes place . . .'[9]

*   *   *

Mozart and Vincenzo Righini had been requested by the Society in January 1785 to provide new vocal works for the forthcoming concerts in Lent. Mozart at first thought of setting a psalm, but soon hit on the idea of adapting the completed parts of his recent Mass in C minor as a cantata, to which end he seems (the evidence is scanty but based on an unimpeachable source, Abbé Stadler) to have secured the collaboration of Lorenzo Da Ponte. On their visit to Vienna in 1829, Vincent and Mary Novello visited the venerable Abbé, who showed them Haydn's Longman & Broderip piano[10] (on which Vincent 'rolled forth some chords and resolutions') and

On enquiring on what occasion Mozart had put the 'Davidde Penitente' into its present form, he informed me that when Mozart came to Vienna he was applied to for some piece in the Oratorio style. As the time allowed was not sufficient to write an entirely new piece he took the greater part of a Mass . . . to which the poet Da Ponte adapted other words and that Mozart added the fine Terzetto in E minor and two new solos in order to complete the work required.[11]

There was a great deal of argument among the directors of the Society as to the exact programme; at one point there were three Haydn symphonies, of which 'The beginning should be the new Symphony in D minor [no. 80] . . .' In the end, only this symphony remained, and the programmes for the two concerts were as follows:

1 Haydn: Symphony no. 80, D minor
2 F.L. Gassmann: Chorus, 'Amore e Psiche'
3 Haydn: Chorus 'Svanisce in un momento' from [the 1784 version of] *Il ritorno di Tobia*

In the interval of the first of the two evenings (13 March), there were two arias (sung by Stefano Mandini and Franziska Lebrun) and an oboe concerto (Lebrun); in the interval on 15 March there was Mandini, then an aria sung by Cavalieri and a chorus and aria by Sacchini, followed by a violin concerto played by Heinrich Marchand. In the second part was Mozart's new cantata, with Cavalieri, Elisabeth Distler and Johann Valentin Adamberger. It was suggested at first that Antonio Salieri should conduct, but in the protocol Salieri's name was crossed out and that of Mozart substituted. The orchestra consisted of some twenty violins, six to eight violas, seven cellos, seven double basses, two flutes, six or seven oboes (one could play clarinet, required in the new aria No. 6), six or seven bassoons, six horns, two trumpets, two trombones, and drums. The chorus was some sixty strong (the boys from St Michael's, the Schottenstift and St Stephen's). It made a substantial total of some 150 performers. At the first concert there was an audience of 660, but in the second only about 225, with most boxes of the nobility empty. Mozart's magnificent and powerful music – the two new arias are worthy of the Mass at its best – did not, it seems, draw more than one full house.[12] The same thing was to happen in 1824 when Beethoven gave his Ninth Symphony in two concerts in the Kärntnerthortheater: the second performance was poorly attended.

The letter in which Leopold Mozart probably described this event is lost, except for the following lines: 'If my son has no debts, I think he could now deposit 2,000 f. in the bank: the money is surely there, and as far as eating and drinking is concerned, the housekeeping is economical to the highest degree . . .'[13]

On Good Friday (25 March), Leopold reports to his daughter:

Just as I am writing, the weather is changing from sunshine to heavy snow: a few days ago it snowed heavily and the wind whistled, and that changed into a bright day, where the streets were frozen solid just as if it were New Year's. I've ordered the copyist to come here, and just now he is at work on three different sets of variations for you [K.398, 455 and 460?] which I shall pay for. Then I shall press for the cadenzas [for Wolfgang's piano concertos] and shall buy whatever [of his] is engraved. . . . During

Lent, *Madame Lang* [Aloysia Lange] – the sister-in-law of your brother was in Munich, where both [she and her husband Joseph] played guest roles in the theatre, and were well paid . . . Now I've heard [Mad.] Lang twice sing 5 or [blank] arias at the piano, which she sang very gladly. One can not deny that she sings with the greatest expression: I often asked people about her, and now at last I can understand why some said she had a very weak voice – and others said she had a very loud voice. Both are true: her sustained notes, and all those she sings with expression, are astonishingly loud; the intricate sections, passage-work, ornamentation and the high notes are very delicate, so that as far as I'm concerned there is too great a contrast between the two, and *in a room* the loud notes offend the ear, whereas in the theatre the delicate passages demand great silence and attention on the part of the audience. More about this when I see you. . . . Mad^me Lang's . . . husband is a fine painter and he sketched me yesterday evening on red paper, completely realistically and very beautifully drawn [this likeness is lost] . . .'[14]

Joseph von Sonnenfels, engraving by Andreas Leicher after a painting by Anton Graff.

Something which Leopold was very careful not to write in his letters to St Gilgen was that, no doubt encouraged by his son and perhaps other members of the Craft (Haydn, the Barons Tinti, Sonnenfels, Prince Paar, and not least Lange himself), he had decided to apply to join the Freemasons. According to records in the secret files of the Vienna State Archives, on 28 March 1785, Leopold Mozart and one Joseph Bashy were proposed and 'because both must soon leave, a special dispensation is requested.'[15] The usual delay – Leopold was initiated on 6 April – was thus considerably shortened, as also was the time taken to attain the second and third degrees, which he did on 16 and 22 April in the Lodge 'Zur wahren Eintracht'. In his letter of 16 April to his daughter, Leopold writes: 'next Tuesday the B[aroness] [von] Waldstetten [*sic*] is sending her horses to us and we are to drive out to see her in *Kloster Neuburg* (where she now lives permanently) to have lunch with her and return in the evening: I am curious to meet this *woman of my heart*, since I have invisibly been the *man of her heart* . . .'[16]

On 24 April there was a celebration in the Viennese Lodge 'Zur gekrönten Hoffnung' ('Crowned Hope') in honour of the famous mineralogist Ignaz von Born, Master of Haydn's Lodge 'Zur wahren Eintracht'. Leopold Mozart and his son were present, Wolfgang having a few days earlier composed a cantata, 'Die Maurerfreude' (K.471), for the occasion. On that day Emperor Joseph II bestowed on Born the title of *Reichsritter* (Knight of the Empire).[17]

Next day, Leopold Mozart left Vienna at 10.30 a.m., as he wrote in a letter from Linz on 30 April to his daughter, 'in the company of your brother and his wife, we ate lunch together in Burkerstorf [Purkersdorf, a post station 12 km. distant], then they returned to Vienna . . .'[18] Father and son were never to see each other again. It was high time Leopold left: Archbishop Colloredo had noticed that his *Vice Kapellmeister* had overstayed his leave and, in a decree dated 2 May 1785, stated that if 'Leopold Mozart is not here by the second half of this month, his salary is to be stopped until further notice . . .'[19]

Leopold arrived in Salzburg just before Whit Sunday (15 May). From this moment onwards, he and his son were to draw apart, although Leopold was in many respects his son's most perceptive and sympathetic critic, friend and

Title page of Mozart's cantata 'Die Maurerfreude' (K.471), for solo tenor, male-voice choir and orchestra. Its first performance was in honour of Ignaz von Born, portrayed (ABOVE) in an engraving by J.G. Mansfeld after a lost painting by F.H. Füger, 1787.

adviser. It would have been better if Wolfgang had heeded his father's advice on many matters; but it is likely that he did not even ask for it any more.

*   *   *

Mozart now accepted a composition pupil from London named Thomas Attwood (1765–1838), who was astute enough to preserve his written studies, thus providing us with a unique record of Mozart's teaching methods. The Prince of Wales (later George IV) had provided Attwood with a purse for studies on the Continent, and the young man went first to Italy where he found in Naples two *maestri*, Felipe Cinque and Gaetano Lattila (1711–88), with whom he studied for two years. He arrived in the Austrian capital about the middle of 1785 and remained with Mozart (but not in his flat) for a year and a half. Master and pupil communicated in Italian, but Mozart was trying to learn English again – he had obviously forgotten much of what he learned in London twenty years earlier – and often wrote notes to Attwood in English and vice versa, e.g. 'Thos. Attwood's com[ts] to Mr Mozardt, hoping this example will meet his approbation, as he has taken all possible Care to leave no room for Correction. Tuesday 23[d] August in the year of our Lord 1785.'; (Mozart:) 'This after noon I am not at home, therefore I pray you to come tomorrow at three and a half. Mozart'; and (at the end of a counterpoint exercise): 'You are an ass.' But Mozart took great pains with his English pupil, sometimes even refashioning an Attwood exercise. Attwood became a successful organist and composer, prominent in British musical life.[20]

Thomas Attwood who, as a young man, was a pupil of Mozart in Vienna; anonymous portrait in oils.

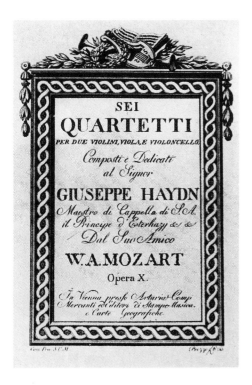

*Title page of
Mozart's six String
Quartets dedicated to
Joseph Haydn,
published in 1785 by
Artaria & Co. as the
composer's 'Opera X'.
In about the same year
Haydn was portrayed
in an anonymous
miniature on ivory*
(RIGHT).

On 1 September 1785 Mozart wrote an Italian dedication to Artaria's edition of the six quartets dedicated to Haydn. It has rightly gone down in history as one of the noblest documents between friends:

To my dear friend Haydn:

A father, having resolved to send his sons into the great world, finds it advisable to entrust them to the protection and guidance of a highly celebrated man, the more so since this man, by a stroke of luck, is his best friend. – Here, then, celebrated man and my dearest friend, are my six sons. – Truly, they are the fruit of a long and laborious effort, but the hope, strengthened by several of my friends, that this effort would, at least in some small measure, be rewarded, encourages and comforts me that one day, these children may be a source of consolation to me. – You yourself, dearest friend, during your last sojourn in this capital, expressed to me your satisfaction with these works. – This, your approval, encourages me more than anything else, and thus I entrust them to your care, and hope that they are not wholly unworthy of your favour. – Do but receive them kindly, and be their father, guide and friend! From this moment I cede to you all my rights over them: I pray you to be indulgent to their mistakes, which a father's partial eye may have overlooked, and despite this, to cloak them in the mantle of your generosity which they value so highly. From the bottom of my heart I am, dearest friend,

Your most sincere friend,
W.A. Mozart

Vienna, 1st September 1785[21]

The quartets were announced in the *Wiener Zeitung* on 17 September,[22] but a week earlier Mozart and Artaria must have been furious at reading, in the

Ignaz Pleyel, as portrayed (when in London in 1792) in an engraving by W. Nutter, 1793, after a painting by Thomas Hardy. His Six Quartets, op. 1, were published in Vienna by Rudolph Graeffer in 1783; the title page bears a dedication to Count Ladislaus Erdödy.

same paper, a little advertisement by Artaria's rival, Christoph Torricella, stating that 'Mozard's [*sic*] 6 Quartets for 2 violins, viola and violoncello are to be had at a very cheap price in my art shop in the Kohlmarkt next to the [coffee-house] Milano.' These were ms. copies in parts of Mozart's early quartets (K.168–173), copies of which Torricella had procured and was pirating. Artaria and Mozart replied as follows:

In the art shop Artaria and Comp. . . . are to be had: by Herr Kapellmeister W.A. Mozart 6 brand new Quartets . . . Opus X, engraved, pr. 6. fl. 30 kr. – Mozart's works require no praise, and to do so would be therefore quite superfluous; one can only confirm that this [work] is a masterpiece. One can be all the more confident since the composer has dedicated it to his friend, Joseph Haydn, princely Esterhazy Kapellm., who honoured it with all the applause due only to a great genius. In consequence the publishers have spared no costs in supplying this work to the connoisseurs – not only as concerns the beauty and clarity of the engraving but also paper and printing – in the assurance that the price which is being charged should not be thought too high, considering that these Quartets consist of 150 pages, which would cost not less than 12 fl. to have copied.

Since in recent newspapers the art-dealer Torricella has also announced 6 Quartets by Mozart at a very cheap price, without remarking whether they are written or engraved, old or new, Hr. Mozart considers it his duty to inform an esteemed public that these Quartets are not new, but old works which he wrote fifteen years ago. He says this so that connoisseurs who are awaiting his new ones will not obtain the wrong works.

Torricella immediately replied, saying that Artaria's announcement was 'an almost totally unnecessary' warning, since, Torricella assures the public, his quartets 'need no other recommendation than that they bear the name [of Mozart]'. He adds an oblique criticism of the 'newest' quartets 'because of their very particular taste', and says that the old works will be new to many connoisseurs and that they will not be fobbed off with spurious works 'since these works, too, are surely Mozart's children'.

* * *

The names of Joseph and Michael Haydn occasionally appear in the correspondence of the Mozart family, but (for obvious geographical reasons) it is Michael who is more often the subject of their comments. In fact nothing of any significance concerning Joseph appears until Wolfgang's letter to his father of 24 April 1784: 'Then: quartets by a certain Pleyel have recently appeared; he is a pupil of Joseph Haydn. If you do not know them, try to procure them; you will find them worth the trouble. They are very well written, and very pleasant; you will at once recognize his master in them. Good – and fortunate for music, if Pleyel will be able in time to replace Haydn for us.'[23] It is – if we consider what Haydn would subsequently compose – a rather astonishing statement, suggesting as it does that Haydn was 'written out' and that his pupil, Ignaz Pleyel (1757–1831), who was about to embark on a spectacular career, could replace him. But in defence of Mozart, it needs

Mozart's corrections to the score of the closing duet in Act I of Haydn's opera Armida, *first produced at Eszterháza in 1784. The changes suggest that Mozart probably intended to include a performance of this duet in one of his Vienna concerts.*

to be pointed out that this was an opinion shared by many for whom Pleyel's music was easier to comprehend than Haydn's.

The Haydn-Mozart relationship has been the subject of much comment, most of it (as far as nineteenth- and twentieth-century Mozart scholarship is concerned) of a slightly surprised nature, considering that Mozartians – but not Mozart – have always tended to consider Haydn a second-rate composer and unworthy of the loving attention with which the younger master treated him and his music. That Mozart actually did revere Haydn is attested in many contemporary and near-contemporary documents, for instance in Franz Xaver Niemetschek's Mozart biography of 1798, based on information given by Constanze Mozart and other authentic sources.[24]

Mozart . . . became a most sincere admirer of the great and incomparable Joseph Hayden, who had already become the pride of music, and now, since Mozart's death, remains our favourite and our delight. Mozart often called him his teacher.

[Quartets dedicated to Haydn 1785:] Not only does the homage of an artist like Mozart enhance Hayden's fame, but it is also to Mozart's credit, and makes us realize the tenderness of his feelings, considering that he himself had such wonderful talent.

Certainly Mozart could not have honoured Hayden with a better work than these quartets, which contain a mine of precious thoughts and which are, indeed, models of composition.

In the eyes of the connoisseur this work is of importance equal to any of his operatic compositions. Everything in it has been carefully thought out and perfected. One can see that he has taken the trouble to deserve Hayden's praise.

We can judge what fine sensibility he had, and how keen his artistic feeling was, when we hear that he was wont to be moved to tears during the performance of good music; particularly when listening to something composed by the two great Haydens.

He was always very touching when he spoke of the two Haydens or other great masters. One would not have suspected that one was listening to the almighty Mozart, but rather to one of their enthusiastic pupils.

His greatest pleasure was music. If his wife wanted to give him a special surprise at a family festivity, she would secretly arrange for a performance of a new church composition by Michael or Joseph Haydn.

Mozart's reactions to Haydn's music were in part simply those produced by a normal interaction between two great artists – the same phenomenon may be observed between Leonardo da Vinci, Michelangelo and Raphael: to emulate, and if possible attempt to surpass, the model. In Mozart's case, one can cite some characteristic examples:

1   Mozart had a chance to hear Haydn's opera *La fedeltà premiata* when it was performed in German by the Kumpf-Schikaneder Troupe just before Christmas 1784 at the Kärntnerthortheater before Joseph II and the whole court. In this opera there are two fascinating and brilliant finales (Acts I and II), multi-movement sections which in their tonal and vocal instrumental richness, length and psychological complexity surpass anything that had been written by Italian composers (who had invented and perfected such finales). A year later, Mozart was to turn the style of these Haydn finales into something even more spectacular – in Acts II, III and IV of *Figaro*. And five years later, he was to adopt Haydn's key structure when composing *Così fan tutte*.

2   When Mozart conducted the Lent concerts of the Tonkünstler-Societät in Vienna in 1785, the programme opened with Haydn's Symphony no. 80 in D minor – a curious work which begins with a dark-hued and relentless section in its main key but soon turns to a waltz-like flippancy for the second subject; the same alternation of mood continues later in the work, with a pensive slow movement and a syncopated finale which not only switches to D major but turns a serious work into comedy. Mozart must have known of the Society's choice of this Haydn symphony by the beginning of 1785. By 10 February, Mozart had composed his D minor Piano Concerto (no. 20, K.466), which utilized the key not only of this Haydn symphony, but also of that composer's seminal String Quartet, op. 9 no. 4 (*c.* 1768–70) and Mozart's own Quartet (K.421) of 1784. Mozart has intensified all the serious aspects of Haydn's treatment of D minor and raised it to a new plane of musical experience.

3   Haydn completed his six 'Paris' Symphonies in 1785 and 1786. By the time Haydn arrived in Vienna from Eszterháza at Christmas 1786, Mozart could have seen copies of all six works. But he will have had a more leisurely opportunity to study them when they were issued a year later by Artaria in Vienna. The first three 'Paris' Symphonies (in the order in which Artaria issued them) were in C major, G minor and E flat. Mozart's last three symphonies were begun in June 1788. Significantly he placed them in E flat (no. 39, K.543), G minor (no. 40, K.550) and C major (no. 41, K.551); and the similarities to the 'Paris' set go further. One of the more striking features is the particular kind of 3/4 metre in the opening movement of K.543 (after the introduction), a soft, singing, legato theme, which is rare in the first movements of Mozart's mature symphonies – from nos. 35 (K.385) to 41 only no. 39 employs one, whereas it is a typical and indeed very striking feature of Haydn's 'Paris' Symphony no. 85 ('La Reine'), in the opening movement (also after the slow introduction).

4   Haydn's Symphony no. 78 in C minor – another work which begins in a serious vein and ends with a popular finale, this time containing alternating C minor and C major tunes, the latter key winning the battle with no 'serious' opposition – was published by Artaria in the spring of 1785. The work opens with a very unusual unison theme, which surprisingly leads to a mysterious passage for the strings, marked *pianissimo*:

A year later, Mozart wrote his C minor Piano Concerto no. 24 (K.491), which certainly 'remembers' Haydn's opening (we quote the theme of K.491 from the entry in Mozart's catalogue):

It also recalls the audacity and subtlety with which Haydn's first four notes are made to combine with themselves in contrapuntal displays that sound not only natural but easy. And yet Mozart has raised Haydn's C minor to new heights of passion, and the clothing – simply because the orchestration is much larger and more complex (against Haydn's flute, oboes, bassoons and horns, Mozart's score requires a flute, oboes, clarinets, bassoons, horns, trumpets and drums) – is infinitely more varied and daringly glittering. This Haydn symphony is practically forgotten today, whereas Mozart's Concerto is universally revered.

How many works by Mozart from the years 1781–90 did Haydn know? It is difficult to establish, but from available evidence it is certain that he heard *Le nozze di Figaro*, *Don Giovanni* and *Così fan tutte*, and there were ample opportunities for him to have heard *Die Entführung aus dem Serail*, e.g. in January 1786.[25] Haydn was, of course, familiar with the six Quartets dedicated to him (K.387, etc.) and at Eszterháza he knew, but did not perform, the Arietta 'Un bacio di mano' (K.541). The Esterházy Archives in Budapest own ms. copies of the last three Symphonies (K.543, 550, 551), but it is not known when they were acquired and it is difficult to imagine their performance, prior to 1790, because Haydn's band lacked trumpets and, of course, clarinets (no problem in the first version of K.550). How, in fact, did Haydn intend to cope with this problem in staging *Figaro*? He was preparing this opera for performance in 1790, but Prince Nicolaus Esterházy died and the opera company was disbanded. He was probably the witness to some of Mozart's piano concertos, and we know that Haydn played in performances of the late Quintets (K.515, 516, 593).

While there are passages in Mozart's Viennese compositions in which we can clearly trace Haydn's influence – a typical case is the finale of the Piano Concerto no. 16 in D (K.451) – they are relatively few and far between. In Haydn's case, we believe that prior to the 'Prussian' Quartets, op. 50 (1787), Mozart's influence is negligible, and largely negative. As would be the case with Beethoven, Haydn either withdrew (no more operas, piano concertos, or quintets) or he was at great pains to try to preserve his own personality. The occasional chromatic 'slither' back to the tonic in Haydn's music, and other such borrowings do not alter the fact that, however massive Mozart's

The first violin part intended for the leader of Haydn's orchestra, Luigi Tomasini – specially prepared for the planned production of Mozart's Le nozze di Figaro *at Eszterháza in 1790.*

136

personality was, its direct influence on Haydn was far less than is usually asserted: most of the critics who have written on the subject were acquainted with less than one-tenth of Haydn's music and quite simply were in no position to write authoritatively about Haydn.

The principal differences between the two composers are almost too well known to require comment, but perhaps a few technical details might be mentioned. The main feature in orchestration is Mozart's density, which is of course part of his density of thought. The trumpets are used in a lower *tessitura*, whereas in Haydn they are still very Baroque, or at best pre-classical, in texture. The cor anglais in Haydn is the clarinet in Mozart, but overall, it is astonishing what a difference a second flute, two clarinets, two bassoons (Haydn often had only one) and two trumpets make in Mozart's scoring. Haydn's fastidious, spare orchestration has its own delicate beauty, but inevitably the sound pales before the gorgeous wash of colour displayed in Mozart's scores. Haydn was a master of irony, and Mozart a master of ambivalence, where the subtlety goes so far (as in *Così fan tutte*) that, as it were, the emotion is sometimes turned totally on its head.

It is a pity that the word 'courtly' has acquired a slightly pejorative significance which has nothing at all to do with its original meaning, one which can well be applied to the great scenes in *Don Giovanni* (Act I, sc. 20; Act II, sc. 13; *NMA* 11/5 [1968], 212, 393). At the risk of belabouring a point made in connection with the all-pervasive rhythm ♩ ♫♩ ♩ , it is an integral feature not only of the courtliness which is so much a part of Mozart's intricate personality, but also a sign of the tighter, more exciting rhythm that informs his score. The intellectual fascination of Haydn's scores is matched in those of Mozart, and the latter are clothed in radiant colours.

Another aspect of Mozart's scores which springs to mind is the accelerated tempo of the allegros, 4/4 instead of 8/8 and barred C instead of 4/4; but these faster tempi must be considered in a broader context. Haydn's operas move slowly; at Eszterháza audiences had unlimited time, especially Prince Nicolaus, 'for whom nothing was too long': Mozart's move quickly, and not only within the allegro.[26] Mozart's mercurial sense of tempo was, I believe, the one aspect of his multi-faceted style that immediately gripped Haydn's imagination. If the reader finds difficulty in applying this theoretical concept to the actual scores, consider Part I of *The Creation*. Here we have that same sense of forward-moving drive which is not in the least retarded either by the slow-moving opening Largo which is 'Chaos', nor by the other slower-than-allegro sectons (e.g. 'Nun schwanden', Andante; 'Nun beut die Flur', Andante; the Sunrise, Andante); the whole moves forward as inexorably as Genesis itself. And we must not forget that the alternative title for Beaumarchais's *Le Mariage de Figaro* is *La folle journée*, indicating that the entire action of the play (and of the opera based on it) takes place within twenty-four hours.[27] It is in the opera's concept of time that we realize that Mozart was a young man of twenty-nine when he composed this masterpiece.

Haydn's opinion of Mozart is summed up admirably in a now-famous letter to a steward in Prague named Franz Roth (or Rott), who gave concerts

OPPOSITE *The opening of Mozart's insertion quartet 'Dite almeno' (K.479) in Bianchi's* La villanella rapita, *from a contemporary Viennese copy (possibly by Wenzel Sukowsky).*

*Mozart's insertions were performed in November 1785 by, among others, the soprano Celesta Coltellini (*TOP*) and the tenor Vincenzo Calvesi, who later created the role of Ferrando in* Così fan tutte *(1790); engraving by G. Struppi and silhouette by Hieronymus Löschenkohl.*

*A page from the printed libretto (*BOTTOM*) notes Mozart's contributions.*

in his house several times a year. This letter, dated December 1787, was first published in the Niemetschek biography (which is dedicated to Haydn) in 1798.

You ask me for an *opera buffa*. Most willingly, if you want to have one of my vocal compositions for yourself alone. But if you intend to produce it on the stage at Prague, in that case I cannot comply with your wish, because all my operas are far too closely connected with our personal circle (Esterház, in Hungary), and moreover they would not produce the proper effect, which I calculated in accordance with the locality. It would be quite another matter if I were to have the great good fortune to compose a brand-new libretto for your theatre. But even then I should be risking a good deal, for scarcely any man can brook comparison with the great Mozart.

If I could only impress on the soul of every friend of music, and on high personages in particular, how inimitable are Mozart's works, how profound, how musically intelligent, now extraordinarily sensitive! (for this is how I understand them, how I feel them) – why then the nations would vie with each other to possess such a jewel within their frontiers. Prague should hold him fast – but should reward him too; for without this, the history of great geniuses is sad indeed, and gives but little encouragement to posterity to further exertions; and unfortunately this is why so many promising intellects fall by the wayside. It enrages me to think that this incomparable Mozart is not yet engaged by some imperial or royal court! Forgive me if I lose my head: but I love the man so dearly. I am, &c.

Joseph Hayden [*sic*].

And so we find Mozart very nearly at the summit of his career, his concerts mostly (but with important exceptions) filled to overflowing, his works gladly published by Torricella and Artaria, who were even starting to issue his juvenilia – so magic had the name of Mozart become by 1785. Leopold Mozart, back in Salzburg and avid for news from his son – usually not forthcoming, or not to the degree Leopold would have liked and expected – writes to his daughter on 3 November that an acquaintance had said to him:

It is quite astonishing how many works your son is now publishing: in every musical announcement I read only the name Mozart. The Berlin announcements put the following after the mention of the Quartets [dedicated to Haydn]: 'suffice it to say, they are by H. Mozart.' I couldn't make any reply, because I didn't know, inasmuch as it is now 6 weeks since I've had a letter from him [Wolfgang]. He [the acquaintance] also said something about a new opera [*Figaro*]. Basta! We'll hear soon enough, no doubt. . .[28]

There were two immediate and pressing musical matters in Vienna with which Mozart was concerned. The first was the Masonic Funeral Music (K.477) for Georg August, Duke of Mecklenburg-Strelitz, and Franz, Count Esterházy de Galántha. A Lodge of Sorrows for the two was held on 17 November, and Mozart's new work – with players augmented at the last minute by travelling brethren to provide an immense wind band (oboes, clarinet, three basset horns, double bassoon and two horns) – was given its first performance, at least in this guise.[29] It is Mozart's magnificent attempt to fuse the two worlds of the Catholic Church and Masonry, with symbols of which the work is replete. It is in three parts (a typical Masonic concept), with the

middle section in E flat, the basic key of the work being C minor. Here Mozart uses an old plainchant known as the *Tonus Pellegrinus*, a melody closely related to the 'Lamentation' chants used in Passion Week. Mozart himself had used it in his oratorio *Betulia liberata* of 1771; but more important, Michael Haydn had turned to it that same year during the middle of the opening section of his Requiem for Archbishop Schrattenbach. And it is astonishing to find Mozart using it again in 1791, in his Requiem, and at exactly in the same place as in Michael Haydn's work. The *Tonus Pellegrinus* was the melody used in the 'Miserere' of the Requiem ceremony and, as noted above, during Passion week – thus its symbolism in a ceremony of a Lodge of Sorrows is deeply appropriate. With its message of comfort – the last chord, in C major, envelops one like the Madonna enclosing the mourners with her widespread cloak in a medieval painting – the Masonic Funeral Music is the essence of Mozart, his humanity and (in all senses) his passion.

The next major contribution that Mozart made was in the opera house – a far cry from the Lodge of Sorrows. On 25 November 1785, the popular opera by Francesco Bianchi (1752–1810), *La villanella rapita*, first given at the Teatro S. Moisè in Venice, was staged in Vienna (Burgtheater) with Celesta Coltellini, Vincenzo Calvesi, Stefano Mandini and Francesco Bussani in the leading roles. Mozart wrote two substantial numbers for insertion in this opera, first (5 November) a quartet 'Dite almeno' (K.479) and later (21 November) a trio 'Mandina amabile' (K.480). These two ensemble pieces go far beyond the normal kind of insertions in Italian operas by other composers, both in size, scope and in that speciality of Mozart's: character delineation – here in a rich comedy. The orchestration (with clarinets) and the content of the scores have that magic, ambivalent profundity which we rightly associate with the greatest Mozart; both pieces have a 'finale' quality, and indeed one of them actually served as such. As Einstein says, 'All Mozart's musical forces were gathering for an outburst',[30] and that outburst was to be *Figaro*.

Before moving to the two worlds in which Mozart was supremely predominant – piano concerto and opera – let us take stock of his situation at the end of 1785. The Niemetschek biography provides interesting vignettes:

In Vienna, especially, his piano-playing was admired; for although Vienna had many great masters of this instrument, which had since become everyone's favourite, nobody could rival our Mozart: His admirable dexterity, which particularly in the left hand and the bass were considered quite unique, his feeling and delicacy, and beautiful expression . . . were the attractions of his playing, which together with his abundant ideas and his knowledge of composition must have enthralled every listener and made Mozart the greatest pianist of his time. . . .

[*Entführung*] created a stir; and the cunning Italians soon realized that such a man might pose a threat to their childish tinkling. Jealousy now reared its head with typical Italian venom. The monarch, who at heart was charmed by this deeply stirring music, said to Mozart nevertheless: 'Too beautiful for our ears and an extraordinary number of notes, dear Mozart.' 'Just as many, Your Majesty, as are necessary,' he replied with that noble dignity and frankness which so often go with great genius. He realized that this was not a personal opinion, but just a repetition of somebody else's words. . . .

I cannot describe the sensation it [the opera] made in Vienna from my own experience – but I was a witness to the enthusiasm which it aroused in Prague among knowledgeable and ignorant people alike. It was as if what had hitherto been taken for music was nothing of the kind. Everyone was transported – amazed at the novel harmonies and the original passages for wind instruments.[31]

And what, for instance, did Giovanni Paisiello, who visited Vienna in 1784 and heard Mozart perform several times, think of him? An extract from the extremely valuable little book, *Aneddoti piacevoli e interessante, Occorsi della vita di G.G. Ferrari*, as translated in *The Harmonicon*, will help to redress the picture:

Shortly after this, I was so unfortunate as to lose the society of my good friend Attwood, who set out for Vienna, in order to complete his studies under the celebrated Mozart. He arrived in that metropolis at the very moment this great composer published his six Quartets, dedicated to Haydn, and sent me a copy as a present, with a letter, in which he advised me not to form an opinion of them till I had heard them executed several times over. I accordingly tried them with some dilettanti and professors, who were friends of mine, but we could execute only the slow movements, and even those indifferently. I scored several of the parts, and among others the fugue in G, in the first quartet. I showed it to the [celebrated composer Gaetano] Latilla, who, after looking over the first movement, pronounced it to be a masterly piece; but when he had examined the ingenious combinations and modulations of the second part, and came to the bars where the subject is resumed, he laid down the copy upon the table, exclaiming in perfect ecstacy, 'This is the most magnificent piece of music I ever saw in my life' . . . A manager of one of the theatres at Rome, of the name of Gasparoni, paid Paisiello a visit. He came to know whether the composer could

Wax relief portrait of Mozart, c. 1785, preserved in the Theatrical Museum of La Scala, Milan.

Silhouette portrait of Mozart executed in 1785 by Hieronymus Löschenkohl for inclusion in the Musik- und Theater-Almanach *published in 1786.*

recommend him a maestro of abilities, one above the common; for since he was unable to engage either himself, Guglielmi, or Cimarosa, he could not find a composer in Italy who was worth two farthings. Paisiello immediately proposed Mozart, as a young man of transcendent talent. He added, 'that he could not say for certain whether his music would please at first, being somewhat complicated; but that should Mozart once take, it would be all over with several masters in Europe.'[32]

This episode occurred in Italy, where Mozart's and Haydn's music was little known and little appreciated; it also shows that, as far as the eighteenth century is concerned, not all Italians were as chauvinistic as writers from north of the Alps often consider them.

That Mozart's music was difficult and met with resistance is, of course, all too true. In an article about Mozart in the *AMZ* in 1799,[33] further details of his life are given (as told by his widow), among other things that the Minuet and Trio of the Quartet, K.421, were written as Constanze was having her first child. The report continues:

The Quartets [referring to the set of six dedicated to Haydn] occasionally had a curious fate. When the late Artaria sent them to Italy, they were returned 'because there were so many printer's errors'. Gradually they were accepted. But all the same, even in Germany these Mozart works fared no better. The late Prince Grassalkowich, for example, had these Quartets performed by some of the players in his *Kapelle*. Time and again he cried, 'You're not playing correctly,' and when they assured him that they were, he tore up the notes on the spot.[34]

*   *   *

We have seen that not only was Mozart the most popular non-operatic composer in Vienna, apart from Haydn, but that his concerts were bringing in a great deal of money. What, then, is one to make of the following letter, dated 20 November 1785, from Mozart to his new publisher, Franz Anton Hoffmeister, in Vienna?

I turn to you with my problems and beg you to assist me with some money, which I need most urgently at present . . .

Excuse me if I bother you constantly, but you know me, and are aware how anxious I am for your affairs to flourish, and thus I am persuaded that you will not take offence at my insistence, but will gladly be of help to me, as I to you.[35]

Hoffmeister's note on the envelope reads simply 'two ducats'.

Franz Anton Hoffmeister, composer and publisher; engraving by F.W. Nettling.

This is surely the stone statue at the feast: Mozart had persuaded Hoffmeister – a very successful composer, and later Lodge Brother – to publish piano quartets (K.478, 493), a novel form in which Mozart thought he could afford to be entirely unconventional. He composed the first about 16 October 1785 and it was issued in December by Hoffmeister.[36] Mozart apparently believed that he could raise some money on the strength of his next quartet (which, however, he did not complete until after *Figaro*). But the fact that he needed to approach Hoffmeister for a loan provides a sombre note on which to end this account of what should have been very nearly the apex of Mozart's career.

VIII

The String Quartets dedicated to Haydn Mozart and the Piano Concerto

---

I N THE COURSE of his career, Mozart composed a vast amount of chamber music, beginning with four Violin Sonatas (K.6–9) (which his father had engraved in Paris in 1764) and ending with the String Quintet in E flat (K.614), completed in April 1791, and the exquisite Adagio and Rondo (K.617) for glass harmonica, flute, oboe, viola and cello, written for the blind harmonica player Marianne Kirchgessner. Between 1764 and 1791, he composed a formidable array of violin sonatas, piano trios, string quartets, string quintets, piano quartets and all sorts of works for special instrumental combinations, such as the famous Clarinet Quintet (K.581) or the extraordinary Quintet in E flat for piano, oboe, clarinet, bassoon and horn (K.452), which made such an impression on the young Beethoven, who closely modelled his own beautiful Quintet, op. 16 (completed in 1797), on Mozart's work, using the same key and instrumentation. Mozart wrote superb chamber music, some of it daringly original, almost all of it – if we except some youthful studies – revealing an astonishing technical ability which is, however, always cloaked in a beautifully polished exterior – what Hans Keller has described as Mozart's 'simultaneous depth and finished surface, his originality and appeal . . . his public privacy'.[1]

Bearing in mind that Mozart wrote in various chamber musical combinations, we would single out two categories for brief examination: the string quartet and (later) the string quintet. There are several reasons for the choice of these two genres: in the first place, all the late works in both categories are masterpieces – a description one would, perhaps, hesitate to apply to every one of the violin sonatas, some of which are 'showpieces' written with the broad public in mind. Secondly, there are numerically many great quartets and quintets, ten of the former and five of the latter, so that one has great variety – whereas there are only two piano quartets (albeit both masterpieces, K.478 in G minor being even more impressive than its later companion, K.493 in E flat), one oboe quartet, one clarinet quintet, one clarinet trio, and so forth. Finally, it is clear that there are many 'private' thoughts that lend themselves especially to chamber music; in the 'public' forms of opera and symphony, these 'private' and generally intricate, complex thoughts have to be rewritten to fit on the broader canvas. Mozart's chamber works, and especially his quartets and quintets – not just the famous 'Dissonance' Quartet – contain dissonances that are hardly encountered in his symphonies, concertos or operas. Naturally, it is difficult to get forty players to execute intricate modulations in tune, whereas four or five, once they have played together often, can accomplish all sorts of subtleties that an orchestra cannot: sharpening a leading note (the winds would have much more difficulty, for obvious technical reasons), playing an accompaniment ♪ ♫ in such a way that the notes are de-accented, and so forth. In the same way that Haydn's and Beethoven's quartets have many things to say that are not found in their respective symphonies, Mozart's string chamber music reveals a whole new side, and certainly the most complex, of his multi-faceted personality.

Haydn's chamber music is very close to Mozart's quartets and even to the quintets (though Haydn never wrote any mature quintets). Mozart, like every thinking man of music, had been impressed by Haydn's opus 20 quartets (1772) which, with Mozart's six 'Haydn' Quartets and Beethoven's opus 18, may be considered the three most revolutionary groups in this genre composed in the eighteenth century (the Beethoven set was already in existence by 1799). As was often his way, Mozart immediately sat down and wrote a set of six himself (K.168–173, composed in 1773), modelled on Haydn's opus 20. Haydn, meanwhile, had applied his vast intellectual abilities to the symphony, and wrote no more quartets until 1781, when his opus 33 appeared. Shortly after that date, Haydn and Mozart met and, as is well known, became close friends. By 1783, Mozart had evolved a grand scheme – to write six string quartets and dedicate them to Haydn, 'from whom,' said Wolfgang, 'I learned how to write quartets.' On 14 January 1785 – a day before it was performed – Mozart completed the last of these, the 'Dissonance'.

The six works are: K.387 in G, 421 in D minor, 428 in E flat, 458 in B flat ('Hunt'), 464 in A (Beethoven's favourite) and 465 in C ('Dissonance'). As I have already noted, these new quartets were often misunderstood by conservative music lovers; their enormous compression, their density (a feature of Haydn's opus 20 and Beethoven's opus 18, too), their anguished chromaticism and their extreme modernity – all these features alarmed and confused many people. But there must have been others who recognized the beauty of these 'Haydn' Quartets – not only the dedicatee, but cultivated Viennese such as Prince Lichnowsky and Baron van Swieten; and we may be sure that they were assiduously studied by a young pianist and composer in Bonn on the Rhine – Beethoven.

Mozart and the Piano Concerto

In the eighteenth century most composers were also virtuoso performers. (Haydn is a notable exception, which is a major reason why the concerto form comprises so little of his extensive *œuvre*). This meant that not only did composers perform, but performers composed. Part of the reason for performers composing lay in the fact that, if the instrument were new, there might not be much good material available, or that perhaps the available material did not display to best advantage the technique of a particular virtuoso. Mozart's clarinet and basset-horn player, Anton Stadler, also wrote for the basset horn, an instrument for which there was practically nothing available. On the other hand, these performers often requested well-known composers to write concertos for them, and thus we owe Haydn's Trumpet Concerto to a Viennese trumpeter named Anton Weidinger and Mozart's Clarinet Concerto (K.622) to Stadler. In Mozart's *œuvre*, most of the concertos were written for the composer himself – first the famous series of violin concertos written in the 1770s and then, as Mozart's interest turned ever more to the piano, the piano concertos, which occupy a central part of his artistic career.

The formal pattern which was invariably used (though with a great amount of flexibility in its details) for the first movements of all Mozartian concertos is set out below. In its simplest form the scheme is:[2]

Anton Stadler, the famous clarinet player for whom Mozart wrote the Clarinet Quintet (K.581) and the Clarinet Concerto (K.622); anonymous silhouette.

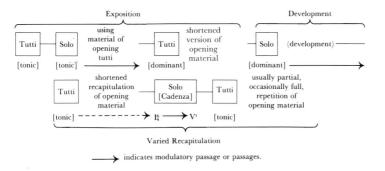

The principal advantage of this kind of formalized scheme was that it automatically imposed a beautifully proportioned symmetry on the whole, while allowing a great deal of freedom within a seemingly strict mould. What Mozart did with particular skill was to combine a rich symphonic scoring with this traditional Baroque concerto form. If it were not for the obvious fact that the music is not going to move to the dominant, the beginning of the magnificent but underrated Piano Concerto no. 13 in C (K.415) could come out of a symphony in the grand manner; the symphonic principle is perhaps applied most impressively to a pair of C major concertos, no. 21 (K.467) and no. 25 (K.503). Gradually Mozart also begins to take over a further, typical aspect of the Viennese symphony – 'working with motifs'. The Viennese masters used this *motivische Arbeit*[3] both to satisfy the demands of their intellectual Viennese audiences and also as a way of creating tension. Used contrapuntally, these transformed motifs could give an entirely new dimension of richness and depth to the symphony and, in Mozart's hands, the concerto as well.

Adalbert Gyrowetz (1763–1850), a prolific and popular composer who left Vienna in 1786 for Italy. Mozart conducted one of Gyrowetz's symphonies at a subscription concert in the Mehlrube. Engraving by J.G. Mansfeld, 1793.

The second movements were more flexible in their formal patterns. We have works in rather simple three-part sections A–B–A, slow movements in variation form, in rondo form – in short, almost anything was permissible. Mozart, of course, did things that flouted all the rules: for instance, in the slow movement of Concerto no. 22 in E flat (K.482) he simply introduces a whole episode for wind band without the solo piano. Very often in this kind of movement, the strings are muted, and Mozart liked to use the minor key to set off particularly forceful or lively outer movements, again as in K.482 and, in a particularly moving fashion, in Concerto no. 23 (K.488).

The final movements generally incorporate something of the rondo form: A–B–A–C–A is a typical rondo pattern. But on more than one occasion (e.g. K.482) Mozart introduces a slow section in the middle, and the variety of his final movements is altogether astonishing. He reserves every kind of surprise, even to ending the grand C major Concerto no. 13 in a whisper.

In those days, the keyboard instrument fulfilled a dual function: it played *basso continuo*, which meant filling in the chords over the bass line rather in the manner of the organ in a setting of the mass; and it was at the same time the solo instrument. Nowadays, this *basso continuo* function of the Mozart piano concerto is coming back into fashion, for it serves to make the soloist more a part of the whole ensemble, sitting, as it were, in the middle of events and having a function throughout. Part of the reason why this *continuo* function fell into disuse was the nineteenth-century attitude towards a virtuoso – like Liszt – who had to preside in solitary splendour, set apart from the common members of the orchestra. A second, equally important, reason was the fact that the sound produced by a Steinway concert grand piano is singularly unfitted for this *basso continuo* function. Mozart's piano, with its more delicate and metallic attack, blends admirably with the orchestra and with its varying instrumental colours – something that a modern piano can achieve only with extreme difficulty.

In the process of enriching the pre-classical concerto as he did, Mozart succeeded in raising the entire intellectual level of the form. It is hard for us to realize today how bad many of these performer-written concertos really were; to show the general mentality, we might illustrate our point with an episode from the autobiography of the Bohemian composer, Adalbert Gyrowetz, whom Mozart introduced to Vienna musical society at one of his concerts; Gyrowetz tells us that *he* was asked to compose the tuttis of violin concertos by the celebrated violinist Giovanni M. Giornovichj (Jarnowic), the result being a typical hotchpotch.[4]

By having so many members of Vienna's aristocracy and bourgeoisie as his pupils, Mozart was able to pass on his entire approach – not only through public concerts, but also via talented individuals such as Prince Lichnowsky (who later became Beethoven's most prominent patron). Thus Beethoven had a lot to thank Mozart for, particularly in preparing the ground for him; so that when he finally arrived to study with Haydn in 1792, the same Viennese who had known and appreciated Mozart were ready to encourage morally and to assist financially the young Beethoven in these formative years of his career. It

Ludwig van Beethoven, aged sixteen; silhouette by Joseph Neesen, 1786.

Title page of Mozart's Piano Concerto no. 15 in C. major (K.415), published in Vienna in 1785. In this publication the trumpet and drum parts, which were added after the original autograph was written, were omitted.

is certainly part of the Mozartian heritage that in 1795 Beethoven made his first public appearance in Vienna at the Burgtheather as soloist in his own Piano Concerto in B flat (op. 19), which, of course, he conducted from the keyboard.

Count Waldstein had written in Beethoven's commonplace book that he should 'receive Mozart's spirit from Hayden's hands'; and it is pleasant to think that Haydn himself conducted many of the concerts in which Beethoven introduced the Viennese public to his latest piano concertos. It was almost literally the fulfilment of Waldstein's prophetic wish.

*   *   *

It is, above all, the enormous stylistic diversity which sets Mozart's piano concertos above and beyond all those of his contemporaries. (As noted earlier, Haydn's Piano Concerto in D [XVIII:11], composed *c.* 1779, which is a very attractive work, marked the end of his activities in the genre.) Some of Mozart's earlier Viennese concertos are deliberately fashioned like chamber music – the most famous one of this kind is perhaps no. 12 in A (K.414), which even begins *piano* to show what kind of a work we may expect. And indeed, as we propose to show, many different kinds of music served Mozart in fashioning these concertos. A grand, symphonic concerto can also begin *piano*. That is possibly a kind of 'surprise' technique: the listener is not sure what is in store for him when Concerto no. 13 in C (K.415) begins, and it is not until the first grand tutti that it becomes clear that this is a symphonic work (particularly in the second version, with trumpets and drums). The symphony, as has been

said above, is one of the main influences on the sound (orchestration) of these grand concertos, of which the principal ones are no. 16 in D (K.451), no. 20 in D minor (K.466), no. 21 in C (K.467) – another work which announces its symphonic thought even while still remaining in the *piano* context with which it begins; no. 22 in E flat (K.482), and especially no. 25 in C (K.503) – the grandest, most difficult and most symphonic of them all; culminating with no. 26 in D ('Coronation'; K.537). There is also the striking and unusual Rondo finale (K.382) for the less than fascinating earlier Concerto no. 5 in D (K.175).

Another major influence is the Imperial wind band, without whose presence the concertos would sound more like Haydn's, or like the chamber concertos: the use of the wind band is occasionally so omnipresent as to stop 'concerto proceedings' entirely, as noted above in respect of K.482. The excellence of the *Harmonie* group is felt in other ways too, in a more chamber musical context: one of the most original instrumental layouts is in the B flat works – no. 15 (K.450) and no. 18 (K.456) – with those piercingly high B flat *alto* horns which are so characteristic of Mozart's scoring in this key (also markedly felt in the pre-Viennese Symphony no. 33 (K.319) and in one of the horns in the G minor Symphony no. 40 (K.550).

Also a strong influence on these concertos is opera, both serious and comic. Comic opera is often suggested by the witty exchanges between piano and orchestra – like a singer commenting on some amusing action – and serious opera in the slow movements, especially those in the minor, which often recall a lonely heroine in an *opera seria*. Such a moment is surely the slow movement of the A major Concerto no. 23 (K.488), one of the most subtle of all, with its gossamer scoring and its sense of gentle melancholy. And the beginning of the last Concerto, no. 27 (K.595), is almost like an aria: one might almost expect a solo soprano rather than a piano to enter at the end of the orchestral section.

Two of the concertos combine all these elements and another as well – a sense of foreboding and fear, of the ominous, an extreme feeling of drama: the Concerto in D minor, no. 20 (K.466), of 1785, and that in C minor, no. 24 (K.491), of 1786. They are perhaps the most remarkable of the whole series, and certainly the most forward looking. In the D minor work, an unsettled mood – almost a kind of dark warning – is established by the syncopations and the growling bass line. What must the Viennese have thought of this extraordinary music, so different from anything they had heard for many years? – not, in fact, since the great wave of minor-key music of the late 1760s and early 1770s: mainly Haydn, of course, with his famous symphonies in F sharp minor, E minor, C minor, F minor and G minor, and his minor-key piano sonatas and quartets from opus 9 and, even more, opus 20; but also other composers such as J.B. Vanhal, imitating Haydn with a whole series of symphonies in minor keys; and the young Mozart himself, with Symphony no. 25 in G minor (K.183).

We might illustrate, with one rather technical but breathtakingly original device, the kind of ends to which Mozart has recourse in the concertos of the early 1780s, raising this device to high drama in the D minor Concerto. We refer to so-called 'stopped' notes in the horn. The hunting horn of Mozart's youth had been made smaller and was soon called a 'hand horn' because it fitted comfortably on the player's right side *and the right hand could be inserted into the bell*, thus lowering the note played by a half note, a whole note (hand inserted more deeply) and even one-and-one-half notes if absolutely necessary. In those days the horns (and the trumpets) could only play the notes of the harmonic scale

↑ = impure notes

In horn concertos, solo players were beginning to develop a very audacious technique, using stopped notes but also having recourse to 'overblowing', a technique by which certain notes in the bass clef could be produced. Mozart had a horn-playing friend from Salzburg who had come to Vienna and was in the court orchestra for *Entführung* – Joseph Leutgeb (or Leitgeb). Mozart began to write horn concertos for his friend, who also owned a cheese shop (when a horn player's teeth started to go, he was finished as a musician). There are four such works of the Viennese period that were completed: K.412, 417, 447 and 495. Leutgeb was obviously equipped to deal with stopped notes, as the following extract from K.447 will show:

('real' notation)

+ = stopped note

But no one expected the horn players of an average orchestra to cope with problems of this kind. There must have been many 'average' players who could not play stopped notes at all. Imagine our surprise, therefore, if we start to examine the Ployer Piano Concerto (no. 14, K.449) to find in the Andantino the following passage for the first horn at bars 15ff. (also 112ff.):

and later, in the finale (bars 24f.):

But it is not until Concerto no. 19 (K.459) that we find the first horn employing stopped notes to increase the tension just before the cadenza in the opening movement as follows:

Cadenza pianoforte

All the cases cited above might be classified as 'tricks of the trade', but with Concerto no. 20 (K.466), Mozart starts to use stopped notes as a dramatic effect, first, coming in 'cold' (without preparation, that is, it being easier to move into a stopped note from an adjacent, non-stopped or 'open' note) in F major (bars 174ff.):

The next series of stopped notes is (as in K.459) the preparation for the cadenza:

In the most dramatic and unsettling section (bars 183ff.) of the finale, the horn is again expected to deliver the following –

– and this time the second horn is also expected to play. Now we must imagine, I think, that the horn player in all these examples was Leutgeb. But Mozart could hardly have expected horn players abroad to be able to execute such passages. Perhaps that is one more reason why – with the exception of Concerto no. 17 (K.453) – he never allowed any of the concertos between no. 14 (K.449) and no. 27 (K.595) to be published. (The other reason was to keep the music as his exclusive property.) What must be said is that, today, we are not able to hear this music as it was written, for the sound of a stopped note is *entirely different* from an open note. This long horn note before the cadenza in no. 20 (K.466) should sound (literally) muted and sinister. It has not been heard that way for 150 years, or since valves for horns came into fashion.

In Concerto no. 22 (K.482), that lovely and mellow work in E flat with its prominent role for wind band – clarinets instead of oboes, but for the first time in an E flat concerto trumpets and drums as well as the other usual wind instruments (flute, bassoons, horns) – there are also spectacular examples of horn stopping, even in the opening tutti –

– and again when the piano enters (bars 99f.) and in the recapitulation (bars 269f.). For the third time, stopped horn notes increase the tension in the final tutti before the cadenza (with the horn coming in 'cold' as well):

There are also stopped notes in the Andante (bars 70f.) and (for the second horn) in bars 89ff.:

This kind of writing is also found in Haydn's *La fedeltà premiata*, which Mozart probably heard performed in December 1784.[5]

The finale contains one of the most audacious series of stopped notes in any of the concertos to date:

and in the movement's middle, slow section Mozart writes the following:

In the C minor Concerto no. 24 (K.491), on the other hand, there is only one horn stopped note (again in the tutti preceding the cadenza, at bars 485f.), possibly because the horns and trumpets are laid out in a manner different from that in K.466: in that work both are pitched in D (the tonic), while in K.491 the trumpets are in C and the horns are in the relative major, E flat, which means that without having recourse to any stopped notes, Mozart can produce C minor 'chords' in his horns and trumpets. One ought to add that there are no stopped notes at all in the C major 'symphonic' Concertos no. 21 (K.467) and no. 25 (K.503). Nor are there any in *Der Schauspieldirektor*, whereas in *Figaro* they appear in the spirited Terzetto (Susanna, Countess, Count) No. 14 (*NMA*; in others No. 13), 'Susanna or via sortite', in Act II just before the Count leaves to fetch the key to the closet in which Cherubino is hiding. There, in bars 49f., are the only stopped notes in the whole opera.

A small point, and highly technical, but one which illustrates the fastidious sense of attention to detail which informs all Mozart's scores. In the D minor Concerto no. 20 (K.466) the sinister stopped horns increase the dramatic tension; in the E flat Concerto no. 22 (K.482) they contribute to displaying the skills of the Imperial *Harmonie*, which of course included stopped notes in the horn department; in *Figaro* they contribute to the sense of tension, but perhaps in an ironic way. It must be remembered that horns were always symbolic of adultery, apart from everything else. We are already in the middle of *Le nozze di Figaro*, the first of the great trilogy of widely contrasting operatic masterpieces written by Mozart in collaboration with Lorenzo Da Ponte.

IX

The Da Ponte Operas

———

THREE IMMORTAL OPERAS were conceived by the poet Lorenzo Da Ponte and Mozart. Their great collaboration began officially in 1785, but we owe it in part to an event which had occurred five years earlier, when Mozart was preparing his first great opera, *Idomeneo*, in Munich. On 29 November 1780, two days before the first orchestral rehearsal, Empress Maria Theresa died. In October 1762, when Mozart was only six, he had bewitched the Court at Schönbrunn Castle with his incredible proficiency; sadly, however, the Empress, who accomplished such political wonders as a young ruler, never took Mozart very seriously. Her son, Archduke Ferdinand, Governor and Captain-General of the Italian province of Lombardy, had commissioned Mozart to write an opera, *Ascanio in Alba*, to celebrate his marriage to Princess Maria Beatrice d'Este. The opera, performed in October 1771, was such a success that Ferdinand seriously considered engaging Wolfgang. Being a dutiful son, he wrote to his mother about the matter. But on 12 December 1771 she replied:

Lorenzo Da Ponte, Mozart's collaborator as librettist; anonymous watercolour (lost).

You ask me if you may take the young Salzburgian into your service. I cannot imagine as what, since I cannot believe you require a composer or such useless people. But if it will give you pleasure, I would not wish to stand in your way. What I say is, do not burden yourself with useless people and never grant titles to that kind of person who would misuse it, running about in the world like beggars. Apart from that, he has a large family.[1]

Maria Theresa had, to say the least, an imperfect understanding of music. The Empress was also rather prudish, particularly with regard to the theatre. She had caused Haydn's opera *Der krumme Teufel* to be banned, because of its political satire and its sexually compromising sections. As long as she reigned, it was quite inconceivable that the libretti of *Figaro*, *Don Giovanni* or *Così fan tutte* would have got past the censors. The Empress had a strict censorship organization, led by van Swieten, which prevented compromising books from being imported into Austria. As a result, the taste and knowledge of the Austrian literary world lagged far behind that of England and France, even of Germany. The Empress interested herself in all this censorship, arguing with

Pope Pius VI, who came to Vienna in 1782 to meet Emperor Joseph II; engraving (commemorating the visit) by J.F. Beer. The papal procession through the city on Easter Sunday (31 March) was recorded in an engraving by Hieronymus Löschenkohl; the façade of the Kirche am Hof (from the balcony of which the Pope blessed the people of Vienna) can be seen in the left background.

van Swieten. On the subject of a Bavarian monthly magazine which ridiculed good-humouredly the dialect and other characteristics of the people, she forbade its importation, adding 'I for one have no love whatever for smacks of irony. . . . It is inconsistent with the love of one's neighbour. Why should people waste their time writing such stuff, or reading it?'[2]

From 1765, Maria Theresa had allowed her son Joseph to act as a co-regent, but Joseph, a child of the Enlightenment, longed to put into practice a whole series of reforms which his mother, becoming more conservative as she grew older, sought to hinder. Joseph II was the most interesting, if deeply problematical, monarch ever to occupy the Habsburg throne, and it is in large part to him that we owe the existence of two Da Ponte-Mozart operas – *Figaro* and *Così* – as well as the Vienna performances of *Don Giovanni*. As soon as he was able, after his mother's death, Joseph – who would be forty on 13 March 1781 – set about propelling the Austrian monarchy into the world of the Enlightenment, and one of his early concerns was to impose restrictions on, though not to abolish, the censors' office. As the 1780s progressed, Austria was witness to a vast flood of political pamphlets, satires, articles and books, such as would have horrified Maria Theresa. The power of the Church was broken politically and economically. The Pope came to Austria in 1782 to reason with Joseph, but to no avail. The numerous monasteries within the monarchy were drastically curtailed. To a detached observer it must have seemed that Austria was approaching Arcadia. Torture was abolished, and barbarous methods of execution such as breaking on the wheel became the exception, not the rule.

154

When the French Revolution broke out in 1789, it was certainly in part Joseph's earlier reforms which saved Austria from a similar fate; but the Church and the nobility (whose vast feudal power had been broken) loathed Joseph II. On the other hand, the peasantry, literary men, merchants, Jews, Protestants, the downtrodden and the poor, came to regard him as a god. When he stopped his carriage, jumped out, and took the plough in his own hand, he became a hero to the farmers: it was a trick that Napoleon was to remember.

It is against this background that we now focus on events of 1785 in Vienna, to which had come the extraordinary figure of Lorenzo Da Ponte, libertine, *poseur*, converted Jew, cultivated man of letters, failed priest and protégé of Antonio Salieri, the court composer. Da Ponte had become personally and politically compromised in his native Italy, first in Venice and then in Treviso; he found it expedient to go to Dresden, where he procured a letter of recommendation to Salieri, which he presented early in 1782. Salieri was well known, had the ear of the new Emperor, and Da Ponte was introduced to Joseph II, who impressed the Italian 'by the utter simplicity of his manner and his dress'.[3] In his *Memoirs* (written many years later and therefore not wholly reliable) Da Ponte makes a special point that it was because of his 'perseverance and firmness alone that Europe and the world in great part owe the exquisite vocal compositions of [Mozart] that admirable genius'. Da Ponte further states that he met Mozart at the home of Baron Wetzlar, and shortly thereafter proposed to Mozart an operatic collaboration. Mozart answered, 'I would do so most willingly, but I am certain that I should never get permission.' Da Ponte answered, 'That will be my business.'

Da Ponte's account of the conception of *Figaro* is as follows:

In conversation with me one day . . . he asked me whether I could easily make an opera from a comedy by Beaumarchais – *Le Mariage de Figaro*. I liked the suggestion very much, and promised to write one. But there was a very great difficulty to overcome. A few days previous, the Emperor had forbidden the company at the German theatre to perform that comedy, which was too licentiously written, he thought, for a self-respecting audience: how then propose it to him for an opera? Baron Wetzlar offered, with noble generosity, to pay me a handsome price for the words, and then, should we fail of production in Vienna, to have the opera presented in London, or in France. But I refused this offer and proposed writing the words and the music secretly and then awaiting a favourable opportunity to show them to the Directors [of the Opera], or to the Emperor himself, for which step I confidently volunteered to assume the responsibility. Martini [Da Ponte's friend and the composer of the very successful *Il burbero di buon cuore* for which Da Ponte had adapted the text] was the only one who learned of the beautiful secret from me, and he, with laudable high-mindedness, and because of his esteem for Mozart, agreed that I should delay working for him until I should have finished the libretto for *Figaro*. I set to work, accordingly, and as fast as I wrote the words, Mozart set them to music. In six weeks everything was in order. Mozart's lucky star ordained that the Opera should fail of scores at just that moment. Seizing that opportunity, I went, without saying a word to a living person, to offer *Figaro* to the Emperor. 'What', he said. 'Don't you know that Mozart, though a wonder at instrumental music, has written only one opera, and nothing remarkable at that?' [Joseph meant *Entführung*, Vienna 1782; he apparently knew nothing of Mozart's earlier operas, and understood nothing of *Entführung*.]

'Yes, Sire', I replied quietly, 'but without Your Majesty's clemency I would have written but one drama in Vienna!'

'That may be true', he answered, 'but this *Mariage de Figaro* – I have just forbidden the German troupe to use it!'

'Yes; Sire', I rejoined, 'but I was writing an opera, and not a play. I had to omit many scenes and to cut others quite considerably. I have omitted or cut anything that might offend good taste or public decency at a performance over which the Sovereign Majesty might preside. The music, I may add, as far as I may judge of it, seems to me marvellously beautiful.'

'Good! If that be the case, I will rely on your good taste as to the music and on your wisdom as to the morality. Send the score to the copyist.'

I ran straight to Mozart, but I had not yet finished imparting the good news when a page of the Emperor's came and handed him a note, wherein he was commanded to present himself at once at the Palace, bringing his score. He obeyed the royal order, allowed the Emperor to hear various selections, which pleased him immensely, or, to tell the truth without exaggeration, astounded him.

Naturally, one's first reaction to such dialogue reported so long after the event is one of considerable scepticism, the more so since John Stone discovered an earlier version of the 1823 *Memoirs* (here referred to as *Extract*),[4] in which many of these elaborate conversations do not feature. Among the significant differences, in 1819 Da Ponte praises the 'first buffo' as an integral ingredient in the success (or conversely failure) of a comic opera – by whom Francesco Benucci was meant in this context. By 1823, the 'first buffo' had disappeared. In the *Extract*, the Italian impresario Domenico Guardasoni, making a guest appearance in Prague, suggested to Mozart that he set Giovanni Bertati's new opera, *Don Giovanni* – a fact which Da Ponte removed in the *Memoirs* because he hoped that Bertati's share in the proceedings would have been forgotten by most of his readers, if indeed they ever knew about it. Finally, in the *Extract*, Da Ponte confuses the chronology of events in 1785 and 1786 by suggesting that Salieri – arch-enemy – was absent from Vienna in 1785 to write for the Paris Opéra, whereas this (no doubt for Mozart) happy event did not occur until 1786. 'Contradictions,' says Daniel Heartz, 'accumulate to a point where it becomes difficult to lend credence to Da Ponte's main claim, about how he won the day for the new opera in a personal interview with the Emperor . . . If we believe Da Ponte, the Emperor capitulated with the speed of an *opera buffa* clown. This demands a credulity of the reader that few can possess. By suggesting that the play be revised to make it more respectable, Joseph had, from the beginning, shown more interest than Da Ponte let on . . .'[5]

Is the entire Da Ponte story of *Figaro*'s birth therefore a fabrication? Possibly not. In the *Memoirs* Da Ponte actually states that he invited Joseph II to attend the dress rehearsal. Although such a procedure would have been most unusual – the Emperor did not normally attend dress rehearsals of plays or operas – the story is in fact true. Count Zinzendorf relates that on that day – 29 April 1786 – 'I went to find the Emperor in the Augarten [where he often resided], but he had gone to town to attend the rehearsal of the opera . . .'[6]

Now let us break into Da Ponte's *Memoirs* and buttress his tale with some other contemporary evidence. For a long while it was fashionable to treat with scepticism Da Ponte's claim that *Figaro* was written and composed within six weeks. Mozart's autograph – the first two acts are in Berlin and the last two acts are among the rediscovered treasures of the former Silesian monastery of Grüssau, now lodged in Cracow – shows that the score was first laid out in a kind of musical shorthand, i.e. the essential instruments were noted, along with *all* the vocal parts. The editor of the new edition of *Figaro* for the *NMA*, Ludwig Finscher,[7] considers that the period of six weeks is entirely plausible, and from a variety of evidence it seems that the work was put down during October and November 1785. The singers' parts could be copied from this short score, and Mozart could then fill in the orchestration during the vocal rehearsals.

Our next news also serves to confirm the extreme speed with which the opera was composed. In the Mozart biography by Edward Holmes, we are told that the composer wrote the finale to Act II during two nights and a day; on the second night he felt so ill that he had to break off, leaving only a few pages to orchestrate (another piece of evidence concerning Mozart's method of composition).[8] That he was under a great physical strain is also shown in an unpublished memoir (sold at Sotheby's, London, May 1981) by his English pupil Thomas Attwood, who was with Mozart from June 1785. Attwood writes: 'Mozart at the time I was with him, appeared to be of a cheerful habit, his health not very strong. In consequence of being so much over the table when composing he was obliged to have an upright Desk and stand there when he wrote . . .'

There were several reasons why Mozart chose Beaumarchais' sequel to *Le Barbier de Séville*, and perhaps the most obvious is that *Il barbiere di Siviglia* was already famous as an opera in the version by Giovanni Paisiello. Paisiello had first given it at the Court of Catherine the Great in St Petersburg and from there, in 1782, it had spread across Europe, arriving in Vienna in 1783. Its success had persuaded the Emperor to ask Paisiello for a new opera, *Il rè Teodoro in Venezia*, which had likewise been an enormous success in 1784. Paisiello's recent *Barber*, then, was in the forefront of Mozart's and Da Ponte's minds, as it was also in the minds of the opera-going public in Vienna. First performed on 13 August 1783, it took Vienna by storm, and with sixty performances became the most popular single opera in the history of the Vienna theatre in the eighteenth century.

It was therefore clear that the public in the Burgtheater would regard Mozart's setting of *Figaro* as the natural sequel to Paisiello's *Barber* (just as the two were in sequence as originally written by Beaumarchais). When Mozart started to write the music for *Figaro*, he was at great pains to emphasize the sequential nature of his characters who had started life in the *Barber*. Let us take one case: in Paisiello's masterpiece – for it is that, despite the fact that it is now largely (though not entirely) forgotten – Rosina, not yet married to Lindoro (disguised as the Count), appears for the first time at the end of Act I –

alone – in one of the most beautiful numbers in the opera: the cavatina 'Giusto ciel, che conoscete'. The tempo is slow (Larghetto), it is love music (she is pouring out her necessarily secret feelings for Lindoro), it contains prominent parts for clarinets and is in E flat. In *Figaro*, when the Countess makes her first appearance, she is now unhappily married to the Count, and pours her heart out – in E flat, alone on the stage, and with prominent clarinets. The point would have been at once clear to the Viennese audience, for as Daniel Heartz has indicated, Mozart 'chooses the same key, metre, tempo and rhythmic motions, and the same harmonic rhythm. The similarities do not stop there. He uses a *messa di voce* on B flat . . . His instrumentation is surprisingly similar, with paired clarinets responding to paired bassoons. Their whispered sighs include many of the same chromatic shadings. Does the emphasis on the modal degrees (e.g. II and VI in bar 22) not sound familiar? Also the lingering sweetness of subdominant six-four to tonic? Perhaps the syncopated rise and fall of the melody in bars 11–13 testify most minutely to his fascination with Paisiello's cavatina.'[9] In fact, *Le nozze di Figaro* was planned in minute detail to be a worthy successor to *Il barbiere di Siviglia*.

Beaumarchais' sequel, *Le Mariage de Figaro*, had engendered one of the greatest theatrical scandals in history. When its author offered the piece in 1781 to the Comédie Française, Louis XVI actually read the manuscript and declared, 'This is atrocious, this will never be played! ('Cela est détestable, cela ne sera jamais joué'), but after endless intrigues, counter-intrigues and pressures of all kinds, it was given privately in the Château de Gennevilliers with royal permission. Then, on 27 April 1784, *Le Mariage de Figaro* was finally given by the Comédie Française in Paris and became the greatest hit of its period, with sixty-eight further performances.

The question of the political content of the play has been ardently discussed. Was it a forerunner of the French Revolution? How much of the supposedly dangerous political content influenced Mozart and Da Ponte in their choice of the subject as an operatic libretto? In 1785 several German translations of the play appeared, including an official one, *Figaros Hochzeit, oder Der tolle Tag*; sanctioned by Beaumarchais; it was published in Kehl across the Rhine from Strasbourg (then as now in France). Mozart owned one of the translations which is catalogued under No. 41 in the list of his effects made after his death to value the estate.

Whatever we may think of the political and moral content of the piece, it is clear that Joseph II considered it too dangerous to stage but, as we have seen, not too dangerous to read: anyone was allowed to own the book. We have no idea how much of the overall plan of the operatic libretto is Mozart's and how much Da Ponte's, but we may assume that it was a real collaboration. Of the many changes that were made vis-à-vis Beaumarchais, we might single out two: Act V of the play included a long monologue for Figaro – highly political, highly inflammatory – which runs to several printed pages.[10] In the opera this becomes Figaro's celebrated warning about women in Act IV, 'Aprite un po' quegl'occhi, uomini incauti e sciocchi' ('Open your eyes a little, you incautious and silly men'). This substitution will have found Imperial favour

Figaro, the stage hero created by Beaumarchais, characterized in a watercolour illustrating the text of La Folle Journée ou Le Mariage de Figaro, *published in Paris in 1785.*

OPPOSITE *Beaumarchais and the title page (1785) of his highly controversial play which had become a hit at the Comédie Française in Paris in 1784. The accompanying illustration, showing the discovery of Cherubino by Count Almaviva, appeared in the official German translation,* Figaros Hochzeit oder der tolle Tag, *published in Kehl in 1785.*

LA
FOLLE JOURNEE,
OU LE
MARIAGE
DE FIGARO,
COMEDIE EN CINQ ACTES
ET EN PROSE.
PAR Mr. CARON DE BEAUMARCHAIS.

Repréſentée, pour la premiere fois , à Paris par les
Comédiens ordinaires du Roi , le 27 Avril 1784.

✳

À PARIS, chez les Libraires aſſociés.

M. DCC. LXXXV.

Count Orsini-Rosenberg, Director of the Court Opera in Vienna; engraving after Jacob Adam, 1783.

for two reasons: first, it removes entirely the political satire of the French original; secondly, it describes in rich detail how men are traduced by women, ending with the famous lines, 'il resto nol dico, già ognuno lo sa' ('I won't say the rest, everybody knows it already'). This is followed by solos for the French horns, in Italian *corni*, which term also means horns on the head, the traditional symbol of a cuckold. This accorded perfectly with Joseph II's ambivalent attitude towards women, and we can visualize him chortling over the horn solos, as Mozart played him the music from the score.

In fact one of the many glories of Da Ponte's libretto and Mozart's score is precisely the great understanding shown for all the women in *Figaro*: in the case of the Countess they go in quite a different direction from Beaumarchais. Her appearance in Act II, in splendid isolation, was meticulously prepared both by Da Ponte and by Mozart. Whereas in the play the Countess makes her entrance late in Act I, together with numerous other characters, in the opera she appears first at the beginning of Act II. Mozart has laid the ground for this moment tonally and in a strikingly simple but effective way: the Countess sings her first, slow aria alone, and in a key radically different from that of the overture. The opera begins in D major, but Act I ends with Figaro's great military scene, appropriately in the martial key of C major; the Countess's aria, however, is in E flat, a long way from the opera's opening.

Most of the letters Wolfgang wrote to his father during the period when he was composing *Figaro* are lost, but sometimes the contents are relayed by Leopold to his daughter. On 11 November 1785, for example, Leopold writes:

At last I received a letter from your brother consisting of twelve lines. He excuses himself because he is head over heels in the midst of finishing the opera, *Le Nozze di Figaro* . . . I know the piece, it is a very difficult play, and the translation from the French into an opera must certainly be free, if the opera is to be effective. God willing, the action will be good, and I don't doubt for the music; but it will cost him much running back and forth and disputing until the book is organized in such a way that he can set to work on it – and he will have put it off and taken his good time with it, as is his usual pretty way, now he must go to work in earnest since Count Rosenberg is pressing him.[11]

Leopold thought that Wolfgang had put off the work; in fact *Figaro*'s score is not only a piece of meticulous planning but shows no traces of disorganization at all – quite the contrary.

While the rehearsals of *Figaro* were going on, Mozart had to overcome a whole series of cabals and difficulties. There was (and is) a short ballet in the opera, but ballets were in principle forbidden. Count Orsini-Rosenberg, Director of the Court Opera, sent for Da Ponte, who records the following dialogue.[12]

'So, the *signor poeta* has used a ballet for Figaro?'
'Yes, Excellency.'
'The *signor poeta* does not know that the Emperor has forbidden dancing in his theatre?'[13]
'No, Excellency.'

'In that case, *Signor poeta*, I will tell you so now.'

'Yes, Excellency.'

'And I will tell you further, *signor poeta*, that you must take it out!'

His '*signor poeta*' had a significant tone of its own which gave the phrase the meaning of 'Signor Jack-ass' or something of the sort. But my 'Yes, Excellency' and 'No, Excellency' had their innuendo too.

'No, Excellency.'

'Have you the libretto with you?'

'Yes, Excellency.'

'Where is the scene with the dance?'

'Here it is, Excellency.'

'This is the way we do [it].'

Saying which he took two sheets of my manuscript, laid them carefully on the fire and returned the libretto to me, 'You see, *signor poeta*, that I can do anything.' And he honoured me with a second *Vale*.

I hurried to Mozart. On hearing such a story from me, he was desperate – he suggested going to the Count, giving [the Inspector] Bussani [who had started the intrigue] a beating, appealing to Caesar, withdrawing the score. It was a task for me to calm him. But at length I begged him to allow me just two days' time, and to leave everything to me. The dress rehearsal of the opera was to be held that day. I went in person to invite the Sovereign, and he promised to attend at the hour set. And in fact he came, and with him half the aristocracy of Vienna. . . . The first act went off amid general applause, but at the end [of Act III] comes a pantomimic scene between the Count and Susanna, during which the orchestra plays and the dance takes place. But the way His Excellency . . . had adapted the scene, all one could see was the Count and Susanna gesticulating and there being no music, it all looked like a puppet show. 'What's all this,' exclaimed the Emperor . . . His Majesty, therefore, sent for me . . . and [upon the Emperor's intervention] the scene which had been suppressed was in shape to be tried and the Emperor cried, 'Oh, now it's all right.'

Perhaps this episode was the reason for the première being postponed from 28 April to 1 May. Leopold Mozart, writing to his daughter, mentions the intrigues that were besetting the opera and its authors. He had his information from friends of Wolfgang's, the soprano Josepha Duschek and her husband from Prague, who had shortly before arrived in Salzburg to give concerts. On 28 April, Leopold writes:

Today your brother's opera, *Le Nozze di Figaro*, will be staged for the first time. It will be remarkable if it succeeds, for I know that extraordinary cabals have been mounted against him. Salieri with his followers have set heaven and earth in motion yet again to defeat him. Mr and Madame Duscheck have already said to me that your brother has so many cabals against him because he has gained such a great reputation through his special talent and cleverness . . .[14]

In the memoirs of Michael Kelly, we have a first-hand account by one of the singers who took part in the first performance (as Don Basilio and Don Curzio). Although written much later, in 1826, Kelly's reminiscences provide many delightful details about the first performance. He writes:

Of all the performers in this opera at that time, but one survives, – myself. It was allowed that never was opera stronger cast. I have seen it performed at different

The singer Michael Kelly, whose Memoirs *provide valuable information about the staging of Mozart's* Figaro *in 1786; anonymous watercolour (lost).*

Josepha Duschek, the celebrated soprano, friend of the Mozarts and their hostess in Prague; engraving by August Clar after J.F. Haake, 1796.

periods in other countries, and well too, but no more to compare with its original performance than light is to darkness. All the original performers had the advantage of the instructions of the composer, who transfused into their minds his inspired · meaning. . . . at the first rehearsal of the full band, Mozart was on the stage with his crimson pelisse and gold-laced cocked hat, giving the time of the music to the orchestra. Figaro's song, 'Non più andrai, farfallone amoroso', Benucci gave, with the greatest animation and power of voice. I was standing close to Mozart, who, sotto voce, was repeating, Bravo! Bravo! Benucci, and when Benucci came to the fine passage, 'Cherubino, alla vittoria, alla gloria militar', which he gave out with Stentorian lungs, the effect was electricity itself, for the whole of the performers on the stage, and those in the orchestra, as if actuated by one feeling of delight, vociferated Bravo! Bravo! Maestro. . . .[15]

Da Ponte wrote a foreword to the original printed libretto, in which he attempted to explain its complications and inordinate length. He mentions specifically 'the vastness and grandeur, the multiplicity of the musical pieces' and 'our particular desire to offer a quasi new kind of spectacle to the public.' Obviously the novelty of the opera was considered so extreme as to require such an explanation, and certainly one aspect of this novelty is the necessity for

the cast not only to sing beautifully, but also to act, and act brilliantly.[16] We have heard of the 'Stentorian' voice of Figaro, Francesco Benucci. Susanna was sung by Anna Storace (the family pronounced her name in the Italian fashion), who had conquered Viennese hearts. Count Zinzendorf, a better connoisseur of the female form than an operatic critic, described her appearance in some detail.[17] Luisa Laschi, as the Countess, was a famous Italian soprano more appreciated, for some reason, in Italy than in Austria. Stefano Mandini, the Count, was also praised by Kelly and others; like Benucci, Mandini was also a fine actor.

Anna (Nancy) Storace, the first Susanna, who returned to England in 1787; engraving by Pietro Bertelini, 1788.

At the first performance, which Mozart led from the fortepiano,[18] the public was divided in its reactions, probably because the piece did not yet 'sit' well with the singers and also because many in the audience had first to come to terms with its novelty. Yet we have Leopold Mozart's quotations from his son's letters which show that at the second performance five numbers were repeated, at the third seven, the little duet 'Aprite presto', between Susanna and Cherubino being given three times. The day after this third performance, Emperor Joseph ordered Count Orsini-Rosenberg to limit the encores, and to this effect an announcement was issued on 12 May, saying that no pieces for more than one voice could be repeated.

What was the critical reaction? Christopher Raeburn, who has uncovered many vital documents about the Da Ponte-Mozart operas and their singers, located a significant review in the *Wiener Realzeitung* of 11 July 1786. It begins with a slightly Bowdlerized quotation from *Le Barbier de Séville*, in which Figaro says, 'That which cannot be said nowadays, will be sung',[19] alluding to the fact that in Austria the play (*Figaros Hochzeit*) was still forbidden, although the opera based on it was not. The writer continues:

Francesco Benucci, who created the role of Figaro; engraving by Friedrich John after Dorfmeister.

The music by Herr Mozart was admired generally by the public at the first performance, and I make an exception only for those whose self-love and pride do not allow them to find anything good except in that which they themselves have composed. On the other hand, the public – and the public often finds itself in this position – did not actually know on that first day what to think. Moreover, it is fair to say that the first performance, because of the fact that the composition is very difficult, was not of the best. But now after several repeats, one would have to side with the cabals or with tastelessness if one were to entertain a different opinion than that which admits the music of Herr Mozart to be a masterpiece of the Art; it contains so many beauties, and such a richness of thoughts as can proceed only from the born genius. Some newspaper writers have taken it upon themselves to relate that Mozart's opera was no success at all. It can be imagined what kind of correspondents they are to circulate such lies.[20]

Scholars have amused themselves in tracing some of the prototypes for certain scenes or ideas in the music of *Figaro*. For example, that Susanna emerging from the cupboard in Act II derives from a scene in Grétry's *L'amant jaloux* which was on the boards of the Vienna Opera in 1780; or that the horns of the husbands referred to by Figaro in Act IV hark back to a similar passage in Paisiello's *Il rè Teodoro*, composed for Vienna in 1784; or that the huge finale in Act II – 940 bars – were inspired by the large-scale finales in Act I and

particularly Act II of Haydn's *La fedeltà premiata*, which Mozart probably heard before Christmas 1784; or that the Fandango in *Figaro*'s ballet derives from Gluck's ballet *Don Juan* (1761).

But essentially all these reminiscences are beside the point: they are merely contemporary aspects of the opera which have but little bearing on the work's timelessness. Even taking the opera strictly from the standpoint of 1786, its innovations are spectacular. One is the question of time and how it is used in the work. The whole action takes place within one day, as the alternative title of the play and opera indicates, 'The Mad Day' – Act I in the morning at breakfast time, Act II at high noon, Act III in the afternoon with, as it were, the hot Spanish sun streaming over the castle, and Act IV in the evening, with – if we follow the conceit of Luchino Visconti – the sun coming up as the Countess forgives her husband and everybody joins in 'Questo giorno di tormenti, di capricci, di follia, in concenti e in allegria solo amor può terminar' ('This day of torments, of whims, of madness can be terminated in agreement and happiness only through love'). It is a young man's opera: Mozart was twenty-nine when he wrote it, Count Almaviva and his lady are both young, as of course are Figaro and Susanna, Cherubino is a mere boy, Barbarina a girl of twelve or thirteen. It is a young man's music, then, and part of the brilliance of Act I is its very tempo. And one may show another way in which Mozart keeps this succession of fast tempi intact. Originally, the overture was not in the form we know it. When Mozart arrived at the end of the second subject, there was to have been a small slow movement in 6/8 time, a siciliano with oboe solo.

Mozart decided, very late in the proceedings, perhaps even after the first performance, to delete this slow movement; as a result of theatrical exigencies the overture in its final state contains a striking innovation, namely, it is perhaps the first overture to use sonata form without a development section (such as we know it in the later overtures to *Così* and *Die Zauberflöte*, where the recapitulation is prepared by such a long development). Another innovation is a lopsidedness in the way the overture begins, symbolic perhaps of a 'Mad Day's' beginning. This effect results from the main theme being seven bars long, rather than the usual eight. A lesser composer would have written:

One of the most profound innovations in *Figaro* is the orchestration, and especially the use of the woodwind – richer, of course, because larger than the band customary in Italian operas. The innovations comprised not just the increased size, however, but the complex fashion in which Mozart orchestrates. One of the characteristics of Italian opera overtures is the heavy use of pedal point (a term derived from organ language, meaning simply that the harmonies shift while the bass notes remain the same). Mozart considered this an eminently satisfactory stylistic trait and his scores contain many pedal points, but in his hands they often assume blazing inspiration. The forward motion is taken from a very old tradition, whereby basses and cellos play repeated notes, quavers or semiquavers, depending on the basic tempo. This use of pedal point combined with a crescendo was a standard device of the Mannheim school. If we examine the *Figaro* overture, we find that, out of its 294 bars, 119 – a significant percentage – are in the form of a pedal point. Now let us turn to the overture to Paisiello's *Barbiere di Siviglia*, which preceded *Figaro* in Vienna by three years. In it pedal point and Mannheim crescendo are also employed, but with a much smaller orchestra, and the wind instruments are more conservatively used. Compared with Paisiello's modest orchestra – no trumpets or timpani – Mozart's with its richer scoring, sounds immensely more exciting, notably in the *Figaro* overture.

And finally a word about keys. Like all Mozart's later operas, *Figaro* basically revolves around one central key, in this case D major, that is to say, the overture begins and the opera ends in D, and in between D is also often used for crucial pieces, such as Bartolo's aria 'La vendetta' in Act I, or the Count's great, dark-hued aria 'Vedrò, mentr'io sospiro, felice con servo mio' in Act III. But within the arch of this D major beginning and ending, we find an extraordinary subtlety and symmetry in the intervening keys. Act II, the first grand dénouement of the opera, is in the remote key of E flat, while Act III begins in A minor and ends, as does Act I, in C. The garden scene of Act IV begins in F minor, but the work ends in D. Even within acts, Mozart sets up brilliant mirror-like patterns for his finales: the progression in Act II works

Joseph Weigl (1766–1846), godson of Joseph Haydn, conducted Mozart's Figaro *in Vienna in 1786 (after the second performance) and again when the opera was revived in 1789; anonymous silhouette.*

Vincente Martin y Soler (also known as Martini), composer of the popular opera Una cosa rara *and of* L'arbore di Diana, *the libretto for which Da Ponte wrote simultaneously with those for* Don Giovanni *and Salieri's* Axur, Rè d'Ormus; *engraving by Jacob Adam after Joseph Kreutzinger, 1787.*

thus: E flat – B flat – G – C – F – B flat – E flat. In Act IV a similar pattern occurs: D – G – E flat – B flat – G – D. It is, in a way, formally perfect and almost a symbol of the rational century it represents.

Moreover, there are whole series of tonal subdivisions that illustrate the action, and these, too, have their own mirror-like perfection. Mozart's ability to provide this kind of finely balanced design may be illustrated in one last example. Mozart thought highly of the so-called Mannheim crescendo, a device he used in many of his instrumental works. In *Figaro*, the first example occurs at the end of the overture (the last part of the work to be composed). At the end of Act IV, after all has been – for the moment – settled, a similar crescendo occurs, also in D, also in fast 4/4, and even with the violin figures based on the interval of the fourth – all is part of this sense of formal perfection and symmetry, right down to the Mozartian hallmark ♩ ♩. ♪♩ ♩ in the drums and trumpets, the same in the overture's ending as in the work's conclusion.[21]

In his biography Niemetschek relates the scandals and difficulties which Mozart was submitted to as a result of *Le nozze di Figaro* – but it also provides a neat transition from Vienna to Prague, where the opera met with a better fate.

[*Le nozze di Figaro*] was performed in Vienna by the Italian Opera Company. If it is really true, as has been definitely asserted – and it is difficult to disbelieve reliable eye-witnesses – that disgruntled singers, out of hate, envy and ill-will, tried to spoil the opera by continually making mistakes at the first performance, the reader may gather how much the whole coterie of Italian singers and composers feared the superiority of Mozart's genius . . . They slandered him and did their best to belittle his art . . . [In Prague] the enthusiasm shown by the public [for *Figaro*] was without precedent; they could not hear it enough. A piano version was made by one of our best masters, Herr Kucharz; it was arranged for wind band, as a quintet and for German dances . . . in addition, there was the incomparable orchestra of our Opera, which understood how to execute Mozart's ideas so accurately and diligently . . . The well-known Orchestra Director Strobach, since deceased, declared that at each performance he and his colleagues were so excited that they would gladly have started from the beginning again in spite of the hard work it entailed.[22]

In Vienna, performances of *Figaro* were given throughout the season, the last on 18 December; then it was taken off, for on 17 November Martini's (or properly Martin y Soler's) new opera *Una cosa rara*, also with libretto by Da Ponte, was staged. The first performance of this lyrical work elicited, according to its poet, 'howls of enthusiasm'. For the next two years, *Figaro* was not played in Vienna, but in Prague, where the nearly bankrupt Bondini Company took it on in 1786, the opera proved such a success that (1) the members of the Bondini Company, instead of disbanding as they had planned to do, reconstituted themselves, and (2) they decided to invite Mozart himself to come to Prague and hear the performance. After New Year's 1787, Constanze and Wolfgang left for the Bohemian capital, where they were received with acclaim. The composer was a triumph, *Figaro* was a triumph, and after hearing one performance on 17 January, Mozart conducted the next one, five days later. On the 19th he gave a concert, at which the 'Prague'

166

Symphony was first performed and the public cheered his improvisations on 'Non più andrai'. The quality of the performance of *Figaro* in Prague seems to have been even better than in Vienna, particularly in the orchestra. A Bohemian newspaper wrote: 'Connoisseurs who have seen the opera in Vienna would like to assert that the performance here [in Prague] went off much better; and very likely because the wind instruments, on which the Bohemians are well known to be the finest masters, have a great deal to do in the whole piece; particular pleasure was given by the interchanges of the horns and the trumpets. . . .'[23] This, too, was a Mozartian speciality, the fine differentiation between these two members of the brass family. Pasquale Bondini naturally wanted to capitalize on Mozart's popularity in Prague and offered him 100 ducats to compose a new opera for the 1787 season, when *Figaro* was no longer in the repertoire in Vienna, *Una cosa rara* was the toast of the town, and the German Opera and concert repertoire was dominated by Carl Ditters von Dittersdorf, a composer much appreciated by the Emperor. Mozart watched while Ditters produced extremely successful German *Singspiele*, an oratorio, an Italian opera and twelve new symphonies based on Ovid's *Metamorphoses*. At the beginning of October 1787, he returned to Prague with a new libretto by Da Ponte – *Don Giovanni*. Da Ponte explains that he wrote the libretti for three operas simultaneously: for Martini 'L'arbore di Diana', for Salieri 'Tarare' and for Mozart 'Don Giovanni'. He recalls:

Carl Ditters von Dittersdorf, whose compositions found great favour with Emperor Joseph II; anonymous pastel, 1764.

> The three subjects fixed on, I went to the Emperor, laid my idea before him and explained that my intention was to write the three operas contemporaneously.
>
> 'You will not succeed', he replied.
>
> 'Perhaps not', said I, 'but I am going to try. I shall write evenings for Mozart, imagining I am reading the *Inferno*; mornings I shall work for Martini, and pretend I am studying Petrarch; my afternoons will be for Salieri. He is my Tasso! . . .' I returned home and went to work. I sat down at my table and did not leave it for twelve hours continuous – a bottle of Tokay to my right, a box of Seville [tobacco] to my left, in the middle an ink-well. A beautiful girl of sixteen – I should have preferred to love her only as a daughter, but alas . . . ! – was living in the house with her mother, who took care of the family, and came to my room at the sound of the bell. To tell the truth, the bell rang rather frequently . . .'[24]

What Da Ponte does not say is that he and Mozart had laid their hands on a new opera on the old subject of Don Juan entitled *Il convitato di pietra*, with libretto by Giovanni Bertati and music by Giuseppe Gazzaniga, who had been composing successfully since 1762. This Gazzaniga work had been launched in Venice in January 1787 and was soon being given all over Italy, but its only claim to fame nowadays is its tenuous connection with Mozart's masterpiece. Mozart and Da Ponte made brief use of some of the details, musical and literary; but as in *Figaro*, there are so many astounding new features in *Don Giovanni* that any reminiscences of other men's works are not only inessential but irritatingly inconsequential to our understanding of this complex opera.

When Mozart arrived in Prague to begin rehearsals, he saw at once that a fortnight was totally insufficient and that the opera could not be given on 14 October. This date had been chosen, probably in haste, to celebrate the

Archduchess Maria Theresa, niece of Joseph II; Don Giovanni was to have been performed in Prague on the occasion of her marriage to Prince Anton Clemens of Saxony, but on the day (14 October 1787) the opera was not ready and Le nozze di Figaro was substituted; silhouette by Franz Deiwel.

arrival in Prague of Archduchess Maria Theresa, a niece of Joseph II, on her wedding trip en route to Dresden, the home of her husband, Prince Anton of Saxony. For this purpose a libretto of *Don Giovanni* had been hastily prepared and printed for the censor in Vienna – one single copy has survived[25] – but in which Da Ponte carefully omitted the end of Act I, with its attempted seduction scene of Zerlina as well as Donna Anna's description of Don Giovanni's attack on her honour. The libretto states specifically that the performance is in celebration of the arrival of the royal couple, but in fact *Don Giovanni* was not yet ready. Alfred Einstein, in a fascinating article[26] written shortly before his death, proposed that Mozart deliberately caused *Don Giovanni* not to be given as being unsuitable for the eyes and ears of a royal bride, but in its place *Figaro* was performed, and at least one diarist (Zinzendorf) thought it in very poor taste to do so (*L'arbore di Diana* had been performed for the young pair in Vienna on 1 October, and on 19 October he noted, with some justification, that *L'arbore*, with its delicate ridicule of chastity, was also a most unsuitable piece for the young couple).

For once in his life, Mozart might have been diplomatically adroit. On 9 October, Da Ponte also came to assist with the rehearsals, and being an old intriguer, he may have smoothed over any difficulties, but the opera was certainly causing problems. The day after the supposed première, Mozart wrote to a friend: 'You will probably think that my opera has now been performed – but you will be slightly mistaken. First, this local theatrical troupe is not as clever as that in Vienna, in being able to rehearse such an opera in so short a time. Secondly, I found upon my arrival so little preparation and organization that it would have been quite impossible to have given it on the fourteenth . . .'[27]

The première finally took place on 29 October, still not quite properly rehearsed and the overture, apparently, completely unrehearsed. The first newspaper report admits that 'The opera is in fact exceedingly difficult to perform, and everybody nevertheless admired how good the performance was, considering how little time there had been to rehearse.'[28] The opera was an enormous success, and Mozart wrote that he wished his good friends 'could have been here for just one evening to share my pleasure! – Perhaps it will yet be performed in Vienna? – I hope so. – They are trying everything to persuade me to stay here for a few months and to compose yet another opera, but flattering though this offer is, I cannot accept it. . . .'[29]

As to the libretto and its music, the very figure of the Don has always been an enormous challenge for any singer, because like the opera itself, the part is ambivalent in the extreme and therefore, like Hamlet, lends itself to a variety of different meanings. The same ambivalence extends to the other roles as well. Was Donna Anna seduced by the Don? What is the character of Don Ottavio? Mozart himself may even have been puzzled by this figure, for, as if to make up for Don Ottavio's stiffness, he composes music of particular poignancy and beauty for him. Is the work a comic opera or a great tragedy? When Mozart and Da Ponte wrote it for Prague, there was the beautiful sextet that followed the Don's descent to Hell, but all this was changed in Vienna when the work was put on there in 1788. Mozart omitted the final sextet, thus producing a tragic ending.[30]

Of the various innovations, two seem remarkable even today, and especially if we try to imagine the effect the work will have had on cultivated audiences of 1787 and 1788. The first is Mozart's introduction of terror into the world of music. Previously, Handel had produced passages of stunning power, hailstones and thunderbolts, J.S. Bach had rent the veil of the Temple in twain, and the Italian madrigalists had lingered chromatically over death; but never before had a deliberate attempt been made to portray naked fear on the stage or in the concert hall – or certainly not at this level.[31] To aid his already rich orchestral score, Mozart took the trombones from the choir loft and once again, following Gluck's experiment in *Alceste* (1768) – which was not adopted in those days by others in Vienna – placed them in the orchestra pit. Here they symbolize hell's demons as the Commendatore's statue appears on stage to condemn Don Giovanni for seduction, rape and murder.

Many centuries before Mozart was born, Flemish composers were famous for their ability to construct the most complicated scenes using contrapuntal forms, in some cases so complicated that they cannot readily be apprehended aurally, even by trained musicians. This fascination with the mathematical side of music flourished in J.S. Bach's writing and, nearer to Mozart, in that of Haydn. The year that *Don Giovanni* was performed in Vienna, Mozart demonstrated his contrapuntal prowess in the finale of the 'Jupiter' Symphony, which rivals J.S. Bach in its ingenuity and complexity. But in *Don Giovanni* Mozart may be said to have achieved an even more exalted plane of instrumental complexity. In the Act I finale there is a ball scene in which three orchestras on stage enter one after another until all three are playing simultaneously. The first plays the famous Minuet in G in 3/4 time, scored for oboes, horns and strings; next, Orchestra II tunes up and plays a Contredanse in G in 2/4 time; finally, Orchestra III tunes up and joins in with a German Dance in 3/8 time. One might add a final example of Mozart's extraordinary use of form in this Act I finale, which is constructed along the following strikingly original symmetrical lines:

```
                            6. Allegro
                    5. Adagio   7. Maestoso
              4. Minuet              8. Minuet
          3. Allegretto                  9. Allegretto
      2. Andante                            10. Andante
  1. Allegro                                    11. Allegro
```

The use of keys in this opera is equally extraordinary. To take one example, in Act II the music moves away from the work's principal key of D minor-major and, after Zerlina's 'Vedrai carino', we find ourselves in E flat, the key of the celebrated sextet at the beginning of which Elvira thinks she is with her faithless lover, Don Giovanni (actually Leporello in disguise). In Da Ponte-Mozart fashion she has forgiven Don Giovanni, and this reminds us that forgiveness is an essential factor in all three Da Ponte operas. Since it occurs with such emphasis, it is clear that Mozart and his poet regarded this loving forgiveness as crucial to their concept of life and drama. So here we are in E flat, with Elvira and Leporello (disguised as the Don), hiding in 'un buio loco' (in a dark place). Suddenly, as Don Ottavio enters with Donna Anna, the key moves from E flat to D major and Mozart brings in the trumpets and drums, softly, in one of those great orchestral washes of colour that so often transfigure his music. And from D major the key changes abruptly to D minor. Why? Because Don Ottavio says, 'L'ombra omai del tuo genitore pena avrà de tuoi martir' ('Your father's spirit will be saddened at your distress'), and we are swiftly confronted with the work's basic key, D minor, the punishment key for murder. As swiftly as the music enters D major and D minor, it is back in E flat. Leporello (as Don Giovanni) is discovered, reveals himself, and the sextet ends in general confusion.

Act I, scene 20, calls for special comment. The hall where Don Giovanni will give his reception is 'illuminated and prepared for a grand *festa di ballo*'. After the introductory scene with Don Giovanni, Leporello, Masetto and Zerlina, the key changes to C major as Don Ottavio, Donna Anna and Donna Elvira – all three masked – enter to martial music. After the three masked figures have greeted their host politely, Don Giovanni answers rather obliquely 'E aperto a tutti, a tutti quanti, viva, viva la libertà' ('It is open to everyone, long live liberty!'). Now this little phrase 'viva la libertà' is suddenly seized on by everybody and turned into a triumphal march with Mozart's inimitable trumpets and drums in his 'fingerprint' dotted rhythm – bar after bar. In the context, this makes no apparent sense whatever. But it is obviously a crucial point in the drama. What can it mean? Clemens Höslinger, of the Haus-, Hof- und Staatsarchiv in Vienna, has proposed that it is Da Ponte's and Mozart's scarcely veiled personal tribute to Joseph II, to his ideas of liberty (freedom) and enlightenment. Everyone in the eighteenth-century audience would have understood the hint. We may suppose that even if he only heard the opera in private, Joseph II understood the message. Almost immediately thereafter, he appointed Mozart 'Imperial Royal Chamber Musician', at a salary of 800 gulden. Was that a coincidence?

Da Ponte's *Memoirs* are the principal source for what happens next.

I had not seen the première of *Don Giovanni* at Prague, but Mozart wrote to me at once of its marvellous reception. The Emperor sent for me, and overloading me with gracious felicitations, presented me with another hundred ducats [for having completed all three libretti in time] and told me that he was longing to see *Don Giovanni*. Mozart returned, and since Joseph was shortly to depart for the field, hurried the score to the copyist, to write out the parts. The opera went on the stage and . . . need I recall it? . . . *Don Giovanni* did not please! Everyone, except Mozart, thought that there was something missing. Additions were made; some of the arias were changed; it was offered for a second performance. *Don Giovanni* did not please! And what did the Emperor say? He said, 'That opera is divine; I should venture that it is more beautiful than *Figaro*. But such music is not meat for the teeth of my Viennese!' I reported the remark to Mozart, who replied quietly: 'Give them time to chew on it!' He was not mistaken. On his advice I strove to procure frequent repetitions of the opera: at each performance the applause increased. . . .[32]

One is loath to spoil a good story, but in fact Joseph II never heard *Don Giovanni* on the stage in Vienna. He could not have done so, because he left for the field on 25 March and was away until 5 December. The opera was not staged in Vienna until May and on the day of the last performance (15 December 1788), the Emperor was ill.[33]

Mozart made widespread changes and substitutions, one of which, 'Dalla sua pace', has achieved immortality, whereas the duet between Zerlina and Leporello is never performed; and Elvira's new scene with the aria 'Mi tradi' is dramatically senseless, as Einstein says, but has now become part of our view of the opera. It seems certain that Mozart planned to omit the final sextet after the Don is dragged to Hell, for the manuscript score (now in Paris) shows a conclusion with all the other characters closing on a cadential 'Ah!' But this 'Ah!' was later cancelled. The Vienna libretto for 1788 certainly omits the final sextet, but perhaps Mozart later restored it. The original performance material has not survived, so we cannot be sure. There is also another ending

Set design by Joseph Quaglio for the graveyard scene in Act II of Don Giovanni, *performed in German in Mannheim in 1789.*

for the overture in D major rather than modulating to the opening F major number of Act I. All these changes are not only superfluous but damaging to the clear design of the Prague version.

After the première of *Don Giovanni* on 7 May 1788, 'Prince R' (unidentified) gave a large party, which was later reported in the *AMZ* (I, 52):

Most of the musical connoisseurs of Vienna were present, also Joseph Haydn. Mozart was not there. There was much talk about the new work. After the fine ladies and gentlemen had talked themselves out, some of the connoisseurs took up the work. They all admitted that it was the valuable work of a versatile genius and was of an endless imagination; but for one it was too full, for another too chaotic, for a third too unmelodic, for a fourth it was uneven, etc. In general one cannot but admit that there is something true in all these opinions. Everyone had spoken by now only – not Father Haydn. At last they asked the modest artist for his opinion. He said, with his usual fastidiousness: 'I cannot settle the argument. But one thing I know' – he added very energetically – 'and that is that Mozart is the greatest composer that the world now has.' The ladies and gentlemen were silent after that.

On 29 August 1789, *Le nozze di Figaro* was revived in Vienna. We may suspect that Da Ponte was behind this event, simply because Mozart was obliged to compose two new insertion arias for his own opera. Nancy Storace had gone back to England and the new Susanna was Adriana Ferrarese del Bene, who had recently become Da Ponte's mistress. The two new arias 'Un moto di gioia' (K.579) replacing 'Venite, inginocchiatevi' in Act II (*not* entered into Mozart's thematic catalogue) and the Rondo 'Al desio di chi t'adora' (K.577), which is in the catalogue under the month of July 1789. Constanze was in Baden, taking the cure, and about 19 August Mozart wrote to her, 'The little aria which I wrote for Ferraresi [*sic*] will be a success, I trust, if she is capable of singing it naively, which I very much doubt. She liked it very much, I ate there – I think *Figaro* will surely be on Sunday, but I'll let you know before – . . .'[34] Other additions and changes were also made in the 1789 revival.[35]

Let us consider for a moment the ramifications of Joseph II's decision to re-introduce Italian opera at the Burgtheater. The immense success of Paisiello's *Il barbiere di Siviglia* shows that Joseph's decision was a measure of his ability to judge popular taste and preferences (also his own, in the case of Italian opera). Between 22 April 1783, when the Italian opera opened again, and 25 January 1790, the eve of Mozart's third Da Ponte opera, *Così fan tutte*, fifty-nine *opere buffe* were performed in Vienna. Among the German composers represented, Mozart was by far the most successful, with twenty performances of *Le nozze di Figaro* and fifteen of *Don Giovanni*, but in terms of popularity Mozart lagged far behind the most successful composers of Italian opera – Sarti (91 perfor-mances), Martin y Soler (105), Cimarosa (124), Salieri (138) and Paisiello (166).[36] Whereas in the twentieth century Mozart has swept the Italian composers of his day off the boards, as it were, the situation was very different in the eighteenth century. The only successes Mozart's Italian operas enjoyed outside Vienna and Prague were performances in German translations given in German-speaking countries. During Mozart's lifetime not one of his Italian operas was given complete in England, France, Russia, Spain, Portugal or Italy (when *Figaro* was put on in Monza in the autumn of 1787, and in the Teatro della Pergola, Florence, in the spring of 1788, the last two acts were newly composed by Angelo Tarchi).[37] In fact, apart from Vienna and Prague, the only known Italian-language performances of *Figaro* in Mozart's lifetime were at Potsdam (autumn 1790) and probably at Eszterháza (August–September 1790).[38] In the case of *Don Giovanni*, two performances in Italian are known to have taken place (apart from Prague and Vienna) when the Guardasoni Troupe (Bondini's successor) from Prague took it to Leipzig as a *Gesamtgastspiel*, performing it for the first time there on 15 June 1788, and to Warsaw (14 October 1789). *Così fan tutte* was performed in Italian during Mozart's lifetime: in Prague some time in 1791 (the libretto is dated), in Leipzig in the summer of 1791 and in Dresden on 5 October 1791.[39]

The rehearsals of *Don Giovanni* were the subject of a long exchange of letters between Count Orsini-Rosenberg in Vienna and Joseph II in the field. In April Rosenberg had to admit that the music was exceptional, to which the Emperior replied sarcastically in a *Handbillet* of 3 May that 'votre goût commence à devenir raisonnable' ('your taste is beginning to become reasonable'). The Emperor continues that it would hardly surprise him if the opera were to fail, since he knows what is appreciated in Vienna; and the right course would be to have one year with no opera at all in order to make the public more moderate in its expectations. When Rosenberg noted that the opera made enormous demands on the singers,[40] the Emperor replied tersely that he realized that 'the music of Mozard [*sic*] really is too difficult in the vocal department,'[41] which suggests that he found Mozart altogether problematical in the theatre. Because of illness, Joseph II did not attend *Don Giovanni* in the Burgtheater on 15 December; after this the opera was taken off and never given again in the Austrian capital during Mozart's lifetime.[42] Count Zinzendorf, always a barometer of taste in high places, thought *Figaro* a bore when he first heard it in the company of his mistress Louise von Diede, though he eventually came to like it better. When *Don Giovanni* was given in Vienna, Zinzendorf wrote in his Diary that his friend Madame de la Lippe 'found the music learned, little suited for singing.'[43]

'In the existing political climate of Vienna', writes Michael Robinson, 'Mozart . . . was an outsider, a man who although recognised as possessing exceptional talent did not have the right qualifications (because not an Italian and not recognised by the Italian musical world as its equal) to become pre-eminent among the opera composers commissioned by the court. How was he to establish his rightful place among them? Naturally he had to show that he understood all the conventions of Italian comic opera and work within these conventions. But this was not enough. Not only had he to compose like an Italian; he had to do better than most Italians to obtain equal status with them.'[44]

Mozart's success with his Italian operas was, in the event, posthumous, particularly in the case of the most perfect example, musically and formally speaking – *Così fan tutte*, the most maligned, misunderstood and for a long period ignored of the three Da Ponte operas. Its librettist is curiously discreet about its origins, saying almost nothing except that it had been performed. Constanze, speaking to the Novellos in 1829, was equally reticent. 'She did not admire the plot of *Così fan tutte*,' wrote Vincent Novello, 'but agreed with me that such music would carry any piece through . . .' His wife Mary then adds, 'Salieri's enmity arose from Mozart's setting the *Così fan tutte* which he [Salieri[had originally commenced and given up as unworthy [of] his musical invention.'[45] Even more oblique is a reference in Niemetschek, taken over partly by Nissen: 'Mozart completed *Così fan tutte* in the year 1790 . . . One wonders in general how that great intellect could lower himself to waste his heavenly and sweet melodies on such a miserable and trashy text. But it was not within his powers to turn down the commission, and the text was specifically recommended to him.'

Now it has always been maintained that Joseph II commissioned this new opera from Da Ponte and Mozart, and there is one curious and interesting fact that may suggest the Emperor's hand in the proceedings: on or about 29 December 1789, Mozart writes to Michael Puchberg as follows: '. . . next month I shall receive from the direction (according to the present arrangement) 200 ducats for my opera [*Così fan tutte*] . . .'[46] The 200 ducats equalled 900 gulden, double the usual honorarium paid by the Court Theatre for new operas in those days. And Zinzendorf, for the first time in his criticisms of Mozart operas, found that 'The music is charming and the subject quite amusing.'[47]

In the customary description of the opera's origins we are told the following (in some versions, the story takes place in Istria,[48] on the Adriatic coast; in others, in Vienna). It seems that in 1788, shortly after the outbreak of the war with the Ottoman Empire, one of the annual masked balls was held in the Redoutensaal. Two gentlemen of the Court were to escort their two ladies there, but explained at the last minute that they had been called up by the Imperial Royal War Ministry and must leave at once to fight the Turks. They did not leave, however, but disguised themselves completely and, using a friend, arranged to be introduced to their ladies, but each, as it were, to the wrong lady. The seduction seemed not only possible, but was put to the test, and with success.

Joseph II, returning from the Ottoman Wars in the autumn of 1789, remembered this incident, which of course appealed to his ambivalent, not to say negative, attitude towards women in general; the plot, of course, is the basis for *Così fan tutte*. In fact, however, there is no evidence for this story (which in any case sounds too good to be true) during the eighteenth century: the earliest dated reference to the 'real life' version dates from 1837.[49] Perhaps one day more evidence along these lines will come to light.

The title of the opera has its own special history. The words of *Così fan tutte* come from *Le nozze di Figaro*, Act I, No. 7, the Terzetto between Susanna, Don Basilio and the Count, which begins with the words 'Cosa sento!' ('What do I hear'). Cherubino has overheard the Count making advances to Susanna, and the Count takes Cherubino to task for trying to seduce the peasant-girl

Barbarina. Don Basilio, the sophisticated cynic, sings 'Così fan tutte le belle, non c'è alcuna novità' ('That's what all beautiful women do, there's nothing new in that'). Not only do the words contain the title of the later opera, but in the following phrase, when Don Basilio repeats the words –

– the undulating passage in quavers will become part of *Così fan tutte*'s overture (in the Presto section, after the slow introduction):

This reference is an 'in' joke so obscure that only highly trained musicians would recognize it; but perhaps Mozart was so bold as to point it out to his by no means unmusical Emperor, by then a very sick man. In the middle of April 1789 Joseph nearly died; but he recovered, though coughing constantly. His lungs were ruined, and by the time he returned from the wars in November it was clear that he had not long to live. Mozart and Da Ponte knew what would happen to their opera if the Emperor should die before it was staged, and we may presume that they worked at full speed, which as we have seen was quicker than anyone else. By the end of December, the first vocal rehearsals were under way. On 30 December, Haydn left Eszterháza for Vienna, and on the day before, Mozart wrote to Michael Puchberg:

. . . Tomorrow evening on account of the appointment there can be nothing at our house. – I have too much work – if you see Zisler anyway, please tell him – Thursday [31 December] however, I invite you (but just you alone) to come at 10 o'clock in the morning to me, for a small opera rehearsal – only you and *Haydn* are invited. Then I'll tell you *a viva voce* about all the cabals of Salieri, which however came to nothing . . .[50]

A few weeks later, on 20 January 1790, Mozart wrote again to Puchberg:

Tomorrow is the first orchestral rehearsal in the theatre. Haydn will go with me – if your affairs allow of it, and if perhaps you would like to attend the rehearsal, you need only have the goodness to come to me tomorrow morning at 10 o'clock, and we will all go together . . .[51]

Haydn could have heard any of the first three performances, which took place on 26, 28 and 30 January, before he returned to Hungary.

On 20 February, Joseph II died. *Così* had to be taken off until the official mourning period was over; it then received six more performances in June, July and August.

Da Ponte was a great cynic, as his *Memoirs* show, and no doubt he intended *Così fan tutte o sia La scuola degli amanti* to be monumentally cynical, as the

Joseph Eybler (1764–1846), who assisted in the preparation of Così fan tutte *in 1790; anonymous silhouette.*

opera's full title shows, with its reference to 'The School for Lovers'. Mozart, however, has removed a great deal of the cynicism. As we have seen, in the previous two operas, two of the pillars on which the music was built are love and forgiveness, the deepest love and the deepest forgiveness of which human beings are capable. I submit that *Così fan tutte* is the supreme example of Mozart's loving forgiveness because, in this most musically perfect of all his operas, there is the most to forgive, and consequently the greatest demand on true love. Mozart himself forgave Constanze when she was taking the cure in Baden in August 1789 – for what? In his letter to her he wrote:

> Dear Little Wife: – I want to speak very frankly to you. – You have no reason to be sad. – You have a husband who loves you, who does everything for you of which he is capable – as far as your gamy leg is concerned, you have only to be patient, this [cure] will quite certainly do you good; I am of course delighted when you are happy – really – but I wish that you would not behave so commonly as you sometimes do – you are far too free with N. N., also with N. N. when he was still in Baden – consider that N. N.s are not so coarse with other women, whom they perhaps know better than you, as they are with yourself, and even N. N., who is otherwise a decent chap and especially respectful to women, even he as a result allows himself in his letters to write the most appalling and rude remarks – a woman has to keep her respect, otherwise she becomes a topic of conversation – Dear, excuse me that I am so open with you, but my peace of mind and the happiness of us both demand it – remember that you yourself once admitted that you *give way* too easily – you know what then happens – remember too the promise you made to me – O God! just try it, My Dear – be cheerful and happy and be nice to me – don't vex yourself and me with unnecessary jealousy – have faith in my love, you have enough proof of it – and you will see how happy we can be, you must believe that only the wise conduct of a wife binds the husband to her with hoops of steel – adieu – tomorrow I shall kiss you from my heart.
>
> Mozart.[52]

Mozart evidently thought he had reason to forgive Constanze, but perhaps there was less to forgive than he imagined, otherwise Constanze would hardly have preserved the letter after Mozart died.

When the lovers say farewell in Act I of the opera, we are treated to the great and melting quintet, 'Di scrivermi ogni giorno' ('Write to me every day'). But the unbelievable then begins to happen, not only between these lovers, but in Mozart's music: for the listener has to be convinced, just as the 'Turkish' suitors have to persuade the young women to be false to their lovers; and the only way that this is remotely possible is, of course, via the music. And touching though the farewell music of Act I is, as also in 'Soave sia il vento' ('May the wind be gentle') when the men sail away from the Bay of Naples to the war, the music that Mozart writes at the point when the pairs of lovers are reversed reaches depths of eroticism and passion undreamt of at the beginning. For the great scene in the garden, 'Secondate, aurette amiche' ('Help me, gentle breezes'), Ferrando and Guglielmo engage a wind band (*Harmonie*) to assist them in their designs. How remarkable that the music is reminiscent of the Serenade for Thirteen Instruments (K.361), itself perhaps real marriage music. All this is in deadly earnest. Concerning the two

manipulators of the action, Don Alfonso and Despina, Richard Mohr has this to say:

> As for Despina and Don Alfonso, presented in their entirety they are more than stock jesters. It is even possible to feel a little uneasy about them and to regard their harmless joke in a more sinister light. They come upon the scene at that critical moment when the four lovers are totally immersed in each other and immediately become the serpent in the Garden of Eden. They find only the beginnings of love charming, and their instant response is to create dissension and misunderstanding.[53]

When Ferrando and Guglielmo return from the Turkish wars and reveal themselves, we are confronted with Mozart's (and Da Ponte's) greatest act of forgiveness. Perhaps the whole perfidy can never be forgiven, for all four – or rather all six, including Despina and Don Alfonso – are equally guilty of a gross act of deception, but more – of traducing love.

The seduction plot has, perhaps, a very eighteenth-century quality, something that the nineteenth century found repugnant and the twentieth finds fascinating. There is, I believe, a parallel in the cruel and heartless treatment of woman in the literature of the period, e.g. in Laclos' ruthless *Les Liaisons dangereuses*, which appeared in Paris just a few years before Mozart composed *Così*. Nowadays, we are no longer shocked by the open sexuality in Laclos or Mozart (Da Ponte), but we are appalled by the way in which the seduction and ruin of the women are coldly plotted. The book was banned in

Paris after the Bourbon kings had been restored in 1814, and at that same time moves were made to rewrite the plot of *Così*, especially in Germany, where the opera was frequently performed. The calculated seduction in *Così* is in fact the one aspect of Da Ponte's (and Mozart's) thinking which is almost totally alien to many people today.

Mozart recognized the enormous difference in emotional texture between *Così* and the previous Da Ponte operas. His treatment of the keys is more intricate and formally perfect than ever before, and here it can be demonstrated that Mozart owes something to Haydn.

In Haydn's *La fedeltà premiata* (which Mozart probably heard in Vienna at the end of 1784), the finales of Acts I and II are based not on the usual tonic-dominant-subdominant relationship, but in *keys of thirds*. This was a complete novelty and must have fascinated Mozart, particularly since Haydn uses the third keys in chains to follow the *downwards* progression of the plot; as things become increasingly complex and unsatisfactory, the keys proceed to illustrate the situation. In Haydn's Act I finale, the scheme is:

– in other words, four moves down a third and then down half a step. And what do we find in *Così*, right after the overture? Almost the same progression:

In Mozart's Act I the tonic (C major) is carefully avoided until No. 13, the sextet 'Alla bella Despina'. This is the stage at which Don Alfonso will introduce the new 'Turkish' suitors, and where the gross deception begins; and from here until the end of No. 27 (Ferrando's cavatina, 'Tradito, schernito') and then the famous line 'Così fan tutte' at the conclusion of No. 30 (Duet, Ferrando, Don Alfonso) the use of C major is avoided throughout the rest of Act I and Act II. As in *Figaro*, the two finales of *Così* are in a kind of mirror pattern:

Act I

D – G – B flat – E flat – G – B flat – D

Act II

C – E flat – A flat – E – D – E flat – B flat – E flat – B flat – F – G – C

↑

arrival of soldiers returning from
the wars announced by chorus

If the opening progression of chain thirds downwards (in Act I) must have hinted to the cognoscenti that all will not be well for the lovers, Mozart has reserved his cleverest borrowing from Haydn for Act II, where the borrower expands vastly on the borrowed. In the finale of Act II of *La fedeltà premiata*, Haydn sets up the following third-relationship:

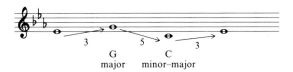

G major   C minor–major

That significant rise of a third followed by a downwards move from the fifth to the tonic is now put to extraordinary use in Act II of *Così*:

E flat triad
- No. 19 – G = Aria, Despina
- No. 20 – B♮ = Aria, Dorabella
- No. 21 – E♭ = Duet with chorus (wind band)

B flat triad
- No. 22 – D = Quartet
- No. 23 – F = Duettino
- No. 24 – B♮ = Aria

C triad
- No. 25 – E = Rondo
- No. 26 – G = Aria
- No. 27 – C minor–C major = Aria

Mozart's orchestration of this operatic masterpiece of 1789 and 1790 is quite different from anything before: there is something glassily brilliant about his use of C major, and the trumpets have far more to do than in the previous two Da Ponte operas – they are even used in the (for Mozart) unusual key of B flat ('Come scoglio'). The differentiation between horns and trumpets – which critics had noted at once in *Figaro* – is further refined here. In the grand Terzetto (No. 3) in Act I, in C major, Mozart used trumpets and drums, but not horns, which he is saving for the introduction of the two ladies in the next number (in A major). Similarly the little chorus (No. 8), the 'Military march at some distance' which summons the two lovers to the wars, has trumpets and drums, but not horns; Mozart is saving the horns for the E major Terzettino (No. 10), the lovely farewell 'Soave sia il vento'. The orchestration of the entire opera is of immaculate precision, pointing up subtleties of the plot. However, there seems for once to be a slight but nonetheless definite division of intent between Da Ponte's text and Mozart's music. The composer, unlike Da Ponte, was not a perfect cynic, and he involves himself far more than the text warrants in the fates of the ladies when the roles are reversed. This is partly because Mozart always showed a special perception for the problems, aspirations and motivations of women, and partly because he has gone to great lengths to convince the audience of the new state of affairs, having perhaps even persuaded himself of the validity of the untruthful situation.

Hence I believe that the particular poignancy of *Così fan tutte* lies in the fact that the necessity for forgiveness is present not only at the end of the opera but throughout the scenes of deception, when the audience know – although the ladies do not yet – that their actions require more forgiveness than does any other action, perhaps, in any other Mozart opera. The emotions generated are therefore doubly powerful and the cynicism of the libretto is in part assuaged.

X

The End of Mozart's Subscription Concerts Austria's Folly and Mozart's Misery

---

Johann Nepomuk Hummel; miniature portrait on ivory by Nannette Rosenzweig.

Among Mozart's pupils during 1787 and 1788 was a boy (born at Preßburg in 1778) named Johann Nepomuk Hummel, who later became Haydn's successor with Prince Esterházy in Eisenstadt, and was well known both as a pianist and as a composer. Hummel left a sketch for the beginning of a Mozart biography: 'He was of a small build, his face was pale; his physiognomy contained much that was pleasant and friendly, combined with something of a melancholy seriousness; his large blue eyes gleamed brightly. In a circle of good friends he could also be quite merry, lively and witty; sometimes he could be sarcastic about sundry matters! . . .'[1]

Another description of Mozart comes from the pen of the singer Michael Kelly (O'Kelly). He records his introduction to Mozart, who

favoured the company by performing fantasies and capriccios on the pianoforte. His feeling, the rapidity of his fingers, the great execution and strength of his left hand particularly, and the apparent inspiration of his modulations, astounded me. After this splendid performance we sat down to supper, and I had the pleasure of being placed at table between him and his wife. After supper the young branches of our host had a dance, and Mozart joined them. Madame Mozart told me, that great as his genius was, he was an enthusiast in dancing, and often said that his taste lay in that art, rather than in music.

He was a remarkably small man, very thin and pale, with a profusion of fine fair hair, of which he was rather vain. He gave me a cordial invitation to his house, of which I availed myself, and passed a great part of my time there. He always received me with kindness and hospitality. He was remarkably fond of punch, of which beverage I have seen him take copious draughts. He was also fond of billiards, and had an excellent billiard table in his house. Many and many a game have I played with him, but always came off second best. He gave Sunday concerts, at which I never was missing . . .

My friend Attwood (a worthy man, and an ornament to the musical world) was Mozart's favourite scholar, and it gives me great pleasure to record what Mozart said to me about him; his words were, 'Attwood is a young man for whom I have a sincere affection and esteem; he conducts himself with great propriety, and I feel much pleasure in telling you, that he partakes more of my style than any scholar I ever had; and I predict, that he will prove a sound musician.' Mozart was very liberal in giving praise to those who deserved it; but felt a thorough contempt for insolent mediocrity . . .

[The English group in Vienna also included Nancy Storace's brother, Stephen, who] gave a quartet party to his friends. The players were tolerable; not one of them excelled on the instrument he played, but there was a little science among them, which I dare say will be acknowledged when I name them:

The First Violin . . . . HAYDN.
The Second Violin . . . . . . BARON DITTERSDORF.
The Violoncello . . . . VANHALL.
The Tenor Viola . . . . MOZART.

The poet Casti and [the Italian composer] Paesiello [*sic*] formed part of the audience. I was there, and a greater treat, or a more remarkable one, cannot be imagined. . . .

Paesiello's Barbiere di Siviglia, which he composed in Russia, and brought with him to Vienna, was got up . . . There were three operas now on the tapis, one by Regini [Vincenzo Righini's *Il Demogorgone ovvero Il filosofo confuso*], another by Salieri (the Grotto of Trophonius), and one by Mozart, by special command of the Emperor. Mozart chose to have Beaumarchais' French comedy, 'Le mariage di Figaro', made into an Italian opera, which was done with great ability, by Da Ponte. These three pieces were nearly ready for representation at the same time, and each composer claimed the right of producing his opera for the first. The contest raised much discord, and parties were formed. The characters of the three men were all very different. Mozart was as touchy as gunpowder, and swore he would put the score of his opera into the fire, if it was not produced first; his claim was backed by a strong party: on the contrary, Regini was working like a mole in the dark to get precedence.

The third candidate [Antonio Salieri] was Maestro di Cappella to the Court, a clever shrewd man, possessed of what Bacon called, crooked wisdom; and his claims were backed by three of the principal performers, who formed a cabal not easily put down. Every one of the opera company took part in the contest. I alone was a stickler for Mozart, and naturally enough, for he had a claim on my warmest wishes, from my adoration of his powerful genius, and the debt of gratitude I owed him, for many personal favours.

The mighty contest was put an end to by His Majesty issuing a mandate for Mozart's 'Nozze di Figaro', to be instantly put into rehearsal; and none more than Michael O'Kelly, enjoyed the little great man's triumph over his rivals . . .[2]

In February 1785, Emperor Joseph II had given a luncheon party in the orangery in Schönbrunn Castle. The festive table was placed in the middle of the room, and at both ends were small stages; the guests were entertained first at one end and then at the other, the chairs being moved as appropriate. On 7 February 1786, Joseph II offered another such 'spring festival on a winter's day' in the orangery, this time in honour of his sister, Archduchess Marie Christine and her consort, Duke Albert of Sachsen-Teschen, now Governor-General of the Austrian Netherlands. Apart from various scenes from German plays, the two *pièces de résistance* were *Der Schauspieldirektor* (*The Impresario*), a German play by Gottlieb Stephanie Jr with an overture and four vocal pieces

The orangery at Schönbrunn, where Mozart's Der Schauspieldirektor was first performed in February 1786. This engraving by Hieronymus Löschenkohl entitled 'Frühlingsfest an einem Wintertage' ('Spring festival on a winter's day') records the occasion, showing the Emperor's banquet in progress and the two stages specially built for the entertainments.

(K.486) by Mozart – some of incredible difficulty – and a small opera by Salieri entitled *Prima la musica e poi le parole* ('First the music, then the words'), performed at the other end of the hall. Zinzendorf was there and thought this room 'much better decorated than last year', but of the German offerings he noted that they were very mediocre. The audience then went to the other end of the room for the Italian contribution; the Count thought Nancy Storace very amusing. Mozart's singers were Aloysia Lange, Caterina Cavalieri and Johann Valentin Adamberger. The Imperial *Harmonie* played Salieri's *La grotta di Trofonio* during the meal, which began at 3 o'clock. The entire affair lasted six hours. The order for payment has survived on a sheet sent by Joseph II to Count Orsini-Rosenberg:

I send you herewith 1,000# [ducats] which you will distribute to the artists who took part in today's festival at Schönbrunn, namely

To Salieri	100#
. . . Mozart	50
The 10 German players at 50#	500
. . . 4 Italian opera singers at 50#	200
For Bussani	50
For the Orchestra	100
	1,000#

(The famous *buffo*, Bussani, was stage-manager for the Italian part of the festivities.)

Both the play and the opera were then put on in the Kärntnerthortheater (première: 11 February), and Mozart's music was singled out as 'containing some special beauties' in a review in the *Wiener Realzeitung* of 21 February; the next day, another paper described the German part as being infinitely

superior to the Italian, and 'that is surely not the result of national pride.'[3]

On Sunday, 19 February, Mozart went to a masked ball at the Redoutensaal dressed as an Indian philosopher. He distributed a printed sheet with eight puzzles and fourteen 'Fragments from Zoroaster's writing'; the sheet has not survived, but extracts were printed in a Salzburg newspaper from a copy Wolfgang sent to his father. Among the puzzles were 'One can have me without seeing me'; 'one can wear me without feeling me'; 'one can give me without having me.' The 'fragments' included: 'It is not for everyone to be modest: it is appropriate only for great men.'; and 'You can praise a woman in the surest and gentlest fashion if you relate bad things about her rivals. How many men are not women in this respect?'; 'If you are a poor but noble fool – become whatever you can, to earn your bread. But if you are a rich, noble fool, become whatever you want: only not a man of understanding, I won't have that.'[4] All this is further evidence of the rather arcane side of Mozart's personality. It goes hand in hand with his becoming a Freemason.

Even apart from composing *The Impresario*, Mozart's life was as full as ever. Before Christmas 1785 he had participated in the Tonkünstler-Societät's second performance of a new oratorio by Dittersdorf (*Ester*), playing the new Piano Concerto no. 22 in E flat (K.482), completed on 16 December. In a lost letter to his father, he wrote that 'the *Andante* had to be repeated (something rare)'.[5] On 2 March 1786, Wolfgang completed another superb Piano Concerto, no. 23 in A (K.488). It was probably played a day or two later at one of the three Mozart subscription concerts (with 120 subscribers, as he wrote to his father) of which no record whatever survives.

We fare better with his next compositions: two new insertions for a performance of *Idomeneo*, with a cast mostly of noble amateurs, held in the private theatre in the palace of Johann Adam, Prince Auersperg (1721–95): the first is a duet for Ilia, soprano (Anna von Pufendorf), and Idamante, tenor

(Baron Pulini), 'Spiegarti non poss'io' (K.489), instead of the older duet No. 20; and the *Scena con Rondò* with a ravishingly beautiful violin solo (Mozart's friend, the young Count August Hatzfeld, a canon of Eichstätt Cathedral in Germany) and tenor (Baron Pulini), 'Non più, tutto ascoltai' (recitative) and 'Non temer, amato bene' (K.490), to replace the beginning of Act II. 'Non temer' must be accounted one of the most touching arias in all Mozart – the equal of anything in *Figaro*. The other singers in this performance, on which Mozart obviously lavished his frustrated love for an opera he could not hope to see staged, as it should have been, in the Burgtheater, included Countess Hortense Hatzfeld, *née* Comtesse Zierotin (the wife of August's half-brother, Clemens), as Elettra, and Giuseppe Antonio Bridi from Rovereto as Idomeneo (he later erected a memorial to Mozart's memory in his garden in Rovereto).

The *Wiener Zeitung* of 8 April reported that on 'Friday the 7th Herr Mozart gave a grand musical academy, the last to be given [this season] in this [Burg] Theatre . . .' It has been supposed that he played his new Piano Concerto no. 24 in C minor (K.491), but that is pure speculation; he had completed it on 24 March, and may have performed it shortly thereafter.

Between the première of *Figaro* (1 May 1786) and the following autumn, there is not much news about the Mozarts: Constanze became pregnant again; their third child, Johann Thomas Leopold, was born on 18 October but died of asphyxiation on 15 November.[6] Otherwise, Mozart could rejoice in the continued success of *Entführung*, which had had two performances in 1783, another three in November 1785, and in 1786 received no fewer than eleven (followed by ten more in 1787 and 1788). However, Mozart earned nothing from these repeat performances, since his work was now the property of the Court Theatre.

It is once again Leopold Mozart in Salzburg who informs us of the contents of a lost letter from Wolfgang, 'very illegible' but from it 'you will see . . . that he will give 4 academy concerts in the Casino', by which is probably meant the hall in the Trattnerhof.[7] For these concerts Mozart composed two new and splendid works, the Piano Concerto no. 25 in C (K.503) – completed in 4 December and probably played next day – and the Symphony no. 38 in D (K.504) completed on 6 December. This symphony was probably the principal new work of the second concert, the date of which is unknown. The symphony was later dubbed the 'Prague', when it was performed in that city. This, Mozart's grandest symphony to date, opens with a majestic and sombre introduction marked Adagio mostly in the minor, followed by a complex and contrapuntally subtle Allegro section. The work has no minuet, but if performed uncut (i.e. with all its repeats) its three movements still last nearly forty minutes.

Mozart had been forming a plan: to go to England when a large part of the English contingent were due to leave Vienna in the coming year. He wanted to take his children to Salzburg and leave them with Leopold, who was horrified by the idea. Wolfgang had learned that his father had taken little Leopold (Nannerl's son) into his house – 'something I never wrote to him', Leopold

tells his daughter, 'so he or perhaps his wife conceived that great idea. That wouldn't be bad at all, they can quietly travel, they could die, could stay in England, then I would run after them with the children . . . Basta! . . .'[8] Mozart's proposed trip was announced in a Prague newspaper: 'The famous Compositeur Hr. Mozart intends to travel to London next spring, where he has the most flattering offers. He will pass through Paris *en route*.'[9]

On 27 December 1786, Wolfgang completed his farewell gift to Nancy Storace, the *Scena con Rondò* with piano solo – 'For Mad:selle storace and me', wrote the composer in his catalogue. The Storaces, Michael Kelly and Thomas Attwood were preparing to leave Vienna. But if, in the face of his father's refusal, Wolfgang could not feasibly leave with them, he and Constanze could undertake a journey to another much nearer capital city – Prague.

We have seen that Prague entertained a special affection for Mozart and his works. As is evident from a lost letter Wolfgang sent to his father, *Figaro* was such a resounding success in the Bohemian capital that 'the orchestra, and a group of *great* connoisseurs and amateurs have sent him a letter of invitation, and a poem in his honour . . .'[10]

Early on 8 January 1787, Mozart and Constanze left Vienna, together with the violinist Franz Hofer (who would marry Constanze's sister Josepha in 1788), the clarinet player Anton Stadler, a young friend and pupil from Salzburg, Franz Jacob Freystädtler (who would later help complete Mozart's Requiem), two ladies from Mannheim, the Mozarts' dog 'Gauckerl' and a valet named Joseph – probably the same 'Joseph Primus' who catered for Mozart in 1791.[11] This journey was one of the happiest and most carefree of Mozart's life: Prague welcomed him, as his letter of 15 January 1787 to his friend Gottfried von Jacquin shows:

The National Theatre in Prague, where Figaro *was played with enormous success in 1786;* Don Giovanni *was first performed there in 1787 and* La clemenza di Tito *received its première on the occasion of the coronation of Leopold II as King of Bohemia in 1791. This is the only major theatre having direct associations with Mozart that is still extant.*

Immediately upon our arrival (Thursday the 11th at 12 noon), we had to rush headlong to make ourselves presentable for lunch at 1 o'clock. After table the old [Joseph Anton] Count Thun gave us a concert, performed by his own people, which lasted nearly one-and-a-half hours. I could enjoy such *real entertainment* every day. At 6 o'clock I went with Count [Joseph Emanuel] Canal [Senior Warden of the Prague Lodge 'Zur Wahrheit und Einigkeit' ('Truth and Unity')] to the so-called Breitfeld [*recte*: Johann, Baron Bretfeld] Ball, where the cream of Prague's beauties likes to gather. That would have been something for you, my friend! I mean, I can see you chasing after all those beautiful girls and ladies – chasing, do you think? – no, limping after them! – I didn't dance and didn't flirt. – The first because I was too tired and the second because I was born stupid; – but I saw with the greatest pleasure how these people happily leapt about to the music of my *Figaro*, all arranged as contredanses and German dances – for here, nothing is talked of except – *Figaro*; nothing else is played, blown, sung or whistled except – *Figaro*: no opera is attended except – *Figaro* and always *Figaro*; certainly a great honour for me. . . . Next Friday the 19th my academy concert will take place in the theatre; I shall probably have to give a second one; that will, alas, prolong my stay here . . .

NB I shall hear and see *Figaro* on Wednesday, if I am not deaf and blind by then. Maybe that will happen to me after the opera[12]

At Mozart's concert on 19 January he performed three fantasias on the piano and improvised variations on 'Non più andrai' from Act 1 of *Figaro*. Niemetschek, his later biographer, was present and reported that

In response to a universal demand, he gave a piano recital at a large concert in the Opera House. The theatre had never been so full as on this occasion . . . We did not, in fact, know what to admire most, whether the extraordinary compositions or his extraordinary playing: together they made such an overwhelming impression on us that we felt we had been bewitched . . . The symphonies he composed for this occasion are real masterpieces . . . full of surprising modulations and have a quick, fiery gait, so that the very soul is transported to sublime heights. This applies particularly to the Symphony [no. 38] in D major [K.504], which remains a favourite in Prague, although it has doubtless been heard a hundred times.[13]

On 22 January Mozart conducted *Figaro* (which he had heard on the 17th), and on 6 February he completed a set of vivacious German Dances for orchestra (K.509) – the first of a new series of such late dance music which displays his skill in the same consummate way as do the bigger forms. But he had to be tricked into composing the dances at short notice. In his biography Nissen writes:

Mozart was requested by Count P – [probably Count Pachta, a great music-lover who maintained his own orchestra in Prague] to compose some contredanses for the Ball of the Society of Nobles, of which he was Director. [Mozart] promised to do so, but it simply did not seem to happen. The Count prepared a trap, invited Mozart to a meal, with the proviso that on this occasion the meal would take place an hour earlier than usual. As soon as Mozart arrived at the appointed time, his host caused the necessary writing material to be brought and insisted that he fulfil that request for the ball, which was due to take place the next day. Faced with this situation, Mozart sat straight down at the desk and in less than half an hour was ready with four contredanses for large orchestra.[14]

In fact, there are six dances, and – while allowing for a little poetic licence – Mozart probably was 'trapped' into writing them punctually; their scoring includes 1 piccolo flute, 2 flutes, 2 oboes, 2 clarinets, 2 bassoons, 2 horns, 2 trumpets, drums and strings, and they are written in the quicker than usual metre of 3/8 (rather than 3/4).

A rather offended Leopold Mozart reports to his daughter in St Gilgen on 2 March:

... since I wrote to Prague, I have had no answer [from Wolfgang]; [but I have since learned that] he earned (so they say) 1,000 f. in Prague, that his last boy Leopold has died and that, as I said, he wants to go to England, but he will have his pupil [Attwood] make some firm arrangements in London, i.e. a contract to write an opera, or a subscription concert, ... Since I wrote telling him in a fatherly way that he won't earn anything if he goes there in the summer, and will arrive there at the wrong time, and that he must have at least 2,000 f. in his pocket to undertake this trip ... he will have lost heart ...[15]

On 23 February 1787, Nancy Storace gave a farewell benefit concert at the Kärntnerthortheater (at which she supposedly made 4,000 gulden).[16] Why this immensely successful singer wanted to leave Vienna is unclear, but it seems that after she and her husband separated, she had become Benucci's mistress and had recently (1786) formed an attachment to the young Lord Barnard (later Duke of Cleveland), one of the many rich young Englishmen who had settled for a time in the Austrian capital. Mozart practised his English in various commonplace books and had plenty of titled Englishmen with whom to converse. The English formed a club and took quarters in a house on the Graben, where the wine flowed freely. Lord Barnard kept a diary (in French), in which his dates with Nancy are amply documented:

[11 May 1786:] I rose at nine o'clock, played tennis, dined at Milord Granard's, went to the ball at Monsieur Manners', where I danced until seven o'clock in the morning. [12 May:] I stayed in bed all day ... [20 January 1787:] I spent the evening at Madame Storace's. [21 January] I supped at La Storace's. I took her dancing to the Redoubt, where we stayed until four o'clock a.m. [3 February:] I have a ball at my quarters for La Storace. It was very fine and mild weather.

Lord Barnard went to Storace's concert on 23 February and afterwards took her home for supper before leaving next day for England. Count Zinzendorf was also at the concert and wrote that one duet from *Una cosa rara* was repeated three times, a bravura aria (possibly Mozart's K.505, though it seems unlikely that the Count would have failed to mention Mozart's participation) was 'rather boring' and she sang an air from Stephen Storace's Vienna opera, *Gli Equivoci*.[17] Wolfgang gave them a letter of introduction to his father; when the English group arrived at Salzburg, they noted that the Archbishop was very attentive to the ladies in the party.

In the spring of 1787 Leopold Mozart became seriously ill. On 4 April Wolfgang wrote what would prove to be his last extant letter to his father. It is, justly, one of Mozart's most celebrated letters.

Now I hear that you are really ill! I hardly need tell you how much I hope to receive some comforting news from you personally; and I surely hope so – although I have made it a habit to imagine the worst in every situation – since death is (strictly speaking) the true goal of our lives, for a couple of years I have made such a close acquaintance with this true and best friend of humanity that his image is not only no longer frightening, but rather contains a great deal that is comforting and consoling! And I thank my God that He has granted me the opportunity (you understand what I am saying) of learning that he [death] is the *key* which unlocks the door to our true state of happiness. At night I never lie down in my bed without thinking that perhaps (young as I am) I shall not live to see the next day and yet not one among my acquaintances – could say that in my intercourse with them I am stubborn or morose – and for this source of happiness I thank my Creator every day and wish with all my heart the same for my fellow-creatures. – I have already explained in the [lost] letter (which Mad. Storace put in her luggage) my way of thinking in connection with the very sad death of my dearest and best friend Count von Hatzfeld – he was just 31 years old; like me – I am not sorry for *him* – but I am most heartily sorry for myself and all who knew him as I did. – I hope and wish that as I write this letter you will be feeling better; but if you should against all expectations not be better, I ask you in the name of . . . [Mozart's dots] not to hide it from me, but to write, or cause to be written, the entire truth so that I can fly as fast as any human being can, to your arms. I entreat you by everything – which is sacred to us. – But I hope soon to receive a reassuring letter from you, and in this pleasant hope I and my wife and Carl kiss your hands a thousand times and I am ever

> your obedient son
> W.A. Mozart.[18]

Freemasons have always considered that this letter – the only one referring to Masonry which was not destroyed by Constanze and/or Nissen – alludes, in the oblique 'you understand what I am saying', to the secret ritual of initiation into the Third Degree (Master Mason) of the Craft, with its emphasis on death.

A few days after this letter was written, Ludwig van Beethoven came to Vienna for the first time, supposedly to study composition with Mozart. In practice, it is unlikely that he received any lessons at all. In later years, Beethoven said only that he had heard Mozart play frequently and found his execution staccato, in other words choppy. Concerning this visit to Vienna, Carl Holz, a close friend of Beethoven, recalled that 'When he was a boy, Beethoven was taken to Mozart, who told him to play; whereupon he improvised. "That is very pretty," said Mozart, "but studied." Beethoven was vexed and asked for a subject on which to improvise; after hearing his efforts, Mozart said to some friends, "Watch out for him, he will have something to tell you."'[19] At that point, however, Beethoven's mother became ill and the young man had to return hurriedly to Bonn.

Mozart's thematic catalogue records the completion, on 19 April, of the first of the mature string quintets, the one in C (K.515). A few days later, on 24 April, the Mozarts took a much less expensive apartment in the suburb of Landstraße; Mozart must have become concerned about the expenses of the large flat in the Domgasse.[20] On 16 May, he finished the second quintet, in G minor (K.516). Shortly thereafter, he arranged his wind-band Serenade in C minor (K.388) for string quintet (originally 406 in the Köchel listing, now renumbered as K.516b). It would seem that Mozart was playing these extraordinary new works, for in a letter to an unidentified friend he wrote:

Please forgive me for recently taking the liberty of removing the Haydn Quartets [op. 50, just about to be issued by Artaria and circulating in pirated copies in Vienna] – but I always think that, *clown* as I am, I should deserve an exceptional treatment. – Please, pray do let me borrow, tomorrow, my 6 quartets [dedicated to Haydn], the Quintet ex G minor and the new one ex C minor. – I will send everything back the day after tomorrow with thanks. . . .[21]

Engraving from the title page of the first edition of 'Ein musikalischer Spaß' (K.522), published by J. André in Offenbach.

On 28 May, Leopold Mozart died in Salzburg. Wolfgang wrote to his sister on 2 June that he was unable to leave Vienna; he supposed that, as far as his father's estate was concerned, it was not worth making the trip, 'and I must admit that I am entirely of your opinion to hold a public auction of his effects; only I would like to have an inventory of them so that I can choose some items . . .'[22] In the event, the St Gilgen relatives offered Mozart a lump sum of 1,000 gulden, which he accepted, asking only to have it paid not in Imperial currency (*Reichsgeld*), such as was then in use in Salzburg, but in Viennese currency and as a bill of exchange (letter of 1 August). (This made a difference: 1,000 gulden in Viennese currency equalled 1,200 in *Reichsgeld*,) Nannerl's husband, Berchtold von Sonnenburg, who was managing her affairs, agreed to his stipulation, whereupon Wolfgang wrote (29 September), asking that the bill of exchange be 'sent to Michael Puchberg, at Count Walsegg's house on the Hoher Markt, because he [Puchberg] is authorized to accept the money, since on Monday I must leave very early for Prague . . .'[23]

During the summer of 1787, Mozart composed or completed two notable works. The first is *Ein Musikalischer Spaß* (K.522), written a fortnight after the notice of his father's death (it is dated 14 June in the catalogue). This wicked parody of contemporary music (in which even Haydn does not escape: the finale, with its catchy tune and pauses, is like an amateur version of Haydn's rondos),[24] seems to have been composed in instalments (as Alan Tyson has shown) for some special occasion, now forgotten. Some biographers – as might be expected in our post-Freudian world – have accused Mozart of being heartless in penning such a flippant piece right after his father's death; they have also seen in *Don Giovanni* a kind of mad release from a father-complex (the figure of the Commendatore). Such 'insights' serve only to reveal a lack of understanding concerning Mozart's way of thinking: when composing, he was always in a special world of his own, and his inner world had very little to do with external realities of life.

The second work of that summer is 'Eine kleine Nachtmusik', finished on 10 August. This Serenade (K.525) originally had five movements (the first minuet and trio have not survived). The public has always been attracted by its formal perfection and by the beauty and delicacy of the slow movement: this might, quite simply, be considered the most beautiful piece of occasional music ever written, hence its enduring appeal.

Mozart's second journey to Prague, on which Constanze again accompanied him, began on 1 October 1787. On the previous journey they had – before being invited to stay with the 'old' Count Thun – stayed at the Inn 'Zu den drei Löwen' (Three Lions), and this time they lodged there again, but made frequent trips to visit their friends the Duscheks, whose country house, the Villa Bertramka, on the outskirts of the city, is now a museum. The history of this second visit has been related in the preceding chapter. By the middle of November 1787, the Mozarts were back in Vienna, where events of extreme importance were to greet them.

The first was that on 5 December the German opera troupe in Vienna was dissolved; Aloysia Lange was taken into the Italian company. But it meant that Italian opera had, at least temporarily, ousted German operas from the Court theatres in Vienna. The reason is probably the simplest one possible: the Italian operas were infinitely superior to those in German, which had mediocre librettos and, except for Mozart and perhaps – on a lower level, Dittersdorf – inferior music. Moreover, Italian operas were international, or rather supranational, and better suited to a great Court opera house than any local product. That, at least, must have been behind Joseph II's decision – that and his usual sense of economy. The Italian company was very expensive; why have a German troupe as well, especially if the operas it performed were not very good?

The day afterwards, Count Orsini-Rosenberg wrote a protocol requesting confirmation of the Emperor's verbal order that Mozart be engaged as court chamber musician (*Kammermusicus*) with an annual salary of 800 fl.[25] The salary was perhaps less than he would have wished, but by the Emperor's standards, it was by no means ungenerous. In 1787 the salary of a *Kammerdiener* (gentleman attendant) was 800 fl., the same as that of the *Schloßhauptmann* (castle captain) at the Belvedere: it was an income of the middle range, which was subject to tax.[26] Gluck had been paid 2,000 gulden, but he was old and famous. His death in 1787 opened the way for Mozart at Court, and the composition of *Don Giovanni*, intended for the Prague wedding ceremonies of Joseph's niece, may have been a further factor in the Imperial decision. Later, Wolfgang wrote in a letter to his sister: 'P.S. to answer you concerning the point about my engagement, the Emperor has taken me into his chamber, . . . *for the time being* at only *800* fl., but no other member of the chamber receives *as much* . . .'[27]

At the end of the year, on 27 December, the Mozarts' fourth child, Theresia, was born: she would survive for only a few months.

Friedrich Baumann, Jr (1764–1841), the actor and bass singer for whom Mozart composed a 'German War Song' (K.539) in 1788; anonymous engraving.

*   *   *

On 6 January 1788, Joseph II's nephew Archduke Francis married Princess Elisabeth Wilhelmine of Württemberg. To celebrate the occasion, Joseph gave the bride jewellery worth 24,000 gulden,[28] and on 8 January the Court Opera performed Salieri's latest stage work. This was Lorenzo Da Ponte's adaptation of *Tarare*, which had been such a revelation in Paris the year before, and was now retitled *Axur, Rè d'Ormus*. The opera had a splendid cast, with Benucci in the title role, and was the event of the season; the whole theatre was brightly lit with candles ('some extinguished before the end', wrote Zinzendorf, who also thought the piece 'flat').[29] All the same, a première under such circumstances ensured continuing success, and Salieri was in any case a very clever manipulator.

The theatrical situation in Vienna was further changed when, on 6 February, the old Kärntnerthortheater was closed (and remained so until 16 November 1791). It was an economy measure, dictated in part by the dissolution of the German opera company. Henceforth, both German plays and Italian operas were given only in the Burgtheater. (In 1791 the Kärntnerthortheater was opened briefly for a concert, given by the blind glass-harmonica player Marianne Kirchgessner, in which Mozart was obliquely involved.) On 9 February 1788, war was declared between Austria and the Ottoman Empire: a mistaken and badly led war which was to have disastrous effects on Mozart's fortunes. At the outset, as with most wars, patriotic feelings ran high, and at the beginning of March even Mozart contributed a 'German War Song' (*Ein teutsches kriegs-lied*, K.539), 'Ich möchte wohl der Kaiser sein', for a young actor, Friedrich Baumann, who was playing at the suburban Theatre in the Leopoldstadt.

Mozart's concert activities still included guest appearances at soirées of the aristocracy. Zinzendorf heard him play at a large concert given by the Venetian Ambassador on 10 February, in which singers from the Opera participated. The Ambassador, Daniele Andrea, Count Dolfin – a scion of an illustrious Venetian family which had supplied several Doges to the Serenissima – lived in the Dorotheergasse (No. 9 today).[30]

The big event of the winter season in 1788 was Mozart's arrangement and performance of C.P.E. Bach's *Die Auferstehung und Himmelfahrt Christi* [or *Jesu*], organized by Gottfried van Swieten for his Gesellschaft der Associirten. A report in Forkel's *Musikalischer Almanach* states that 'on 26 February . . . and on 4 March this Cantata . . . was put on at *Count Johann [Baptist] Esterhazy's*, with an orchestra of 86 persons in the presence of and under the direction of that great connoisseur of music, Freyherr *von Swieten*, to general applause on the part of all the distinguished audience. Hr *Mozart* gave the tempi and read from the score, Hr·Umlauf was at the keyboard [*Flügel*]. The performance was the more excellent because it was preceded by two full rehearsals . . . among the singers were Madam *Lange*, the tenor *Adamberger*, the bass *Saale* [Ignaz Saal], and 30 members of the chorus. On the 7th this same piece was performed in the I.R. National Theatre [Burgtheater].'[31] This was not such a waste of Mozart's time as might at first be thought. He was genuinely interested in 'old' music and, apart from everything else, these congenial commissions by two of his leading patrons were an additional source of income. What is not generally realized is that it was probably in the interval of the first of these concerts that Mozart played his 'Coronation' Piano Concerto no. 26 (K.537), completed two days before the first performance of the C.P.E. Bach Cantata. This work – which already suggests that Mozart realized that his 'severe' style was going out of fashion (if indeed it had ever really been fashionable) – was entered under that date (24 February) in the catalogue; and the next entry is even more significant, listing the last great bravura aria (K.538), sketched out a decade earlier, for Aloysia Lange. The entry reads '*Eine Arie in f dur. – Ah se in ciel benigne stelle* etc: für Mad:me Lange . . .' and is dated 4 March 1788, the very day of the second performance of the Bach Cantata. It seems likely that in that concert interval Aloysia sang the new/old aria by her brother-in-law. Which, if any, of the two new Mozart compositions were played at the Burgtheater on 7 March cannot now be determined.

We now come to the public announcements of Mozart's string quintets. Various theories have been put forward as to the origin of the late quintets. In 1786, Luigi Boccherini became Court Composer to King Frederick William II of Prussia, who had succeeded Frederick the Great. Like his predecessor, the new king was passionately fond of music and was, moreover, a fine cellist, for whom Haydn also composed quartets. Alfred Einstein[32] considered that Mozart may have composed these quintets with the King of Prussia in mind. This might be thought doubtful, in view of the following notice that Mozart inserted (a) in the *Wiener Zeitung*, on 2, 5 and 9 April 1788, and (b) in the *Journal des Luxus and der Moden* of June 1788, published in Weimar:

MUSICAL NOTICE

Three new Quintets for 2 Violini, 2 Violas, and Violoncello, which I offer on subscription, handsomely and correctly written. The price for subscribers is 4 ducats or 18 fl. [gulden] Viennese currency. – The subscription formulae are to be had daily of Herr *Puchberg* in the Sallinz [firm of Michael Salliet] offices on the High Market, where the works will be available from 1 July.

Kapellmeister Mozart.

in actual service of His Majesty.[33]

It is now thought that Mozart simply wrote this set of three works on speculation and intended to sell them by subscription. He played them with his friends for a year and then decided to sell them in manuscript copies. What a shame for Mozart to announce in the *Wiener Zeitung* of 25 June 1788 the postponement of the issuing of his quintets until 1 January 1789.[34] In January 1783 he had more or less successfully sold his three new piano concertos (K.413–15) by subscription, but times had changed. In 1783, Mozart had been the darling of the Viennese public, but by 1788 he was no longer in such favour. He was, moreover, in debt to Michael Puchberg.

The music of these three quintets can only be described as alarming in the extreme. Those familiar with the six quartets dedicated to Haydn will remember that one of the greatest (K.465) was clothed in the radiant garb of C major and showed that, in the course of this piece, Mozart was eminently capable of making that key one of yearning pathos. Here, in K.515, the highly original opening theme uses an old device (broken triad) in a new way. Tension is generated, and maintained, by the repeated quavers in the middle voices; while the broken triad in the cello is answered by the first violin in a phrase of peculiar poignancy. This formula is repeated three times before the theme comes to fruition. But hardly has Mozart completed the theme than the music comes to a halt. After a bar's rest, the whole process is repeated in *C minor* and the roles of the first violin and cello reversed: the poignancy of what was formerly the first violin's 'answer' becomes darkly ominous when brought down *three octaves* to the cello's lowest register.

At the risk of becoming fanciful, we must nevertheless reiterate that even to the relatively untrained ear, this was a very upsetting transformation; and that, moreover, it is *not* the kind of music Mozart had been writing five years earlier. In the case of the G minor quintet, the atmosphere becomes even more emotionally charged. Its unusual key, its dramatic power, its combination of tragedy and tenderness, have assured it a special place in the chamber music repertoire. This and the great G minor Symphony no. 40 (K.550, completed 25 July 1788) constitute perhaps the most personal music that Mozart ever wrote. By May 1787, when he composed the quintet, it must have been obvious to Mozart that, at least as far as the Viennese were concerned, his popular appeal had in some way begun to fail. The G minor Quintet is a mirror of Mozart's personal tragedy: the greatest musical genius of the day becoming misunderstood and even rejected, as well as sliding into debt.

There can be little doubt that in recent times many in the Viennese audiences will have been perplexed and disturbed when presented with the Piano Concertos no. 20 in D minor (K.466, completed in February 1785) and no. 24 in C minor (K.491, completed 24 March 1786); but these concertos are in the main public works of public drama, whereas the quintet is essentially a private work of private anguish. Nothing quite like it had ever been heard before: Haydn's great minor-key quartets from op. 20 (1772) were also private works, but the tragedy in them is more classic, less personal. Part of the trouble with selling 'private' works like Mozart's quintets was that the composer was appealing precisely to a group that was beginning to distance itself from his 'public' works. Thus, on 15 May 1788, Archduchess Elisabeth Wilhelmine could write to her husband, the future Emperor, '. . . in the last few days they have put on a new opera by Mozart [*Don Giovanni*], but it did not enjoy much success . . .'[35]

Since Mozart's failure with his Viennese public was a crucial development, we propose to examine the phenomenon from two different standpoints. First the documentation. In the reviews of the quartets dedicated to Haydn, some opinions were expressed about their difficulty, but one writer in the influential German magazine, Cramer's *Magazin der Musik* (23 April 1787), stated that Mozart is

the best and most accomplished piano player I have ever heard; it is only a pity that in his artful and really very beautiful writing, by searching for novelty, he reaches too high, which means that sensibility and heart gain but little: his new Quartets . . . which he dedicated to Haydn are really too highly seasoned – and which palate can withstand that for long? Forgive the metaphor from the cookbook . . .'[36]

And now we may return to the Piano Quartet in G minor which Mozart wrote for Hoffmeister in 1785. As we have hinted before, it was in its very scoring an avant-garde work for Vienna, and was so full of technical difficulties in the piano part that it required not only expert execution but attentive listening. The following report (here in summary) was contributed in June 1788 to the fashionable *Journal des Luxus und der Moden*:[37]

Mozart has now arrived in Vienna as Imperial Chapel Master [an appointment that took place in 1787]. And now a few words about a bizarre phenomenon which he (or his celebrity) brought about. A little while ago, there appeared a single Quadro (for piano, violin, viola and violoncello), each single part engraved separately, and which is very intricate, requiring the greatest precision in all four parts; but even in a very successful performance, this 'musica di camera' can and should please only musical connoisseurs.

The rumour was: Mozart has composed a new and very special Quadro, and this or that princess or countess has it and plays it. The rumour spread quickly, excited general curiosity and was responsible for the witless idea of performing this original work in large, noisy concerts.

Many another piece can sustain a mediocre performance; this product of Mozart's is, however, scarcely bearable if it is performed by mediocre dilettante hands and carelessly presented. This was what happened countless times during the past winter; just as I arrived from my journey and was taken to some concerts, there would appear a certain Fräulein or demoiselle of the middle class, or some arrogant dilettante, and would roll off this Quadro at a noisy party and pretend to appreciate it. It *could not* please; everyone yawned with boredom at this incomprehensible noise for four instruments, but it *had* to please, it *had* to be praised.

What a difference, when this much discussed work of art was played in a quiet room by four skilled musicians who have studied it well, where the suspense of each and every note did not escape the attentive listener's ear, and which was played with the greatest precision in the presence of only two or three attentive persons. But then there would have been no *éclat*, no brilliant and modish applause to be reaped, no conventional praise to be culled.

Hoffmeister had issued the G minor Quartet in December 1785 as part of a series of chamber music pieces by various composers. Sales of Mozart's contribution to the series were disappointing, and Hoffmeister lost money on his edition of the work. He nevertheless began engraving the second of the projected set of three, the Quartet in E flat (K.493), but became discouraged after completing the violin part and decided to cut his losses (engraving a work as considerable as a quartet was an expensive process). According to the account in the Nissen biography, Hoffmeister 'made the master a present of the advance payment already given' and asked to be relieved of his contract with the composer. Fortunately, Mozart was able to persuade Artaria & Co. to take over the project. Artaria bought the plates of the violin part from Hoffmeister, engraved the others, and issued the work in July 1787. Apparently the sales were not such as to encourage Mozart to write the projected third quartet.[38]

*　　*　　*

It has been suggested by the distinguished Australian physician, Dr Peter J. Davies,[39] that Mozart had manic-depressive tendencies, something that many lay people had felt intuitively about those many minor-key works of the 1780s. Now, while it is a commonplace that tragedy is not necessarily confined to minor keys, and that Mozart is often as yearning and poignant in major keys (notably in the slow movements of the G minor Quintet and the 'Jupiter' Symphony) we must, I think, nevertheless regard most of these minor-key works of the 1780s as going far beyond the normal range of expression (say, in Haydn's works of the same period) and that Mozart reserved his most troubled, alarming and even dangerous music for works composed in the minor. While not attempting either a complete list, or concealing that tragic major-key works may have been omitted, as well as individual minor-key movements within major-key works, e.g. slow movements of Piano Concertos such as no. 22 (K.482) and no. 23 (K.488), here is the selection for further scrutiny:

1782
Serenade in C minor for wind band (K.388; exact date?)

1783
Quartet in D minor (K.421) – June (Constanze related that her labour pains coincided with the composition of the Minuet, 17 June).
Fugue in C minor for two pianos (K.426) – 29 December.

1784
Piano Sonata in C minor (K.457) – 14 October.

195

1785
Piano Concerto no. 20 in D minor (K.466) – 10 February.
Fantasia for piano in C minor (K.475) – 20 May.
Piano Quartet in G minor (K.478) – 16 October.
Masonic Funeral Music in C minor (K.477) – 10 November (?)[40]

1786
Piano Concerto no. 24 in C minor (K.491) – 24 March.

1787
Rondo for piano in A minor (K.511) – 11 March.
Quintet in G minor (K.516) – 16 May.
Quintet in C minor (K.406) (arrangement of the Serenade in C minor, K.388; see 1782) – end of May(?)
Don Giovanni (K.527) – penultimate scene, D minor – 28 October.

1788
Adagio for piano in B minor (K.540) – 19 March.
Adagio and Fugue for strings in C minor (K.546) – 26 June.
Symphony no. 40 in G minor (K.550) – 25 July.

1791
Requiem in D minor (K.626) – October–November(?).

Dr Davies produces a long and scholarly analysis of Mozart's personality, concluding part I as follows: 'There is convincing evidence for the insidious onset during Mozart's early adult life of a chronic mood disturbance, which persisted until his death, and which was associated with pathological mood swings of hypomania and depression. It will become apparent that the diagnostic criteria for cyclothymic disorder (which is related to manic-depressive personality) are fulfilled.' This study is full of descriptions of Mozart's 'flamboyant, hypomanic behaviour'. Sophie Haibl, Mozart's sister-in-law, stated that

He was always good-humoured, but even in his best periods very thoughtful, looking at one with a sharp expression. He answered everything carefully, whether the subject was merry or sad, and yet he seemed to be thinking deeply about something entirely different. Even when he washed his hands in the morning, he paced up and down the room, never standing still, tapping one heel against the other, and deep in thought. At table he often took the corner of his napkin, crumpled it up tightly, rubbed it up and down his upper lip, and appeared to be unaware of what he was doing, and often making grimaces with his mouth at the same time. In his leisure he was always passionately attached to the latest fad, whether it was riding or billiards. To keep him from company of an unworthy kind, his wife patiently shared everything with him. Otherwise his hands and feet were always in motion, he was forever playing with something, for instance his hat, pockets, watch-chain, tables, chairs – as if he were playing the piano.[41]

'From the viewpoint of his mental health,' continues Dr Davies in another passage of great insight,

1787 was the most crucial year of his life. Even his triumphant success in Prague in January was marred by the death of his friend Count August Hatzfeld. Then he had to contend with the departure of his English friends in February, and recurrence of serious illness in April. . . . Then in September, his protector and childhood friend Dr Sigmund Barisani suddenly died.

The monumental significance of Leopold Mozart's death cannot be overstated. When his father died, a vital part of himself ceased to exist . . .[42]

Actually, these bouts of acute depression had begun well before, and (as the list of works in the minor shows) was particularly prominent in 1785 and the first part of 1786 (Piano Concerto no. 24). 'Hypomanic spells last from days to months,' explains Dr Davies, 'and may sometimes intermingle or alternate with periods of depression . . . Intervening intervals of normal mood may last for several months. Artists with cyclothymic disorder are capable of amazing productivity during their hypomanic periods, when there is inflated self-esteem, excessive energy, sharpened creative thinking and decreased need for sleep. Mozart is the ultimate example of a composer in this category . . .'

After the death of his father, Mozart drew even closer to Constanze, and became increasingly dependent on her. He took her on long trips, even immediately after a pregnancy (as in 1791). But there can be no doubt that Wolfgang's utter dependence on her was a source of strain, and her visits to Baden to take the cure were one of the few forms of escape she could legitimately manage. 'It has to be emphasised,' says Dr Davies, 'that cyclothymics are very difficult people to live with.'

This deep-seated imbalance in Mozart's personality provides, in my opinion, the only satisfactory explanation for this series of violent depressive works in the minor key. There could have been no *question* in his mind of writing 'popular' works when these black moods were upon him: if anything could bring relief, it was the therapy of composing these baleful pieces. It has often been asserted that the corrections and symptoms of disorganization found in the autograph copy of the C minor Piano Concerto no. 24 (K.491) were simply the result of Mozart's hectic concert life with all its concomitant problems: I suggest, however, that the existence of many erasures and particularly of widespread changes may suggest a state of violent inner tension, which is reflected in this, the most impetuous and aggressive of all the piano concertos. The Adagio and Fugue in the same key (1788) and the Symphony no. 40 in G minor (1788) also reflect the same desperate disruptions.

*   *   *

The summer of 1788 saw the series of letters[43] seeking help from his fellow Mason, Michael Puchberg, who almost always sent him some money. In all, he sent Mozart 1,415 gulden – a very substantial sum. Mozart was, then, in serious debt by 1788. This was due in part to growing economic pressure brought on by the Turkish war, which was going badly for Austria; the nobility began to conserve resources, and concert-going was less important to them than opera-going. Mozart and his wife were beginning to live beyond their means, and Constanze was now beginning to feel the strain of repeated pregnancies and having to take the very expensive cure in Baden.

One of these letters to Puchberg is undated and has been placed in the canon of Mozart's correspondence under June 1788. I consider, however, that it must have been written considerably later. Mozart reminds his 'Brother' that he is still eight ducats in debt, but is unable to repay them at present; he asks a new favour – an additional 100 gulden, 'but only until next week (when my academies in the Casino begin) . . .; by then, my subscription money must necessarily have come in, and I can then quite easily repay you 136 fl. with warmest thanks.

'I take the liberty of offering you 2 tickets which I ask you, as a Brother, to accept without any payment, since in any case I shall never be able adequately to recompense the friendship you have shown me . . .'[44] I have suggested elsewhere[45] that these Casino concerts actually took place, though probably not in June, and that the last three Symphonies (nos. 39–41, K.543, 550, 551), completed respectively on 26 June, 25 July and 10 August 1788, were the principal new works destined for the new concert series. Since these three works and Symphony no. 38 in D major ('Prague', K.504) constitute a new departure in the history of the symphony, we will examine them briefly.

The 'Prague' is generally treated separately from the final trilogy, but this practice is surely a great mistake. For with K.504 Mozart leaves his Haydn models forever and moves into the kind of new world that we also find in *Don Giovanni*, written shortly thereafter. There are, indeed, facets of K.504 which are unique in Mozart's whole symphonic output; and nowadays many scholars consider the first movement to be the greatest single symphonic movement ever composed by Mozart. Standing, as it does, chronologically on the brink of the French Revolution, musically it transcends its age and enters that world of sublime thought which lies outside such concepts as time or place.

In the last three symphonies we have a kind of bird's-eye view of Mozart as composer. From the warmth and autumnal beauty of the E flat Symphony no. 39 (with clarinets but no oboes)[46] we move to the frantic and anguished neuroticism of no. 40 in G minor (to which clarinets were added later) and finish with no. 41, the majestic 'Jupiter' (no clarinets), where the fruits of Mozart's interest in counterpoint and his involvement with Bach and Handel reveal themselves in the spectacular finale, one of the greatest contrapuntal achievements of the eighteenth century. The overall mood of each one of these symphonies is, however, staggeringly diverse – in the slow movement of no. 39 the autumnal serenity is disturbed as if by a violent storm; amid the near-hysteria of no. 40 we are, again in the slow movement, introduced to a magical world which has the same kind of depth as those mysterious landscapes in the background of many a *quattrocento* Italian painting; and, in the 'Jupiter' Symphony, the slow movement introduces a note of violent unrest into the otherwise rather detached and lofty C major world of the rest of the work.

We have discussed the sudden changes of mood in Mozart's music at this critical period: the point is further illustrated during the summer of 1788, when the day (11 August) after completing the 'Jupiter' Symphony, Mozart turned to yet another War Song (K.552, 'beym auszug in das feld', 'when leaving for the field') followed by a series of canons (2 September), which range from the gravely beautiful 'Alleluja' (K.553, based on the famous Gregorian chant for Easter Sunday) to the popular 'Bona nox, bist a rechta Ox' (K.561, in Viennese dialect, still the delight of students today in Austria). At the end of the month (27 September) he completed a large-scale Divertimento for string trio (K.563), the greatest of its kind in the eighteenth century. In the late autumn, he was again earning a welcome fee for arranging Handel's *Acis and Galatea* (K.566) 'for Baron Suiten'. It was performed at Count Johann Baptist Esterházy's quarters on 30 December.

The year 1789 witnessed another crisis in the Vienna Opera. When – in view of the economic situation arising from the vast expenditures required to pursue the Turkish war – the Emperor, then in the field, heard from Rosenberg that the Italian Opera required an additional sum of 80,000 gulden, he ordered it to be closed (letter from Semlin, 29 July). Rosenberg had been attempting to save the Opera and on 15 January, Zinzendorf went to a reception at Rosenberg's and heard Da Ponte's proposals to salvage the situation. (Da Ponte was successful, which means that without his intervention we would not have had *Così fan tutte*.)[47]

On 6 March, Mozart's (now controversial) arrangement and re-orchestration of Handel's *Messiah* was given, under van Swieten's aegis, at Count Johann Baptist Esterházy's, with Aloysia Lange, a Mademoiselle Altamonte (a friend of Gottfried von Jacquin), the tenor Adamberger and Ignaz Saal as soloists. A word-book was printed, and an extant copy (in Klosterneuburg Abbey) also bears the above cast-list in a handwritten addition. Zinzendorf attended a later performance, on 7 April, and found it slightly boring 'even though the music was really very beautiful.'[48]

At the end of March, Mozart wrote to Franz Hofdemel, an official in the Upper Law Chambers (later Private Secretary to Count von Seilern) asking for a loan of 100 gulden. At the end of the letter[49] he noted 'We shall soon be able to call each other by a *more attractive* name' – referring to the fact that Hofdemel was about to join Mozart's Masonic Lodge. Hofdemel lent Mozart the money, on the promise of repayment four months from the date of signature, 2 April 1789. Mozart probably needed the money for his planned concert tour of Germany. The day after the last *Messiah* performance (7 April), Mozart set off with Prince Carl Lichnowsky, full of hope for a better future. He might have remembered what Count Arco, the Master of Archbishop Colloredo's Kitchen, had said to him in June 1781,[50] as Mozart was starting his triumphant rise to fame and fortune: 'here [in Vienna] a man's success is of short duration – at the outset one reaps all possible praises and earns a great deal of money as well, that is true – but for how long? – after a few months the Viennese want something new again.' Perhaps Berlin would be different.

Mozart's re-orchestration of 'I know that my Redeemer liveth' from Handel's Messiah. *A copyist prepared the original orchestration of Violins I and II and the bass line, to which Mozart has added parts for violas, flute, clarinet and bassoon, and has inserted 'Sop:' (soprano).*

XI

Two Trips to Germany
The Decline and Fall of Wolfgang
Amadeus Mozart

An eighteenth-century engraving suggesting the nature of long-distance travel by carriage.

Travel in the eighteenth century was at best unpleasant and at worst dangerous. In spring and autumn, most of the roads were a quagmire, bridges were easily washed away (and often not repaired for weeks), and in many parts of Europe, brigands abounded. In December 1788, Mozart's pupil J.N. Hummel set off with his father on a concert tour which would eventually bring them to London, where young Hummel appeared in one of the Haydn-Salomon concerts. The Hummels went first to Berlin, where they met Mozart. During this trip, Johannes Hummel, the father, kept a journal which describes travelling conditions and records precise details of expenses and income.

The trip from Vienna to Prün [Brünn] is twenty miles. . . . It was extremely cold with heavy snow, so that we often had to get out of the carriage in order to proceed . . . in the worst possible weather we arrived in Prün using the sledges we had organized. I tried the 'Hirsch' [Stag] Inn at first; that was very bad; then I went to the 'Three Princes' and agreed daily terms with the host for four weeks, and in this period we put on concerts twice, the first time in the Tavern, the second in the 'Three Princes', but both were bad because the gentlemen are, I think, poor as church mice and would rather whore and gamble than appreciate art; the women spend everything on clothes etc. Finally, I came to pay the bill and my arrangement amounted to 3 fl. 34 xr., but I had to pay the bastard 5 or 6 fl. and 60 xr. I asked how it was possible since we had agreed terms. He answered that the restaurant had written this sum, I asked after the waiter, the host said he wasn't there any more; and by God! I had to pay because the stage-coach was already outside the door . . . From Prün to Iglau the weather was very bad . . . When I reached Prague, I had trouble with the coachman, who would not take us to the inn where we wanted to stay. I stayed at first in a miserable inn, in a few days I had to move to H. Duschek's, where we had everything and were extremely well treated . . . Prague is very dirty, with narrow streets, here they eat much game and you can live well. The music [they were playing *Figaro* and *Don Giovanni* in the theatre] is not very well done. Madame Duschek has a beautiful property [Villa Bertramka] . . . the nobility wear the same kind of dress as in Vienna . . . To Dresden with the diligence, we paid 9 Reichstaler to the Saxon border, then we had to take sledges because of the deep snow, we suffered a great deal because of the cold and the sledge overturned. The inns are very poor, most of the time you have to sleep on straw. We stopped at the 'Post', where on the first day we were badly served. Dresden is a rather pretty town but there's not much to be done as far as the fine arts go . . . The people promised much and did little, a very hungry people, we weren't even invited to eat because they themselves have nothing to eat, and if you are a guest, there are no more than three courses, soup, beef and roast; during the day they mostly drink tea . . . The music at the concerts is very poor . . .

From Dresden to Berlin we took our own carriage, which cost us 20 Thaler. At the 'Great Rooster' Inn is the daughter of a captain who plays [the piano] very nicely, but she can't play anything except Mozart. The inns are again very bad, we mostly had to sleep on straw . . .[1]

The costs of the Hummels' trip (1788–91) and the receipts for the period amounted to:

Travelling for 3 years	182 (fl.)
Music paper for 3 years	39
Laundry bills	156
Cobbler's bills	150
At the tailor's and other purchases	300

Concerts, printed announcements
Concert tickets } Germany 150
Concert advertisements in newspapers

Music purchased	650
[Ditto] André Offenbach	150
Scotland and England, concert bills, tickets, announcements, music and engraving of music, paid	850
[sub-total]	2,627 (fl.)

From Holland returning through Germany, paid for music, concert bills, announcements	200
Tips for coachmen and inns	50
Money sent home	588
From Hanover to Piermond [= Pyrmont, a spa], travel . . .	10
Food for twelve days	24
[total]	3,499 (fl.)

Gross receipts	13,276
Fortepiano [sold at end?]	1,000
Petty cash	30
	14,306 (fl.)[2]

In other words, a profit of 10,807 gulden, which shows that it was quite possible to undertake a successful concert trip, even if, as in young Hummel's case, the artist was quite unknown. It also shows that it was necessary to keep careful accounts, and if you were to avoid overspending, you had to sleep in ordinary inns.

When, in 1789, Mozart undertook his own trip to Berlin (Potsdam), he was invited to travel there with Prince Carl Lichnowsky (later an admirer of

Prince Carl Lichnowsky (1756–1814), with whom Mozart travelled on his trip to Berlin in the spring of 1789; anonymous portrait in oils.

Beethoven). No doubt travelling in the carriage of a wealthy and cultivated prince made life much more pleasant on the journey, but it was in turn much more expensive. Whatever Mozart may have saved by staying in bad inns and eating miserable food, he would have spent in keeping with the Lichnowsky standards. For this journey we have the best possible witness – Mozart himself. Wolfgang's letters to Constanze provide not only a vivid running commentary, but also illustrate his passionate devotion to her. The series begins after the coach crossed into Bohemia:[3]

Budwitz [8 April]

Dearest Little Wife!

While the Prince is occupied bargaining about horses, I am delighted to seize this opportunity to write a few words to you, wife of my heart. How are you? Do you think of me as often as I think of you? I look at your portrait every other moment – and weep – partly for joy, partly for sorrow! Keep your health, so precious to me, and farewell, dear! Do not be worried on my account, for on this trip I know of no discomforts – or annoyances – nothing that is except for your *absence* – which, since it can't be helped, can't be changed. I write this with tears in my eyes; – adieu – I shall write you more, and more legibly, from Prague,

Prague, Good Friday, 10 April 1789

Dearest and Best Little Wife!

We arrived here safely at 1.30 in the afternoon . . . We alighted at the 'Unicorn', and after I shaved, had my hair done and dressed, I went out with the intention of lunching with [Count] Canal, but since I had to pass the Duscheks, I called there first and learned that Madame had left yesterday for Dresden!!! – So we shall meet there. He lunched at the Schönborn's [name almost illegible], where I used to eat frequently; – so I went there. – I had Duschek called (as if someone had business to discuss with him). Now you can imagine the joy. . . . After table I went to [Counts] Canal and Pachta, but found no one at home; – so I went on to Guardasoni [the impresario of the Italian company in Prague] who has almost arranged for me to write an opera for next autumn with him for 200# [ducats] and 50# travelling expenses.[4] – Then I went home to write this letter to my dear little wife. – Another thing; – [the oboist] Ramm just left here for home a week ago, he came from Berlin and said that the King had asked often and insistently if I were really coming, and since I hadn't arrived, he said, I suppose he isn't coming. – Ramm got very upset and sought to persuade him to the contrary; – on the basis of this news, my affairs will not proceed badly. – Now I shall drive with the Prince to Duschek, who is expecting us, and at 9 o'clock p.m. we leave for Dresden . . . – Dearest little wife! I so long for news from you – perhaps there will be a letter waiting for me in Dresden! O God! Make it come true. . .

At 7 o'clock in the morning
Dresden, 13 April 1789

Dearest, Best Little Wife!

We expected to arrive in Dresden after lunch, but we didn't get here until yesterday, [Easter] Sunday, at 6 in the evening; so bad were the roads.

I went yesterday to the Neumans,[5] where Mad:me Duschek is living, to give her the letter from her husband. – They live on the third floor on the corridor: and from the room you can see everybody who arrives; – when I arrived at the door, H: Neumann

202

was already there, and asked me, with whom he had the honour of speaking; – I answered: 'I shall tell you right away who I am, but you must be good enough to have Mad:me Duschek called out, in order not to spoil my joke.' But at that,moment Mad: Duschek stood before me, for she had recognized me from the window, and said at once, 'There comes someone who looks like Mozart' – now everyone was delighted. – The company was numerous and consisted mostly of ugly women, but they replaced their lack of beauty by their charm; – today the Prince and I shall go there for breakfast, then to [Kapellmeister Johann Gottlieb] Naumann, then to the chapel. – We shall leave for Leipzig tomorrow or the day after. . . .

Dearest little wife, if only I had a letter from you! – If I could tell you everything I do with your dear *portrait*, you would often laugh. – For example, when I take it out of its cover, I say: 'God greet you, Stanzerl! – God greet you, God greet you; – little rascal; – pussy-kitty; – little turned-up nose – little bagatelle – schluck und druck!' – and when I put it back again, I let it slip in bit by bit, and always say, Stu! – Stu! – Stu! but with that *certain emphasis* which such an important word requires; and at the very end, 'good night, little mouse, sleep well'; – now I suppose I have written the silliest things possible (at least as far as the great world is concerned) – but for us, who love each other so dearly, it is certainly not silly; – today is the 6th day I have been away from you, and by God! it seems like a year. . . .

Dresden, 16 April 1789
Half-past eleven at night

Dearest, Best Little Wife!

What? – Still in Dresden? – Yes, my dear; – I will relate everything to you in detail; – Monday the 13th, after we breakfasted at the Neumanns, we all went to the court chapel, and Mass was by Naumann (who also conducted it himself) – very mediocre; – we were in the oratory opposite; – all of a sudden, Neumann nudged me and introduced me to Herr von König, who is the Directeur des plaisirs (the plaisirs of the

View of Dresden, showing the bridge over the Elbe; engraving by Bernardo Bellotto after an original painting of 1749.

sad Elector [of Saxony, Frederick Augustus III), and who asked me if I would not like to perform before his Highness. I answered that although that would be a mark of the highest favour, it did not depend on me alone and thus I could not stay [longer than planned] – and that was the end of it. My princely travelling companion invited the Neumanns and Duschek to lunch: – during lunch came the news that I was to play at court next day, Tuesday the 14th, at 5.30 in the afternoon. – That is quite exceptional for it is very difficult to gain a hearing here; and you know I had no pretensions about this place. – We had a quartet party at our quarters in the Hotel de Boulogne. We held it in the chapel with Antoine Tayber (who, as you know, is the organist here), and with Hr: [Anton] Kraft (violoncellist with Prince Esterhazy) who is here with his son [Nikolaus]; in this little concert I offered the Trio [either the Piano Trio in E (K.542) or the Divertimento for string trio in E flat (K.563)] which I composed for Hr: v. Puchberg – it was quite tolerably performed – Duschek sang a great deal from *Figaro* and *Don Juan*; – the next day I played at court the new Concerto in D [no. 26, 'Coronation', K.537]; the day after, on the morning of Wednesday the 15th, I received a rather pretty snuff-box. – We then lunched at the Russian Ambassador's [Alexander Mikhailovich, Prince Beloselsky], where I played for a long time. – After lunch, it was arranged that we go to an organ. – We went there at 4 o'clock – Naumann was also there. – Now you should understand that a certain [Johann Wilhelm] *Hässler* (organist from Erfurt) is here; he was also present; – he is the pupil of a pupil of Bach. His forte lies in the organ and the piano (clavichord, rather). – Now everybody here thought that since I come from Vienna I would have no knowledge of this taste and this style of playing. – So I sat down at the organ and played. – With much effort, Prince Lichnowsky (because he knows Hässler well) persuaded him to play, too; – the strength of this Hässler is in his use of the organ pedals which, since the pedals are graduated here, is not such a great skill; otherwise, all he has done is to learn the modulations and harmony of the old Sebastian Bach by heart, and is incapable of performing a proper fugue – and has no solid way of playing – and thus falls far short of [the Viennese organist and composer J.G.] Albrechtsberger. – After that, it was decided to go to the Russian Ambassador's again, so that Hässler could hear me play the forte piano; – Hässler also played. – On the forte piano I find [my pupil] the Auernhammer girl just as good; so you can imagine how his reputation soon sank with me. – After this we went to the opera, which is really awful . . . – After the opera we went home; now came the happiest moment for me; I found the long expected and eagerly awaited letter from you, dearest, best one! – Duschek and Neumann were there as usual, I went in triumph to my room, kissed the letter numerous times before I broke the seal, then – I gulped it down rather than read it. – I stayed in my room for a long time; for I couldn't read it enough, kiss it enough. When I reappeared in company again, the Neumanns asked if I had received the letter, and when I said yes, they all congratulated me heartily, because I was lamenting every day that I had received no news; – the Neumanns are dear people. – Now, about your dear letter. . .

1   Please do not be sad;
2   Be careful of *your health* and *do not trust* the spring air;
3   That you do not go out alone, on foot – but preferably – do not *go out on foot at all*;
4   That you should be assured of my love; – I have not written a single letter to you without placing your dear portrait in front of me.
5   Please conduct yourself so as to take into consideration *your* and *my honour*, but also consider *appearances*. – Do not be annoyed at this request. – You must love me the more for thus valuing honour.

Portrait of Mozart by Dorothea (Doris) Stock, Dresden, 1789; silver-point on ivory paste board, height 7·5 cm.

6   et ultimo please be more detailed in your letters. – . . . do the Lang[e]s visit
     sometimes? – Has he made any progress with the portrait? – What kind of life do
     you lead? – All things in which I am naturally very much interested. –
     Now farewell, dearest, sweetest one, . . .

Mozart's reference to the unfinished portrait of himself by Lange (which may be dated, on the basis of this letter, *c.* 1789–90; it used to be dated, wrongly, *c.* 1782) was perhaps prompted by the fact that on this very day in Dresden, a portrait of him had been drawn in silver-point by Doris Stock (1760–1832), a talented artist.

There follows a considerable gap in the family correspondence, because at least four letters written by Wolfgang and five by Constanze are lost. The next big event was the academy concert in Leipzig, held at the old Gewandhaus on 12 May. The announcement stated that tickets cost 1 gulden and that the concert would begin at six o'clock, the programme on this occasion consisting of:

First Part	*Second Part*
Symphony	Concerto for the pianoforte
Scena (Mad. Duschek)	Scena (Mad. Duschek)
Concerto for [the] pianoforte	Fantasy for pianoforte
Symphony	Symphony [perhaps Finale only]

Mozart had great trouble with the rehearsals, for the members of the orchestra were rather old, but by dint of much tact and flattery, he persuaded them to play as he wished (he broke a shoebuckle in one of the rehearsals, stamping his feet). The German critic, Friedrich Rochlitz, was present and it is thanks to him that we know the actual programme, which included the Piano Concertos in B flat (no. 18, K.456) and C (no. 25, K.503), the *Scena* 'Ch'io mi scordi di te' (K.505), and probably the *Scena* composed for Madame Duschek in Prague, 'Bella mia fiamma' (K.528). The symphonies, unidentified, were probably two of the last four – nos. 38–41. There were in fact two piano pieces, the Fantasia in C minor (K.475) and a set of variations (probably K.354, as it is referred to by Rochlitz as being in E flat).

Despite everything [continues Rochlitz] the costs of the concert were not even covered, for the hall was almost empty. No wonder! For he stood too tall above his time for them to be able to appreciate him, even for them to understand him at all.

Everyone who knew [Mozart] had received free tickets, and certainly half of the recipients appeared at the concert. Mozart paid no attention, for he could not have been in better humour even if the room had been crowded with paying customers. Since the programme included no chorus, the members did not qualify for free tickets in the usual way. Several came to the box office and requested tickets. – 'I will ask the Herr Kapellmeister,' said he. 'Oh, let them in, let them in!' answered Mozart, 'who wants to be pedantic in such matters?'[6]

Only on 16 May does the series of Mozart's surviving letters to Constanze begin:[7]

Dearest, Best Little Wife-of-my-Heart! –

What? Still in Leiptzig? My last letter of the 8th or 9th [lost] told you I would leave at 2 o'clock in the morning, but the many requests of my friends persuaded me not to insult leiptzig [*sic*] (on account of the mistakes of one or two people), but to give an academy concert on the 12th. – This [occasion] was, as far as applause and honour [went], brilliant enough, but the income was correspondingly meagre; Duschek, who is here, sang in it; the Neumanns from Dresden are all here; – the pleasure of being as long as possible in the company of these nice people . . . delayed my trip up to now; – yesterday I wanted to leave, but could find no horses; – the same today; – for everybody wants to leave just *now*, and the number of travellers is exceptionally large; – but tomorrow morning, at 5 o'clock, off I go. – My dear! – I am very sorry, and half glad almost, that you find yourself in the same state as I have been; but no! – I wish that you would never be in this position and I certainly hope that even as I write this you will have at least *one* of my letters to hand . . . I shall *have* to stay at least 8 days in Berlin; and thus I probably won't be in Vienna before 5th or 6th June – i.e. 10 or 12 days after you receive this letter; another thing concerning the non-arrival of my letters: on 28th April I wrote to our dear friend Puchberg – I pray you, present him with 1,000 compliments and thanks in my name. . . .

In fact, Mozart did not leave Leipzig as planned, for in his catalogue (which he carried with him even on his travels) he notes: '17th May. in Leipzig. A little Gigue for the piano in the commonplace book of Hr: Engel, court organist to the Elector of Saxony in Leipzig.' This is the extraordinary Gigue in G (K.574), whose eccentric tonal patterns approach twelve-note music (eleven of the twelve notes in the first two bars), and the general effect of which is Kafka-like: spidery and slightly sinister.

Mozart proceeded to Berlin, where he and his pupil Hummel met (23 May), and where he was flatteringly received by Frederick William II and his consort, Queen Friederike. In the Nissen biography we read:

. . . This Prince loved and valued music in general, but he was really – if not a connoisseur, then at least an amateur of taste. As long as he was in Berlin, Mozart had to improvise in his presence almost daily, and often played quartets in the King's chambers with members of the royal Kapelle. Once, when he was alone with the King, the latter asked him how he judged the Berlin orchestra. Mozart, for whom any flattery was totally alien, answered: 'It has the greatest collection of virtuosi in the world; and also I have never heard such quartet playing as here; but when all the gentlemen play together, it could be improved.' The King was pleased by this frankness, and with a smile, said to him: 'Come and stay with me, you could see to it that it could be improved! I will offer you 3,000 thaler a year.' – 'Should I completely abandon my good Emperor?' said the faithful Mozart, who remained moved and silent. . . . The King, too, seemed moved by all this and after a while added: 'Consider the matter – I shall keep my word, even if you don't take advantage of it until much later.'

The King related this conversation to various people, also to Mozart's wife [widow], when she came to Berlin after her husband's death, and was materially supported by the protector of her late husband.[8]

Mozart's pen now takes up the narrative again on 19 May:

Well now, I hope that you will have received some letters from me, for they can't all have been lost; – I can't write much this time, because I must pay calls; I write only to tell you of my arrival . . . I shall be so glad to be with you again, my dear!

On 23 May he writes:

Where do you think I am writing this? In my room in the inn? – No; – in the Thiergarten in a tavern (in a garden building with a beautiful view), where I ate today

The Royal Palace in Berlin, seen from the east, with the equestrian statue of the Great Elector of Brandenburg, Frederick William (died 1688), by Andreas Schlüter; engraving by J. Rosenberg, 1781.
Mozart was received by Frederick William II (ABOVE), who offered him a post at the Prussian court; engraving by J. Adam, 1793, after a painting by Anton Graff.

all *alone*, so that I could devote my thoughts entirely to you. – The Queen wants to hear me [play] on Tuesday; *but there is not much to be had from that quarter.* I had myself announced only because it is the custom here, and otherwise they would take offence. – My dear little wife, you will have to content yourself with looking forward to seeing *me*, more than seeing any *money*. – 100 Friedrichs' D'or are not, however, 900 fl. but 700 fl. [probably an advance honorarium for six string quartets intended for the king and for six piano sonatas for the King's daughter, Princess Friederike];[9] at least that is what they told me. – 2ndly, Lichnowsky had to leave me because he was obliged to hasten away in the morning and hence I was forced to look after myself (in that expensive place, Potsdam). – 3rdly, I had to lend him 100 fl., because his purse was emptying; – I could hardly avoid doing so, you know why [the Prince was a fellow Mason]. – 4thly, the academy concert in Leipzig, just as I forecast, was a failure, so I had to backtrack 32 miles almost for nothing; Lichnowsky is entirely to blame for it, because he would not leave me in peace unless I returned to Leipzig. – Still – more about this when I see you. – There is, firstly, not much to be made from an academy concert and 2ndly – the king does not look upon it with favour. – You must be satisfied *with me* and with *this*, that I am fortunate enough to be in the king's good graces; what I've written to you must remain between us. – Thursday the 28th I shall go to Dresden, where I shall spend the night. On the 1st of June I shall sleep in Prague, and the 4th: – the 4th? *With my darling little wife*: prepare your dear and loveliest nest very daintily, for my little piece has really earned it, he has behaved very well and wants only to possess your loveliest [c——; word crossed out]. Imagine that rascal, as I write he is crawling on to the table and looking at me questioningly, but I smack him down properly – that chap is still [raging; word crossed out] and I can hardly keep that villain in his place. I hope you will come to meet me at the first post-station? – I shall arrive there on the 4th at noon. – I hope Hofer (whom I embrace 1,000 times) will be there too – if H: and Fr: von Puchberg were also to come, everybody I love would be together. Don't forget Carl either. – Now the most important thing: you must get hold of a reliable person (Satmann or someone like that) and take him with you, and he must then accompany my carriage and my luggage to the customs officials, so that *I* . . . can go home with all you dear ones. – but make sure! . . .

The musical connoisseurs in Germany had been astounded by Mozart. *Die Musikalische Real-Zeitung* in Speyer (17 June) included reports from Dresden that the composer had played for the Elector 'and in many noble and private houses, with the most boundless success; his dexterity at the piano is quite indescribable – to which must be added his exceptional ability to play at sight, which approaches the incredible; – for he is hardly able to play a piece better after practising than when he reads it for the first time. He also displayed his great ability to play the organ in the grand tradition . . .'[10]

But none of this had improved Mozart's financial situation. Quite the contrary, for shortly afterwards he wrote the now famous, and shaming, letter begun on 12 July to Michael Puchberg:

Dearest, best Friend! . . .

God! I am in a position in which I would not wish my worst enemy to be; and if you, best friend and Brother, forsake me, I, *unhappy and innocent* though I am, together with my poor, sick wife and child, am lost. Only the other day when I was with you I wanted to pour out my heart to you – but I had not the courage! – and I should not

Friedrich August, Elector of Saxony; engraving by I.F. Bause after a painting by Anton Graff.

have done so now – I only dare to do so trembling and in writing – and I wouldn't dare to write it either – if I didn't know that you know me and all my circumstances, and are convinced of my *innocence* regarding my unfortunate and very unhappy situation. Oh, God! Instead of coming to you with thanks, I approach with fresh requests! – instead of solutions, new petitions. If you knew my heart thoroughly, you must be able also to feel my pain; that through this unfortunate illness I have been prevented from fulfilling my commissions, I need not repeat to you; I must only relate to you, that despite my miserable situation, I nevertheless decided to give subscription academies in my quarters, in order to enable me to cover all the large, frequent and immediate expenses, for I was entirely convinced of your friendly assistance; but in this, too, I did not succeed; my fate is alas, *but only in Vienna*, so against me that I cannot earn money even if I wish to; for the last fortnight I have circulated a list [for subscribers] and on it is one name – Swieten's! – Since, however, it now (the 15th) seems that my dear wife is improving daily, I expected to be able to work again, had not this blow, this heavy blow, arrived; – they tell us that she is improving – although yesterday evening her condition left me feeling stunned and in despair, so much did she suffer and I – with her, but last night (the 14th) she slept so well and this morning she feels so improved that I have the highest hopes; now I am beginning to be in a condition where I can work, but I find myself in a different unhappy situation – if only temporarily! – Dearest, best friend and brother – you know my *present circumstances*, but you also know *my prospects* . . . Meanwhile, I am composing 6 easy piano sonatas [only one, K.576, was ever completed] and 6 quartets for the king,[11] all of which I shall have engraved by Kozeluch at my own expense; apart from everything else, the dedications will bring in something; in a few months my fate must be decided *at least in some small fashion*, therefore you, best friend, have nothing to lose with me; it is now up to you, my only friend, if you can and will lend me 500 fl. – I offer, until my situation is resolved, to repay you 10 fl. per month; then (as is bound to happen in a few months) I shall repay the whole sum with whatever interest you require, and shall be indebted to you for the rest of my life, since I shall never be capable of thanking you for your friendship and love; – well, thank God, it is done, now you know everything, do not take my confidence in you amiss, and consider that without your support, the honour, the peace-of-mind and perhaps the life of your friend and brother would be ruined; always your most grateful servant, true friend and brother

W. A. Mozart.

From home, 14 July 1789.
Oh, God! I can hardly bring myself to send this letter! but I must! If this illness had not occurred, I would not have been obliged to behave so shamelessly towards my only friend; – and yet I hope for your forgiveness, since you know the good and the *bad of my situation*. The bad is temporary, but the good is surely lasting, if this momentary evil can be removed. – Adieu! – for God's sake forgive me, please forgive me! – and – Adieu!

17 July 1789

. . . You must be annoyed with me, for you give me no answer. . . . since in my last letter to you, best friend, I told you in all honesty everything that was burdening my heart, only a repetition of that letter would be necessary now, but I must only add that: 1. I would not need such a large sum were it not for the appalling costs in connection with the cure of my wife, especially if she has to go to Baden. 2. Since in a short while I shall be in better circumstances, the amount I must repay is a matter of indifference to me, but for the moment it would be better and more certain if it were large. 3. I must entreat you, if it is quite impossible for you to spare me such a sum at present, to show your friendship and brotherly love for me by supporting me *with whatever funds you can spare at once*; do not doubt my integrity. . . .

P.S. Yesterday my wife was in miserable health. Today since the leeches were applied she is better, thank God; – I am still very unhappy! always between fear and hope! – and then! – Dr Closset [later Mozart's doctor in his last illness] was here again yesterday.
[In Puchberg's handwriting: 17 July 1789, answered the same day and sent 150fl.][12]

Constanze was seriously ill, and developed bed-sores which the doctors thought might reach the bone. 'She has submitted to her fate in an astonishing way', wrote Mozart to Puchberg, 'and awaits improvement or death with genuine philosophical calm, I write this with tears in my eyes . . .'[13] During this July, Mozart even managed to finish one of the works for the Prussian court, the only piano sonata (K.576) of the intended set of six, written in the easy, popular style which he was a master of (if he wanted to be; no doubt, he could not bring himself to finish the rest in a style that was becoming alien to him). Immediately after his return from Germany, he had started work on the quartets, completing the first (in D, K.575) in June.[14] The other two (K.589 in B flat and K.590 in F) were to follow in May and June of 1790.

Some time had elapsed since Mozart had worked on string quartets in a concentrated fashion; the last of the 'Haydn' series had been completed in 1785. After that, he composed a single quartet in 1786, possibly commissioned by the publisher F.A. Hoffmeister. Although this work (in D major, K.499) is in some ways less complicated and less difficult of interpretation than those of the 'Haydn' series, it is nonetheless both beautiful and profound (and contains one of the most original minuets in all eighteenth-century music). The last three quartets, written for the royal cellist, subtly flattered the king by allotting a much more prominent cello part than is usual, and this led the composer to re-think the whole layout. Mozart was trying to create a new popular style, similar in scope (but not in content) to that which Haydn had perfected and with which he had already won the hearts of musical Europe. So in a real sense, the 'Prussian' Quartets – as they are called – are 'easier' and more approachable than the austere 'Haydn' series. One aspect of the difference has been suggested by the late Hans Keller:

On the one hand, there is no doubt that [in the 'Haydn' Quartets] Mozart made, if the phrase be permitted, a special effort in view of his expert dedicatee, to whom he would also be psychologically prepared to confide his deepest secrets. On the other hand, His 'cello-playing Majesty created very particular and grave textural problems with which any other composer, including probably Haydn and Beethoven, would have been unable to cope at a high creative level. Mozart's solutions show an almost incredible capacity for adjustment, a mastery of the medium in circumstances that were nothing short of a textural emergency. . . .[15]

Constanze went off in August to take the cure at Baden. Mozart had recovered his equanimity and was composing a number of works in

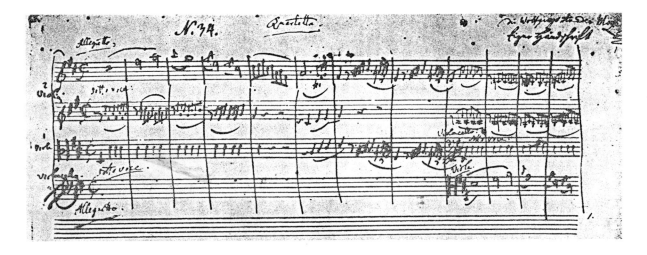

August/September and October – mostly insertion arias in operas by other composers being staged at the Burgtheater.[16] But there was also another, more personal work which Mozart found time to write, the Clarinet Quintet in A (K.581) for his friend and fellow Mason, Anton Stadler. If there is any one work that sums up this unhappy year, this must be it – parts of it seem to reflect a state of aching despair, but the whole is clothed not in some violent minor key, but in a radiant A major. The music smiles through the tears. It displays all the composer's love for and understanding of the clarinet and has rightly become one of the touchstones of clarinet writing in chamber music. It may be that it was composed with the Tonkünstler-Societät in mind, for its first public performance took place at its first Christmas concert that year (on Tuesday, 22 December) in the Burgtheater. The quintet was played between the parts of Vincenzo Righini's Cantata *Il natale d'Apollo*.[17]

The opening of the autograph of Mozart's String Quartet in D (K.576), the first 'Prussian' quartet.

A fortnight after Mozart completed his Clarinet Quintet (entered in his catalogue on 29 September), news arrived of a great victory over the Turks at Belgrade. In his diary (13 October), Zinzendorf relates how the people thronged the streets of Vienna all night, hoping that peace had come and that the frightening inflation could be halted. A day later, Zinzendorf noted that one lady had tied her skirts round her arms and head; and a bourgeois girl was stripped naked by the revelling crowd. The war was producing very odd side-effects, and there was no end in sight. Prices continued to soar.

In the midst of this unsettling scene, the Mozart family had to endure yet another personal tragedy: on 16 November their fifth child, Anna Maria, died of cramps only an hour after being born.[18] At the end of the year, Mozart again approached Puchberg for money – this time 400 gulden. *Così fan tutte* was about to be given and the composer told Puchberg that he could soon expect repayment. 'I really must pay off the chemists and doctors,' added Mozart and begged his friend 'to rescue me from this ghastly situation.' He hoped to finish his set of quartets for the Prussian court, so as to convince Puchberg of his 'complete honesty'.[19] It was in this letter that he invited Puchberg and Haydn to a rehearsal of *Così fan tutte*. Puchberg responded by sending 300 gulden.

On 20 February 1790 – the year in which he composed hardly anything – Mozart again approached Puchberg for money – 'it's a matter that can't be postponed' – and received 25 gulden.[20] And on that day Joseph II died, to be succeeded by his brother, as Leopold II. Joseph had been a controversial and difficult monarch, whose decisions, if made with the best of intentions, often resulted in catastrophic situations – especially in regard to the futile war with Turkey. But although he had a very imperfect understanding of Mozart's music, Joseph supported the composer to the end. Now, under a new monarch, Mozart could not be sure that his position as chamber composer to the court would be confirmed.

Week after week, he continued to borrow money from Puchberg. At the end of March or the beginning of April, Mozart received a letter from van Swieten, the contents of which he communicated to Puchberg. Swieten had hopes of persuading the new monarch to engage Mozart as first or, more realistically, second Kapellmeister, and Mozart had hopes of persuading Puchberg to disgorge more money; the response to this particular letter was 150 gulden. On 8 April, Mozart discusses a performance of one of the new trios, as well as of the 'Stadler' Quintet, at the house of Johann Carl, Count von Hadik (son of Field-Marshal Andreas von Hadik), and seizes the opportunity to dredge up another loan, this time a meagre 25 gulden. A fortnight later, Puchberg was sending him another 25 gulden, and at the beginning of May, Mozart again pressed his friend and received 100 gulden. In that letter, Mozart complains of toothache and headache, relates his plans for subscription concerts at home and then tells Puchberg of a debt of 100 gulden to a haberdasher, 'who is now seriously and violently demanding payment.' On 17 May, Mozart writes:

You will no doubt have heard from your household that I called on you yesterday, uninvited (as you had given me permission to do), to lunch with you. – You know my circumstances; in short – since I cannot find any true friends, I am forced to raise money from the usurers; but as it takes time to seek out and find the most Christian among this un-Christian class of people, I am at the moment so destitute that I must entreat you, my dearest friend, in the name of all we hold sacred, to assist me with the bare necessities . . . If you knew how much sorrow this causes me – it has prevented me all this time from finishing my quartet [K.589]. – I now have great hopes for an appointment at court, for I have reliable information that the Emperor has kept my petition and not referred it back with a favourable or condemning remark, as he has with the others. That is a good sign. . .

It was not a good sign, however, though Puchberg sent along another 150 gulden. Mozart actually began a petition to Archduke Francis in which he humbly requested that he might be considered for the position of second Kapellmeister, 'especially,' as he put it, since 'the very clever Kapellmeister Salieri has never applied himself to the church style, whereas I have made this style my own from my earliest youth.' He also hoped that he might teach members of the royal family. But there is no evidence that this petition – if indeed that is the one Mozart was referring to in the letter to Puchberg – was ever written or sent (none has survived in the court archives).[21] Salieri remained as 'Hofkapellmeister' (court chapel master) with Ignaz Umlauf as the official 'Hofkapellmeister-Substitutus'.[22] But at least Mozart soon learned that his own previous appointment and salary had been confirmed by Leopold.

At the end of May 1790, Constanze went to Baden once again to take the cure. Mozart wrote to her early in June, saying that if she came back to town on Saturday, she could stay 'for half of Sunday as well'. His pupil and friend, Joseph Eybler, was conducting a mass at his parish church in Schwechat, a town near Vienna on the road to Hungary. 'Take care of your health, apropos – N.N. (you know who I mean) is a bastard – first he flatters you so sweetly to your face and then in public he runs down *Figaro* . . .'[23]

Ten days later, he writes to Puchberg:

The violinist and impresario Johann Peter Salomon; portrait by Thomas Hardy, 1791. Salomon met Mozart in Vienna before leaving for England accompanied by Joseph Haydn.

I'm here to conduct my opera [*Così*, now back in the repertoire after the closing of all theatres following Emperor Joseph's death] – My wife is a little better. – She feels some relief already, but she will have to bathe at least 60 times . . . Dearest friend, can you, in view of my pressing necessities, be of some assistance to me. Oh, please do it! – for the sake of economy, I stay in Baden and come in only when strictly necessary. – Now I am forced to give away my quartets (this laborious work) for a trifling sum, just to get some money in hand . . .; tomorrow a Mass [K.317?] of mine will be performed at Baden [by my friend Anton Stoll, director of music there]. Adieu – (at 10 o'clock) . . . P.S. Please send the viola.
[In Puchberg's hand: 'sent 25 fl. 12 June']

It used to be thought that the sale of the quartets was to Artaria, but this must be wrong:[24] Artaria would not have taken a year and a half to publish them. The sale was probably to one of the firms of Viennese copyists (Traeg, Lausch, etc.) or to a private individual such as Johann Tost (for whom Mozart wrote his late quintets). What Mozart *had* done was to sell two of the first set of three Quintets to Artaria who brought them out in 1789 (K.515) and August 1790 (K.516).[25] Yet despite all these sources of extra income, Mozart was now living permanently beyond his means – and principally because of the costs incurred by Constanze's lengthy cures. But Puchberg's supply was drying up – he obviously regarded Mozart as a bottomless pit – for in the middle of August Mozart applied to his friend yet again, with the usual anguished remarks ('. . . picture to yourself my condition – ill, full of trouble and worries . . . can you not extend a helping hand with a trifle? . . .'); for which he received a mere 10 gulden, the lowest sum yet offered.[26]

It was time to take drastic action. Mozart had formed yet another scheme to raise money – a concert tour through southern Germany, ending in Frankfurt, to coincide with the coronation festivities of Leopold II as Emperor of the Holy Roman Empire of German Nations. Mozart was still an unknown quantity to Leopold, and the composer hoped his concerts would be noticed by the court. He travelled in his own carriage (at great expense), leaving on 23 September accompanied by his violin-playing brother-in-law Hofer.[27] On his return, Mozart raised a huge sum – 1,000 gulden – from a merchant named Heinrich Lackenbacher by pawning the family's entire household furnishings. Constanze, who since her marriage had lived in ten different rented lodgings, had moved yet again, during Wolfgang's absence, to a flat in the Rauhensteingasse.[28] It was a roomy, if rather dark, apartment, but it cost considerably less (330 gulden p.a.) than the Domgasse quarters (460 gulden).

On this second tour the German connoisseurs were again lavish in their praises – one of the most interesting contemporary descriptions of a concert conducted by Mozart and including his solo performance in concertos comes from the pen of Count Ludwig von Bentheim-Steinfurt,[29] who was present at the historic concert in Frankfurt on 15 October. The hall was half-empty, however, due to other events at the same time – and Mozart returned to Vienna with empty pockets.

There were interesting offers from London – first from the manager of the Italian Opera there, Robert Bray O'Reilly, who wanted Mozart to compose 'at least two operas, serious or comic' for the forthcoming season. His letter,[30] written on 26 October 1790, reached Mozart after his return. Then, a few weeks later, came Johann Peter Salomon, the leading impresario of the day, intending to bring Haydn and Mozart, together or separately, to London.[31] Prince Nicolaus Esterházy had died, thus freeing Haydn from his responsibilities as Kapellmeister (though he received a handsome pension from his late employer, as well as his salary) and permitting him to travel abroad. He came to Vienna where he could participate in Mozart's latest String Quintet (K.593), apparently a commission from Haydn's former leader of the second violins at Eszterháza, Johann Tost. Abbé Stadler related how the quintet of players was organized, with Haydn and Mozart alternating as first and second viola. They played the C major Quintet (K.515), 'and still more that in G

The final entries in Mozart's catalogue of his own compositions (begun in 1784, see pp. 106–7). The entries record the last two operas – Die Zauberflöte and La clemenza di Tito – and the Clarinet Concerto in A (K.622), the final item, listed under the date 15 November, being Eine kleine Freymaurer-Kantate (K.623); the detail from the first page of the cantata bears Mozart's signature and the corresponding date of completion – 15 November.

'minor' (K.516) and (related Vincent Novello)[32] Stadler 'particularly mentioned the 5th in D major, singing the Bass part' (i.e. K.593).

Haydn and Mozart were together on 15 December, the day Salomon departed for London with Haydn. When the moment of parting arrived, tears came to Mozart's eyes and he said 'We are probably saying our last adieu in this life.' Haydn, who was 58, took this to refer to his own mature years, for it could not have occurred to him that he might outlive his young friend.[33]

*　　*　　*

In 1791, the Mozarts' financial situation began to show a distinct improvement.[34] The large sum that Mozart borrowed in 1790 (1,000 gulden) had been absolutely necessary for them to get back on their feet. Then came the two big opera commissions, for *Die Zauberflöte* (which was started first) and the unexpected bonus of composing the Coronation Opera for Prague, *La clemenza di Tito*. Unlike 1790, which was a disastrous year for Mozart's creative output – almost nothing of any significance was composed except for the remaining two 'Prussian' Quartets, the string Quintet in D (K.593) and the 'Piece for a musical clock' (K.594) – 1791 proved to be one of Mozart's most prolific years, as a simple list reveals: the Piano Concerto no. 27 (K.595) completed; three Lieder (K.596–8), Six Minuets for full orchestra (K.599), Six German Dances for full orchestra (K.600), Four Minuets and Four German Dances (K.601, 602), Two Contre-Danses for orchestra (K.603), Two Minuets (K.604) and Two German Dances for orchestra (K.605), Contre-Danse 'Il trionfo delle donne' (K.607) and Six Ländlerische (K.606), another piece for musical clock (K.608), a Contre-Danse 'Die Leyerer' (K.610), One German Dance with Leyerer trio (K.611), Aria 'Per questa bella mano' for bass and double-bass solo (K.612), Variations for piano on the song 'Ein Weib ist das herrlichste Ding' (K.613), the String Quintet in E flat (K.614), a final chorus 'Viviamo felice' (K.615) for the opera *Le gelosie villane* by Sarti, an Andante for musical clock (K.616), Adagio and Rondeau for glass-harmonica etc. in F minor (K.617), the motet 'Ave, verum corpus' (K.618), the Small German Cantata 'Die ihr des unermeßlichen Weltalls Schöpfer ehrt' (K.619), *Die Zauberflöte* (K.620), *La clemenza di Tito* (K.621), the Clarinet Concerto in A (K.622), *Eine kleine Freymaurer-Kantate* (K.623) and a whole series of single pieces and fragments, including most of the Requiem (K.626). Given such an impressive list of works, there was every reason to suppose that Mozart was about to embark on a new and spectacularly successful stage in his career.

La clemenza di Tito, composed for the coronation celebrations in Prague,[35] brought Mozart back once more to the Bohemian capital, where his music was much appreciated. It is to this city that we now return, not so much to relive the excitement surrounding Leopold II's coronation (see p. 227), but to examine another, more sinister side of life in high places – a suspected conspiracy of the Freemasons.

XXV-XXVIII PRAGUE

The people of Prague, capital of Bohemia, held Mozart and his music in high regard. His opera Le nozze di Figaro *went into rehearsal there shortly after its première in Vienna in 1786, and the following year Mozart travelled there twice, on the second occasion to compose and conduct his next opera,* Don Giovanni. *In 1791 he was commissioned at short notice to write a new opera,* La clemenza di Tito, *to be performed at the National Theatre in September as part of the celebrations associated with the coronation, as King of Bohemia, of Emperor Leopold II (see p. 327).*

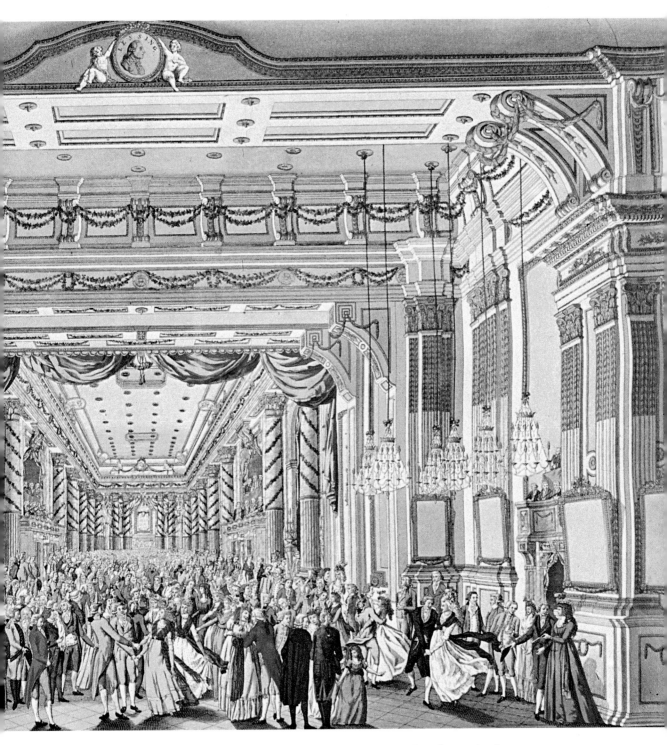

(TOP LEFT) *General view of the city from the west; coloured engraving by Leopold Peuckert.*
(CENTRE LEFT) *One of a series of engravings showing the progress of the coronation procession of Leopold II and his consort, Maria Luisa, to the cathedral; engraving by Franz Heger.*
(BELOW LEFT) *The baroque church of St Nicholas, seen in a contemporary engraving; following Mozart's death, a Requiem mass was held here.*
(ABOVE) *A special chamber built next to the National Theatre in 1791 to provide space for some of the many festive events; engraving by C. Plush after P. and F. Heger.*

XXIX *An unsigned painting, dating from* c. *1790, showing a meeting of the Viennese Masonic Lodge 'Zur gekrönten Hoffnung' ('Crowned Hope') in which Prince Nicolaus Esterházy is officiating as Master of Ceremonies and Mozart is depicted, seated in the foreground on the right, holding a conversation with his neighbour (see pp. 115f.).*

*(*OVERLEAF*)*
XXX *One of the celebrated stage designs by Karl Friedrich Schinkel for the Berlin production of* Die Zauberflöte *in 1816. The monumental entrance to the palace of the Queen of the Night, for whose entry this architectural design – strongly reminiscent of ancient Egyptian architecture – gave way to a backcloth (partially visible) representing the night sky, featuring a striking, symmetrically arranged, all-over pattern of stars on a blue background, together with delicate clouds and a crescent moon.*

PAMINA Du hier! — Güttige Götter=
Achzehenter Auftritt. II. Act.

TAMINO — Hier sind die Schreckensforten
Achtundzwanzigster Auftritt. II Act.

XXXI, XXXII Die Zauberflöte, *first produced in Vienna at the*
Theater auf der Wieden (Freihaus-Theater) in 1791, rapidly became
popular throughout German-speaking countries. In 1795 the monthly
Allgemeines Europäisches Journal, *published in Brünn (now Brno),*
included a series of six scenes from the opera, two of which (from Act II)
are shown here; coloured engravings by Joseph and Peter Schaffer.

XII

A Freemasons' Conspiracy in 1791?

O N 14 OCTOBER 1791, Mozart was in Vienna, writing an affectionate letter to his wife, who was taking the cure in Baden.[1] He describes, in an outburst of naive optimism, how he took Salieri and his mistress, the singer Caterina Cavalieri, to *Die Zauberflöte*. 'They both said it was a grand opera . . . they have never seen a more beautiful or pleasant production.' It is Mozart's last letter known to survive.

On that same day, Emperor Leopold II, in the Hofburg in Vienna, received an unsigned letter from a confidant (Leopold would, of course, have recognized the handwriting):

With a feeling of horror I beg to inform your Majesty . . . of a most curious report which was conveyed to me yesterday evening . . . by a man not unknown to Your Majesty, *Ehrenberg*, who wishes to repeat the matter in person and to inform you of various other dubious circumstances as soon as Your Majesty is graciously pleased to grant him a private audience. . . .

On the very first day after the arrival of His Royal Highness the Archduke Francis [from the Prague Coronation, Cabinet Secretary Johann Baptist von] Schloißnigg entered the Cabinet office of Ehrenberg and delivered the following sermon, which I am in the position of being able to repeat, partly *verbatim* and partly based on its most significant content.

'Thank God the Archduke has finally arrived. He could in fact have stayed away longer, *because he has ruined my pheasant hunt*. But I already feared he had been subjected to some influences *because he is taken everywhere*, and his father [Leopold II] doesn't want to let him out of his sight, *so that he will not see or experience certain things*. But all has been arranged and I have to say, everything is still all right, as it was before.

'You know that marvellous story, too, about the 16,000 military being called up in Vienna. They want to stave off the coming *Revolution. But that won't help them at all. A revolution is necessary, because . . . a ruler who simply enjoys life does not deserve to occupy the throne* [here the handwriting becomes shaky and the underlining uneven].

A shock passes through my veins as I write this, but Ehrenberg has offered to swear before Your Majesty that he heard these *words* from Schloißnigg's lips.

This person, this Cromwell, this perpetrator of *high treason* is the private tutor and daily confidant of the Crown Prince of Austria; he is at the head of the Illuminati; he was placed in this position by Baron Swieten; he permits himself such speeches in front of third parties in whom he otherwise shows no particular trust, speaks thus in an Imperial building and in the chancellery of the Crown Prince!!! What might he say in other circumstances, and what designs and plans might be maturing in this man's mind!²

This letter started a chain of investigations into Schloißnigg's activities, but its most interesting feature is the reference to Baron van Swieten, Imperial and Royal Librarian and patron of Mozart and of music in general. It is the first hint that Swieten might not have been considered a thoroughly loyal member of the Austrian establishment.

Before we proceed further, some explanation is necessary to distinguish several different kinds of Freemasonry with which this chapter is concerned: first, the Illuminati. The standard work on the subject, published in 1886, is by Robert F. Gould, who wrote: 'The secret society of the Illuminati of Bavaria is connected with the Masonic Brotherhood by the feeblest thread imaginable . . . its suppression entailed the extinction of Freemasonary throughout Bavaria and a great part of Southern Germany, a blow from which, after the lapse of a century, the Fraternity has not yet recovered.'³

Professor Adam Weishaupt, founder of the Illuminati movement in Bavaria; engraving after G.V. Mansinger.

The founder of the Illuminati was Professor Adam Weishaupt (1748–1830), born in Ingolstadt, Bavaria, and educated there by the Jesuits. At the university there he was appointed to two chairs, in 1772 and 1775 respectively, both formerly occupied by members of the Society of Jesus, whose aims Weishaupt had come to hate. He proceeded to form his own society with the objective of destroying evil and promoting good causes. The first members were enrolled in May 1776; novices knew only their teacher, but later, on being promoted, came to know other members. At the outset, none was a Freemason, but Weishaupt himself was initiated into a 'Strict Observance' lodge in Munich at the end of 1777 and thereafter introduced Masonic practices.

In the early stages, the society was active only in southern parts of Germany and in Roman Catholic areas of the country. By 1780, however, Marquis Constanzo von Constanzo, a Privy Councillor of the Elector of Bavaria, was deputed to spread the society's influence to northern Germany. He succeeded in converting many members of 'Strict Observance' lodges, who in turn expected a new ritual, which Weishaupt had still not perfected. On the completion of a new set of rituals, Weishaupt quarrelled with his leading disciple, Baron von Knigge, who withdrew in 1784.

With the advent of revolutionary sentiments in France, the threat posed by a secret society such as the Illuminati led to an Electoral edict of 22 June 1784, by which they were suppressed, along with all Masonic lodges throughout Bavaria. Although, in Gould's words, 'some of the greatest names of the age' were members of the Illuminati, the highest estimate of their membership at any time during the society's ten-year existence was no more than 2,000.⁴

The 'Strict Observance'⁵ branch of Freemasonry referred to above developed slowly during the first twenty years of its existence in the mid-eighteenth century, but in the following twenty years it spread throughout

Maria Luisa Röm. Kaiserin. Leopold II. Röm. Kaiser.

The Empress, Maria Luisa, and her
husband Leopold II, who had been
crowned as Holy Roman Emperor in
Frankfurt in 1790; engraving by
Franz Heger.
In September 1791, their coronation as
King and Queen of Bohemia took
place in St Vitus' Cathedral, Prague.
A series of contemporary engravings
were published charting the ceremonial
procession (cf. pl. XXVI) through the
city; one of these (RIGHT, ABOVE)
shows the royal party outside the
Cathedral. The coronation itself is
also shown (RIGHT).

continental Europe. This organization originated in Scotland and was based on the historical fiction that an unbroken succession of Grand Masters had existed for centuries since the destruction of the Knights Templar, some of whom had managed to find a place of refuge in Scotland (where Freemasonry had its origins). The identity of each successive Grand Master was secret during his lifetime, and it was believed that Prince Charles Edward Stuart (the Young Pretender) held that office in the 1740s, though Lord Kilmarnock[6] was thought by some to have been Grand Master.

Karl Gotthelf, Baron von Hund und Alten-Grotkau, born in 1722, is recorded as having received all three degrees of conventional Freemasonry in 1742. He was subsequently active in Paris (where he probably came under the influence of Lord Kilmarnock and other Jacobite supporters), Frankfurt etc. and c. 1750 he became Grand Master of the VIIth Province (Germany between the Elbe and the Oder) and soon sought to revive the Order of the Temple in continental Europe, which was divided into nine provinces. Baron von Hund issued a new warrant to the Naumberg lodge in 1753, having previously established a lodge and provincial chapter on his own estate at Unwurde. It was at Naumberg that plans for financing the restoration of the Order of the Temple were laid.[7] Within the new system each novice (Entered Apprentice) was bound by an oath of unquestioning obedience to his superiors, hence the title 'Strict Observance'. Promotion was through five further degrees, the highest being that of Knighthood (at first restricted to members of the nobility, but later open to wealthy merchants, e.g. in Hamburg, on payment of exorbitant fees).

In September 1780, Duke Ferdinand of Brunswick put forward a plan for a Convent to review the origins, aims, rituals etc. of contemporary Freemasonry, but it was not until July 1782 that it finally opened in Wilhelmsbad. Thirty-five delegates were present, and members of other systems, including the Illuminati (represented by Knigge), were also permitted to address the congress. The outcome was a reverse for the Strict Observance, which went into decline.

The files in the Haus-, Hof- und Staatsarchiv in Vienna, from which all the unpublished material for this chapter has been taken, show that c. 1790 the authorities in Vienna became increasingly concerned about the (as they believed) secret operations of the Illuminati, the Strict Observance and, ultimately, all aspects of Freemasonry. European Masons were increasingly being influenced by the ideas of the French Revolution, and the Austrian authorities were under the impression that French lodges were exerting pressure on their Austrian counterparts to follow France in establishing a constitutional monarchy – in 1790–91 the idea of regicide had not yet entered most people's minds, even in France.[8]

The Austrian secret police, aided by Austrian embassies abroad, wanted to establish: (1) Who were the leading Illuminati and where did they primarily operate? (2) Who were members of the Strict Observance, and where? (3) Were members of (1) and (2) also straightforward Masons as well? (4) Were any or all of these groups actively fomenting French Revolutionary ideas in the Austrian crown lands? From the outset, the authorities seem to have considered Bohemia a potential hotbed of revolution. The following were considered to be Bohemian Illuminati:[9]

Kollowrat, Count, known as the Reichenberger, First Lord Chancellor of Bohemia.
Kollowrat, Count, his brother
Del Cuito, now in Vienna
Count Philipp Clary
Sauer, Judge of the Appeal Court
Canal, Joseph private [i.e. having no official position]
Lazansky, President of the *Landrechte* [courts]
Prince Pignatelli, Spanish General, absent
Baron von Taubenheim, *Rittmeister*

Baron Gottfried van Swieten, who on 5 December 1791 was dismissed from all his official appointments on suspicion of being involved in a Masonic conspiracy; engraving by François Gonard, 1781.

It was not exactly a list to raise a cheer in the offices of the Vienna secret police, for it included too many names of high officials. But was it all true? Ordinary Masonic lodges kept detailed membership lists; the Illuminati and Strict Observance did not. The Vienna police continued to send lists of names of probable Illuminati to Bavaria: among the names were those of many of Mozart's friends and patrons[10] – Count Seeau, the music Intendant of Munich, Christian Cannabich, the composer and conductor in Munich, Count Friedrich Spaur, canon of Salzburg cathedral, and of course Sonnenfels, the great theatrical reformer, and even Count Cobenzl, Vice-Chancellor, Mozart's host in 1781 and 1782.

On 14 February 1790, it was found that a secret Lodge of the Illuminati existed in Prague, with the name 'Liebe und Wahrheit' ('Love and Truth'). Accompanying a list [3 January 1792?] of Illuminati for Bavaria prepared by Professor Leopold Alois Hoffmann, a covering letter stated that 'his High Count Excellency should have the list copied secretly and send the original back to Count Lehrbach', who was a councillor in the Bohemian and Austrian Court Chancellery, and Minister at the Palatine Court. This amazing document is reproduced in Appendix 5.[11]

Again we encounter the name van Swieten, as No. 14. Remembering that the Baron had been in Berlin for many years, and considering the inclusion of Prussian names in the list (including two princes of the realm), one may suppose that Swieten became a member of the Illuminati while in Berlin. Baron Jacobi (Jacoby), No. 15 on the list, was the Prussian Ambassador in Vienna, and a member of Mozart's Lodge. By now the Austrian authorities were very alarmed. Johann Baptist von Schloißnigg (No. 26) had, by the time the list was prepared, already lost his position, 'former tutor of Archduke Francis' being written beside his name. There can be little doubt that Mozart, as a leading Mason, will have been under suspicion as well and perhaps would have lost his position as I.R. Chamber Composer had not other events intervened. On 5 December 1791, a note was delivered by hand to Baron Gottfried van Swieten, informing him that he had been summarily dismissed

Heinrich Franz, Count Rottenhan, who, as Lord Lieutenant of Prague, was commanded by Leopold II to investigate reports of a Masonic conspiracy in the city; engraving by Johann Boehm.

OPPOSITE
The Rauhensteingasse, Vienna (ABOVE), showing (left) the house in which Mozart died; watercolour by J. Wohlmuth, c. 1820. (BELOW) The suburban setting of St Marx, where Mozart's remains were interred in the local cemetery; coloured engraving by Carl Schütz, 1792.

from his official positions. In the 1792 Illuminati list he is already described as 'former President of the Studies Commission'. (Swieten was not a diplomat for nothing, however: Leopold II died on 1 March 1792 and by the time the next *Schematismus* was printed, in 1793, Swieten had managed under the new Emperor, Francis II, to recover his former position.)

A short walk from the imposing building on the Josephsplatz which housed the Imperial Royal Court Library was the composer's home, a modest house at Rauhensteingasse No. 970. There, 'in the hour after midnight, as the fifth of December 1791 began, Wolfgang Amadeus Mozart died.'[12]

*   *   *

One of the men with whom Mozart had been closely associated in Prague was the Lord Lieutenant, Heinrich Franz, Count Rottenhan (1737–1809), formerly President of the Government of Upper Austria. He had become a confidant of Leopold II, who had created the post of *Burggraf* of Prague for his liegeman – an appointment so discreet that Rottenhan's name simply disappears from the 1791 *Schematismus*. But courtiers knew that Rottenhan's position remained one of enormous hidden power; Zinzendorf especially noted that at the first performance of *La clemenza di Tito* in Prague (6 September 1791) 'Rottenhan was in the box with the Emperor...'[13] Francis II, when he became Emperor in 1792, remembered those civil servants who had been loyal to his father, and we find Rottenhan a member of the State Council for Internal Affairs, listed with all his titles (lord of the estates Rothenhaus, Edlitz, Platten, Neosoblitz [Neosablaz] and Bielenz in the Kingdom of Bohemia, Knight Grand Cross of the Royal Order of St Stephen, actual privy councillor, living at Krugerstraße No. 1074.)

As the new year dawned without Mozart, one of Leopold II's confidants, *Rittmeister* (Captain of the Horse) Prochaska (Prohaska), wrote to Rottenhan on 26 January seeking information on the famous actor, Carl Wahr, a leading Shakespearean interpreter in his day. Wahr had retired to Prague and it was rumoured that as well as being a Mason he was a leading member of the Illuminati. Rottenhan answered that Wahr was indeed a respected member of the old-Scots-Lodge 'Zu den drei Sternen' ('Three Stars'), whose Masters were the Illuminati Count Künigl and Baron Schmidburg, Royal Captain of the District.[14] By now, Leopold II was beginning to suspect that there was a conspiracy of the Freemasons in Prague. That city had always been a kind of rival to Vienna and there were many 'dissidents' there, political and otherwise. The Emperor then wrote personally to Rottenhan, and the Count promptly replied in a long letter dated 29 January 1792:

Your Majesty

Your most gracious letter of the 26th inst. was delivered to me by *Rittmeister* Prohaska: . . . Your Majesty may rest assured that I shall pursue with the utmost attention the business graciously entrusted to me. I am not able to judge on what ground the suspicion is based . . . that the persons named on the list given to me are in dubious association with others of ill intentions; but I shall be the more attentive to

what is happening, although if my humble impressions are not greatly mistaken I may reassure Your Majesty completely concerning the public safety of this province [Bohemia], and [that] the persons entered on that list do not in themselves appear to me to be at all dangerous. With the exception of Dr Mayer, they are all Freemasons; there is indeed a great deal of fanaticism among the Masons here, and I believe that at the time when the Illuminati sect was being established, many of the Masons here joined *Weishaupt* and other apostles of this dangerous order in Vienna . . . But if I consider the everyday activities and the family background of these men, the whole organization is, in my view, rendered very innocuous.

Freemasonry has certainly caused a very great deal of harm: it encourages prejudice, it discourages a true public spirit. The worst is that this proselytizing, and the deviousness with which those who manipulate the masses use every possible opportunity to secure appointments or any other advantage in order that the Craft or rather the individuals themselves are viewed in the best possible light. Under the previous government this mischief reached such proportions that many young people had no hopes of a career unless they became Masons . . . I shall here limit myself to saying that at present – unless I were to receive information of a more critical nature – there is no reason for concern about the Masons in this district. [Concerning the Illuminati] The men of this Order (in part hypocrites and in part fanatics) attempt to impose their will with an indescribable intolerance and arrogance and have as their goal nothing less than the overthrow of all positive religion and law-and-order, . . .

These reformers – to whose intellectual principles almost all scholars in Germany, especially those in Prussia and the small principalities of Saxony, belong – are the implacable enemies of all monarchs, but are also the declared opponents of all classes of citizens who, under the protection of the laws of the monarchy, are possessed of some advantages over others because of their position in society within this system. Just because of this situation, I believe that Illuminatism, given the present constitution of the Austrian State, cannot become dangerous. Apart from the fact that fortunately we have not yet reached the degree of immorality which *must* of necessity lead as in France to Revolution, most of the Masons here who might have been considered to be Illuminati are *property owners*. The horrors of the French Revolution must have taught them what would happen to them if they were to raise a traitorous hand against the laws of the land. . . . Finally, the reasons which are producing rebellious actions in France do not obtain here – . . . In view of the present situation there is no possibility that the downfall of the present order of things would enrich anyone here. In France, certain members of the nobility could forfeit their property and title because through the Revolution they could hope to steal ten times what they owned before; the operation of the assignat [paper money] alone made millionaires out of bankrupt property owners. But all this would be quite impossible on German territory, so that whatever the learned Illuminati 'Republic' in Germany tries to hatch (and even their projects are less dangerous than those of the French clubs, because German scholars always remain pedants), they will have no effect on Your Majesty's German provinces, as long as financial order, the continuing exercise of the government administration supported as hitherto by the public spirit, watchfulness against false Enlightenment, serious support of a religion which has a positive effect on the populace, strict discipline in the army, and the proper balance between the various classes of citizens, are adhered to.

As far as the personal character of those persons suspected of being Illuminati is concerned, I cannot of course prove everything I think about them, but also from this

232

standpoint they do not appear to me to be dangerous. [There follows an assessment of the characters of Count Lazansky, Count Friedrich Nostiz, Count Kollowrat, Baron Putiany, Count Canal, Professor Meissner, the actor Spies, the retired actor Carl Wahr, Count Künigl, Dr Mayer and Count Laurus. Rottenhan continues:]

How Dr Mayer came to be on this list I cannot understand. Long before I had the least prospect of securing my present position, at a time therefore when he could have had no possible reason for deceiving me by his observations, Dr Mayer kept bitterly objecting to the increase of Illuminatism and to the pressures of the Masons. He discussed the perniciousness of this secret society so frequently that I presumed it was partly due to his melancholy state of mind. I know for certain that he belongs to no lodge here. . . . Dr Mayer must conduct much correspondence with foreign scholars in connection with his work on physics and chemistry, but I cannot imagine that he has allowed himself to dabble in politics. Altogether Dr Mayer has more relations with men who, according to French terminology, belong to the aristocrats rather than to the democrats. But I shall do my best to uncover any disguise the man may have donned if he is not the solid, honest scientist I take him to be. . .[15]

Leopold II, a careful ruler who became increasingly devious as the political situation in Europe deteriorated, was bombarded with demands from his sister Marie Antoinette to undertake some military action to save the French monarchy. He hesitated, being aware of the far-reaching consequences of such action, but on 7 February 1792 he signed a defensive alliance with Prussia, each side promising to supply, if necessary, 10,000 troops to aid the other country if either were invaded. A secret clause also provided for mutual aid in the case of internal disturbances (i.e. revolution); but Leopold II was still opposed to military intervention in France and said so in a note drafted by Minister Kaunitz for Prince Reuss in Berlin.[16]

DIE ZAUBERFLÖTE

Though imbued with the ideas and symbolism of Freemasonry, Mozart's opera is also characterized by a fairy-tale atmosphere which helped it to gain widespread popularity in German-speaking countries in the years following its first performance in 1791 at the Theater auf der Wieden in Vienna (see also plates XXX–XXXII). Attempts made in the 1790s – in the wake of the French Revolution – to reinterpret the meaning and the message of the opera as a political allegory are discussed in Appendix 6.

ABOVE *Frontispiece from the original printed libretto of 1791, engraved by Ignaz Alberti, a fellow Mason; the scene, which includes Masonic symbols and features ancient Egyptian motifs, was omitted from later editions.*

ABOVE, RIGHT *Announcement of the first performance, given on 30 September 1791.*

ABOVE *Stage design by Joseph Quaglio for the 1793 Munich production: pen and wash drawing.*

RIGHT *Tamino fleeing from the serpent in Act I, scene 1, as illustrated in the* Wienerische Opernkalender, *Vienna 1796; engraving by Mathias Ludwig.*

LEFT *The actor-manager Emanuel Schikaneder (1751–1812), who in addition to writing the libretto with C.L. Giesecke, created the role of Papageno; engraving by Philipp Richter.*

Leopold II's last public act as Emperor was to receive the new Turkish Ambassador on 26 February 1792, ratifying the exchange of ambassadors with the Pforte in Istanbul, which had been celebrated by the festive arrival of Ratif Effendi and his suite in Vienna on 11 February. The dreadful war with Turkey was now officially at an end.

The day before this audience – it was a Saturday – Leopold had ridden to Schönbrunn to supervise preparations for the court's transference there in summer. He returned overheated from the ride and threw open the windows of his apartments. On Tuesday, 28 February, he awoke with sharp pains in his left chest and spleen. By 9 a.m. he was drenched in perspiration and bright red in the face, with excruciating abdominal pains. Leeches were applied four times in two days. In the afternoon of 1 March, Empress Maria Luisa sat knitting by the window of his bedchamber; about 3.30 Leopold called out, saying he must vomit. She rushed to his bedside and he died in her arms.

Soon sinister rumours began to circulate: Leopold had been poisoned by the Freemasons, the Jesuits, by emissaries from Paris. It was, of course, pure fiction. The Empress never recovered from the shock, and she too died not long afterwards, on 15 May. The new Emperor, Francis, was young (twenty-four) and inexperienced, and politically Austria gradually drew further and further to the right. The situation was not helped by the deterioration of the monarchy in France, and by Francis' decision to go to war (although in the event the French declared war on Austria on 20 April 1792). The Austrians promptly lost Belgium and were disastrously defeated in France and the Netherlands in June and July 1794. 'All the normal resources of the monarchy were exhausted; it was impossible to see where the means to finance a new campaign would come from.'[17]

Austria was on the way to becoming a police state. Pressure on the Masons was so severe that by 1793 many lodges had voluntarily closed. Capital punishment for high treason was reintroduced and some 'Jacobin' conspirators were hanged in 1794. In January 1795, a new law prohibited all secret societies, which were associated in the official mind with high treason, and in June 1795 an official order 'went out to close all surviving Masonic lodges'.[18] It was a *Handbillet* by Francis to Counts Károly, Pálffy (Hungarian Court Chancellor) and Heinrich von Rottenhan, now Court Chancellor.

But what were they to do with *Die Zauberflöte*, clearly a Masonic opera with a Masonic message?[19] By 1794 and 1795 the work was so popular and so widely diffused that it could hardly be forbidden without causing an immense and unwelcome scandal (and the mechanics of forbidding it would have been hopelessly impractical). The police state found a way. It caused a brochure (see Appendix 6) to be printed in 1794 in which the villains of the opera were seen as Jacobins (The Queen of the Night = Jacobinism; her daughter, Pamina = the Republic). In 1795 a new view was promulgated, in which the Queen of the Night personifies the former government in Austria, etc.

In Masonic language, it was high midnight. One by one, all the lights of the temples were extinguished and darkness descended until 1918. The Mozartian era was at an end.

Notes on the text

INTRODUCTION

1 Only recently I had to insist on the use of the *NMA* for the Deutsche Grammophon recordings of the Mozart symphonies played by the Vienna Philharmonic and conducted by James Levine; they had begun to record the music using the old Breitkopf edition, because the Archives of the Vienna Philharmonic did not possess most of the scores and parts of the *NMA*.
2 Cliff Eisen, 'New Light on Mozart's "Linz" Symphony, K.425', *Journal of the Royal Music Association*, vol. 113, Part 1 (1988), 81ff.
3 Isak Dinesen (Baroness Blixen), *Seven Gothic Tales*, New York 1934, 120.

CHAPTER I

1 Mozart, *Briefe*, IV, 199. This is part of a postscript to a very long letter, from which we shall be quoting other parts in another place, written by Mozart's sister Maria Anna ('Nannerl' or 'Nannètte') *c.* April 1792 and consisting of valuable notes towards a biography of Wolfgang which in the event was incorporated into Friedrich Schlichtegroll's *Nekrolog auf das Jahr 1791* (Gotha, 1793). (In fact this particular section was added as a kind of postscript by a friend of the Mozart family, Dr Albert von Mölk, a lawyer, obviously using information provided by Maria Anna.)
2 Leopold's father and godfather were both named Johann Georg. See Mozart, *Briefe*, VI, 434. Concerning Mozart's mother, ibid., 435.
3 The original *Cassatio* by Leopold Mozart, edited by the present writer, is published by Doblinger in Vienna.
4 Mozart, *Briefe*, VI, 434. Deutsch, *Dokumente*, 11.
5 Deutsch, *Dokumente*, 14.
6 Mozart, *Briefe*, 199. Dr von Mölk's postscript to Maria Anna's letter, also quoted above (see note 1).
7 *Hochfürstlich-Salzburger Kirchen- und Hof-Kalender für 1770.*
8 Deutsch, *Dokumente*, 84f.
9 Mozart, *Briefe*, IV, 181f.
10 Mozart, *Briefe*, III, 373; and VI, 217.
11 R. Angermüller, *W.A. Mozart's musikalische Umwelt in Paris (1778)*, Munich–Salzburg 1982, LVI.
12 So named because it was used at the coronations at Frankfurt in 1790 and 1792 and at Prague in 1791: see Landon, *1791*, 50, 104.
13 The first complete recording, conducted by Meinhard von Zallinger and produced by the present writer, was issued by the Haydn Society in 1950.
14 Sold on 22 May 1987 to a New York private collector. 'This is undoubtedly the most important music manuscript offered for sale at auction this century,' noted the beautifully prepared catalogue.
15 Novello, 76f.
16 Mozart, *Briefe*, III, 93–5.

CHAPTER II

1 Otto Michtner, *Das alte Burgtheater als Opernbühne*, Vienna etc., 1970, 21ff.
2 Joseph Gerold, Vienna, preface dated 1 December 1781, and *avant-propos* 14 February 1782; 232 pp. in 8° (author's collection).

3 Works from the 1780 season and those produced in 1781 include:

(1) Grétry: *Die Freundschaft auf der Probe* (Marmontel), 22 Jan. (1 repeat)
(2) Ruprecht: *Was erhält die Männer treu* (Zehnmark), 5 Feb. (1 repeat)
(3) Grétry: *Der eifersüchtige Liebhaber* (trans. Stephanie Jr) 8 Feb. (3 repeats)
(4) Gluck: *Die Pilgrime von Mecca* (Dancourt), 12 Feb. (6 repeats)
(5) Holly: *Der Sklavenhändler von Smyrna* (C.F. Schwan) 13 Feb. (1 repeat)
(6) Gassmann: *Die Liebe unter den Handwerksleuten* (Goldoni, trans. Neefe) 15 Feb. (3 repeats)
(7) Umlauf: *Die schöne Schusterin* (trans. Stephanie Jr) 25 Feb. (2 repeats)
(8) Audinot & Gossec: *Der Fassbinder* (Poinsinet) 27 Feb. (2 repeats)
(9) Anfossi: *Die verfolgte Unbekannte* (trans. Stephanie Jr) 19 Apr. (3 repeats)
(10) Grétry: *Der Hausfreund* (trans. Stephanie Jr) 24 Apr. (3 repeats)
(11) Mitschka: *Adrast und Isidore* (Molière, trans. Bretzner) 26 Apr. (1 repeat)
(12) Salieri: *Der Rauchfangkehrer* (Auenbrugger) 30 Apr. (8 repeats)
(13) Paisiello: *Die eingebildeten Philosophen* (trans. Stephanie Jr) 22 May (9 repeats)
(14) Grétry: *Die abgeredete Zauberei* (trans. Stephanie Jr) 11 July (2 repeats)
(15) Zanetti: *Die Wäschermädchen* (trans. Bock) 11 July (2 repeats)
(16) Grétry: *Zemire und Azor* (Marmontel) 19 July (4 repeats) (This opera had been in the repertory for some years [1779] with Aloysia Lange in the title role.)
(17) Monsigny: *Der Deserteur* (trans. Stephanie Jr) 1 Aug. (not repeated until 1782)
(18) Piccinni: *Die Sklavin und der grossmütige Seefahrer* (Stephanie Jr) 7 Aug. (1 repeat)
(19) Grétry: *Die unvermuteten Zufälle* (trans. Stephanie Jr) 1 Sep. (1 repeat)
(20) Gluck: *Iphigenie in Tauris* (trans. Alxinger) 23 Oct. (6 repeats)
(21) Guglielmi: *Robert und Kalliste* (trans. Eschenburg) 5 Nov. (not repeated until 1782)
(22) Gluck: *Alceste* (perf. in Italian) Schönbrunn Castle Theatre 25 Nov., Burgtheater, 3 Dec. (3 repeats)
(23) Gluck: *Orfeo ed Euridice* 31 Dec.

4 Michtner, op. cit. (note 1), 141; the coppersmith Anton Schauer was paid 155 gulden for this device.
5 Statistical analysis from Michtner, op. cit., 117.
6 *Adrast und Isidore*; *Die Wäschermädchen*; *Die Sklavin . . .*; and *Die unvermuteten Zufälle* (see note 3 above).
7 Michtner, op. cit., 99.
8 V.J. Sykora, *František Xaver Dušek*, Prague 1958, 214ff. For the Haydn works, see Landon, *Haydn: Chronicle and Works, The Early Years 1732–1765*, 269ff.
9 A wind-band arrangement of Mozart's *Entführung* for the

Schwarzenberg *Harmonie* exists in the family archives at Český Krumlov (then called Böhmisch-Krumau); it was published by the late E.F. Schmid (Bärenreiter Verlag, Kassel) as Mozart's, which it is not.

10 One such is Haydn's 'Marche Regimento de Marschall' (1772), discovered by the present writer in Prague in 1958 (Verlag Doblinger, Diletto Musicale No. 34/1).

11 Unpublished. Diary of Count Carl Zinzendorf, Haus-, Hof- und Staatsarchiv, Vienna. Translations: (Krumau): 'The opera of *Figaro* played on wind instruments, I didn't listen. Those gentlemen dined here.' (Frauenberg): 'After dinner, music from *Figaro*'. (Vienna): 'In the evening to the concert where the Emperor's musicians played the whole of *Cosa rara*, of which the music made a charming effect.'

12 *Entführung*, *NMA* 11/5 (G. Croll), 1982, p. xix, n. 56.

13 In the Library of Congress, Washington, D.C.

14 The original reference to this work's being played at Baroness Waldstätten's comes from Nissen (p. 466), but in the following curious fashion: in the biography, at this point, Mozart's letter of 7 August 1782 to his father is cited, and after discussing the wedding reception at the Baroness's – quoted from the autograph, see p. 82 – Nissen *inserts* the following sentence: ['The souper was . . . "more princely than baronial."] During the souper I was surprised by a sixteen-part *Harmonie* [wind-band music] of my composition. Now my dear Konstanze. . . .' (etc., as on p. 82). I suggest that this insertion is simply Constanze's recollection of the event: it was of course not sixteen-part but thirteen-part. I must in fairness add that Daniel N. Leesen and David Whitwell, in their article 'Concerning Mozart's Serenade in B♭ for Thirteen Instruments, K.361 [370a]', *Mozart-Jahrbuch 1976–77*, Kassel etc. 1978, 108f., do not agree with this theory. They suggest that Nissen 'wanted to make the wedding sound more glamorous than it really was'; but they then add that possibly 'he was influenced by Constanze who may have recalled that a work of some sort was played at the wedding.' The proposed date of *c*. 1784 for the Serenade given by the authors (p. 106) is contradicted by some of the watermarks, which suggest a date some two years earlier.

15 Deutsch, *Dokumente*, 202f.

16 The basic research on the Imperial *Harmonie* was made by Roger Hellyer and incorporated into his now famous thesis, *Mozart's Harmoniemusik*, Oxford 1973. For a very interesting recent publication, see Bastiaan Blomhert, *The Harmoniemusik of Die Entführung aus dem Serail by Wolfgang Amadeus Mozart. Study about its Authenticity and Critical Edition*, The Hague, 1987, esp. pp. 26ff. A description in Cramer's *Magazin der Musik* is taken from two players of the Batthyány *Harmonie* on a concert tour in Germany in 1783. They said the group consisted of 'a society of virtuosi containing only wind instrumentalists who have reached a high degree of perfection, known in Vienna under the name of Imperial–Royal *Harmonie*. This group, which includes 8 persons, gives a fully "voiced" concert, in which they play only things actually written for the voice, which one of them, the virtuoso and composer Wehend [*sic*] arranges for wind band, i.e. choruses, duets, trios and even arias from the best operas are played, in such a way that the oboe and the clarinet take the part of the voice. The following names of the musicians were given, viz.:

1 Hr. Trimsee [Triebensee] 1st oboe
2 Hr. Wehend [Vent, Went] 2nd oboe
3 Hr. Stadler, 1st clarinet
4 Hr. Stadler, 2nd clarinet, brother of the above
5 Hr. Rupp, 1st hunting horn
6 Hr. Eisen, 2nd hunting horn. Is supposed to be even superior to Hr. Rupp
7 Hr. Kautner [Kauzner], 1st bassoon
8 Hr. Druben [Trubur, Drobnay], 2nd bassoon, also even better than the first.'

The official listing (with individual addresses) in the *Schematismus* is as follows:

OBOISTS
Hr. Georg Triebensee
Hr. Johann Went

CLARINETTISTS
Hr. Anton Stadler
Hr. Johann Stadler
BASSOONISTS
Hr. Wenzel Kauzner
Hr. Ignaz Drobnay
HUNTING HORN PLAYERS
Hr. Martin Rupp
Hr. Jakob Eisen

17 Op. cit. (footnote 2), 122ff.

18 Alexander Weinmann, *Beiträge zur Geschichte des Alt-Wiener Musikverlages. Kataloge Anton Huberty (Wien) und Christoph Torricella*, Vienna 1962. For Artaria, see Weinmann, *Vollständiges Verlagsverzeichnis Artaria & Comp.*, Vienna 1952.

19 Ralph Kirkpatrick, *Domenico Scarlatti*, Princeton, N.J. 1953, 178.

20 In one instance, the use of a fortepiano in a Viennese concert of 1763 has been recorded. See Eva Badura-Skoda, 'Prolegomena to a History of the Viennese Fortepiano', *Israel Studies in Musicology*, vol. II, Jerusalem 1980, 77–9.

21 Mozart, *Briefe*, II, 68–70. Mozart used a Stein piano in his Frankfurt concert of 1790 – see Landon, *1791*, 14.

22 Landon, *Beethoven*, 111, also p. 62.

23 Beethoven performed the work, according to his pupil Carl Czerny, with the *sopra una corda* pedal held down for the whole of the first movement; the first edition, on the other hand, requires no pedals whatever ('Si deve suonare tutto questo pezzo delicatissimamente e senza sordini').

24 (a) *Konzert zur Wiedereröffnung der Sammlung alter Musikinstrumente am 1. Juni 1966*: W.A. Mozart, *Sonata für 2 Klaviere*, K.448, Robert Schumann, *Kinderszenen*, op. 15; Jörg Demus and Norman Shetler. Harmonia Mundi. Two Walter pianos in the collection, one *c*. 1785, the other *c*. 1795, are used.

(b) *Mozart in Paris – Mozart in Wien*. Jörg Demus. Harmonia Mundi, 2 LPs.

Both recordings are highly recommended.

25 Not to speak of the famous 'gliding octaves' in the finale, which were written with a shallow key in mind.

26 One is owned by Paul Badura–Skoda in Vienna: it has been used by him on some excellent recordings of Haydn and Mozart (Harmonia Mundi). Another, almost identical, instrument is owned by Alan Rubin in London. A third, in the Holburne of Menstrie Museum, Bath, has a range up to *a'''* (i.e. three octaves above middle C) in the top register.

27 Thirty years ago, the present writer discovered a handsome and very early grand fortepiano in Rosenburg Castle (Lower Austria); this had never been restored and was in excellent condition. It is unsigned and may be either a German instrument or perhaps a very early Walter – some of his instruments are not signed. The Rosenburg piano would appear to be the earliest fortepiano known in Austria.

28 Mozart, *Briefe*, III, 99.

29 Ibid., 106 and 101 resp. K.338 has only oboes and bassoons (apart from the brass and drums); K.297 flutes, oboes, clarinets, bassoons, horns, trumpets and drums.

30 Charles Burney, *The Present State of Music in Germany, the Netherlands and United Provinces* (2 vols.), London 1773 and 1775.

31 Otto Biba, 'Die Wiener Kirchenmusik um 1783', *Beiträge zur Musikgeschichte des 18. Jahrhunderts*, Eisenstadt 1971, 7–79.

32 *Maria Theresa*, Englewood Cliffs, N.J. 1973, 177.

CHAPTER IV

1 Mozart's complaints letter, 17 March 1781: *Briefe* III, 93–5; also 98 (24 March 1781). Galitzin: Deutsch, *Dokumente*, 73.

2 Mozart, *Briefe* III, 98; VI, 56, Landon, *Beethoven*, 64. Alfred Stix, *H.F. Füger*, Vienna–Leipzig 1925. 86 (picture of the three 'Graces' by Füger, 1788. Österreichische Galerie, Vienna, reproduced as Tafel XXIII). Deutsch, *Dokumente*, 250.

3 Zinzendorf, ms. Diary: Elisabeth's marriage (4 November 1788); wedding night (9 November); also entries for 10, 11 and 12 November.

4　Mozart, *Briefe*, III, 139.
5　Ibid., 102f.
6　Ibid., 105, 108, 109.
7　Servants and the like were addressed in the third person.
8　Mozart, *Briefe*, III, 110–12.
9　Ibid., 146.
10　Ibid., 107.
11　Ibid., 120f., 127.
12　Ibid., 132.
13　Ibid., 138.
14　Ibid., 143f.
15　Ibid., 160.
16　Ibid., 162–4.
17　Ibid., 165.
18　Ibid., 167f.
19　Ibid., 175.
20　Ibid., 196.
21　Ibid., 212f.
22　This version was performed during the Mozartwoche in Salzburg in January 1988. See *The Harmoniemusik of Die Entführung aus dem Serail by Wolfgang Amadeus Mozart – Study about its Authenticity and Critical Edition*, The Hague, 1987. An edition of the Donaueschingen ms. has been prepared by Dr Blomhert (Bärenreiter Verlag, Kassel).
23　Mozart, *Briefe*, III, 246.
24　Haberkamp, Textband, 177–80. Blomhert, op. cit., 122–4.
25　Mozart, *Briefe* III, 239.
26　Ibid., 343f.
27　Ibid., 346.
28　Deutsch, *Dokumente*, 187.
29　Nissen, 465.
30　Mozart, *Briefe*, III, 112.
31　Ibid., 116f.
32　Ibid., 129f.
33　Leopold's letter to his daughter, 8 April 1785, Mozart, *Briefe*, III, 386.
34　Ibid., 140f.
35　Ibid., 153, 154 (5 September).
36　Ibid., 171f.
37　For the probability that the enlarged orchestration of the Concerto was made for the concert, see Köchel, p. 335.
38　Mozart, *Briefe*, III, 176 and VI, 94.
39　Ibid., III, 179–82. Archduke Maximilian proposed Mozart as Princess Elisabeth's teacher, and she answered that if it had been up to her she would have taken no one else. But 'the Emperor had suggested Salieri'.
40　For this part of the letter, see Landon, *1791*, 196.
41　Mozart, *Briefe*, III, 186. For further details, see Landon, *1791*, 196f.
42　Nissen, 415.
43　Mozart, *Briefe*, III, 191.
44　'. . . *l'Empereur*, qui parla infiniment [de la] musique, du combat entre Mozhardt et Clementi' (Zinzendorf, Diary, ms.).
45　Mozart, *Briefe*, III, 190.
46　Ibid., 194.
47　Ibid., 196.
48　Letter of 13 February 1782. *Briefe*, III, 197f.
49　Ibid., 199.
50　Ibid., 208f.
51　Ibid., 214ff.
52　Ibid., 216f.
53　Ibid., 217f.
54　Ibid., 218f.
55　Ibid., 220.
56　Deutsch, *Dokumente*, 182.

CHAPTER V

1　Weather: Mozart's letter of 13 November 1782: *Briefe*, III, 241. Archbishop: letter of 21 May 1783: *Briefe*, III, 269f. In a later missive (5 July 1783: *Briefe*, III, 277f.) Mozart quotes people in Vienna as saying 'You'll see, you will never get away again. You've

no idea of what that nasty, wicked Prince is capable . . .'. Leopold's soothing reply is reflected in Wolfgang's letter of 12 July (*Briefe*, III, 279f.).
2　Mozart, *Briefe*, III, 245; VI, 124.
3　Ibid., III, 251f.
4　See William Sandys and Simon Andrew Forster, *The History of the Violin*, London 1864, 310, for the dates (14 February, 24 February, 6 May) when Radnitzky's copies arrived in London. Also *Joseph Haydn: Critical Edition of the Complete Symphonies* (ed. Landon), vol. VIII, Philharmonia No. 596, Vienna, 2nd ed., 1981, where the frontispiece shows a facsimile of a page from Symphony no. 77, copy signed by Radnitzky.
5　There are also Mozart's Concertos no. 6, K.238, no. 17, K.453 (incomplete) and no. 26, K.537 ('Coronation') in ms. parts in Cheb. There are Radnitzky parts of a Koželuch piano concerto. None of the Mozart copies is listed in Köchel.
6　Mozart, *Briefe*, III, 313f.
7　*The Collected Correspondence and London Notebooks of Joseph Haydn* (ed. Landon), 71.
8　Mozart, *Briefe*, III, 257f.
9　Ibid., 251f.
10　Ibid., 259.
11　Ibid.
12　Ibid., 261f.; also VI, 137.
13　*NMA*, Werkgruppe 15, Band 3 (Christoph Wolff, 1976), p. VIII.
14　Mozart, *Briefe*, III, 268.
15　Ibid., 273.
16　Ibid., 199f.
17　Landon, *1791*, ch. XIII.
18　Mozart, *Briefe*, III, 282–8.
19　Nissen, 475–7.
20　Published anonymously as *Biographische Skizze von Michael Haydn*, Salzburg 1808 (by G. Schinn and F.J. Otter).
21　Letter of 7 Feb. 1778: Mozart, *Briefe*, II, 265.
22　Mozart, *Briefe*, III, 288. The editor of the notes (VI, 154), the late J.H. Eibl, believes that the quartet is from Luigi Gatti's *Olimpiade*, first performed in Salzburg in 1775. Bologna = Michelangelo Bologna, a castrato, as was Francesco Ceccarelli. Joseph Fiala (*c*. 1754–1816) was a composer and a member of the Salzburg orchestra: he was an oboist, but also played cello. Abbé Joseph Bullinger was a tutor to Count Arco's family and a family friend of the Mozarts. Ludwig Feiner was second oboist in the Salzburg orchestra. Abbé Henry, an ex-Jesuit and violinist. The theatre put on Shakespeare's *Romeo and Juliet*. Novello, 114f.
23　Mozart, *Briefe*, III, 247f.; Nissen, 476.
24　Mozart, *Briefe*, III, 202f.
25　Hermann Abert, *W.A. Mozart* (2 vols.), 7th ed., Leipzig 1956, II, 122.
26　Mozart, *Briefe*, III, 290.
27　*NMA*, Werkgruppe 1, Abteilung 1, Band 5 (Monika Holl, Karl-Heinz Köhler, 1983), pp. IX–XIX.
28　Letter of 31 October 1783; *Briefe*, III, 291.
29　C.F. Pohl, *Denkschrift*, 60f.; Mozart, *Briefe*, III, 299.

CHAPTER VI

1　The title in full is 'Verzeichnüss aller meiner Werke vom Monath Februario 1784 bis Monath . . .' (from the month of February 1784 until the month of . . .). The volume, owned by the heirs of Stefan Zweig, is on permanent loan to the British Library. A facsimile was issued by O.E. Deutsch, Vienna 1938, and again in New York 1956. A new publication, edited by Alan Tyson, is in preparation.
2　Reproduced in Deutsch, *Bilder*, no. 25. Mozart, *Briefe*, VI, 162–4.
3　Deutsch, *Dokumente*, 198. Zinzendorf, Diary (ms.).
4　Mozart, *Briefe*, III, 303f.
5　Ibid., 305ff.; also reproduced from the original in the Österreichische Nationalbibliothek, Vienna, in pls. VII and VIII. See Appendix I.
6　Deutsch, *Dokumente*, 198.
7　Mozart, *Briefe*, III, 309f.

8 Ibid., VI, 704.

9 Ibid., III, 201. A description of Swieten's apartment in the Hofburg is given by Count Zinzendorf (Diary, 14 June 1782). After dining at Prince Galitzin's, he and other members of the party walked to the National Library. Zinzendorf thought the flat delightful: it included a pretty room for his servant, an attractive dining room with blue and white damask without gold ornaments, the Baron's bedroom in yellow damask, his study (green background with yellow arabesques on the wall) containing attractive consoles and a handsome desk. There was direct access to the famous gallery of the Court Library. Zinzendorf thought the gallery magnificent. The ladies in the party looked at engravings in the celebrated royal collection.

10 Mozart, Briefe, III, 264.

11 Most of the information thus far in this section has been taken from the standard article on the subject: Edward Olleson, 'Gottfried van Swieten, Patron of Haydn and Mozart', Proceedings of the Royal Musical Association, 1962–3, 63ff.

12 Concerning Heintl, see Landon, Haydn: Chronicle and Works, The Early Years, 1732–1765, 75f.

13 Schematismus, p. 341. The house, no. 1046, was rented from Joseph Cavallion, Count von Salmour (Salmor). It is now Krugerstraße 10.

14 Wiener Zeitung, 9 October 1782.

15 Taken from Albert Elmar, 'Demetrius Michalowitsch Fürst von Galitzin', in Wiener Geschichtsblätter, 33. Jg, 1978, Heft 2, 77–82.

16 Mozart, Briefe, III, 244.

17 Income (today equivalent to nearly £17 million/$28 million). See also J. Harich, 'Das fürstlich Esterházysche Fideikomiß', Haydn Yearbook IV (1968), 29.

18 Else Radant, 'The Diaries of Joseph Carl Rosenbaum 1770–1829', Haydn Yearbook V (1968), 18.

19 Mozart, Briefe, III, 256f., and VI, 133.

20 Landon, Haydn: Chronicle and Works, Haydn at Eszterháza, 1766–1790, 70, 75. C.F. Pohl, Haydn, vol. II, Leipzig 1882, 143. Colombazzo was a member of the Tonkünstler-Societät. He also gave benefit concerts at the Burgtheater in 1784 and the Kärntnerthortheater in 1787. It was, I submit, for such a benefit concert that Colombazzo wanted Mozart's oboe concerto. It used to be thought (Köchel, 3rd ed.) that the fragmentary Oboe Concerto in F (K.293), with orchestration including clarinets, may have been started in Vienna in 1783, but the NMA, Serie v, Werkgruppe 14 (Franz Giegling, 1981), now places this interesting fragment – of which the opening ritornello (bars 1–50) is fully orchestrated – in the years 1778–9, probably in the autumn of 1778.

21 Landon, Mozart and the Masons, London 1982, passim.

22 His eldest son, Anton (hereditary prince 1790–4), was also a Mason. See Landon, Mozart and the Masons, 66 ('Gerubell').

23 First published in Landon: Haydn: Chronicle and Works, Haydn at Eszterháza, 1766–1790, ills. 7, 8.

24 László Berényi adds the following, interesting note on Count Johann Nepomuk Esterházy's activities in Transylvania:

The importance of his appointment to the presidency of the School Commission seems to require a brief explanation. This has to do with the sweeping changes of the education system planned by Joseph II in 1785 which, among other fundamental reforms, curtailed the control of education by the Catholic clergy. Very special people had to be selected to oversee the introduction of the reforms against fierce opposition from the Church and ultra-conservative elements in the counties: thus, the hitherto insignificant presidency of the School Commission became a most sensitive appointment of trust and it became quite important to have the 'right' people heading the counties as well. Hence the appointment of Count Johann to two Lord Lieutenancies in Transylvania, even though he did not own a home or estates in either of them, normally a condition of such an appointment. Therefore, it is obvious that he had an important job to perform, and this most likely kept him away from Vienna and his home, Castle Oszlop in western Hungary. As a Catholic magnate with a wife from the foremost Protestant aristocracy of Transylvania who 'traitorously converted to popism', Count Johann most likely did not exactly cherish the idea of spending more time than absolutely necessary among the clannish, puritanical and Protestant aristocracy of Transylvania.

However, according to records, he found a way to mitigate his difficult circumstances by enlisting the aid of Brother Masons in Hermannstadt and it is noted that during the mid-1780s he was a permanent fixture at the meetings of the Lodge 'St Andreas zu den drei Seeblättern'. It is said that by 1785 this lodge counted 132 members and this represented the political and intellectual élite of Transylvania at the time. The Grand Master of the Lodge was Count Georg Banffy de Losoncz, governor of Transylvania from 1789 till the end of his life and Count Johann Esterházy's brother-in-law.

It appears that by 1790 Count Johann finished his assignment in Transylvania for, as we see, his son László (Ladislaus) was born in Vienna in that year. It can be assumed that he spent 1791 and at least part of 1792 also in Vienna when he was made a Privy Councillor.

Apparently, between 1793 and 1795 he had to spend some further time in Transylvania, at least until his appointment as Councillor of the Court Chancellery for Transylvania on 16 March 1795, a post which no longer required his continuous presence in Transylvania.

László Berényi has furnished the date and place of birth of each of Count J.N. Esterházy's children:

Name	Date	Place
Ferenc (Franz)	16 March 1778	Vienna
János (Johann)	4 February 1779	Vienna
Alajos (Aloysius)	19 February 1780	Vienna
György (Georg)	21 July 1781	Vienna
Mihály (Michael)	9 February 1783	Hermannstadt
Marianna	23 January 1786	Hermannstadt
Josepha	12 July 1787	Hermannstadt
Dénes (Denis)	7 March 1789	Hermannstadt
László (Ladislaus)	29 June 1790	Vienna
Agnes	19 January 1793	Kolozsvár (Klausenburg)
János (Johann) and Maria	19 November 1793	Kolozsvár

The Lodge 'Crowned Hope', of which the Count was a member, was renamed following the reorganization of Viennese lodges in response to an Imperial decree dated 11 December 1785; two other lodges – 'Beneficence' (Mozart's lodge) and 'Three Fires' – were amalgamated with 'Crowned Hope' and the newly constituted Lodge 'New Crowned Hope' met for the first time on 14 January 1786. Surviving lists of members provide further evidence of the Count's presence (1781–3) and absence from Vienna after 1781.

Year	No. and Name	Occupation	Office
1781	1 Johann Gr Eszterhazy	k.k. Kämmerer (I.R. Chamberlain)	Meister v. Stl. (Master)
1782 (8 Feb.)	11 Johann Graf Eszterhazy	K.K. Kämmerer	[added in ink:] abgegangener Logenmeister (departed [Lodge Master])
1783 (9 Feb.)	12 Johann Graf Eszterhazy	k.k. wirklicher Kämmerer	Abgegangene[r] Logenmeister

In subsequent years the Count is listed among 'Abwesende Brüder' (Brothers absent) as follows: 1784, 30 March, 'No. 110 . . . in Herman[n]stadt'; 1785, No. 186; 1786, March, No. 25; [1789] (year established by other evidence), 'No. 31 . . . in Hermannstadt.' For a printed list of 1790 see Appendix 2.
Source: Haus-, Hof-, und Staatsarchiv, Vienna. Vertrauliche Akten 72 (alt 114), fol. 3 (1790); 10 (1789); 113 (1786); 238 (1783); 243 (1782); 249 (1785); 265 (1781); 295 (1784).

25 See also Bardos Kornel, A tatai Esterházyak zenéje 1727–1846, Budapest 1978.

26 Haus-, Hof- und Staatsarchiv, Vienna. Vertrauliche Akten 76 (alt 118), fol. 72. Fol. 37–60 for other printed Paris lists.

27 Deutsch, Dokumente, 206 (and 198).

28 When Regina Strinasacchi appeared in Salzburg, Leopold Mozart noted in a letter to his daughter dated 7 December 1785: 'She doesn't play a note without expression . . . Altogether I must

say that I consider a woman who has talent plays with more expression than a man . . .'. Mozart, *Briefe*, III, 467.

29 *NMA*, Serie VIII, Werkgruppe 23, Band 2 (Reeser), 1965, p. xiv.

30 Mozart, *Briefe*, IV, 313. Paisiello's letter in Landon, *Haydn: Chronicle and Works, Haydn at Eszterháza, 1766–1790*, 491.

31 Mozart, *Briefe*, III, 318.

32 Ibid., 331.

33 Deutsch, *Dokumente*, 204.

34 For the circumstances surrounding Mozart's death, see Landon, *1791*, ch. XI.

CHAPTER VII

1 Mozart, *Briefe*, III, 361.

2 Ibid., 368.

3 Ibid., 370.

4 Deutsch, *Dokumente*, 208.

5 The standard article on the subject is Joachim Hurwitz, 'Haydn and the Freemasons', *Haydn Yearbook* XVI (1986), 5–98.

6 Mozart, *Briefe*, III, 372–4.

7 Ibid., 374–7.

8 Deutsch, *Dokumente*, 211f.

9 Mozart, *Briefe*, III, 378f.

10 Now owned by the present writer.

11 Novello, 158. Actually the 'Terzetto' was not newly composed, but is an adaptation of the 'Quoniam tu solus sanctus' from the Mass. The two new pieces are (1) No. 6, Tenor Aria, 'A te, fra tanti affani' (K.469, no. 6) and No. 8, Soprano Aria, 'Tra l'oscure ombre funeste' (K.469, no. 8); Mozart also added a kind of cadenza for the two soprano and tenor soloists at the end of No. 10, the Chorus 'Chi in Dio sol spera' (adaptation of the 'Cum Sancto Spiritu' from the Mass). The additional arias provided a more even distribution of the solo parts, viz. No. 1, Chorus 'Alzai le flebili voci al Signor' (= Kyrie); No. 2, Chorus 'Cantiamo le glorie' (= opening of 'Gloria in excelsis'); No. 3, Aria (Soprano II) 'Lungi le cure ingrate' (= 'Laudamus te'); No. 4, Chorus 'Sii pur sempre benigno, oh Dio' (= 'Gratias'); No. 5, Duet (Soprano I, II) 'Sorgi, o Signore, e spargi' (= 'Domine Deus'); No. 6, Aria (Tenor): see above; No. 7, Chorus 'Sei vuoi, puniscimi' (= 'Qui tollis'); No. 8, Aria (Soprano I): see above; No. 9, Terzetto (Soprano I, II, Tenor) 'Tutte le mie speranze' (= 'Quoniam'); No. 10, Chorus 'Chi in Dio sol spera' (= 'Jesu Christe') with, in the concluding section, the new cadenza.

12 *NMA*, Serie I, Werkgruppe 4, Band 3 (Monika Holl), 1987.

13 Mozart, *Briefe*, III, 380.

14 Ibid., 380–2.

15 Deutsch, *Dokumente*, 213–6.

16 Mozart, *Briefe* III, 388. Leopold's impressions of the Baroness, if recorded, have not survived.

17 Born celebration: Deutsch, *Dokumente*, 216.

18 *Briefe*, III, 389.

19 Deutsch, *Dokumente*, 217.

20 *NMA*, Serie X, Werkgruppe 30, Band 1 (Erich Herzmann, Cecil B. Oldman, Daniel Heartz and Alfred Mann; 1965). Mozart was forever insisting on singing lines – 'meglio ancora per la Cantilena', he wrote ('still better because of the cantilena'). Mozart's love for the clarinet is reflected in Attwood's note 'the Clarinett is very useful instead of the oboes'. See also Mozart, *Briefe*, VI, 238.

21 Landon, *Haydn: Chronicle and Works, Haydn at Eszterháza, 1766–1790*, 673.

22 Announcements: Deutsch, *Dokumente*, 220–2.

23 A lost letter, preserved in extract only in Nissen, 481. See Mozart *Briefe*, 311.

24 Niemetschek, 31ff.

25 *Wiener Theaterkalender auf das Jahr 1787* [Vorwort: 1 Dec. 1788]. Mozart's opera was given at the Kärntnerthortheater in January. In February *Der Schauspieldirektor* and Salieri's *Prima la musica, poi le parole* were also performed there.

26 Consider *Le nozze di Figaro*, Act I: Sinfonia: Presto, barred C. No. 1 (Duettino) Allegro, 4/4. No. 2 (Duettino) Allegro, 2/4. No. 3 (Cavatina) Allegretto, 3/4. No. 4 (Aria) Allegro, 4/4. No. 5 (Duettino) Allegro, 4/4. No. 6 (Aria) Allegro vivace, barred C. No. 7 (Terzetto) Allegro assai, 4/4. No. 8 (Coro) Allegro, 6/8. No. 9 (Aria) Vivace, 4/4. No slow movement occurs until the Countess's Cavatina, 'Porgi amor', at the outset of Act II. Let us take Act I of Haydn's *La fedeltà premiata*, perhaps his most successful large-scale opera (in terms of length, number of participants and overall complexity). Sinfonia: Presto, 6/8. No. 1 (Introduzione) Allegro, 3/4 – Adagio, 4/4 – Adagio, barred C – Allegro, 3/4. No. 2 (Aria) Presto, 6/8. No. 3 (Aria & Recit.) [Poco adagio], 3/4. No. 4 (Aria) Presto, 4/4. No. 5 (Aria) Allegro con brio, 4/4. No. 6 (Aria) Adagio, 3/4. No. 7 (Aria) Poco andante, 2/4. No. 8 (Aria) Adagio, 3/4. No. 9 (Aria) Allegro di molto, barred C – Adagio – Presto – Adagio – Presto. No. 10 (Aria) Allegro assai, barred C. No. 11 (Aria) Andante, 2/4 – Largo, barred C – Allegro, 4/4. No. 12 (Aria), Vivace, 4/4 – Adagio, 3/4 – [Allegro], 4/4 – Presto, 3./4. No. 13 Finale: Vivace assai, 4/4 – Adagio, 3/4 – Presto, 2/4 – Presto, 6/8 – Vivace assai, 4/4 – Adagio, barred C – Presto, 2/4 – Presto, 4/4 – Presto, barred C. It is only in the finale, incidentally, that we find the same sense of forward-moving time that is so typical of *Figaro*; and although the forward drive of Act I of *Figaro* is (as it happens) connected with an entire series of rapid or relatively rapid tempi, the presence or absence of an adagio or largo has little to do with this overall concept of swift movement. Quotation about Prince Nicolaus: Edward Olleson, 'Georg August Griesinger's Correspondence with Breitkopf & Härtel', *Haydn Yearbook* III (1965), 36.

27 The first production we have ever seen to take full cognizance of the progression from morning (Act I) to high noon (Act II), afternoon (Act III), and evening (Act IV) proceeding, at bars 445/8 of the Finale (Eulenburg pp. 71of.), to sunrise was Luchino Visconti's magical production at the Rome Opera in the 1963/64 season (conducted by Carlo Maria Giulini).

28 Mozart, *Briefe*, III, 439.

29 For a possible earlier performance, see P. A. Autexier, *Mozart & Liszt sub Rosa*, Poitiers 1984, 19ff. *NMA*, Serie IV, Werkgruppe 11, Band 10 (Landon), 1978.

30 *Mozart, His Character, His Work*, London 1946, 429.

31 Niemetschek, 31ff.

32 Ferrari, 2 vols London 1830; *Harmonicon* 1830, 371f.

33 *AMZ* (1799), I, 854f.

34 This section is based on Landon, *Haydn: Chronicle and Works, Haydn at Eszterháza, 1766–1790*, 510–11.

35 Mozart, *Briefe* III, 454.

36 On 2 December 1785, Leopold Mozart wrote that the previous day the postman had brought a parcel with *inter alia* the new Piano Quartet 'from the 16th October this year'; he also adds that the violin and viola parts were already engraved. Haberkamp, *Textband*, 24of. A copy of the print bearing the ms. note of one of Mozart's subscribers, 'Ernestine Comtesse d'Auersperg née Princesse de Schwarzenberg', has survived.

CHAPTER VIII

1 *The Mozart Companion*, London 1956, 102.

2 Ibid., 239.

3 Working with motifs, i.e. using a single fragment to build up a whole movement: two famous examples are the finale of Haydn's Symphony no. 103 (1795) and the opening movement of Beethoven's Fifth Symphony (1808).

4 *Lebensläufe deutscher Musiker von ihnen selbst erzählt*, ed. Alfred Einstein. Band III/IV: Adalbert Gyrowetz, Leipzig, n.d. [1924?], 13.

5 A musical example in Landon, *Haydn: Chronicle and Works, Haydn at Eszterháza, 1766–1790*, 539.

CHAPTER IX

1 Alfred Arneth, *Briefe der Kaiserin Maria Theresia an ihre Kinder und Freunde*, Vienna 1880, vol. I, 92. Ibid., II, 148f.

2 Robert Pick, *Empress Maria Theresa*, New York 1966, 236.

3 *Memoirs of Lorenzo Da Ponte*, trans. Elisabeth Abbott, New York 1967 (reprint of 1929 edition), 129ff.

4 An Extract from the Life of Lorenzo Da Ponte, with the history of several dramas written by him, and among others, Il Figaro, Il Don Giovanni e La Scuola degli Amanti set to music by Mozart, New York, 1819.

5 See Daniel Heartz, 'Constructing Le nozze di Figaro', Proceedings of the Royal Musical Association, vol. 112, part 1, 1987, 77–98.

6 Zinzendorf, Diary. This passage is missing in Deutsch, Dokumente (and the Errata); the original reads '. . . Je cherchois L'Empereur à l'augarten, il étoit en ville, il étoit à la répétition de l'opéra . . .'.

7 NMA, Serie II, Werkgruppe 16, 2 vols. (Finscher), 1973.

8 Life of Mozart, London 1845, 269.

9 Op. cit., 86.

10 The following extract is quoted from Figaro's monologue (in the excellent translation by John Wood, Penguin Classics, 1964, 199ff.): 'No, My Lord Count, you shan't have her, you shall not have her! Because you are a great nobleman you think you are a great genius . . . Nobility, fortune, rank, position! How proud they make a man feel! What have *you* done to deserve such advantages? Put yourself to the trouble of being born – nothing more! For the rest – a very ordinary man! . . .'

11 Mozart, Briefe, III, 443f.

12 Memoirs, 159ff.

13 Otto Michtner, Das alte Burgtheater als Opernbühne, 206 (n. 15) explains: 'Ballet insertions were forbidden ever since Italian opera had been reintroduced into the Burgtheater. Now it was the singer Bussani, newly designed "Sopraintendente del scenario e vestiario", who sought by a false "reading" of that decision to forbid the ballet in Act III. But the Emperor saw quite correctly that the section in Figaro was not an inserted ballet but a dramatically necessary part of the opera, and hence he allowed the scene to be included.' Among Mozart's enemies was, at least in some part, Rosenberg himself, who in a journal of 1793 (Berlinische Musikalische Zeitung, p. 141) is described as '. . . the avowed enemy of the Germans, who will hear nothing that is not Italian.' (Michtner, ibid., n. 15).

14 Mozart Briefe, III, 536.

15 Reminiscences of Michael Kelly (2 vols.), London 1826, I, 257ff.

16 Joseph II, in a Handbillet to Rosenberg on 14 August 1783, draws special attention to the *acting* in Paisiello's Il barbiere di Siviglia: 'J'ai tardé à répondre à la lettre que vous m'avez écrite pour vous donner nouvelle de la réussite du Barbier de Seville, qu'on a joué hier. Ils s'en sont tiré pour l'action en vérité au delà de l'espérance, surtout Benucci qui dans des certains moments a copié et presque frisé Schroeder. La Storace a très bien chantée un air cantabile et quoiqu'imitant assez les différentes gestes de la Adamberger, dans differentes situations la sguaiatezza prenait pourtant le dessus. Mandini a fort bien joué hors l'ivrogne que ne lui allait pas et Figaro passablement, beaucoup du monde et on a fait répéter plusieurs morceaux . . .' Michtner, op. cit., 158. In other words, the Italian singers had begun to imitate the famous school of acting cultivated in the Burgtheater, especially Friedrich Ludwig Schröder among the males and Maria Anna Adamberger, *née* Jaquet, among the females. As Paisiello's opera was not only well sung but well acted, the same surely applied to Mozart's Figaro when performed three years later by the same singers.

17 Zinzendorf on Anna Storace: 'jolie figure, voluptueuse, belle gorge, beaux yeux, cou blanc, bouche fraiche, belle peau, la naiveté et la pétulance de l'enfance, chante comme un ange.' ('Pretty face, voluptuous, fine bosom, beautiful eyes, a white neck, a fresh mouth, delicate skin, the naivety and petulance of youth, sings like an angel.'), Diary, 22 April 1783.

18 Franz Kazinczy's autobiography; Deutsch, Dokumente, 241.

19 The French original, significantly different, reads: 'Aujourd'hui, ce qui ne vaut pas la peine d'être dit, on le chante.' ('Nowadays, what isn't worth saying is sung instead.').

20 Österreichische Musikzeitschrift, July–August 1957.

21 The above cited timpani rhythm is, of course, the augmentation of the familiar ♩ ♫ ♩.

22 Niemetschek, op. cit., 34f.

23 Deutsch, Dokumente, 246.

24 Memoirs, pp. 174ff.

25 Now available in facsimile, Gesellschaft der Musikfreunde, Vienna 1987.

26 Don Giovanni, Haydn Society, Boston 1951.

27 Mozart, Briefe, IV, 54f.

28 Prager Oberpostamtszeitung, 3 November 1787 (Deutsch, Dokumente, 267).

29 Mozart, Briefe, IV, 58 (Prague, 4 November 1787).

30 See also p. 173. On 16 December 1788 Joseph II wrote to his sister Marie Christine, saying that he had 'not yet been to the theatre' (Deutsch, Dokumente, Addenda and Corrigenda, 58). Is the whole conversation between Joseph II and Da Ponte a fantasy? The Emperor held private musical soirées and heard extracts from the most popular operas; let us say, charitably, that he heard it (perhaps in an arrangement for Harmonie?) at one of them. Otherwise, it is yet another black mark against the whole Da Ponte version of events.

34 Mozart, Briefe, IV, 97.

35 See Alan Tyson, 'Some Problems in the Text of Le nozze di Figaro: Did Mozart have a Hand in Them?', Journal of the Royal Musical Association, vol. 112, part 1, 1987, 99–131. The piano score of 'Un moto di gioia' in Mozart's hand is published in facsimile by the Gesellschaft der Musikfreunde, Vienna.

36 For a detailed list, see 'Mozart and the opera buffa tradition', in W.A. Mozart – Le nozze di Figaro, ed. Tim Carter, Cambridge 1987, 11ff.

37 Alfred Einstein, 'Mozart and Tarchi,' in Monthly Musical Record 65 (1935), no. 768, July–August, 127ff. Alfred Loewenberg, Annals of Opera, Cambridge 1943, 211; Loewenberg says that the Monza and Florence performances 'passed nearly unnoticed.'

38 For these performances in Hungary, see J. Harich in Haydn Yearbook 1 (1962), 91f.; also Landon, Haydn: Chronicle and Works, Haydn at Eszterháza, 1766–1790, 733.

39 Loewenberg, op. cit., 223. Così: 237. Deutsch, Dokumente, 309. Facsimile of the Leipzig playbill of 1788: R. von Freisauff, Mozart's Don Juan . . ., Salzburg 1887.

40 O. Michtner, op. cit., 263f.

41 Deutsch, Dokumente, 277, 290.

42 Op. cit., Addenda and Corrigenda, 58.

43 Zinzendorf, Diary; 'Mᵉ de la Lippe trouve la musique savante, peu propre au chant.' Deutsch, Dokumente, Addenda and Corrigenda, 50, 51, 56. On 4 July 1786 Zinzendorf thought 'La musique de Mozart singulière, des mains sans tête . . . ('singular, all action without brain . . .').

44 Op. cit. (note 36), 12f.

45 Novello, 94, 137. Nissen, 543.

46 Mozart, Briefe, IV, 100.

47 Zinzendorf, Diary: 'La musique est charmante, et le sujet assez amusant.'

48 Da Ponte's original libretto was set in Trieste, not Naples.

49 See Rudolph Angermüller, 'Anmerkungen zu "Così fan tutte"', Österreichische Musikzeitschrift, 7–8 (1982), 279ff., esp.282.

50 Mozart, Briefe, IV, 100.

51 Ibid., 102.

52 Ibid., 96f.

53 Così fan Tutte, New York 1968.

CHAPTER X

1 Deutsch, Dokumente, 452.

2 Reminiscences of Michael Kelly (2 vols.), London 1826, I, 222–5, 237ff.

3 Deutsch, Dokumente, 229–33, also Addenda and Corrigenda, 48.

4 Deutsch, Dokumente, 234f. More puzzles were recently discovered in Leipzig, some very peculiar. Mozart, Briefe, VI, 713f.

5 Mozart, Briefe, III, 484. Concerto: p. 510. Idomeneo: pp. 510f. and Deutsch, Dokumente, 234. Subscription concerts: Briefe, III, 484.

6 Deutsch, Dokumente, 245. Entführung: Peter Branscombe in Landon (ed.), The Mozart Compendium (forthcoming).

7 Mozart, Briefe, III, 618. Works: pp. 616 and 617. Deutsch, Dokumente, 246.

8 Leopold's letter from Salzburg, dated 17 November 1786, to his daughter. Briefe, III, 606.

9 Deutsch, *Dokumente*, 248.
10 Mozart, *Briefe*, IV, 7 (12 January 1787).
11 Mozart signed a commonplace-book of Edmund Weber (one of his wife's cousins), step-brother of Carl Maria von Weber, whose (real) brother Fridolin (Fritz) was engaged in 1788 by Haydn for the Eszterháza orchestra. Mozart writes (*Briefe*, IV, 6): 'Be diligent – cultivate your work – and do not forget your cousin who loves you from his heart Wolfgang Amadeus Mozart [Masonic sign] *Vienna*, 8th January 1787 in the morning at 5 o'clock before leaving.' The Webers, then, were also Freemasons and seem to have been staying in Mozart's apartment. The two brothers were there with their father (Franz Anton) and his new wife, Genoveva (*née* Brenner).
12 Mozart, *Briefe*, IV, 9–11.
13 Niemetschek, 36f. (corrected from original).
14 Nissen, 561.
15 Mozart, *Briefe*, IV, 28f.
16 Reproduced in print by a contemporary that same year: Deutsch, *Dokumente*, 272.
17 S.M. Ellis, *The Life of Michael Kelly* . . ., London 1930, 118ff. Zinzendorf, Diary: '. . . au concert de la Storace. . Le duo de la cosa rara fut répété trois fois, un air de bravoure qu'elle chanta un peu ennuyeux. Son compliment allemand tiré des Equivoci faisait un joli air . . .'
18 Mozart, *Briefe*, III, 40ff.
19 Landon, *Beethoven*, 53f.
20 Deutsch, *Dokumente*, 256.
21 The autograph, which recently came to light, was auctioned by J.A. Stargardt in Marburg/Lahn in 1965 and is now in private possession in the United States. Mozart, *Briefe*, IV, 3, wrongly dated and said to have been addressed to Swieten, but Mozart would certainly have addressed Swieten as 'Excellency', rather than no address at all. See also Mozart, *Briefe*, VI, 324.
22 Mozart, *Briefe*, IV, 49.
23 Method of payment: ibid., 52, 54.
24 The absurd fugue in the finale is based on a C major fugue by Mozart's pupil, Thomas Attwood.
25 Deutsch, *Dokumente*, 269.
26 Landon, *1791*, 221, n.5 (left-hand column).
27 Letter to Nannerl: *Briefe*, IV, 72. In a list dated 7 May 1790 (HHS, Obersthofmeisteramt OMEA SR 109, Intimationsbuch vom Jahr 1775 bis ersten April 793, the salaries of the 'HofMusique' are listed as follows:

Name	Wood, special Augmentations	Salary p.a.	Lodgings reckoned in money
Kapellmeister Salieri		1,200 fl.	152
Substitute Umlauf	1,600 fl. for 8 choirboys	850	
Organist Arbesser		400	
Organist Albrechtsberger		300	92
Violinist Franz Hofer [Mozart's brother-in-law]		150	
Kompositeur Mozart		800	

Salieri had been promoted to Kapellmeister on 16 March 1788 (p. 90) following the death of Giuseppe Bonno. Some other figures may prove useful. In 'Auszug von 1t Octobris bis letzten Decembris 777 dieseits vergangenen Besoldung und Pensions Anweisungen', 'the 18th ditto Order for yearly 7,000 F. salary and 1,000 F. Lodging Money from 1st November for the former Imp. Roy. Ambassador Herr Gottfried Freyherr van Swieten.' During the coronation festivities in Prague, the court kitchen required 115,000 gulden, costs of furnishing apartments for the royal suite 43,000 gulden, and the Oberst Hofpostamtsverwalter (Postal Direction) 18,337 gulden.
28 Haus-, Hof- und Staatsarchiv, Vienna, XII/15 E. Oberst Kammereramt; Sonderreihe. Geheime Kammerzahlamt. A. Amtbücher Bd 8, 9, 10 (187–9).
29 Zinzendorf, Diary, 8 January 1788: 'Le théâtre éclairé mais les bougies en partie éteintes avant la fin . . . La Pièce fort platte.'
30 The Ambassador had previously served as ministre pléni-potentiaire in Paris. I am indebted to M. Philippe A. Autexier for information about Dolfin (letter of 2 January 1988). Deutsch, *Dokumente*, 273, and Addenda and Corrigenda, 55.
31 Deutsch, *Dokumente*, 273.
32 Einstein, *Mozart* . . ., 191.
33 Deutsch, *Dokumente*, 274.
34 Ibid., 280f.
35 Ibid., 276.
36 Ibid., 255f.
37 Ibid., 279f.
38 Nissen, 633.
39 *Musical Times*, March 1987, 123–6.
40 For another possible date see p. 138.
41 In a contribution to the Nissen biography (pp. 627ff.).
42 Davies, op. cit., 191–6.
43 Mozart *Briefe*, IV, 65ff., 69f.
44 Ibid., 65.
45 Landon, *1791*, 31.
46 One of the most interesting and characteristic features of the E flat Symphony is the clever fashion in which Mozart links the introduction with the rest of the movement. Even amateur listeners can appreciate that the dotted French rhythm in the introduction, particularly in the second part (bars 14ff.), returns triumphantly in the trumpets at the end of the movement (bars 299ff.). The long downward scales in the violin in bars 2ff. of the introduction reappear, speeded up, in bars 72ff. of the Allegro. All this is not some mathematical trick, but Mozart's attempt to persuade the listener of the inevitability of the musical evolution experienced both aurally and visually. An even more subtle evolution can be noted in the Allegro of the 'Prague' Symphony, where the music of the second subject (bars 97ff.) turns into a bassoon accompaniment, speeded up and compressed rhythmi-cally, to the third subject (upbeat to 111ff.) – thus another example of seamless evolution. (See Werner Steger, 'Rhythmische Kernformeln in Mozarts letzten Symphonien', *Die Musikforschung* XIII [1970], I, 41ff.) It is even possible to work out an underlying *cantus firmus* for all four movements of the 'Jupiter' Symphony.
47 Deutsch, *Dokumente*, Addenda and Corrigenda, 58. Da Ponte raised 100,000 gulden from Vienna's nobility. Baron Gontard, 'a very wealthy gentleman much respected in Vienna, was to receive the subscriptions and act as manager. I would be assistant director.' Da Ponte, *Memoirs*, 181. The plan was approved by Joseph II.
48 Deutsch, *Dokumente*, 294, and Addenda and Corrigenda, 59.
49 Mozart, *Briefe*, IV, 77f. Hofdemel's name appears in the Lodge list for the first time in 1789.
50 Mozart, *Briefe*, III, 124f.

CHAPTER XI

1 K. Benyovszky, *J.N. Hummel*, Bratislava, 1934, 189ff.
2 Ibid., 197f.
3 Mozart, *Briefe*, IV, 79ff.
4 This project never materialized because Guardasoni was called to Warsaw that same year and did not return to Prague until 10 June 1791.
5 Johann Leopold Neumann (*recte*), secretary to the Saxon War Council, whose wife was a pianist.
6 *AMZ*, I (1798), 20–22, 85f., 179; XXII, 297. Reprinted in Nissen, 527ff. Deutsch, *Dokumente*, 299f.
7 Mozart, *Briefe*, 86ff.
8 Nissen, 535f.
9 It was customary for wealthy dedicatees to reward composers (and indeed authors), but not usually in advance. Ten years later, Prince Franz Joseph Maximilian Lobkowitz paid Beethoven 400 gulden for the dedication of the opus 18 Quartets. Jaroslav Macek in the Beethoven Symposium, Baden, 28–30 September 1987, *Musikforschung*, 41. Jg. (1988), Heft 2, 167.
10 Deutsch, *Dokumente*, 304.
11 See above, p. 208, and below, p. 210.
12 Mozart, *Briefe*, IV, 92–4.

13 Ibid., 95.
14 Ibid., 91, 109, 111.
15 *The Mozart Companion*, 102.
16 Aria, 'Alma grande, e nobil core' (K.578) for Mademoiselle Louise Villeneuve, insertion in Cimarosa's *Li due baroni di Roccazzurra*, performed in Vienna on 6 and 13 September 1789. Aria, 'Schon lacht der holde Frühling' (K.580), for Mozart's sister-in-law Josepha Hofer, currently engaged by Schikaneder in the Theater auf der Wieden, an insertion in a German translation of Paisiello's *Il barbiere di Siviglia* (17 September). Aria, 'Chi sa, chi sa qual sia' (K.582), for Louise Villeneuve, insertion in Martin y Soler's *Il burbero di buon cuore*, a revival staged at the Burgtheater on 9 November. Mozart, *Briefe*, VI, 388f.
17 Deutsch, *Dokumente*, 315.
18 Death of Anna Maria: ibid., 314.
19 Mozart, *Briefe*, IV, 99f.
20 Letters to Puchberg in 1790: ibid., 102–7.
21 Ibid., 107.
22 For the *Schematismus* see Appendix 4.
23 Mozart, *Briefe*, IV, 110. Next letter 110f.
24 See Landon, *1791*, 45.
25 Haberkamp, Textband, 281–5.
26 Mozart, *Briefe*, IV, 111f.
27 Landon, *1791*, ch. 1.
28 For a detailed description by Else Radant, see Landon, *1791*, 200ff.
29 Ibid., 14.
30 Deutsch, *Dokumente*, 332.
31 Landon, *1791*, 18f.
32 Novello, 170 and 347, n. 123.
33 Landon, *1791*, 19f.
34 Ibid., 60ff.
35 For new information on the first audience, see Appendix 7.

CHAPTER XII

1 The whole letter is quoted in Landon, *1791*, 144f. Cf. Mozart, *Briefe*, IV, 161–3.
2 HHS, VA 41 (alt 62), fol. 353f.
3 *The History of Freemasonry* (3 vols.), Edinburgh [1886]: quotation and summary from vol. III, 121–3.
4 Gould (loc. cit.) states that the Illuminati 'ceased to exist, and with them, Freemasonry in the south of Germany'. The authorities in Vienna at the time thought, however, that the movement had simply gone underground. In a letter dated 14 October 1785, Leopold Mozart – himself a recent recruit to the ranks of the Masons – wrote to his daughter: 'I learn that less than one per cent of what is being said here about the Illuminati business in Munich is true . . . some zealots have been banished or have left of their own accord . . . According to what [the oboist] H[err] Rahm [Ramm] tells me, the genuine Freemasons (whose members include the Elector [of Bavaria]) are very annoyed with these strange gentlemen.' (*Briefe*, III, 425). A recent authoritative article on the subject is Heinz Schuler, 'Freimaurer und Illuminaten aus Alt-Bayern und Salzburg und ihre Beziehungen zu den Mozarts', *Mitteilungen der Internationalen Stiftung Mozarteum*, 25. Jg., Heft 1–4 (1987), 11ff.
5 See Gould, op. cit., III, 99ff.
6 Grand Master of Scotland from November 1742 to November 1743. Beheaded for high treason 18 August 1746.
7 Gould footnote: 'All these schemes were so arranged as not only to accumulate a large treasure for the Order, but also to provide the officials, even to the W.M.'s [Worshipful Masters] of the Lodges, with a stipend. They came out beautifully on paper, but failed in practice. It would be wrong, however, to attribute any mercenary views to Hund and his colleagues, for at this time they were all, and afterwards, with very few exceptions, men of large means, proved probity, and high position. Many of them, indeed, made great pecuniary sacrifices for the good of the Order.'
8 See Landon, *1791*, 132ff.
9 HHS, Karton 41, V.A. 62/63, Logenlisten, fol. 156f.
10 HHS, ibid., fol. 163ff., 166 Nota degli Illuminati di Bavaria ed di altri paesi [Acta del Cte di Lehrbach].
11 HHS, ibid., fol. 269–73.
12 See Landon, *1791*, 168 (Nissen's account using material provided by Constanze Mozart).
13 Ibid., 115.
14 HHS, Karton 41, fol. 276ff.
15 Ibid., fol. 324–339v. The list attached to the letter is printed as Appendix 5(b).
16 Adam Wandruska, *Leopold II* (2 vols.), Vienna 1965, II, 381.
17 Ernst Wangermann, *From Joseph II to the Jacobin Trials*, 2nd ed., Oxford 1969, 147.
18 Ibid., 175.
19 See *1791*, ch. x.

Abbreviations of bibliographical sources

AMZ — *Allgemeine Musikalische Zeitung*, Leipzig, 1798 *et seq.*

Da Ponte, Memoirs — *Memoirs of Lorenzo Da Ponte*, trans. Elisabeth Abbott, ed. and annotated by Arthur Livingston, with a new preface by Thomas G. Bergin, New York 1929; reprinted 1967.

Deutsch, *Bilder* — Otto Erich Deutsch, *Mozart und seine Welt in zeitgenössischen Bildern* (with parallel English captions and notes on the illustrations), Kassel etc. 1961 (*NMA*, Serie x: Supplement, Werkgruppe 32).

Deutsch, Dokumente — *Mozart: Die Dokumente seines Lebens*, ed. Otto Erich Deutsch, Kassel etc., 1961. Vol. II, 'Addenda und Corrigenda', ed. Joseph Heinz Eibl, Kassel etc. 1978.

Haberkamp — Gertraut Haberkamp, *Die Erstdrucke der Werke von Wolfgang Amadeus Mozart*, 2 vols., Tutzing 1986: I, 'Textband'; II, 'Bildband'.

HHS — Haus-, Hof- und Staatsarchiv, Vienna.

Köchel — The edition of the Köchel catalogue to which reference is made is, unless stated otherwise: Ludwig, Ritter von Köchel, *Chronologisch-thematisches Verzeichnis sämtlicher Tonwerke Wolfgang Amadé Mozarts . . .*, 8th ed., Wiesbaden 1983. References to works by Mozart occurring in the text and in the notes on the text generally include only the original numbers in the Köchel listing; wherever appropriate, revised numbers are included in the index of works by Mozart on pp. 271–2.

Landon, Beethoven — H.C. Robbins Landon, *Beethoven: a documentary study*, London and New York 1970.

Landon, Masons — H.C. Robbins Landon, *Mozart and the Masons. New Light on the Lodge 'Crowned Hope'*, London and New York, 1982.

Landon, *1791* — H.C. Robbins Landon, *1791: Mozart's Last Year*, London and New York 1988.

Michtner — Otto Michtner, *Das alte Burgtheater als Opernbühne*, Vienna etc. 1970.

Mozart, *Briefe* — *Mozart: Briefe und Aufzeichnungen*, ed. Wilhelm A. Bauer and Otto Erich Deutsch. Letters: 4 vols, Kassel etc. 1962–3. Commentary (ed. Joseph Heinz Eibl): 2 vols, Kassel etc. 1971. Indexes (ed. Eibl): 1 vol., Kassel etc. 1975.

The Mozart Companion — Edited by H.C. Robbins Landon and Donald Mitchell, London 1956.

Niemetschek — *Life of Mozart . . . by Franz Xaver Niemetschek*, trans. Helen Mautner, with an introduction by A. Hyatt King, London 1956.

Nissen — Georg Nikolaus Nissen, *Biographie W.A. Mozarts nach Originalbriefen*, Leipzig, 1828; photographic reprint, Hildesheim 1972.

NMA — *Neue Mozart Ausgabe*, the collected edition of Mozart's works begun in 1955 and in progress.

Novello — *A Mozart Pilgrimage, Being the Travel Diaries of Vincent and Mary Novello in the year 1829*, transcribed and compiled by Nerina Medici di Marignano, ed. Rosemary Hughes, London 1955.

Pezzl — [Johann Pezzl], *Skizze von Wien*, 6 *Hefte* published in 2 vols., Vienna 1786–90; new edition, Graz 1923.

Zinzendorf — Ms. Diaries of Count Carl von Zinzendorf, in the Haus-, Hof- und Staatsarchiv, Vienna.

Select bibliography of recent publications

The article on Mozart in *The New Grove Dictionary of Music and Musicians*, ed. Stanley Sadie, London 1980, includes a good general bibliography, which is reproduced in Sadie, Stanley, *The New Grove Mozart*, London 1982. Books and articles of special interest published in or after 1982 are listed below:

BRAUNBEHRENS, Volkmar, *Mozart in Wien*, Munich and Zurich, 1986. A sensible re-examination of many aspects of Mozart's life in Vienna with some new interpretations of his last years.

DAVIES, Peter J., 'Mozart's Illnesses and Death', *Musical Times*, CXXV (1984), pp. 437ff. and 554ff. The authoritative new study on the subject, superseding all previous studies, great and small.

——, 'Mozart's Manic-Depressive Tendencies', *Musical Times*, CXXVIII (1987): part 1, pp. 123–6, part 2, pp. 191–6.

EISEN, Cliff, 'Contributions to a New Mozart Documentary Biography', *Journal of the American Musicological Society*, XXXIX/3 (Fall 1986), pp. 615–32. This important article is a foretaste of the large volume of supplementary documents (addenda to Deutsch, *Dokumente*), to be published in 1990.

LANDON, H.C. Robbins, *Mozart and the Masons: New Light on the Lodge 'Crowned Hope'*, London and New York 1982. Mozart identified in a group picture of the Lodge 'Crowned Hope' in 1790, with documentation, partly unpublished, of Lodge membership lists.

MAUNDER, Richard, *Mozart's Requiem: On Preparing a New Edition*, Oxford 1988. An essential book on the Requiem.

MORROW, Mary Sue, 'Mozart and Viennese Concert Life', *Musical Times*, CXXVI (1985), pp. 453ff. Re-examination of the evidence.

NEUMAYR, Anton, *Musik & Medizin am Beispiel der Wiener Klassik*, Vienna 1987. A reappraisal, by a Viennese physician, of *inter alia* Mozart's terminal illness.

SCHWERIN, Erna, *Constanze Mozart: Woman and Wife of a Genius*, New York 1981. A sensible reappraisal of Constanze.

——, *Leopold Mozart, Profile of a Personality*, New York 1987. A useful survey of his character.

——, *Antonio Salieri: An Appraisal and Exoneration*: Part 1, New York, 1988. An examination of his life and influence, based on the sources.

STEPTOE, Andrew, 'Mozart and Poverty. A re-examination of the evidence'. *Musical Times* CXXV (1984), pp. 196ff.

——, *The Mozart-Da Ponte Operas. The Cultural and Musical Background to* Le nozze di Figaro, Don Giovanni *and* Così fan tutte, Oxford 1988. This brilliant and subtle study appeared too late for consideration in the present volume.

TYSON, Alan, *Mozart – Studies of the Autograph Scores*, Cambridge, Mass., and London 1987. An essential series of studies concerning dating based on the use of paper types and on watermarks, the evidence of which has resulted in extensive chronological revision of works by Mozart.

VALENTIN, Erich, *Leopold Mozart, Porträt einer Persönlichkeit*, Munich 1987. The first modern assessment of his character, but in very abbreviated form.

Appendix 1

Mozart's list of subscribers, reproduced here, was sent to his father on 20 March 1784. It was discussed by O.E. Deutsch first in *Music and Letters* (July 1941) and also in *Dokumente* (pp. 485ff.), the 174 names being presented in alphabetical order, not as listed by Mozart. Further details based on later research were published in Mozart, *Briefe*, VI, 167ff., where the names follow the composer's original order. Additional information and corrections concerning certain individual subscribers are provided below. Some cumbersome German titles and problematical terms (e.g. 'Truchsess', literally 'carver', but signifying a position of prestige at court) have not been translated.

Additional source material consulted includes: various editions of the *Hofschematismus* (Vienna, 1781–1802); Ignaz, Ritter von Schönfeld, *Adels-Schematismus des Österreichischen Kaiserstaates* (2 vols., Vienna 1824 and 1825); various editions of 'Gotha' – *Genealogisches Taschenbuch der deutschen gräflichen* [*fürstlichen, freiherrlichen*] *Häuser auf das Jahr* [etc.], and *Debrett's Peerage*.

The importance of Mozart's list is very simply that it is unique in giving a cross-section of the cultivated concert-going public in Vienna in 1784. It is not an exhaustive list, of course; if Joseph II wished to attend a concert, he would send a servant in advance – with a 'pourboire' above and beyond the price of entry – to fetch his ticket (see, for example, the case cited on p. 87). Nevertheless, the document serves as a primary first-hand source for Viennese musical history of the period.

New information on and corrections relating to certain subscribers (Mozart's spellings shown in parentheses where different):

APPONYI, Countess ('Apumoni')
Maria Carolina, Countess von Lodron (b. 1756); m. 1779 Anton Georg, Count Apponyi de Nagy-Appony(i) (1751–1817).

AUERSPERG, Prince Adam
Johann Adam Joseph, Prince von Auersperg (1721–95), Knight Grand Cross of the Order of St Stephen, Royal Sicilian Order of St Januarius, Chamberlain and Privy Councillor; m. (1) Maria Catharina, Countess von Schönffield (†1753), and (2) Maria Wilhelmine, Countess von Neipperg (†1775); host for Mozart's *Idomeneo* in 1786.

AUERSPERG, Prince Carl von
Carl Joseph Anton, Prince von Auersperg (1720–1800), *Oberst-Erbland-Kämmerer und Marschall* in Krain, Knight of the Order of the Golden Fleece, I.R. Chamberlain, Privy Councillor.

AUERSPERG, Princess
Maria Josepha Rosalia, *née* Countess Trautson (1724–92), wife of Prince Carl.

AUERSPERG, Count Carl
Carl, Count von Auersperg, *Oberst-Erblandmarschall* in Tyrol, Knight of the Order of the Golden Fleece, Commander of the Order of Maria Theresa, Knight of the Bavarian Order of St Hubertus, Chamberlain, Privy Councillor, Lt-Gen.-Field Marshal; m. 1776 Maria Josepha, Countess von Lobkowitz.

AUERSPERG, Count Wilhelm
Wilhelm, Count (later Prince) von Auersperg (1749–1822), later Maj.-General; m. 1776 Leopoldine Francisca, Countess Waldstein.

BASSEWITZ, Countess ('Passowitz')
Elisabeth Marianne, Countess (Reichsgräfin) Bassewitz (b. 1760); m. 1784 Karl Friedrich Gustav von Holtke, *Jägermeister*.

BRAUN, Baron v.
Ludwig, Reichsfreiherr von Braun (1762–1847), *Reichshofrath* in Vienna, later in Nassau and Hessian service, for thirty years as Ambassador Extraordinary and Minister Plenipotentiary in Vienna; or his father, Karl Adolph (d. 1785), from 1764 *Reichshofrath*, summoned to Vienna in 1760 by Emperor Francis Stephen.

BURKHARDT, Baron
Franz Ludwig Joseph, Herr auf Battelau und Stranka (b. 1746), k.k. niederösterreichischer Regierungsrat [Lower Austrian government councillor].

BURKHARDT, Mad:me
Marie Christine, Freiin von Laykam, wife of the above.

CHOTEK
Johann Rudolf, Reichsgraf Chotek von Chotkowa und Wognin (b. 1749), *Oberstblandthürhüter* in Upper Austria, Knight of the Order of the Golden Fleece, Chamberlain, Privy Councillor etc.; or his father, Johann Karl (1705–87), *Oberstblandthürhüter* in Upper Austria, etc., later Ambassador in Berlin.

DEGLMANN ('Toeglman')
Bernhard, Freiherr von Deglmann, *Hofrat* (later Privy Councillor) of the Bohemian-Austrian Court Chancellery, later (1791) Vice-President of the *Hofkammer, Ministerial-Banko-Hof-Deputation*.

DIETRICHSTEIN, Joseph
Joseph, Count Dietrichstein, President of the Government of Lower Austria; m. 1783 Therese, a niece of Count Carl von Zinzendorf.

EHRENFELD ('Arenfeld')
Joseph Frech von Ehrenfeld, *Konzipist der Staatsratskanzlei*; or Ignaz Frech von Ehrenfeld, *Aksessist der Registratur des Exhibiten-Protokolls der Vereinigten Hofstelle*.

ERDÖDY, Count Ladislaus ('Ertödy')
Probably Ladislaus II, Count von Erdödy de Monyorokerek et Monte Claudio, *Erbobergespann des Warasdiner Comitats* etc., Chamberlain, Privy Councillor; patron of Ignaz Pleyel and Master of the Lodge 'Zum goldenen Rad' ('Golden Wheel') in Eberau. However, other members of the family are also possible candidates, e.g. Ladislaus (1746–86) of the middle line; or Joseph (b. 1754) of the cadet line, who was Haydn's patron; or Johann Nepomuk (1723–89), of the cadet line, joint manager of the Preßburg theatre in the 1780s, Knight Grand Cross of the Order of St Stephen, Chamberlain, Privy Councillor, *Oberstkämmerer* of the Kingdom of Hungary, and Royal Hungarian *Kammerpräsident*.

ESTERHÁZY, Count Franz ('François')
See above, pp. 118f. and Appendix 3.

ESTERHÁZY, Countess
Wife of Count Franz; see above, and Appendix 3.

ESTERHÁZY, Count Johann Baptist ('Jean')
See above, pp. 116f. and Appendix 3.

FRIES, Count
Johann, Reichsgraf Fries (1719–85), industrialist and banker; or his eldest son, Joseph then aged 21.

Mozart's list of subscribers, sent to his father in Salzburg, 20 March 1784; actual size of page 22.8 × 18.0 cm

GALITZIN, Prince ('Gallizin')
Russian Ambassador; see above, pp. 111ff.

GEBSATTEL, Baron
Franz Philipp, Freiherr von Gebsattel (d. 1796), *Ritter Hauptmann des fränkischen Kantons Rhon und Warre, Obermarschall zu Würzburg*.

HARRACH, Count ('Le Conte Harrach l'aïné')
Carl Joseph, Count von Harrach zu Rohrau (1765–1831), who in 1784 was head of the senior line of Rohrau (Haydn's birthplace); or Johann Nepomuk Ernst, Count Harrach (1756–1829), Knight of the Order of the Golden Fleece, Chamberlain, *Reichshofrat*, who was head of the cadet line of Bruck-an-der-Leytha.

HERBERSTEIN, Count
Johann Gundaker, Count von Herberstein (1738–1810), Chamberlain, Privy Councillor, *Oberst-Jägermeister* (Master of the Hunt) of the Prince-Archbishop of Salzburg.

HERBERSTEIN, Count Joseph
Joseph Franz Stanislaus, Count von Herberstein-Moltke (1757–1816), of the cadet Moravian line, *Oberstblandkämmerer und Truchsess* in Carinthia, Chamberlain, Privy Councillor, *Hofkammerpräsident*.

HERBERSTEIN, Count Nep.
Joseph Johann Nepomuk, Count von Herberstein (1727–1809), *Oberstblandkämmerer und Truchsess* in Carinthia, Chamberlain, Privy Councillor, *Oberst-Landrichter* of Lower Austria.

HOYOS, Leopold
Johann Leopold Innocenz, Count Hoyos (1728–96), Chamberlain, Councillor of the Government of Lower Austria.

JACOBI, v.
Konstans Philipp Wilhelm Jacobi (1745–1816; from 1786 'von' and from 1788 Freiherr von Kloest), *Hof- und Legationsrat, Staatsminister*, representative of the Prussian Government in Vienna, 1773–92; member of Mozart's Lodge 'Zur(neu)gekrönten Hoffnung'.

JAHN, Herr v.
Ignaz Jahn, *Hoflieferant* (Supplier to the Court), owner of the traiteur shop in Schönbrunn since 1776, also of that in the Augarten and of the Jahn restaurant (in the rooms of which concerts were held; Mozart played his Piano Concerto no. 27 in B flat, K.595, there in April 1791).

KEES ('Käs')
Franz Bernhard, Edler von Kees(s) (1720–95), Councillor of the Appeal Court and of the Provincial Court (*Landrecht*) of Lower Austria; patron of Haydn; gave orchestral concerts at his house, in which Mozart participated; or Franz Georg, Edler von Kees(s) (b. 1747), Court Councillor under Joseph II.

LICHNOWSKY, Princess ('Lignowsky')
Marie Christiane (Christine), *née* Countess Thun, wife of Prince Carl (see above, pp. 63f.); or Charlotte Caroline, *née* Countess Althann, mother of Prince Carl.

LIECHTENSTEIN ('Prince Louis Lichtenstein')
Aloys Joseph, Prince Liechtenstein (1729–1805), Knight of the Order of the Golden Fleece, Chamberlain.

MARGELI(C)K, Mad^me de ('Margelique')
The wife of Dr. jur. Johann Wenzel, Freiherr von Margelick, Knight of the Order of St Stephen, Court Councillor and *geheimer Referendar bey den Böhmischen und Österreichischen vereinigten Hofstellen* (confidential adviser to the Bohemian and Austrian joint Court department), Vice-President of the Bohemian Gubernium, and of the Gubernium of the Crown Lands of Galicia and Lodomeria; residing in the Trattnerhof.

MARSCHALL, Count ('Marchal')
Christian Karl August Ludwig Marschall von Biederstein (1758–1827), Royal Prussian Colonel and Quartermaster General,

married Amalia von Qualtieri; or, from the Baden line, Karl Wilhelm (1764–1817), in 1792 in the service of the government of Baden.

MONTECUCOLI, Count
Ludwig Franz, Markgraf Montecucoli (1767–1827), later a member of the Lodge 'Zur(neu)gekrönten Hoffnung'.

MORTON, Mylord
Hon. John Douglas (1756–1818), second son of the 14th Earl of Morton; mentioned in Zinzendorf's Diary, 1 March 1784.

NIMPTSCH, Count
Ferdinand, Count Nimptsch, army officer (Infantry Colonel, 1794); or Joseph, Count Nimptsch, Freiherr von Fürst und Kupferberg, Major (later General of the Light Horse [Chevaux-Légers]), Knight of the Order of Maria Theresa.

NIMPTSCH, Countess
The wife of one of the above.

NOSTITZ, General ('Nostiz')
Friedrich Moritz, Reichsgraf von Nostitz-Rieneck, Dienstkämmerer, Lt-Field-Marshal, Colonel of Grand Duke Leopold of Tuscany's Regiment of Cuirassiers, Vice-Commandant of the City of Vienna, 1779.

OTT
Michael von Ott, Titularrath with the Russian Ambassador (Galitzin) in Vienna.

PAAR, Count
Wenzel, Count (later Prince) Paar (1744–1813), Chamberlain, son of Prince Wenzel Johann Joseph (1719–92), who succeeded his father as General-Erbland-Postmeister in the Austrian postal system.

PALM, Prince
Carl Joseph, Prince von Palm (1749–1814), Chamberlain, Privy Councillor, Knight of the Bavarian Order of St Hubertus and of the Order of the Golden Lions.

PASSTHORY ('Paszthory')
Alexander von Passthory, Hofrat des Ritterstandes, Hungarian-Transylvanian Court Councillor, a member of Baron van Swieten's Studies Commission.

PENZENSTEIN ('Pentzenstein')
Johann Penzeneter von Penzenstein, Maj.-General (later Lt-Field Marshal), Artillery Commander in the Low Countries, 1784–5; or, more likely, Karl Anton von Penzenstein, Councillor of the Lower Austrian Government.

PODSTATSKY, Count Joseph ('Potztazky')
Joseph, Count Podstatsky-Liechtenstein-Castelcorn.

PUTHON, v.
Johann Baptist, Ritter (later Freiherr and Reichsfreiherr) von Puthon (1744 [1745?]–1816) etc.; a leading Mason.

ROSTY, DE ('Rosti')
Ignaz von Rosty, Colonel, District Commander of the Ordnance Office; Maj.-General of the Artillery, 1794; member of the Prague Lodge 'Truth and Unity', 1791.

ROTTENHAN, Count
See above, pp. 230ff.

SCHAFFGOTSCH (Schafgotsch), née Countess Kollonitz ('Schafgotsch née Kollnitsch')
Maria Anna, Countess Schaffgotsch (1744–1802), wife of Anton Gotthard, Count Schaffgotsch-Semperfrey von und zu Kienast (1721–1811), Knight of the Order of the Golden Fleece, Knight Grand Cross of the Order of St Leopold, etc., Chamberlain, Privy Councillor.

SEILERN, Count August
Christian August, Count Seilern (1717–1801), Knight Grand Cross of the Order of St Stephen, Chamberlain, President of the High Court (Oberste Justizstelle), Privy Councillor; or Joseph Johann, Count Seilern (b. 1752), Chamberlain, Ambassador of the Elector of Bohemia to the Imperial Assembly (Reichsversammlung) in Regensburg, 1789.

SOLTYK, Count ('Soldyk')
Stanislaus, Count Soltyk, Polish patriot and later (1794) emissary in Vienna, involved with the 'Jacobin' plot (cf. Ernst Wangermann, From Joseph II to the Jacobin Trials, 2nd ed., 1969, 144).

STERNBERG, Count
Christian Philipp, Count Sternberg-Manderscheid (1732–86), Knight of the Order of the Golden Fleece, Chamberlain, Privy Councillor; or Franz Adam, Count von Sternberg (1711–89), Chamberlain, Privy Councillor and Oberst-Landmarschall in Bohemia.

STERNBERG, Count Adam
Adam, Count Sternberg (1751–1811), lord of Serowitz, Chamberlain.

STOPFORD, Lord
James George Stopford (1765–1835), who, as son and heir of the 2nd Earl of Courtown, would in 1784 have used the courtesy title Viscount (or, less formally, 'Lord') Stopford (his father's subsidiary title). He succeeded his father as 3rd Earl of Courtown and 2nd Baron Saltersford in 1810.

SWIETEN, Baron van ('Suiten')
See pp. 108ff., above.

TESCHENBACH, Mr de
Possibly Freiherr von Teschenberg, a member of a Hungarian family ennobled in the mid-eighteenth century.

TRATTNER, Mad:me de
Maria Theresa, Edle von Trattner(n), née Nagel, wife of Johann Thomas von Trattner(n) etc.; she was a pupil of Mozart.

UGARTE ('Hugart')
Johann Wenzel, Count Ugarte (1748–96), Court Councillor of the High Court; or his brother Aloys (1749–1817), who married (1777) Maria Josepha, Countess Czernin-Chuderitz.

WALDSTEIN, Count
Vincenz Ferrerius, Count von Waldstein und Wartenberg (1731–97), Oberst-Erblandvorschneider of Bohemia, Chamberlain, Privy Councillor, Freemason (in Prague); or Franz de Paula, Count von Waldstein (1759–1823), Knight of the Order of St John and Commander of the Order of St Leopold, Chamberlain, Lt-Colonel; or Ferdinand Ernst Gabriel, Count von Waldstein und Wartenberg (1762–1823), Chamberlain, Beethoven's patron from the composer's Bonn period.

WALDSTEIN, Count Georg
Georg Christian, Count von Waldstein und Wartenberg (1743–91), Erbland-Vorschneider in Bohemia, Chamberlain, who married (1765) Marie Elisabeth, Countess Ulfeld (1747–91), sister of Maria Wilhelmine, Countess Thun.

WETZLAR, Baron, father ('Wetzlar Père')
Carl Abraham Wetzlar, Reichsfreiherr von Plankenstern, wholesaler and banker. See p. 75, above.

WETZLAR, Baron ('Raymund')
Raimund, son of the above, friend of Mozart and owner of a flat in which the Mozarts lived for a while. See p. 75, above.

WILCZEK, Count ('Wolschek')
Franz Joseph, Count Wilczek (1748–1834), Chamberlain and Privy Councillor; or Johann Joseph, Count Wilczek (d. 1819), Minister Plenipotentiary in Naples and subsequently in Austrian Lombardy etc.; or Joseph, Count Wilczek (b. 1752), Chamberlain, Captain in the Lascy Infantry Regiment.

WÜRTTEMBERG, Prince ('Würtemberg')
Of the many possible princely candidates the one referred to may be Friedrich August Ferdinand (b. 1763), Imperial Colonel and owner of an infantry regiment.

ZOIS VON EDELSTEIN
Joseph, Freiherr von Zois (b. 1741), married Maria Katharina (1756–1825), elder daughter of Dr Leopold von Auenbrugger (the Auenbrugger sisters were excellent pianists, to whom Haydn dedicated a set of piano sonatas).

'Zur gekrönten Hoffnung', 1790
List of members present ('*Anwesende Brüder*') and absent ('*Abwesende Brüder*') and Serving Brethren ('*Dienende Bruder*').

GENEALOGICAL TABLE

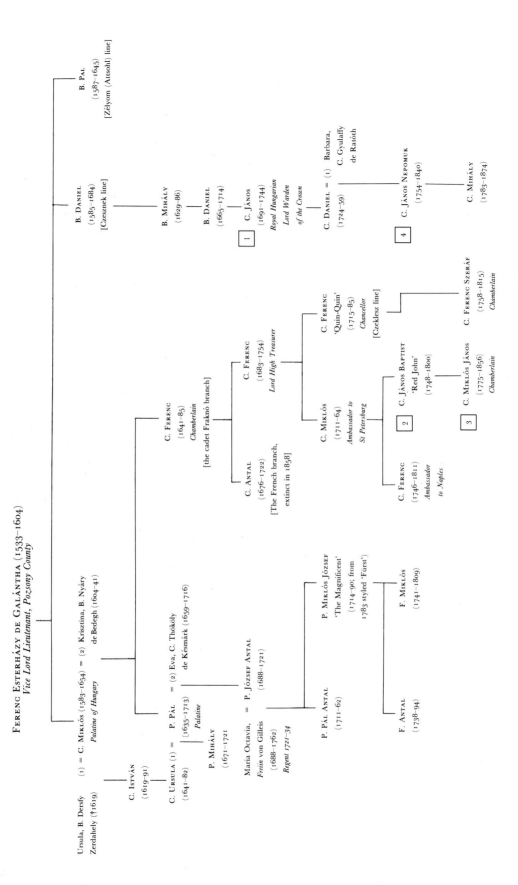

Appendix 3

The genealogy of the Esterházy family, with special reference to the four Counts Esterházy of the eighteenth century bearing the name *János* (*Johann*): genealogical table and biographical details of the four Counts Esterházy.

by László Berényi

The following abbreviations and symbols are used in the table and biographical details:

B.	Baron(ess)	*	born
d.	daughter	†	died
C.	Count(ess)	=	married
F.	Fürst		
P.	Prince(ss)		

The names of individuals are given in their Hungarian form. German equivalents are as follows:

Antal	Anton	Mihály	Michael
Ferenc	Franz	Miklós	Nicolaus
István	Stephan	Pál	Paul
János	Johann	Szeráf	Seraph(im)
József	Joseph		

Biographical details of the four Counts Esterházy noted as 1, 2, 3 and 4 in the genealogical table.

1

János, Count Esterházy de Galántha, hereditary lord of Fort Csesznek.
* 1697; † 3 October 1744 at Pozsony (Preßburg; now Bratislava); created Count 7 December 1721.
Lt-General of Prince Rácóczi; received the *Jus Gladii* (the absolute right to dispense justice within the boundaries of his own domains – a rare honour), 1718; Privy Councillor and member of the Governing Council, 1735; Royal Hungarian Lord Warden of the Crown, 1741.
Married 7 July 1720 at Bodok, Nyitra County: Barbara, C. Berényi de Karancs-Berényi (* 1697; † 3 December 1759), d. of C. György Berényi and his wife, Clara, C. Ujfalussy de Divek-Ujfalu.

2

János Baptist, Count Esterházy de Galántha, hereditary lord of Fort Frakó (Forchtenstein), known in the family as 'Red John'.
* 6 June 1748 in Vienna; † 25 February 1800 in Vienna.
Lord Lieutenant of Bereg and Pozsony Counties; I.R. Chamberlain, 1771; Privy Councillor.
Built the Esterházy palace (designed by Charles Moreau) in the Krugerstrasse, Vienna. Known for his passion for the theatre and for taking part in amateur performances.
Married 11 November 1772 at Pozsony: Maria Anna. C. Pálffy ab Erdöd (* 5 December 1747; † 3 June 1799 in Vienna), d. of C. Miklós Pálffy etc., Chancellor of the Royal Hungarian Court, Knight of the Order of the Golden Fleece, and his wife, Maria Anna, C. von Althan.

3

Miklós János, Count Esterházy de Galántha, hereditary lord of Fort Frakó.
* 1 June 1775 in Vienna; † 18 February 1856 in Vienna.
I.R. Chamberlain, 1796; Privy Councillor, 1832.
Married 1 June 1799 in Vienna: Marie Françoise Isabelle, Marquise de Roisin (* 24 January 1778 at Douai St Jacques, Flanders; † 9 December 1845 in Nice), d. of Marquis Philippe Albert de Roisin and his wife Françoise de Retz de Bressoles, Comtesse de Chanclos.

4

János Nepomuk, Count Esterházy de Galántha, hereditary lord of Fort Csesznek.
* 18 October 1754; † 23 February 1840 in Vienna.
I.R. Chamberlain, 14 January 1775; Councillor of Government (*Landesregierung*) of Lower Austria, 1777; Lord Lieutenant of Hunyad and Zaránd Counties, 1789; Privy Councillor, 6 June 1792; Lord Lieutenant, Veszprém County, 1813; Vice-Chancellor for Transylvania, 1822; Knight of the Order of St. Stephen, 1 March 1824; Chief Usher of the Royal Hungarian Court, 1825.
Noted for his famous numismatic collection.
Married 10 June 1777 in Schönbrunn Palace chapel, Vienna: Ágnes, C. Bánffy de Losoncz (* 19 June 1754; † 14 November 1831 in Vienna), d. of C. Dénes (Dionisius) Bánffy etc. and his wife, Ágnes, B. Barcsay de Nagy-Barcsa.

Appendix 4

(a) *The Hofmusik and National Theatre personnel in Vienna, 1782, from the* Theater-Almanach *of that year, pp. 130ff. Author's collection.*

VI. THE ORCHESTRA

Kapellmeister	Hr. Antonio Salieri.
His Substitute	Hr. Umlauf.
First violins	Hr. Woborzil.
	— Rheinhart.
	— Scheidel.
	— Franz Hoffer.
	— Milechner.
	— Leopold Klemm.
Second violins	Hr. Michael Hoffer.
	— Johann Klemm
	— Millner.
	— Piringer.
	— Plasky.
	— Pachner.
Violas	Hr. Huber.
	— Mathias Zoffer.
	— Nurscher.
	— Purghi.
Violone [double basses]	Hr. Boldai.
	— Schillinger.
	— Weuig.
Violoncelli	Hr. Weigl.
	— Orchsler.
	— Packer.
Oboes	Hr. Tribensee.
	— Vent [Went]
Flutes	Hr. Turner.
	— Menschel.
Bassoons	Hr. Kauzner.
	— Trubur.
Horns	Hr. Leitgeb
	— Krzybanek
Clarinets	Hr. Johann Stadler.
	— Anton Stadler.
Trumpets	Hr. Joseph Mayer.
	— Karl Mayer.
Timpani	Hr. Schulz.

Section VII lists the various officials of the theatre as follows: 'Erster Kassier und Zahlmeister' (First Cashier and Paymaster); 'Erster Controleur . . .' (First Controller of the ticket office and payments); 'Comissair . . .' (Commissioner of the Wardrobe); 'Logenmeister' (Master of the Boxes); 'Dessen Gehülf' (His Assistant and Inspector of the Locked Seats in the Parterre Noble); 'Oberaufseher . . .' (Superintendent and Inspector); 'Unterinspektor' (Assistant Inspector); 'Wärter . . .' (Attendant of the Imperial Royal Court Boxes); 'Billeteinnehmer' (Ticket Collectors); 'Machinist' (Machinist); 'Maler' (Painter); 'Erster Garderobier . . .' (First Keeper of the Wardrobe and Inspector); 'Zweiter Garderobier . . .' (Second Keeper of the Wardrobe and Inspector of the Spoken Theatre); 'Dritter Garderobier . . .' (Third Keeper of the Wardrobe and Inspector of the Sung Theatre). 'N.B. Under them are twelve tailors; if the work proves too great, other persons are engaged from local sources. During the last Carnival, 50 persons were employed in the Wardrobe.'

Section VIII lists the following tradesmen in regular paid employment:

- A chimney sweep and four apprentices
- A ticket distributor
- Six carpenters
- Nine joiners
- Four masons
- Four paint-mixers
- Three lamp-cleaners
- Twenty assistants
- Two corporals, who serve as doorkeepers and as watchmen in the house
- Two footmen with the spoken theatre
- Two footmen with the opera
- A footman for the carriages of theatrical personnel

Opposite, right
Plans of the theatre showing the parterre at ground level and the arrangement of boxes on the upper level. Note that there were two Court Boxes (*Hof Logen*).
Theater = stage; *Orchester* = pit; *Parterre noble* = front seats (pit); *Zweyter Parterre* = rear seats (pit).

(b) *Extracts from the* Hof- und Staats-Schematismus . . ., *Vienna 1791 (from the copy in the Haus-, Hof- und Staatsarchiv, Vienna).* The following list of members of the Hofmusik (addresses in the original here omitted) is taken from pp. 403–6. Among the singers, under the treble ('Sopranist') and alto headings, the boys (unnamed) in the Hofmusikkapelle (Sängerknaben) are also included. The trumpeters and the timpani player are not listed; the string players listed as 'Violinisten' also include viola players. Only one 'Tromponist' is listed, though three were in regular use in 1791; likewise no flutes are mentioned, but they too were in regular demand. Under the heading 'K.K. Kammermusizi' Mozart is listed with address at Währingergasse 135, but in 1791 he was in fact living in the Rauhensteingasse. Those members who appear under both 'Hofmusik' and 'Kammermusizi' headings received additional salary.

Hofmusik- und Theatralrechnu[n]gs-Revisor
Hr. Joh. Baptist Thorwart, k.k. Oberstkämmereramtssekretär, . . . [address]

Hofkapellmeister
Hr. Anton Salieri, . . .

Hofkapellmeister-Substitutus
Hr. Ignaz Umlauf, . . .

Sopranist
Hr. Georg Michael Schlemmer, . . .
Und 4 Sängerknaben

Altist
Hr. Anton Packer, . . .
Und 4 Sängerknaben.

Tenoristen
Hr. Leopold Panschab, . . .
Hr. Adalbert Brichta, . . .
Hr. Jos. Krottendorfer, . . .
Hr. Valentin Adamberger, . . .
Hr. Martin Ruprecht, . . .

Bassisten
Hr. Tobias Gfur, . . .
Hr. Anton Ignaz Ulbrich, . . .
Hr. Cirilins Haberta, . . .
Hr. Jakob Wranezy, . . .
Hr. Joseph Hofmann, . . .

Organisten
Hr. Franz Arbesser, . . .
Hr. Joh. Georg Albrechtsberger, . . .

Violinisten
Hr. Franz Kreybich, . . .
Hr. Anton Hofmann, . . .
Hr. Johann Klemp, . . .
Hr. Joseph Scheidel, . . .
Hr. Franz Hofer, . . .
Hr. Wenzl Müller, . . .
Hr. Karl Maratschek, . . .
Hr. Thadäus Huber, . . .
Hr. Heinrich Bauheimer, . . .
Hr. Joseph Hofmann, . . .
Hr. Zeno Franz Wenzl, . . .
Hr. Peter Fuchs, . . .
Hr. Johann Baptist Hofmann, . . .
Hr. Joseph Pirlinger, . . .

Violoncellisten
Hr. Johann Hofmann, . . .
Hr. Jos. Orßler, . . .

Violionisten [sic]
Hr. Leopold Krebner, . . .
Hr. Franz Balday, . . .

Tromponist
Hr. Ignaz Karl Ulbrich, . . .

Oboisten
Hr. Georg Tribenser [sic], . . .
Hr. Johann Went, . . .

Fagottisten
Hr. Wenzl Kauzner, . . .
Hr. Ignaz Drobnay, . . .

Instrumentdiener
Joseph Federl, . . .

K.K. Kammermusizi
Kompositor
Hr. Wolfgang Mozart, . . .

Violinisten
Hr. Franz Kreibich, . . .
Hr. Heinrich Bonheimer, . . .
Hr. Thomas Woborzill, . . .
Hr. Johann Baptist Hofmann, . . .

Oboisten
Hr. Georg Triebenser [sic], . . .
Hr. Johann Went, . . .

Klarinetisten
Hr. Anton Stadler, . . .
Hr. Johann Stadler, . . .

Fagotisten
Hr. Wenzl Kauzner, . . .
Hr. Ignaz Drobnay, . . .

Waldhornisten
Hr. Martin Rupp, . . .
Hr. Jakob Eisen, . . .

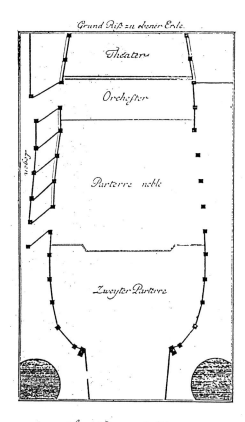

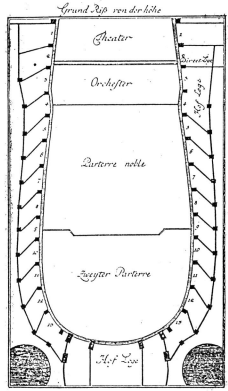

Appendix 5

Lists of members of the Illuminati

(a) *Verzeichnis einiger berühmten Illuminaten*
(List of some famous Illuminati)
Haus-, Hof- und Staatsarchiv, Vienna, Vertrauliche Akten 41 (alt 62), fol. 269–73 [2 January 1792?]

1 Heinrich, Prince of Prussia.
2 Crown Prince of Prussia.
3 Duke of Sachsen Weimar.
4 Duke of Sachsen Gotha.
5 Duke of Orléans.
6 Freyherr v. Dallberg, Coadjutor in Mainz, *Provinzial for Germany.*
7 Count Herzberg, formerly Prussian minister.
8 Count Kollowrath, First Chancellor of Bohemia and Austria.
9 Count Palfi [Pálffy], First Chancellor of Hungary.
10 Count Pamfi [Bánffy], Governor in Transylvania.
11 Count Brigido, Governor at Lemberg in Galicia.
12 Count Stadion, I.R. Ambassador in London.
13 Baron Kressel, Vice-Chancellor of Bohemia.
14 Baron Swi[e]ten, formerly President of the Studies Commission in Vienna.
15 Baron Jacobi, Prussian Ambassador in Vienna.
16 Herr v. Dehm, Prussian Ambassador in Aix-la-Chapelle.
17 Minister of Finances [in France] Neckar.
18 Court Councillor Sonnenfels in Vienna.
19 Count Nicolaus Forkatsch [Forgács] in Hungary, Lord Lieutenant in Neitra. N.B. *stirred up Hungary to mutiny.*
20 Count Stadion, Cathedral Canon in Mainz.
21 Baron Hompesch, Cathedral Canon in Speyer.
22 Baron Hompesch, his brother, an adventurer.
23 Count Kowencel, Cathedral Canon in Eichstätt.
24 Baron v. Podmanizki, Government Councillor in Vienna.
25 Peter v. Ballock, Councillor of Law in Ofen [Budapest].
26 Court Councillor v. Schloisingg [Schloißnigg], Privy Cabinet Secretary and former tutor of Archduke Francis.
27 General La Fayette.
28 Barvave, member of the former National Assembly [in France].
29 Brissot, member of the present National Assembly.
30 Rochefautcault [*sic*], member of the present National Assembly.
31 Bishop Fauchet, member of the present National Assembly.
32 Paine, writer and peoples' representative in Paris.
33 Fabri, mayor of Lüttich [Liège].
34 Van der Noot.
35 Mirabeau, the late [died 2 April 1791].
36 Scheridan [*sic*], Speaker of Parliament in London.
37 Captain v. Archenholz.
38 Manvillon, Lieutenant-Colonel in Brunswick.
39 Wiland [Wieland], Court Councillor [and writer] in Weimar.
40 Privy Councillor Schloser in Karlsruhe.
[Later: '*solemnly renounced*']

41 Professor Spittler in Göttingen.
[Later: '*solemnly renounced*']
42 Professor Meiners in Göttingen.
[Later: '*solemnly renounced*']
43 Professor Feder in Göttingen.
44 Campe, pedagogue in Brunswick.
45 Trapp, pedagogue in Brunswick.
46 Gedicke [Gödicke], pedagogue in Berlin.
47 Villaume, pedagogue in Berlin.
48 Chun, former librarian in Kassel.
49 Biester, librarian in Berlin.
50 Dr and Professor Plattner in Leipzig.
51 Professor Engel in Berlin.
52 Professor Meisner in Prague.
53 Professor Schuz [*sic*] in Jena.
54 Professor Kreil in Pest [Budapest].
55 Professor Klein in Mannheim.
56 Professor Dannenmeyer in Vienna.
57 Professor Zeiler in Vienna.
58 Councillor of Justice Klein in Berlin.
59 Boye, editor of the 'Deutsches Museum'.
60 Professor Rheinhold in Jena.
61 v. Alxinger in Vienna.
62 Blumauer in Vienna.
63 v. Wezer in Vienna.
64 Professor Köfil in Lemberg.
65 Weishaupt and company, p.p. [*per procura*].

(b) *Beigeschlossene Nota des Grafen Rottenhanns* [*sic*]
(Note enclosed with the letter from Count Rottenhan)
Haus-, Hof- und Staatsarchiv, Vienna, Vertrauliche Akten 41 (alt 62), fol. 316

Count Laschantsky [Lazansky], President of the *Landrecht*, and his wife, *née* Kollowrath
Count Philipp Clari [Clary]
Count Kollowrat of Reichenau
Professor Butscheck
Count Kinigl [Künigl]
Count Friedrich Nostitz
Count Joachim Sternberg
Count Prokop Sternberg, Cathedral Canon
Librarian Unger
War [Wahr], the former actor
Abbé Arnold, Hofmeister [major domo] with Count Kollowrath and Canon of Eichstadt [Eichstätt] Cathedral
Spies, former actor and administrator with Count Kinigl
Maier, Doctor
Meisner, Professor
Cornova and Noe, Jesuits and Professors
Captain Bergier, pensioned
Artillery Lieutenant Chapitz
Baron Budiany
Count Laurus
Gürtner, Professor
Gruber, Jesuit
Bletz, administrator with the house of Schwarzenberg

Appendix 6

Die Zauberflöte *as a political opera*

(1) 1794

As the French Revolution moved into the Terror, the Austrian authorities must have become increasingly concerned by the Masonic content and message of Mozart's opera. It was thought that the 'Jacobins' were attempting to subvert the Austrian Monarchy by means of a gigantic Masonic spy-ring with its headquarters near the rolling heads in Paris. Therefore the government in Vienna encouraged any new interpretation of *Die Zauberflöte* which would divert attention from the original Masonic content. One of the earliest of such 're-interpretations' appeared in Linz, 'printed and to be had of Franz Auinger, 1794', with the title *Die Große Oper Zauberflöte deutlich ausgelegt, um den wahren Sinn derselben zu begreifen* (The grand opera, *The Magic Flute*, clearly explained so as to understand its true meaning). The 14-page brochure, which is couched in the form of a dialogue between Thalia and Momus (here disregarded) includes the following description:

> Night, the philosophy of the Jacobins, bore a daughter, the Republic, which she wished to educate in the realms of the Night, so as to enable her to have a Jacobin marriage and relationship . . . The Jacobins are not in agreement whether she should be married to a single Jacobin dictator, who of course is told exactly what to do by the other Jacobins, or to 7000 Jacobin men, or to ten only. . . . The daughter, Republic, was taken by her mother, Night, to a place where there are still temples and priests (for in France there are no more priests, and actors and dentists yell down from the pulpits) – to a place of safety . . . There she is to marry a noble prince who withstands all the trials and thus shows that he is a child of the true light and a proper, legal bridegroom. . . .
>
> In the first scene Tamino the Prince is to receive France and hence to make an end of her unmarried Republican state. The Jacobin snakes threaten him, but some of those living in Night are sympathetic to monarchist ideas and kill the snake. Then, in the second scene, Papageno or the Jacobean bird-catcher appears; he induces people to attend the Jacobin club and be locked in the national bird-cage, where they are delivered to Night. . . . The Jacobins seem not to be able to avoid the truth and reality of a king. . . . If the Jacobin murderers actually shed the innocent blood of their small, innocent king [Louis XVII], they will ruin their cause even further. . . . The three ladies, who I understand to represent the royal entourage, disguise themselves cleverly, because they call the power which holds back the Republic a demon and monster. They must speak the Jacobean language, otherwise they would betray themselves. . . .
>
> In the seventh and eighth scenes the Jacobin parrot . . . has been punished for his lies by having his mouth padlocked, but is pardoned again. . . . The present of the flute for the prince is an excellent conceit; for the Jacobins shall have to dance to his tune. Also the silver bells for Papageno, who is soon of royal persuasion . . . are appropriate, for whenever the silver bells sound . . . those who under the Jacobin government have seen only paper money will be reminded of royal thoughts.
>
> The three boys . . . are the geniuses of France. . . . Monostratos [*sic*] is already a Jacobin emissary and a courtier

of Jacobin persuasion who, while flattering his lord, has the intention of robbing him of France, so as to have the Republic for himself and his followers. Therefore he also receives, in the 19th scene, his just reward [a beating] . . . It is really better to be a slave in a well-ordered state than under Jacobin tyranny, the worst the world has ever seen . . . The description of Pamina as a prisoner . . . reminds the listener of the cruel treatment of the late Marie Antoinette. [In the music of Sarastro's priests] the trombone is a death-trumpet turned towards the Jacobins . . . Excellent, too, and majestic is the 18th scene, where Sarastro displays a united front against the Jacobins. It was quite right that after the many and astonishing defeats suffered by the Jacobins, he should appear in a triumphal chariot . . . where the six lions should bear rich trappings, one with the arms of the German Empire and the Austrian Monarchy, the second with the Imperial Russian arms, the third with the Prussian eagle, the fourth with the arms of England and Holland, the fifth with the Spanish and Portuguese arms, and the sixth with the arms of the Italian kingdom and states.

> In Act II Sarastro explains that only a royal son (not therefore a Jacobin club, or a national convention, or a decemvirate) may have the bride. . . . The three ladies . . . [are like those who,] secretly loyal to the royal party, always preserve in public the language of Night, especially when they receive orders to act against the royal side. . . . [These] three ladies then suffer the same fate as the Jacobins and with Night are destroyed, just as with the blackamoor, who after trying to have the Republic, publicly embraces the Jacobin party. . . . They are against the Queen of the Night, that is the Jacobin philosophy, which is now Queen of France. . . . The armed men show which trials await the bridegroom of France. The fire and water are those dangerous elements through which he, with such heroic force, must fight the Jacobins. . . . This piece [*The Magic Flute*] is one of the most magnificent weapons against the Jacobins. . . .
>
> [Österreichische Nationalbibliothek, Vienna, music collection, cat. 580058-A]

(2) 1795

In this year another attempt was made to 'rethink' *Die Zauberflöte*, The following outline is taken from a brochure entitled *Die geheime Geschichte des Verschwörungssystems der Jakobiner in den österreichischen Staaten, Für Wahrheitsfreunde* (The secret Hisory of the conspiratorial system of the Jacobins in the Austrian States. For Friends of Truth), with the fictive impressum 'London 1795' (read Vienna), pp. 47–54:

> The whole of the famous and well-known opera, *The Magic Flute* (can one believe it?) is an allegory of the French Revolution, according to the situation in the years 1789–90 and 1791, in which latter year the piece was first given in the so-called Wiedner-Theater [Theater auf der Wieden]. But we don't want to accuse the good Mozart of all this; he was merely the creator of the excellent music and had nothing to do with the construction of the piece. Very probably he had no idea of the underlying concept of the piece. That is why some persons, who are not informed, find the plot ridiculous, incomprehensible and tasteless. The success which it [the opera] enjoyed in

259

Vienna was therefore extraordinarily great for two reasons – partly because of the beautiful music, partly because of the hidden message. It had an unbroken run of sixty-two performances; and during the first fortnight. . . it was essential to secure a seat by five o'clock, for later people were turned away in hundreds because the house was full. It was not until the third week that one could, with considerable effort, procure a seat at six o'clock. Naturally an increasing number of persons became acquainted with the message that was hinted at in the piece, until the following written explanation was discovered, whereby also the profane world had the good fortune to receive the light. . . .

Characters

The Queen of the Night	*The former government*
Pamina, her daughter	*The freedom which is always the daughter of despotism*
Tamino	*The people*
The three nymphs of the Queen of the Night [3 ladies]	*The deputies of the three Estates*
Sarastro	*The wisdom of a better set of laws*
The priests of Sarastro	*The National Assembly*
Papageno	*The wealthy*
An old lady [later Papagena]	*Equality*
Monastatos, the Blackamoor	*The emigrants*
Slaves	*The servants and mercenaries of the emigrants*
Three good sprites [3 boys]	*Wisdom, justice and love of the fatherland; they guide Tamino*

The idea on which this piece is based is: the freeing of the French populace from the hands of the old despotism through the wisdom of a better set of laws.

The plot

Tamino is folowed by a huge serpent (the forthcoming state bankruptcy) . . . The Queen of the Night wishes to save him, because her existence is coupled with his. She is unable to accomplish this alone but requires her three nymphs, who destroy the serpent. Tamino is grateful to his saviours and receives from them an excellent present, a *magic flute* (the freedom to speak to his own advantage and to complain). The Queen of the Night asks him to free her daughter from the clutches of a cruel, libidinous and tyrannical king, Sarastro, who stole her and hid her in a cave. In order to encourage Tamino in this endeavour she promises Tamino her daughter's hand in marriage, though this is not her real intention, since she has long promised [Pamina's] hand to Monastatos . . . The Queen, through her nymphs, tells Tamino that in his adventures he must allow himself to be guided by three good sprites. He now joins the company of Papageno (the wealthy who, as is well known, were held in check before the Revolution by the aristocracy and the Church, and who with their influence helped to alter the course of the ship of state); they begin their journey to the lands of the infamous Sarastro. [Tamino] is astonished to find in this figure precisely the opposite of that which he had been led to expect. Sarastro is in fact a powerful and brilliant king, but instead of this power and brilliance being constructed on the ruins of his subjects, they are founded on the best form of government, and hence his subjects adore him. He appears on a triumphal chariot drawn by wild beasts,

which being interpreted means that *lawful wisdom* tames the natural brutality of humankind; and that the *whole world gladly submits to it*.

Instead of treating Tamino with enmity (as he expects), Sarastro welcomes him with love and tells him that he has been betrayed by the Queen of the Night . . . [Sarastro] offers to lead [Tamino] freely to the Temple of Honour and Happiness. . . . Tamino, touched by the goodness of the excellent old man, offers his whole soul to Sarastro, especially since he solemnly promises to give [Tamino] the gracious Pamina in marriage. Sarastro now summons his priests, to inform them that he considers Tamino worthy of being admitted to the Temple of Honour and Happiness and causes them to vote on it. They agree unanimously.

The priests, at Tamino's reception, also illuminate the most terrifying places with torches, to show that at last the torches of the Enlightenment shine into the darkest corners of the earth. But before Tamino may enter the Temple of Happiness, he must submit to all the vexatious initiations which every seeker must undergo.

These include the vows of silence, the tarrying in unpleasant places and finally the terrible trials of fire and water. Tamino passes all the tests, persuaded *of the goodness* of the old Sarastro, with resolute courage; and with his Pamina he is at last received into the Temple of Happiness, where she becomes his bride. His companion Papageno . . . is at bottom a weak and simple person who, much as he longs for happiness, yet hates any exertion and difficulty and is particularly unwilling to make any sacrifices. While Tamino patiently submits to all the trials placed before him, [Papageno] thinks only of his own pleasures, *eating and drinking*. But he soon realizes that all this will not bring him real happiness and therefore decides . . . to hang himself. At the last moment he is saved by the good sprites, and offers his hand, however unwillingly, to an old lady (equality, the oldest component of humankind); she is transformed into a gracious young girl who will make Papageno happy.

The excellence of Papageno consists in: *beautiful feathers over his whole person*, because of his vanity. The *shepherd's pipe* represents his simplicity, the *Glockenspiel* [bells] (to which all must dance, a result of wealth) is like a golden bowl which circulates in the hands of the wealthy.

Monastatos (the emigrants) attempts as best he can to prevent Tamino's happiness, by deceit and fraud, and by violence; so that in the end he even wants to kill Pamina. But Sarastro punishes him. One last time he gathers his forces to storm, with the Queen of the Night, the Temple of Happiness; but he is cast forever into oblivion. . . .

The wild beasts, which are tamed for a while by the sounds of the flute, are lions (arms of the Netherlands), leopards (England), and eagles (Austria, Russia and Prussia). The others are smaller states.

[Stadtbibliothek, Vienna, A 4949]

Is there any element of truth in either of these political interpretations? The 1795 version, which post-dates the 'Jacobin' trials and executions in Vienna, is better written than the rather crude propaganda of the 1794 brochure; but while the 1795 version is a little more plausible, neither seems to be really convincing. It will be noted that any mention of Freemasonry is scrupulously avoided in both articles, and in the last analysis it is the Masonic content of *Die Zauberflöte* which is real, powerful and omnipresent. If writers wished to equate the Masonic 'three' with the concept of 'Liberty, Equality and Fraternity', those words were certainly not inimical to the Masonic message; but they are not the whole story.

Appendix 7

The Audience at the first performance of Mozart's La clemenza di Tito *in Prague, 6 September 1791; a Report based on unpublished documents in the Haus-, Hof- und Staatsarchiv, Vienna*

by ELSE RADANT

The coronation of Leopold II in Prague as King of Bohemia required immense preparations on the part of a committee presided over by the Imperial Lord High Steward (*Obersthaushofmeister*), Prince Georg Adam Starhemberg. From the repairs to the route over which the royal carriages would pass, to the cleaning and illumination of the city of Prague; from the improvement of paving-stones in the city to the 'keeping in order of the students, Jews and working apprentices', who were forbidden to wear a sword during this period; – all these were the kind of matters with which the committee had to concern itself. The ceremony of taking the Oath of Allegiance to the Crown had to be prepared, the route to Prague established. There was also a committee which was concerned with providing entertainment for the guests of the Emperor – balls, concerts and the theatre. Ensuring the smooth operation of all these festivities was the responsibility of Prince Starhemberg. Members of his committee included: *Obristkämmerer* (Lord High Chamberlain) Prince Franz Xaver Orsini-Rosenberg, confidant of the late Emperor Joseph II; Count Leopold Kollowrat-Krakowsky, *Oberster Kanzler* (Lord High Chancellor) of the Bohemian Gubernium (Government); Vice-President of the Court of Appeals, Baron Joseph Kirnmayr; Count Franz Saurau, *Hofrat* (Court Councillor) of the Bohemian Department; and the Lord High Marshal of the Court, Count Ernst Kaunitz. Secretaries were Anton and Merlat, and the *Actuarius* (Registrar) was Count Herberstein-Moltke.

On 25 January 1791, Emperor Leopold appointed the Vice-Chancellor of the Combined Court Department, Count Wenzel Ugarte, as *Obersthofmeister* (Lord High Steward) to the young Archduchesses (his daughters) and at the same time made him *Hofmusikgraf* (Count in charge of court music) and Director of the Court Theatres; these additional duties brought an increase in Ugarte's salary from 8,000 gulden to 12,000. Ugarte thus entered the inner circle of the Emperor's advisors; and as Director of the Court Theatres he was no longer responsible to the office of the Lord High Steward but – as in former times – directly to the Emperor; from this one may surmise that Leopold, like his late brother Joseph, took a close personal interest in opera and spoken theatre as a vehicle for the education of the populace. On 30 January, Ugarte was sworn in, together with another confidant of the new Emperor, Heinrich Franz, Count Rottenhan, who would later be required to investigate supposedly dangerous Freemasons in Prague (see pp. 230ff.). Rottenhan's duties in connection with the coronation included the allocation of free tickets to the first performance of *La clemenza di Tito*, which the Bohemian Estates was financing.

First, however, all the foreign dignitaries had to be invited, and proofs of nobility for all the new Imperial chamberlains had to be submitted. Suitable castles were chosen as overnight stops for the Imperial suite while en route from Vienna to Prague.

In Vienna the infant Princess Maria Ludovika (whose birth in February 1790 had cost the life of her mother, the Princess of Württemberg, first wife of Crown Prince Francis) died at the age of sixteen months. The doctor who attended the birth – 'that animal of a man-midwife', as Count Zinzendorf describes him – had used forceps and injured both mother and child. The little princess was laid to rest in Vienna in the Capuchin Monastery (where all the Habsburgs are buried) on 24 June. On 5 August the Bohemian Delegation under Counts Leopold Clary and Vinzenz Waldstein received the Bohemian coronation insignia and took them from Vienna to Prague under military escort. From Hungary the Hungarian Noble Bodyguard under Colonel Barcsay started to march towards the Bohemian capital. With them was an 'uninvited' *Rittmeister-Auditor* (judge-advocate captain of horse), Franz Vorbringer, who later wanted to submit his bill for expenses to the *Hofmeisteramt*, which summarily rejected the request. The Emperor himself was petitioned, but in vain. In October 1791 the Commander under Salieri and Prince Anton Esterházy (Haydn's patron), submitted to the *Hofmeisteramt* a bill for travel expenses in the amount of 9,485 gulden 59 kreuzer.

In Prague meanwhile, committees occupied themselves with balls, festivities and the problem of guest accommodation. The city was filled to overflowing, and those who, like Prince Colloredo-Mansfeld, could live in their own houses, were fortunate. Antonio Salieri and one of the seven musicians he took with him to Prague were billeted in the Wälscher Platz No. 66; the others were lodged in the Brückengasse, on the Bridge and on the Ring of the Small Side (Kleinseite, Mala Strana). The various servants of the nobility lived in barracks, quickly constructed for the purpose. Prices of food were held down rigidly and an official list shows that, during the coronation period, only the price of beef rose (from 6 to 7 kreuzer per pound). But there was a flourishing black market in tickets for the viewing platforms lining the streets along which the coronation train would proceed; officially, standing room cost 1 fl. 30 kr., a seat 2 fl. 20 kr.

When, after the ceremonies were over, the bills started to arrive at Prince Starhemberg's office, it soon became clear that the actual costs exceeded the estimates. The church music and *Tafelmusik* expenses under Salieri were 883 ducats (3,532 gulden), whereas the *Hofmusikgraf* had apportioned only 1,000 gulden for the music; the court kitchens required 115,000 instead of the estimated 65,000 gulden. The furnishings and decorations of the Imperial household's quarters, the bill for which was submitted by the Court Director of Furnishings, Leopold Le Noble von Edlersberg, cost 43,000 gulden; the *Oberster Hofpostamtsverwalter* (Director of the Court Postal System) and the *Hofreisedirektor* (Director of Court Travel) required 6,337 gulden in postal expenses and 12,000 gulden travel expenses for the Emperor and for Archduke Carl (who with his suite went from Prague to Belgium). The *Oberster Stallmeister* (Lord Master of the Horse), Prince Johann Baptist Dietrichstein, requested the *Obristhofmeister* 'as an act of generosity' to increase the payments *per diem* for some of his servants; this was agreed to, but the trumpeters and timpani players each received in Prague only 3 gulden *per diem* instead of the 4 gulden they had received during the coronation at Frankfurt in 1790.

Within the *Landrechte* (Land Courts) of Prague, a list was circulated in August showing which members of the Estates would follow the Emperor on horseback or in a carriage.[1] Some excused themselves for reasons of health or lack of money (as *Freiherr* Wenzel von Übel did).

In September, Count Rottenhan was informed that 1,358 seats in the Estates' opera house would be required: on the first (U.S. second) floor, boxes 1–4 for the Emperor and his party and the grand central box for the Lord High Steward and the Court Ministers,[2] the grand central box on the second (U.S. third) floor for the ladies-in-waiting. Further, 28 boxes (to seat 112 ladies and 48 cavaliers) were required for 'foreign nobility of the first rank'[3] and 22 boxes (for 88 ladies and 66 cavaliers)[4] for 'local nobility'. The 'remaining nobility' who could not be accommodated in the boxes were allotted places in the parterre (pit) – 200 ladies seated and 150 places for their escorts to stand; while the 'second noblesse', i.e. ministerial officials, were allotted the second (rear) half of the parterre – 250 ladies seated and 100 places standing room for their escorts. The 'places of honour' must have been very crowded, for in each of the four boxes in the gallery there were '16 ladies and 16 escorts', while the 'remaining places of honour' (150 ladies, 150 gentlemen) were in the gallery. Apart from the four Court boxes and the two central boxes, there were in this theatre, according to the list, five boxes to the left and five to the right of the parterre, seven boxes to the right and eleven to the left on the first floor, and on the second floor eleven boxes to the right and eleven to the left; but on the third floor only two boxes to the left and two to the right.

A further list details 'personnel for whom tickets to the opera are suggested'. From Her Majesty's retinue: 3 *Kammerdienerinnen* (ladies of the bedchamber) and 2 *Kammermenscher* (chamber servants). From the retinue of the three Archduchesses: 1 *Kammerfrau* (lady-in-waiting) and 3 *Kammerdienerinnen*. From the Saxon retinue:[5] 1 *Kammerfrau*, 2 *Kammerdienerinnen*, 1 *Kammermensch*. From the private office of Emperor Leopold were listed four persons and in addition: 3 *Kammerfouriere* (quartermaster-sergeants of the chamber), 18 *Kammerdiener* (servants of the bedchamber), 12 *Thürhüter* (doorkeepers), 4 *Kammerheizer* (stokers for the stoves and fireplaces), 1 *Oberstkämmersecretaire* (Secretary to the Lord High Chamberlain), 1 personal physician, 1 personal surgeon, 1 *Kammerzahlmeister* (Master of the Privy Purse), 2 *Officianten* (officials), 1 *Kapellmeister* (sc. Salieri), 7 court musicians, 8 *Edelknaben* (pages), 1 *Hoffuttermeister* (Court Master Fodderer) and 1 Assistant, 1 Clerk to the Fodderers, 1 *Equipageninspektor* (Inspector of Carriages), 1 *Sattelknecht* (groom), 7 *Bereiter* (riding masters), 1 *Pferdearzt* (horse doctor) and 4 *Hoffouriere* (Court quartermaster-sergeants).[6] It was thus a very mixed audience that would witness the première of Mozart's opera. The names of the 'hon. Court suite' had already been sent *breve manu* ('hand carried') to Count Rottenhan, but can no longer be located.[7] The distribution of the tickets presented difficulties since citizens of Prague, who were very fond of Mozart's music, also wanted to attend this gala evening (6 September). The *Land* President therefore issued a printed statement that in allocating tickets the following order of precedence had to be maintained: the Court, their guests, the nobility, foreigners, guests of honour, etc., and hence 'one appeals to the celebrated good nature of the Prague public that they will readily appreciate that the foreign [i.e. non-local] guests' must be given preference. This document also included instructions to the nobility and honorary guests who wished to collect their tickets on 5 and 6 September, to provide their servants with a written document including name and seal, and to have this delivered to the Office of the *Land* President. The remaining tickets were distributed in such a way (among government officials, bankers, wholesalers, lawyers and professors – and not forgetting the military) that for each of these various groups a committee chose three tickets for one lucky family (husband, wife and eldest daughter). Paragraph 7 of this statement warned against futile attempts to secure tickets other than those allotted. Paragraph 8 established the order for the carriages to set down at the opera, for the performance which was to begin at 7.00 p.m. (but in fact the Court arrived late at 7.30); and the public was requested to start driving there at 5.00 so as not to obstruct the Court carriages. Members of the Estates supervised the theatre so that no one could enter without a valid ticket. Many 'persons of rank' had to be turned away because they lacked tickets. The Emperor was received with loud applause, but the opera itself enjoyed only a *succès d'estime* (a moderate success). The second performance was poorly attended, since the tickets for it had to be purchased and the prices were considered very high. On 8 September, the German Sekonda Company performed a prologue by Schlenkert entitled *Habsburgs Meistersänger* in the opera house.

The critics praised the 'true, profound, great scenes it contained' and considered the incidental music 'was worthy of it'. 'The result was that tears flowed and in the parterre people said out loud that it was the perfect vehicle for the occasion.' On 9 September, the Emperor attended the theatre and saw Kotzebue's play *Der Jakobiner Club* and Schröder's *Die Eifersüchtigen*. He remained to the end.

SOURCES

Haus-, Hof- und Staatsarchiv, Vienna: Zeremonialakten Böhmische Krönung 1791, ZA Prot. 38; Zinzendorf, ms. Diaries; Johann Debrois, *Aktenmässige Krönungsgeschichte des Königs von Böhmen Leopold des Zweiten und Marie Louisens*, Prague 1792, Erstes Heft; *Vollständiges Archiv der doppelten böhmischen Krönung Leopold des Zweiten und Marien Louisen, Infantin von Spanien, in Prag im Jahr 1791*, ed. by Albrecht, Prague, n.d.

NOTES

1 This list was signed by 62 members who wished to ride on horseback or in a carriage; the final number was nearly 80 names.
2 *Obersthofmeister* (Lord High Steward) Prince Starhemberg; *Staatskanzler* (State Chancellor) for Interior and Foreign Affairs, Prince Wenzel Anton Kaunitz, by then an elderly gentleman; the presidents of the various Court Chancelleries – the Bohemian-Austrian (Count Kollowrat-Krakowsky), the Hungarian (Count Karl Pálffy von Erdöd) and the Illyrian (Count Franz de Paula Balassa); the Minister Plenipotentiary for Italy, Count Joseph Wilczeck; as Conference Minister Prince Franz Xaver Orsini-Rosenberg and State and Conference Minister Field-Marshal Franz Moritz Lascy; Vice-Chancellor Count Johann Rudolph Chotek. Each was accompanied by his lady (insofar as the ladies did not themselves occupy a position at Court, such as lady-in-waiting to one of the Archduchesses, etc.). Perhaps there were also in these boxes the representatives and ministers of the foreign embassies, etc.
3 To this group belonged the Elector of Saxony as proxy for Lusatia (Laussitz) in Saxony; the Elector Palatine of Bavaria; Prince Franz Sulkowsky as Duke of Bielitz; the Duke of Gotha; Prince Schwarzenberg-Rudolstadt, who sent an emissary (*Freiherr* Lynecker); Prince Liechtenstein (as Duke of Troppau), Prince Lobkowitz and Prince Schwarzenberg (as Duke of Krumau); *Reichspostgeneral* (General of the Imperial Postal Administration) Prince Thurn and Taxis; the Grand Master of the Teutonic Knights (as proxy for Freudenthal in Bohemia).
4 The local and other nobility consisted of: the Bohemian, Moravian and Austrian aristocracy; members of the Estates; persons who held hereditary posts; the dignitaries of the Church – the Archbishops of Prague and Olmütz, the Bishops of Budweis, Brünn and Königsgrätz, the Abbots of Strahof, Ossegg and Töpel, cathedral canons; reigning princes, their cadet lines, and princes 'without vote'. Count Carl von Zinzendorf sat in a box in the first tier together with Fräulein Klebersberg (whose father Adalbert was a member of the Bohemian *Landrecht*), the Venetian Ambassador (Conte Daniele Andrea Delfino) and three further ladies. He noted that Rottenhan was sitting with the Emperor and that leaving the theatre after the performance proved extremely difficult (because of the press of people).
5 Leopold's eldest daughter Maria Theresa was married (1787) to Prince Anton of Saxony. In 1784 Leopold remarked to his brother Joseph II that this was a misalliance. At that time Emperor Joseph answered that it was altogether a great fortune for an Archduchess to find a husband. (She died as Queen of Saxony.)
6 From the Empress's entourage: 3 *Kammerdienerinnen* (Magdalena, Theresia, Katharina Bianchi), 2 *Kammermenscher* (Maria Anna Kröckl, Magdalena Gäschi). The Archduchesses's entourage: 1 *Kammerfrau* (Anna Kock or Kamilla Piquet). The servants and *Kammermenscher* could not be identified; the same applies to the Saxon entourage. Four individuals from the Emperor's personal office (perhaps *Rittmeister* Prohaska and Joseph Sumathing, both of whom were requested by the Emperor in August 1791 and sent to Prague); 3 *Kammerfouriere* (Joseph Strobl, Leopold von Edlersberg, Valentin von Mack), *Kammerdiener*, *Thürhüter* and *Heizer* not identified. One *Oberstkämmererprivatsecretair* (J.F.S. von Kronenfels); 1 personal

physician (Joseph Selb); the 'Hofcapellmeister' and the seven musicians were deleted. One *Hoffuttermeister* (J.P. Sticker von Haymingthal); his assistant (Maximilian von Bressler und Sternau); *Futterschreiber* (Karl Keil); 1 *Equipagen-Inspektor* (F.P. Pechet); 1 *Sattelknecht* (M. Schopp); 7 *Bereiter* (Karl Hübner, Joseph Schönmayer, J.N. Hackh, J.B. Hauser, Karl Esslin, Leopold Gerubel, Franz Gerubel); 1 *Pferdearzt* (Ludwig Scotti). The four *Hoffouriere* (Court quartermaster-sergeants) and the *Leibmedicus* (personal physician) could not be identified.

7 We have a list according to which one can identify the audience at the gala performance with some confidence. We read: 'Allerhöchste und höchste Herrschaften [Imperial and leading nobility], including the Duke of Curland ... 12'. The Emperor and Empress apart, there would have been present in Prague: Archduchess Marie Christine and her consort, Duke Albert von Sachsen-Teschen; Archduke Francis (without his wife, Maria Theresa, not yet recovered from the birth of their daughter); his sister Maria Theresa with her consort, Prince Anton of Saxony; his sister Maria Anna, who, in her capacity as Abbess of Prague, was to crown the Empress; his younger brothers Ferdinand, Carl, Alexander Leopold, Joseph and Anton, and the youngest sister, Amalia, then aged eleven. It is not known if the four youngest sons of the Imperial couple (ranging in age from three to eight) travelled to Prague, but it is reasonable to assume that these children remained in Vienna. The Duke of Curland was an uncle of Prince Anton of Saxony; with his inclusion in the count, we arrive at a total of twelve in the Imperial party, as stated. At the time, Ferdinand, recently married, would not yet have acquired his own retinue.

Otherwise, the list (with descriptions of individuals) reads:
Der k.k. Oberste Herr Oberste Hofmeister [Lord High Steward] (Fürst [Prince] Georg Adam Starhemberg)
Der k.k. Oberste Kämmerer [Lord High Chamberlain] (Fürst [Prince] Franz Xaver Orsini-Rosenberg)
Der k.k. Oberste Hofmarschall [Lord High Marshal] (Graf [Count] Ernst Kaunitz)
Der k.k. Oberste Stallmeister [Lord Master of the Horse] (Fürst [Prince] Johann Bapt. Dietrichstein)
S. Excell. der H. Feldmarschall Gr. [Field-Marshal Count] (Franz Moritz) Lacsy
Gr. v Cobenzel (Ludwig; Hof- und Vizekanzler) [Court and Vice Chancellor]
Arciieren [Imperial] Garde Capitaine Hr. Fürst [Prince] (Joseph) v Lobkowitz
Adj. Capitaine Lieutenant Gr. [Count] (Joseph) v Khevenhüller[-Metsch]
Trabanten Garde Capitaine Gr. [Captain of the Guard of Gentlemen-at-Arms, Count] (Friedrich Moritz) v Nostiz
Der Hr. Oberste Hofmeister Ihrer M. d. Kaiserin [Lord High Steward of H.M. the Empress] (Graf [Count] Anton Thurn)
Die Fr. Oberste Hofmeisterin Ihrer M. d. Kaiserin [Lady High Steward of H.M. the Empress] (Fürstin Antonia Bathyani)
Der wirkl. [actual] Oberste Hofmeister bei Erzhzg Franz [of Archduke Francis] Hr. Gr. [Count] (Franz de Paula) Colloredo
Der Hr. Oberste Hofmeister der Erzherzoginnen [of the Archduchesses] Gr. [Count] (Wenzel) v Ugarte
Die Frau Oberste Hofmeisterin ... [of the Archduchesses] Gräfin [Countess] (Maria Franziska) Boland
Der Oberste Hoferblandpostmeister Hr. Fürst [Lord Postmaster-General, Prince] (Wenzel) v Paar
Der k.k. Oberste Silberkämmerer Hr. Gr. [Lord Silver Chamberlain, Count] (Franz de Paula) v Dietrichstein
2 General Adjutanten S. königl. Hoheit des Erzherzog Franz [Adjutant-generals to H.R.H. Archduke Francis] Hr. Oberster (Franz Xaver) v Rollin (and Count Kamillo Lamberti)
Graf [Count] Palfy (crossed out)
Hr. Freyherr v Worndorf (Gottfried von Warensdorf, Chamber of the young Archdukes, later with Archduke Carl)
H. v Spanocki (Major Lelio von Spannocki, private office of the young Archdukes)
Oberste Hofmeister
Oberste Hofmeisterin } v Sachsen [Saxony]
2 Dames du Palais
Fürst [Prince] Karl v Liechtenstein

4 Kammerherren [Gentlemen of the Chamber] (Marquis Friedrich Manfredini, Count Joseph Esterházy, Count Johann Cristalnig [and ?])
Baron Londriani

Obersthofmeister Stab [staff of Lord High Steward]
Hof Secretair [Court Secretary] v Werlet (Georg Verlet von Löwengreif)
1 Registrator (v Strobel crossed out; possibly Assistant Registrar D.F. Dietz)
2 Hofkanzelisten [Court clerks] (J.A. Morgenbesser and Jakob Zimmer)
1 Hofceremoniarius [Master of Ceremonies] (Franziskus Werner)
2 Hofkapläne [Court Chaplains]
1 Hofmedicus [Court physician] (ev. Johann v Ost)
1 Hofchyrurgus [Court Surgeon] (Anton Brambilla)
1 Hoftappezierer [Court tapestry-maker] (M. Flader)
1 Ungar. Herold [Hungarian herald] (Joseph von Pavich)
2 Hofcontrolleure [Court controllers] (J.A. Wittigauer, Franz Sonnenmayer)
1 Controllschreiber [clerk] (J.N. Schwander)
2 Zöhrgardner [guardians of provisions] (F.J. Herteur, Anton Herteur)
2 Hofkellermeister [cellar masters] (Joseph Schwarz and L. Jordan)
1 Oberzuckerbäcker [pastry master] (Franz Bauer)
3 Kücheninspectores [kitchen inspectors] (A. Joubert, M. Zelena, J. Grimm)
1 Hofapotheker [Court apothecary] (Wenzel v Tzscherni)
1 Hof Capellmeister (Antonio Salieri)
7 Hofmusici [Court musicians]

Leib Garde [Bodyguards]

von d. Arciieren Garde. Exclusive des H Capitain und Capitaine Leut. [Imperial guards, except for Captain and Lt.-Captain] (Fürst Joseph Lobkowitz and Graf Joseph Khevenhüller-Metsch) [both listed above]
1 Oberstlieutn. [Lt.-Col.] (Graf [Count] Joseph v. Sierakowsky)
2 Secondwachtmeister [Second Masters of the Watch]
30 Gardes
1 Chyrurgus [Surgeon] (J.A. Brambilla)
1 Rechnungsführeradjunct [Assistant Master of Accounts] (Franz Rodini)
1 Fourier [Quartermaster-sergeant]

Hungar. Garde, exclusive des Hr. Capitain Lieutn. [Hungarian guards, except for Lt.-Captain] (Baron Michael v. Spleny)
Oberstlieutn. und Oberst [Lt.-Col. and Col.] (Abraham von Barcsay)
2 Secondwachtmeister [Second Masters of the Watch]
30 Gardes
1 Chyrurgus [Surgeon] (Andreas Ullram)
1 Proviantmeister [Quartermaster-Sergeant]

Trabanten Garde, exclusive des [Guards of the Gentlemen-at-Arms, except] *H. Capitaine* (Graf F.M. v Nostiz) [listed above]
1 Oberstlieutn. [Lt.-Col.] (Wenzel v. Müller)
1 Premier Wachtmeister [First Master of the Watch] (Joseph del Core)
3 Second Wachtmeister [Second Masters of the Watch]
1 Rechnungsführer [Master of the Accounts] (J.F. Bünsdorf)
1 Chyrurgus [Surgeon] (F.X. Stiller)

Staatskanzlei [State Chancellery]
H. Baron v Spielmann (Anton; geheimer Hof- und Staatsreferendarius) [privy court and state advisor]
H. Baron (Egydius) v. Collenbach (geh. Hof- und Staatsreferendarius)
2 Officiales (N. Appel, Georg Grosskopf)
1 Postreise Director [Director of Mails] (Joseph Pruckmayr)
8 Postofficiere [postal officers]

Acknowledgments

The author is grateful to the following individuals and institutions for their valuable help in the preparation of this book (sources of specific illustrations are listed separately below):

Albertina, Vienna
Archiv der Stadt Wien
Philippe A. Autexier, Poitiers
Mrs Eleanor Bailie, London
László Berényi, London
Mrs Joan Draper, Llandaff
Countess Monika Esterházy, Vienna
Gesellschaft der Musikfreunde, Vienna
    (Dr Otto Biba)

Galerie Gilhofer, Vienna
Haus-, Hof- und Staatsarchiv, Vienna
    (Dr Clemens Höslinger)
Historisches Museum der Stadt Wien
    (Dr Adalbert Stifter)
Hofkammerarchiv, Vienna
    (Dr Christian Sapper)
Dr Ulrike Hofmann, St Pölten
Mag. Joachim Hurwitz, Rotterdam
Frau Dr Brigitte Kolarsky, Vienna
Stift Melk, Lower Austria
Internationale Stiftung Mozarteum, Salzburg
Österreichische Nationalbibliothek (Musiksammlung), Vienna

Sources of Illustrations

Colour plates are identified by roman numerals and black-and-white illustrations by the page numbers on which they appear. As an aid to identification the following abbreviations are used; *a* above, *b* below, *m* middle, *l* left, *r* right. Apart from items in the author's collection, photographs were supplied by the following:

By gracious permission of Her Majesty the Queen XXIII;
Augsburg: Mozart Gedenkstätte 13, 15, 62, 120, 159*l*; Staats- und Stadtbibliothek 93*al*;
Beethoven Society, Hradec u Opavy, Czechoslovakia 202;
Berlin: Deutsche Staatsbibliothek 164;
Bertarelli Archives, Milan 77*l*, 200;
Bonn: Universitätsbibliothek 133;
Düsseldorf: Goethe-Museum 30*a*, 180;
Eisenstadt: Burgenländisches Landesmuseum 134;
Esterházy Archives, Budapest 136;
Galerie Gilhofer, Vienna IX, X;
Glasgow: Hunterian Art Gallery, University of Glasgow VI;
Collection Ernst Hartmann, Vienna 234*al*;
Leipzig: Musikbibliothek der Stadt Leipzig 205;
London: British Library 37, 54, 56*a&b*, 57*a*, 60–61, 81*b*, 83*r*, 106*r*, 107, 121, 130*r*, 189, 207*l*, 215*l*; National Portrait Gallery 53*a*; Royal College of Music 130, 215*a*; Theatre Museum (Harry R. Beard Collection) 161*a*;
Milan: Museo alla Scala 141*a*;

Munich: Bayerische Staatsbibliothek 27*a&br*, 212; Deutsches Theatermuseum XXX, 27*l*, 171;
Antiquariat Ingo Nebehay, Vienna 83*l*;
New York: Pierpont Morgan Library 80;
Prague: Narodní Gallery 185: Narodní Museum XXVI, 161*b*, 199, 227*a&br*;
Private Collection V, 190;
Private Collection, Vienna 146*b*;
Rohrau: Haydn Gedenkstätte 114;
Salzburg: Internationale Stiftung Mozarteum I, II, III, IV, VII, 11, 12, 50*r*, 73*al&r*, 231*a*, 234*ar*; Museum Carolino Augusteum 94;
Schwarzenberg Archives, Český Krumlov, Czechoslovakia 33*a&b*;
Collection Hans Swarowsky, Vienna 87;
Vienna: Albertina 30*m*, 59*b*, 81*a*, 177, 231*b*; Archiv der Gesellschaft der Musikfreunde XIV, XXIX, 51, 73*am*, 131*r*, 145, 148, 167*b*, 215*br*; Historisches Museum der Stadt Wien XXXI, XXXII, 32, 63*l*, 66, 154*r*, 182–3, 235*b*; Kunsthistorisches Museum XI, XIII, XVII, XXII, 2, 50*l*, 109*l*; Niederösterreichische Landesregierung 77*r*; Österreichische Nationalbibliothek 30*b*, 31, 58*b*, 63*r*, 86, 93*ar&b*, 95, 109*r*, 207*r*, 227*l*;
Washington, D.C.: Whittall Foundation Collection, Library of Congress 34.

Index

Index of Works by Mozart

Each work listed is identified by its original number in the Köchel catalogue (see Abbreviations of bibliographical sources, p. 246), as conventionally used; where appropriate, the revised number is also shown in square brackets, e.g. '*Maurerische Trauermusik* (Masonic Funeral Music, K.477 [479a])'.

Adagio and Fugue in C minor (for strings, K.546) 9, 105, 196f.
Adagio and Rondo (for glass harmonica, K.617) 9, 143, 216
ARIAS, *Scene* etc.: 'Ah se in ciel, benigne stelle (K.538) 192; 'Al desio chi t'adora' (K.577) 172; 'Bella mia fiamma' (K.528) 206; 'Ch'io mi scordi di te' (K.505) 185, 187, 206; 'Mia speranza adorata' and 'Ah, non sai, qual pena' (K.416) 88; 'Misera, dove son!' (K.369) 88; 'Misero! O sogno!' and 'Aura che interno' (K.431 [425b]) 96; 'Non più, tutto ascoltai' (insertion in *Idomeneo*, K.490) 184; 'Non so, d'onde viene' (K.294) 87; 'Per questa bella mano' (K.612) 216; 'Un bacio di mano' (K.341) 136; 'Un moto di gioia' (K.579) 172
CANTATAS: 'Davidde penitente' (K.469) 127f.; 'Die ihr des unermesslichen Weltalls Schöpfer ehrt' (K.619) 216; 'Eine kleine Freymaurer-Kantate' (K.623) 122, 216; 'Die Maurerfreude' (K.471) 129
Chorus 'Viviamo felice' (K.615) for Sarti's *Le gelosie villane* 216
CHURCH MUSIC 16, 25f.;
'Alleluja' (K.554) 199;
Masses 25; — in C (K.317, 'Coronation') 25, 214; — in C minor (K.427 [417a]) 25, 91f., 94f., 127;
Motet 'Ave, verum corpus' (K.608) 9, 92, 216;
Requiem (K.626) 9, 25, 92, 139, 185;
Vespers (K.321, 329) 16
CONCERTOS 9;
— for clarinet in A (K.622) 145, *215*, 216;
— for flute in D (K.314 [285d]) 115;
— for horn (K.412, 417, 447, 495) 149f.;
— for oboe in F (K.293) 241(20);
— for piano: — in D (K.175) 78, 85, 87f., 148, (Rondo finale, K.382) 109; — in E flat (K.271) 15; — in F (K.413 [387c]) 84f., 193; — in A (K.414 [385p]) 84f., 147, 193; — in C (K.415 [387b]) 88, 96, 145, 147, 193; — in B flat (K.450) 107, 108, 148; — in D (K.451)

107, 108, 126, 136, 148; — in G major (K.453) 105, *107*, 108, 120, 151; — in B flat (K.456) 14, 125, 148, 206; — in F (K.459) 105, 150f.; — in D minor (K.466) 25, 123, 125, 135, 148ff., 151f., 193, 196; — in C major (K.467) 127, 145f., 148, 152, 196; — in E flat (K.482) 35, 146, 149, 151f., 183, 195; — in A (K.488) 146, 148f., 183, 195; — in C minor (K.491) 136, 149, 152, 184, 193, 196f.; — in C (K.503) 145, 148, 152, 184, 206; — in D ('Coronation', K.537) 148, 192, 204; — in B flat (K.595) 149, 151, 216, 249;
— for two pianos in E flat (K.365 [316a]) 75
DANCE MUSIC 12, 216
Divertimento for violin, viola and violoncello (K.563) 199, 214
Duet 'Spiegarti non poss'io' (insertion for *Idomeneo*, K.489) 184
Duos for violin and viola in G (K.421) and B flat (K.424) 9, 90
March, A small (K.544) 105
Masonic Funeral Music, K.477 [479a]), see '*Maurerische Trauermusik*
Masses, see above under Church music
Maurerische Trauermusik (Masonic Funeral Music (K.477 [479a]) 118, 138f., 196
Musical clock, pieces for 216
Musikalischer Spaß, Ein ('A Musical Joke') 189
OPERAS:
Ascanio in Alba (K.111) 153;
La clemenza di Tito (K.621) 8, 9, 10, 105, 224, 230, 261–3;
Così fan tutte (K.588) 8, 9, 10, 35, 71, 134, 136f., 153f., 172f., 174–9, 199, 211f., 214; arias from 176, 178, 179; overture 165;
Don Giovanni (K.527) 9, 25, 136f., 153f., 167ff., 170ff., 173, *185*, 189, 191, 194, 196, 198, 200, 204;
Die Entführung aus dem Serail (*The Abduction from the Seraglio*, K.384) 9, 29f., 35, 65ff., 68ff., 71f., 83, 136, 140, 149, 156, 184; arias from 67ff.; overture 68, 70; windband arrangement *33*
Idomeneo (K.366) 25f., 27, 66, 78, 91, 153, 183f.; arias from 26, 91; overture 26;
La finta semplice (K.51 [46a]) 109;
Lucio Silla (K.135) 88;
Le nozze di Figaro (*The Marriage of Figaro*, K.492) 9, 10, 25, 33, 53, 71, 125, 134, 136, 138, 140, 142, 152ff., 155ff., 158, 160ff., 163ff., 166ff., 170, 172f., 182, 184ff., 200, 204, 213; arias from 25, 152, 158, 162, 165, 174f., 186; overture 164ff.

Der Schauspieldirektor (*The Impresario*, K.486) 29, 35, 152, 182f.
Thamos, König in Ägypten (K.345 [336a]) 25f., 30;
Die Zauberflöte (*The Magic Flute*, K.620) 9, *215*, 224, 225, 234–5, 236, 259f., pls. XXX–XXXII; overture 165
ORATORIOS:
Betulia liberata (K.118 [74c]) 139;
arrangement of C.P.E. Bach's *Auferstehung und Himmelfahrt Jesu* (K.537d) 192;
arrangements of works by Handel (K.566, 572) 116, 199
PIANO MUSIC:
Adagio in B minor (K.540) 196;
Fantasia in C minor (K.475) 127, 196, 206;
Fugue in C minor for two pianos (K.426) 195;
Gigue in G (K.574) 206;
Marche funebre (K.453a) 106;
Prelude and Fugue in C (K.394 [383a]) 91f.;
Rondo in A minor (K.511) 196;
Sonatas: — in D (K.284 [205b]) 37, 48, 120; — in B flat (K.333 [315c]) 37, 120; — in E flat (K.457) 127; — in C (K.545) 105; — in D (K.576) 210: — for two pianos in D (K.448 [375a]) 75, 120;
Variations: — on 'Je suis Lindor' from Paisiello's *Il barbiere di Siviglia* (K.354 [299a]) 52, 206; 6 — (K.398 [416e]) 88, 128; 10 — (K.455) 88, 128; 8 — (K.460 [454a]) 128; — on 'Ein Weib ist das herrlichste Ding' (K.613) 216
QUARTETS (piano; K.478, 493) 9, 142f., 194ff.
QUARTETS (string) 9;
— (K.168–73) 132, 144; — in G (K.387) 38, 123, 131f., 133, 136, 138, 140, 142, 144, 194; — in D minor (K.421 [417b]) 38, 123, 131f., 133, 135f., 138, 140, 142, 144, 194f.; — in E flat (K.428 [421b]) 38, 123, 131f., 133, 136, 138, 140, 142, 144, 194; — in B flat (K.458, 'Hunt') 38, 123, 125, 131f., 133, 136, 138, 140, 142, 144, 194; — in A (K.464) 38, 123, 125, 131f., 133, 136, 138, 140, 142, 144, 194; — in C (K.465, 'Dissonance') 38, 123, 125, 131f., 133, 136, 138, 140, 142f., 193f.; — in D (K.499) 210; — in D (K.575) 210, *211*, 214; — in B flat (K.589) 210, 213ff.; — in F (K.590) 210, 214f.
Quartet (vocal): insertion 'Dite almeno' for Bianchi's *La villanella rapita* (K.479) 139f.
QUINTETS 9;
Clarinet; — in A (K.581) 143, 211, 213;

271

Rachel's
favourite food at home

RACHEL ALLEN

Collins

I dedicate this book to my husband, Isaac, whose love, wisdom and inspiration I could not live without.

This paperback edition published in 2008 by Collins

First published in 2006 by Collins,
an imprint of HarperCollins Publishers Ltd.
77–85 Fulham Palace Road
London W6 8JB
www.harpercollins.co.uk

Recipes on pages 214-227 previously published in *Rachel's Diary 2008*

Editorial Director: Jenny Heller
Project Manager: Emma Callery
Editors: Gillian Haslam & Alastair Laing
Design: Smith & Gilmour, London
Photography: Peter Cassidy and Cristian Barnett
Cover photography: Mark Read
Cover design: Anna Martin

ISBN   978-0-00-727579-3

Colour reproduction by Colourscan, Singapore
Printed and bound by Lego, Italy

Contents

Introduction

I think my very earliest memory of food (actually, probably my earliest memory of anything) is of my sister, Simone, feeding me mashed banana as though I were her baby. She's four years older than me and as she was probably only about five or six at the time, I was only about two! Then, when we were a bit older, we loved helping mum in the kitchen (although now I can imagine that we were probably not that much help), and would often bake cakes and biscuits ourselves. We were very lucky that there was always good home-cooked food in the house, even when Mum was working, and we always sat down at the table together as a family and enjoyed great chats. Often there would be friends there too. It is still the same when I stay with my parents in Dublin.

So now that I have children myself, cooking at home is very important to me. It evokes such happy childhood memories. I also love that time of the evening when my husband, Isaac, gets home from work and we have a glass of wine in the kitchen while one of us prepares supper. This is our time for catching up on what's been going on during the day. Of course, there is the added pleasure of our children's company – even if they are fighting!

Many of you may be parents, and working ones at that, so I have included plenty of suggestions in this book for easy meals that all the family can enjoy. Even better, they can be whipped up in no time. But there is so much more to enjoying cooking at home, like those times when you are looking forward to friends or family coming to stay, or when you're planning a big party for a special occasion, or when it's such a glorious day that you decide to have a spontaneous lunchtime barbecue or a little alfresco dinner party on a balmy evening. There are also those important times when only mum's cooking will do – I know that's how I feel about my own mum's food, and hopefully my children will feel the same about mine. You may want to bake a gorgeous cake or some buns for that special somebody on a special day, or even make completely delicious edible gifts. Cooking great food at home is a joy that I wish to pass along to you. Among the many recipes in this book I hope there is inspiration aplenty, and that this book will become a much-loved member of your family. May it last you many happy years, and feed you many joyous meals!

1 Easy Family Food

I love family meals since this is when everyone gets to sit together and talk about what went on during the day. This type of food should be easy to prepare and quick to rustle up, or else made in advance earlier in the day. This is simple food that the whole family will enjoy and the recipes can be easily amended to suit everyone's taste.

Scrambled Eggs with Tomato, Chilli and Coriander

SERVES 2 / VEGETARIAN

I love this scrambled egg variation, which I first tasted in a restaurant looking out over Mexico City. It's full of protein (from the eggs) and antioxidants (from the coriander), and is a great way to start the day. Of course, you can omit the chilli for children, the coriander still makes it special.

15g (½oz) butter
1 ripe tomato, finely chopped
½–1 chilli, deseeded and finely chopped (optional for children)
4 free-range eggs, best quality possible
3 tbsp milk
Salt and freshly ground black pepper
1 tbsp chopped fresh coriander

Melt the butter in a saucepan, add the tomato and chilli and cook for a few minutes until the tomato is just softening. Meanwhile, whisk the eggs with the milk and a pinch of salt and pepper. Add to the saucepan and stir gently until the egg is softly scrambled. Stir in the chopped coriander, and serve.

Fruity Breakfast Muffins

MAKES 12 / VEGETARIAN

These are gorgeous muffins and they make delicious breakfast fare. The best thing about this basic recipe is that you can add whatever fruit you like.

2 eggs
100ml (3½fl oz) milk
100ml (3½fl oz) natural yoghurt
75ml (2¾fl oz) sunflower oil
1 tsp vanilla extract
225g (8oz) plain flour
3 tsp baking powder

¼ tsp baking soda
¼ tsp salt
½ tsp ground cinnamon
100g (4oz) wholemeal plain flour
100g (4oz) brown sugar, plus 1-2 tbsp
    brown sugar, for sprinkling (optional)

Preheat the oven to 180°C (350°F), Gas mark 4. Line a muffin tray with 12 muffin cases. Break the eggs into a large mixing bowl and whisk to break up. Whisk in the milk, yoghurt, oil and vanilla. Add the chopped fruit and stir.

In another bowl sift the plain flour, baking powder, baking soda, salt and cinnamon. Add the wholemeal flour and sugar, and mix. Fold the dry ingredients into the wet ingredients. Stop mixing as soon as it comes together, do not over-stir.

Divide the mixture between the muffin cases, sprinkle the tops with brown sugar, if using, and cook in the preheated oven for 20-25 minutes, or until the tops spring back when gently touched. Allow to stand in the tin for 1-2 minutes, then transfer to a wire rack to cool.

RACHEL'S HANDY TIP

If your children won't eat a whole muffin, you can make these in a normal-sized bun tray. If you halve the recipe, you will get 12 buns. Bake for 11-13 minutes.

VARIATIONS

PEACH OR PEACH AND BANANA MUFFINS

Add 2 peaches that have been stoned and chopped into about 5mm-1cm (¼-½in) cubes after you have whisked in the milk, yoghurt, oil and vanilla. For yet more variety replace half the chopped peach with one mashed banana.

APPLE AND CINNAMON MUFFINS

These are so yummy, the cooking apple works better than plain eating apple. Add 250g (9oz) grated, unpeeled cooking apple as for the peach variation.

RHUBARB AND GINGER MUFFINS

These are great as you can use frozen rhubarb. Use 250g (9oz) trimmed, finely chopped (5mm(¼in)) rhubarb in place of the peach, plus 1 generous teaspoon finely grated ginger (whisked in with the wet ingredients).

BERRY MUFFINS

Fresh of frozen berries are delicious in muffins. It's a great way to get children to eat fruit! Use 250g (9oz) berries, such as raspberries, blueberries or blackberries.

Chicken, Ginger and Cashew Stir-fry with Coconut Noodles

SERVES 4-6

This delicious and easy stir-fry is very quick to prepare for both friends and family; it is a favourite of ours and makes a yummy and healthy supper. If you do not have a wok, use a large, heavy bottomed frying pan.

FOR THE NOODLES:
1 litre (1 3/4 pints) vegetable (or chicken) stock
1 x 410g tin coconut milk
450g (1lb) thin egg noodles
FOR THE STIR-FRY:
2 tbsp sesame oil
1 tbsp sunflower oil
6 large garlic cloves, peeled and finely chopped
1 tbsp finely grated ginger

450g (1lb) chicken, cut into thin strips
1 carrot, peeled, cut in half lengthways and very thinly sliced at an angle
150g (5oz) mangetout, cut in half at an angle
250g (9oz) mushrooms, sliced
150g (5oz) unsalted cashew nuts or peanuts, toasted and roughly chopped
3 tbsp chopped coriander
Salt and freshly ground black pepper

First, prepare the coconut noodles. Place the stock and coconut milk in a saucepan and bring to the boil. Add the noodles and cook according to the instructions on the packet. When cooked, drain. To prevent them from sticking together, add a couple of tablespoonfuls of the cooking liquid to the noodles. Cover and keep warm.

Meanwhile, heat a wok until almost smoking, add the sesame and sunflower oils and the garlic and ginger. Cook for a few seconds, then add the chicken and cook for a few minutes, stirring regularly, until the outside is just golden. Add the carrots, mangetout and mushrooms, toss and stir for another few minutes until the vegetables are just cooked but still slightly crunchy. Toss in the nuts and chopped coriander and season. Serve on top of the noodles.

Broccoli Soup with Parmesan Toasts

SERVES 6-8 / VEGETARIAN

I adore this delicious and nutritious soup. It's great either for family suppers or for a dinner party. The soup can be frozen and the Parmesan toasts prepared in advance, then grilled at the last moment. Ideal if you need a meal in an instant.

FOR THE SOUP:
25g (1oz) butter
2 potatoes, peeled and finely chopped
1 large onion, peeled and chopped
Salt and freshly ground black pepper
1 head of broccoli, with stalk
800ml–1 litre (1¼-1¾ pints) hot vegetable (or chicken) stock
175ml (6fl oz) double cream

FOR THE PARMESAN TOASTS:
8 slices good-quality white bread
75g (3oz) Parmesan cheese, finely grated

Melt the butter in a medium to large saucepan, and add the potatoes and onion, salt and pepper. Cover with a piece of butter wrapper or greaseproof paper and sweat over a gentle heat for 10 minutes.

Meanwhile, cut the broccoli florets from the stalk. Using a small knife, remove the outer layer of skin from the stalk and discard, then chop the stalk into 1cm (½in) pieces. Add to the onion and potato, and sweat for a further 5 minutes.

Add the hot stock to the potatoes, onion and broccoli stalk, bring up to the boil, then add the chopped florets. Boil without the lid over a high heat for 4–5 minutes until soft, then add the cream. Remove from the heat, liquidise and season to taste.

To make the Parmesan toasts, toast the bread on both sides, sprinkle with grated Parmesan and pop under a hot grill or into a hot oven for 2 minutes or until the cheese melts. Cut the toast into fingers and serve on the side with the soup.

Risotto Verde

SERVES 6 / VEGETARIAN

This is a gorgeous, fresh tasting green risotto and is easy to make as it is baked in the oven.

4 tbsp olive oil
250g (9oz) peas, fresh or frozen
100g (4oz) spinach
950ml (1 pint 12fl oz) vegetable (or chicken) stock
1 onion, peeled and finely chopped
2 garlic cloves, peeled and crushed
Salt and freshly ground black pepper
350g (12oz) risotto rice, such as arborio or carnaroli
150ml (5fl oz) white wine
12 stalks of asparagus, ends trimmed and cut in half lengthways
100g (4oz) Parmesan cheese to serve

Preheat the oven to 180°C (350°F), Gas mark 4. On the hob, heat half the olive oil in an ovenproof saucepan, add the peas and spinach and cook, stirring all the time, for 2 minutes, until the spinach wilts. Add about 50ml (2fl oz) of the stock and purée in a blender or food processor. Set aside.

In the same saucepan, heat the remaining olive oil, add the onion and garlic and season with salt and pepper. Cover with a lid and sweat over a gentle heat until soft but not coloured. Add the risotto rice and stir it around in the saucepan for a minute, then add the remaining stock and the wine. Stir and bring it up to the boil, cover with the lid and place in the preheated oven for 15–20 minutes or until the rice is just cooked and all the liquid has been absorbed. Stir in the vegetable purée and set aside with the lid on.

Bring a saucepan of water up to the boil, add a good pinch of salt and the asparagus. Boil for 2–3 minutes or until it is just tender, then drain. Serve the risotto in warm bowls with the asparagus and Parmesan arranged on top.

RACHEL'S HANDY TIP
The alcohol in the wine burns off during cooking and the flavour is lovely, but if you do not want to use it, just replace it with extra stock.

Pasta with Spinach, Bacon and Parmesan
SERVES 4

This is a delicious and super-quick recipe. A firm family favourite!

400g (14oz) spaghetti or tagliatelle
2 tbsp olive oil
125g (4½oz) bacon rashers (10 streaky rashers or 5 back rashers), chopped
2-3 garlic cloves, peeled and finely chopped
150g (5oz) baby spinach leaves
Salt and freshly ground black pepper
50g (2oz) Parmesan cheese, or something similar, freshly grated, to serve

Put a large saucepan of water on to boil and add 1 teaspoon salt. When boiling, add the pasta, stir well and cook rapidly until al dente.

While the pasta is cooking, heat the oil in a large frying pan, add the bacon and garlic and cook on a high heat for about 4 minutes until the bacon is golden and slightly crispy. Add the spinach and stir until it has wilted. Season to taste.

Drain the pasta when cooked and return to the large saucepan. Pour in the bacon and spinach and stir to mix. Serve immediately with the grated cheese.

Creamy Pasta with Sun-blush Tomatoes, Olives and Pine Nuts

SERVES 4-6 / VEGETARIAN

I like to use semi-sun-dried tomatoes for this simple dish, as they are milder and more juicy than the completely sun-dried ones. Leave out the olives if your children don't care for them.

400g (14oz) dried pasta
250ml (8fl oz) crème fraîche
75g (3oz) semi-sun-dried (also called 'sun-blushed') tomatoes
1 tbsp tomato purée
12–16 black olives, pitted and chopped
50g (2oz) pine nuts, toasted in a dry pan until golden
50g (2oz) Parmesan cheese, finely grated
Salt and freshly ground black pepper
Pinch of sugar (optional)

Bring a large saucepan of water with 1 teaspoon salt up to the boil, and cook the pasta according to the instructions on the packet.

Meanwhile, place the crème fraîche in a saucepan and heat to a gentle simmer. Add the sun-blush tomatoes, tomato purée, chopped olives, most of the toasted pine nuts and most of the grated cheese. Season with salt and pepper and taste – it might need a pinch of sugar too.

When the pasta is cooked, drain, leaving a couple of tablespoons of the cooking water with the pasta. Stir in the hot sun-blush tomato sauce, taste and season again if necessary. Sprinkle with the remaining pine nuts and grated Parmesan cheese and serve.

RACHEL'S HANDY TIP
Try drizzling Basil Pesto (see page 233) over this dish. It's also good with slices of chorizo sausage that have been cooked in a hot dry pan for a minute.

Spicy Salmon Cakes

This foolproof recipe makes about 12 salmon cakes for a family supper. You can also use this recipe to make about 40 mini salmon cakes for small bites to serve with drinks for an informal party. They are absolutely delicious served with flavoured mayonnaise (see page 232) and Tomato and Cucumber Salsa (see page 139). Again, if your children do not eat spicy food, you can omit the chilli or Tabasco.

350g (12oz) filleted and skinned salmon, roughly chopped
50g (2oz) butter
2–3 garlic cloves, peeled and crushed
100g (4oz) white breadcrumbs
1 egg, whisked
2 tsp Dijon mustard
2 tbsp lemon juice
2 tbsp chopped coriander (you can chop the small stalks too)
6 spring onions, chopped
2 tsp Worcestershire sauce
1–2 tsp Tabasco sauce or 1 deseeded and chopped chilli (optional for children)

Combine all the ingredients in a food processor and whiz to combine. Taste for seasoning, add more salt, pepper, lemon juice or Tabasco, if necessary. If you do not have a food processor, chop up the salmon as finely as possible and mix together all the ingredients in a bowl. Shape into patties with a 7.5cm (3in) diameter, or 4cm (1½in) diameter patties for mini salmon cakes. Pan-fry in 3–4 tablespoons olive oil on a medium heat for 3–4 minutes on each side (2–3 minutes for mini cakes), or until golden. Serve on warm plates.

VARIATION
This is also delicious with a Mediterranean twist. Omit the Tabasco or chilli and substitute the same amount of basil for the coriander in the salmon cakes, the mayonnaise and salsa.

Pan-fried Mackerel with Herb Butter

SERVES 4 AS A MAIN COURSE OR 8 AS A STARTER

Mackerel is a delicious and healthy fish. It is also serious brain food for children and adults alike. Mackerel is in season from late spring through the summer into September.

FOR THE MACKEREL:
8 fillets of mackerel, with the skins on
75g (3oz) plain flour, seasoned with salt and pepper
25g (1oz) butter, softened
Lemon wedges, to serve
FOR THE HERB BUTTER:
100g (4oz) butter
2 tbsp chopped fresh herbs
1 tbsp lemon juice

First, make the herb butter. Cream the butter in a bowl, add the chopped herbs and the lemon juice. Roll into a sausage shape and wrap in greaseproof paper or cling film. Put into the freezer to chill quickly.

Place a frying pan or a grill-pan on the heat and wait for it to get very hot. When the pan is hot, dip the fillets of fish in the seasoned flour and shake off the excess. Spread the flesh side (not the skin side) with a little soft butter and place butter-side-down on the hot pan. Cook for a couple of minutes, until crisp and golden, then turn over and cook the other side for another 2–3 minutes, turning down the heat if the pan is getting too hot. Serve on hot plates with one or two slices of herb butter slowly melting on the fish, and a wedge of lemon on the side.

Upside-down Rhubarb and Ginger Cake

SERVES 8 / VEGETARIAN

This recipe and the variation opposite are great topsy-turvy puddings and they are wonderfully easy because they are made in a frying pan instead of a cake tin. When I made this for one of my television programmes, the film crew declared it to be the best thing ever!

50g (2oz) butter
250g (9oz) brown sugar
350g (12oz) rhubarb, trimmed and cut into 2cm (3/4in) chunks
200g (7oz) plain flour
1 tsp baking powder
1/2 tsp salt

1/4 tsp bicarbonate of soda
2 eggs
200ml (7fl oz) buttermilk or sour milk
75ml (23/4fl oz) vegetable or sunflower oil
1 generous tsp of grated ginger

Preheat the oven to 180°C (350°F), Gas mark 4. Melt the butter in a medium-sized ovenproof frying pan (measuring 25cm (10in) in diameter). Stir in half the sugar and cook over a gentle heat for about 2 minutes. Add the rhubarb – there's no need to stir – and remove from the heat and set aside.

Sieve the flour, baking powder, salt and bicarbonate of soda into a bowl. Whisk the eggs in a measuring jug or small bowl and add the remaining sugar, buttermilk, oil and ginger. Mix together, then pour into the dry ingredients and whisk to form a liquid batter. Pour this over the rhubarb in the pan. Place the pan in the oven and bake for 30 minutes or until the cake feels firm in the centre.

Cool for 5 minutes before turning out by placing an inverted plate over the top of the pan and turning pan and plate over together in one quick movement. Serve warm or at room temperature with softly whipped cream.

Upside-down Apple and Cinnamon Cake

SERVES 8 / VEGETARIAN

This variation on the upside-down theme is a perfect end to a special family meal or dinner party. If you have any left over (I certainly never do!), have it with a cup of tea the next day.

50g (2oz) butter
250g (9oz) brown sugar
3 eating apples, peeled, cored
   and sliced 5mm (1/4in) thick
200g (7oz) plain flour
1 tsp baking powder
1/2 tsp salt

1/4 tsp bicarbonate of soda
1 generous tsp ground cinnamon
2 eggs
200ml (7fl oz) buttermilk or sour milk
75ml (23/4fl oz) vegetable
   or sunflower oil

Preheat the oven to 180°C (350°F), Gas mark 4. Melt the butter in a medium-sized ovenproof frying pan (measuring 25cm (10in) in diameter). Stir in half the sugar and cook over a gentle heat for about 2 minutes. Add the apple – there's no need to stir – and remove from the heat and set aside.

Sieve the flour, baking powder, salt, bicarbonate of soda and ground cinnamon into a bowl. Whisk the eggs in a measuring jug or small bowl and add the remaining sugar, buttermilk and oil. Mix together, then pour into the dry ingredients and whisk to combine into a liquid batter. Pour this over the apple in the pan. Place the pan in the preheated oven and bake for 30 minutes or until the cake feels firm in the centre.

Cool for 5 minutes before turning out by placing an inverted plate over the top of the pan and turning pan and plate over together in one quick movement. Serve warm or at room temperature with softly whipped cream.

Toffee Sundae

MAKES 500ML (18FL OZ) / VEGETARIAN

My boys and I all love making sundaes. They're a serious treat! The toffee sauce is the best ever, and keeps for months in the fridge. It's especially delicious for drizzling over ice cream. This recipe makes quite a lot, but since it keeps for so long it's great to have some just waiting for an excuse to be used up.

FOR THE TOFFEE SAUCE:
100g (4oz) butter
175g (6oz) brown sugar
100g (4oz) caster sugar
275g (10oz) golden syrup
250ml (8fl oz) single cream
½ tsp vanilla extract

FOR THE SUNDAE:
1 tub vanilla ice cream
TO SERVE:
Pieces of Heavenly Fudge
  (see page 190) (optional)

For the toffee sauce, put all the ingredients into a saucepan, and boil for about 4–5 minutes, until the sauce is smooth, stirring regularly.

Place a scoop or two of vanilla ice cream in each bowl or glass. Drizzle over the warm toffee sauce and, if you like, crumble two or three pieces of Heavenly Fudge (see page 190) over each bowl and eat!

No-pastry Pear and Almond Tart

SERVES 6 / VEGETARIAN

This is a delicious tart and is also perfect for people who don't want to make pastry. You can use a variety of fruit for the filling (see below).

175g (6oz) icing sugar
50g (2oz) plain flour
100g (4oz) ground almonds
Finely grated zest of 1 lemon
5 egg whites
175g (6oz) butter, melted

2 ripe pears, peeled, cored and
    quartered, then cut into long slices
    about 5mm (¼in) thick
25g (1oz) flaked almonds
Icing sugar, to serve

Preheat the oven to 200°C (400°F), Gas mark 6. Lightly grease the sides of a 23cm (9in) tart tin with a removable bottom and place a disc of greaseproof paper on the base. If you prefer, you can serve this tart on the tart tin base, in which case do not use a disc of paper.

Sieve the icing sugar and flour into a bowl and stir in the ground almonds and lemon zest. Whisk the egg whites for 30 seconds, until just frothy, and add to the dry ingredients with the warm melted butter. Mix until smooth.

Pour the mixture into the prepared tin. Arrange the pieces of pear on top and sprinkle with the flaked almonds.

Bake in the oven for 15 minutes, then turn down the oven to 180°C (350°F), Gas mark 4 and cook for a further 10 minutes or until risen and pale golden. The filling should feel firm to the touch in the centre.

Allow to sit in the tin for a few minutes before turning out onto a wire rack. Dust with icing sugar to serve. This is delicious with softly whipped cream.

VARIATIONS

Instead of pears I sometimes use 100g (4oz) raspberries or blackberries (either fresh or frozen) for the topping. Alternatively, I use 50g (2oz) pine nuts instead of fruit. You can also make this with 100g (4oz) peach or nectarine slices, which is particularly nice in the summer!

2 Sweet Celebrations

I adore baking, and love having the excuse to make something sweet. It could be a birthday, anniversary, any other special occasion, or even just for a gossip and a cup of tea with a friend! People always reckon that you are a genius with lots of time on your hands if you have baked something, but really it's often only a matter of getting the oven on, and mixing together a few magic ingredients in a bowl. And what a gorgeous gift it is to make a home-made treat to celebrate someone's special day!

Cardamom Sour-cream Cake

SERVES 6-8 / VEGETARIAN

This is one of the most delicious cakes. It stays wonderfully moist and the flavour of the sour cream or crème fraîche with the cardamom is sublime. This makes a gorgeous birthday cake, or a special gift for Mother's Day.

FOR THE CAKE:
1 egg
200ml tub sour cream or crème fraîche
   (reserve 1 tbsp for icing)
175g (6oz) caster sugar
225g (8oz) plain flour, sifted

½ tsp bicarbonate of soda
Pinch of salt
1 tsp ground cardamom seeds

FOR THE ICING:
125g (4½oz) icing sugar, sifted
1 tbsp sour cream or crème fraîche

Preheat the oven to 180°C (350°F), Gas mark 4. Grease the sides of a 20cm (8in) round cake tin and dust with flour; line the base of the tin with a disc of greaseproof paper.

Whisk the egg in a large bowl. Add all but 1 generous tablespoon of the sour cream or crème fraîche and the sugar and whisk to combine. Add the sifted flour and bicarbonate of soda, then the salt and the ground cardamom. Fold the mixture to combine, do not over-mix. Transfer into the tin and place in the oven. Cook for about 35 minutes until the top of the cake just feels firm to the touch and a skewer inserted into the centre comes out clean. Remove from the oven and let it sit for 10 minutes before removing from the tin and cooling on a wire rack.

When the cake has just cooled, make the icing by mixing the reserved tablespoon of sour cream or crème fraîche with the icing sugar. If it is too stiff add just a drop of water. Spread the icing over the top of the cake, allowing any extra icing to drip down the sides.

VARIATION

CARDAMOM SOUR-CREAM BUNS
This recipe works perfectly when cooked in bun cases. They look so sweet with birthday candles in each one. Just divide the mixture between 12 paper cases in a bun or muffin tray (or use a non-stick 12-bun tray) and cook at the same temperature for 18-20 minutes. Ice as above.

Chocolate Cake for Birthday Parties

SERVES 8 / VEGETARIAN

I often make this for my children's birthday parties. One year my youngest requested a cake in the shape of a boy (well, Bob the Builder actually), and I did not have the cake tin required. So, I multiplied this recipe by three and cooked it in two roasting trays (each measuring 30 x 26cm (12 x 10in)). When the cake was cooked, it took every bit of artistic talent that I had to cut it into something that slightly resembled our friend Bob. At least the guests at the party were only three years' old, and had great imaginations!

FOR THE CAKE:
100g (4oz) butter, softened
350g (12oz) caster sugar
2 eggs
225g (8oz) plain flour
50g (2oz) cocoa powder
1 tsp baking powder
1/4 tsp bicarbonate of soda

250ml (8fl oz) buttermilk or sour milk
1 tsp vanilla essence or extract

FOR THE ICING:
285g (10 1/2oz) icing sugar
2 tsp cocoa powder
3 tsp melted butter
A few tbsp boiling water

Preheat the oven to 180°C (350°F), Gas mark 4. Line the bases of two 22cm (8 1/4in) or three 18cm (7in) cake tins with greaseproof paper, and grease the sides.

Put the softened butter into a large bowl, add the sugar and beat together until light and fluffy; add the eggs one at a time, beating well. Sieve the flour, cocoa, baking powder and bicarbonate of soda into the butter and sugar mixture, then pour in the buttermilk and add the vanilla essence, stirring well to create a smooth cake dough.

Divide between the cake tins and place in the centre of the preheated oven. Bake for 19–25 minutes, until just set in the centre. When cooked, a skewer inserted into the centre should come out clean. Allow to sit in the tins for 5 minutes, then turn out and cool on a wire rack.

Meanwhile, make the icing. Sieve the icing sugar and cocoa powder into a bowl, then beat in the butter and enough boiling (or hot) water to bring it to spreading consistency. It may only take 1 or 2 tablespoons of water.

Sandwich the cakes together with a layer of icing in the middle. To coat the cake in icing, I find it easiest to place it on an upturned plate. Use a small palette knife or a table knife, and dip it into hot water before and during the icing of the cake; I find this helps give a smooth icing with a shiny gloss.

Porter Cake

SERVES 10-12 / VEGETARIAN

This traditional Irish cake uses porter, such as Guinness, Beamish or Murphy's, and is a deliciously rich and moist fruit cake. Make it a few days in advance of the celebratory event (it's perfect for St Patrick's Day) if you like, and it will improve even more!

450g (1lb) plain flour
1 tsp grated or ground nutmeg
1 tsp mixed spice
1 tsp baking powder
Pinch of salt
225g (8oz) butter
225g (8oz) light brown sugar
450g (1lb) sultanas or raisins or a mixture of both
75g (3oz) chopped candied peel
2 eggs
1 x 330ml bottle of porter or stout

Preheat the oven to 180°C (350°F), Gas mark 4. Line the sides and base of a 20cm (8in) high-sided round cake tin (the sides should be about 7cm (2¾in) high) with greaseproof paper.

Sieve the flour, nutmeg, mixed spice, baking powder and salt into a bowl. Rub in the butter, then stir in the sugar, sultanas or raisins and the candied peel.

Whisk the eggs in another bowl, add the porter or stout, then pour into the dry ingredients and mix well. Empty into the prepared tin and bake for about 2 hours in the preheated oven. If it starts to brown too quickly on top, cover it with foil or greaseproof paper after about 1 hour. The cake is cooked when a skewer inserted into the centre comes out clean. Allow it to sit in the tin for about 20 minutes before turning out and cooling on a wire rack.

Orange and Chocolate Chip Celebratory Cupcakes

MAKES 12 / VEGETARIAN

I love the combination of orange and choc chip, but if you just want plain cupcakes omit the zest and replace the juice with an equal quantity of milk. These would be great for a birthday breakfast!

FOR THE CUPCAKES:
2 eggs
150g (5oz) light brown sugar
Finely grated zest and juice of
  two oranges
Milk
100g (4oz) butter, melted
350g (12oz) plain flour, sifted

1 tbsp baking powder
1/4 tsp bicarbonate of soda
1/2 tsp salt
200g (7oz) dark chocolate, roughly
  chopped into chips
FOR THE ICING:
100g (4oz) icing sugar
Juice of 1/2 orange

Preheat the oven to 200°C (400°F), Gas mark 6. Line a muffin tray with 12 paper muffin cases.

Whisk the eggs and add the sugar and grated orange zest. Measure the juice from the oranges and make it up to 175ml (6fl oz) with milk. Whisk the juice, milk and melted butter into the eggs and sugar, then add the sifted flour, baking powder, bicarbonate of soda, salt and the chopped chocolate. Stir to combine but do not over-mix. Spoon the mixture into the muffin cases and bake in the oven for 18–25 minutes until golden on top and the centre is firm to the touch.

When the cupcakes have cooled, make the orange icing. Sift the icing sugar into a bowl and add 1 teaspoon orange juice. Stir and add a little more juice. Beat the mixture until it comes together and add yet another drop of juice to make an icing of spreadable consistency. If you have made it too wet, add a little more sifted icing sugar.

When the icing is made and the buns are cool, take a small table knife and dip it into a cup of boiling water. This will make it easier to spread the icing on the cupcakes and give it a nice glossy shine. Spread the icing (about 1 teaspoon per cupcake) onto each cake, allow the icing to set for a few minutes and then serve. These cakes keep very well for 4–5 days and can also be frozen.

Lemon Biscuits

MAKES ABOUT 25 / VEGETARIAN

These are incredibly simple and gorgeous biscuits. Do make sure that the butter you use is nice and soft. They are very tasty on their own with a cup of tea or with the Lemon and Ginger Pudding (see page 171). The biscuits can be cut into any kind of shape, such as hearts for Valentine's Day, numbers for a birthday party or little holly leaves or Christmas trees during the festive season.

175g (6oz) plain flour
Finely grated zest of 1 lemon
100g (4oz) butter, softened
50g (2oz) caster sugar

Preheat the oven to 180°C (350°F), Gas mark 4. Put the flour and lemon zest into a mixing bowl, rub in the soft butter, add the caster sugar and bring the whole mixture together to form a stiff dough. Do not add any water.

Roll the dough out to a thickness of about 5mm (1/4in) and cut into shapes. Transfer carefully to a baking tray and bake in the oven for 6–10 minutes until they are pale golden. Cool on a wire rack.

RACHEL'S HANDY TIP
I quite often roll out this dough between two sheets of cling film, as I do for pastry. Chill the slightly flattened piece of dough before rolling out and then the butter does not stick to the cling film.

Wholemeal Shortbread Biscuits

MAKES ABOUT 20 / VEGETARIAN

My boys love making these biscuits so they can choose whatever shapes they like. They are great for birthday parties and lunch boxes. They are also good sandwiched together with raspberry jam!

75g (3oz) wholemeal flour
75g (3oz) plain flour
100g (4oz) butter, softened
50g (2oz) caster sugar

Preheat the oven to 180°C (350°F), Gas mark 4. Place all the ingredients in a food processor and whiz until the mixture almost comes together and resembles coarse breadcrumbs. Then tip onto the work surface and bring it together with your hands. If you are not using a food processor, rub the butter into the combined flour and sugar in a bowl and bring together with your hands.

Sprinkle your work surface with a little flour (brown or white) and roll out the dough until it is about 5mm (1/4in) thick (or roll it between two pieces of cling film, as in the note on page 45). Using a biscuit cutter, cut into whatever shapes you like or just simply into squares with a knife. Transfer onto a baking tray (no need to grease or line it) and bake in the oven for 6–10 minutes depending on the size, or until they are pale golden and feel firm on top. Remove carefully and cool on a wire rack.

Little Almond Brittles

MAKES ABOUT 40 / VEGETARIAN

These are divine little petits-fours, great to serve at the end of a special celebratory meal with coffee. They also make a lovely gift when placed in a small see-through bag and tied with a ribbon.

125g (4¹/₂oz) flaked almonds
225g (8oz) caster sugar
100ml (3¹/₂fl oz) water
75g (3oz) butter
125g (4¹/₂oz) good-quality dark chocolate with at least 70% cocoa solids

Preheat the oven to 180°C (350°F), Gas mark 4. Line two trays with greaseproof paper or non-stick paper.

Place the almonds on a baking tray and toast in the oven for 3–4 minutes until golden – watch them carefully to ensure they don't burn.

Place the sugar, water and butter into a saucepan and stir over a low heat until the sugar has dissolved and the butter melted. Remove the wooden spoon or spatula. Bring to the boil, and boil uncovered for 10–15 minutes or until the mixture is golden brown – watch out as it will be very hot. Do not over-stir this, just swirl the mixture in the pan to prevent it from burning on the bottom. Remove from the heat and add the almonds. Stir to combine, do not over-stir or the mix will turn sugary. Working quickly, place dessertspoonfuls of the mixture on the lined trays and flatten with the back of a wet spoon. Return the pan to the heat for a few seconds if it gets too thick.

Melt the chocolate in a bowl over a pan of simmering water, and drizzle over the brittles (or if you prefer, you can dip the tops of the brittles in the melted chocolate). Allow the chocolate to set, then remove them from the tray and serve or wrap up for gifts. They will keep for a couple of weeks in an airtight container.

Chocolate and Almond Cake with Brandy Cream

SERVES 8 / VEGETARIAN

This is a delicious chocolate cake that uses ground almonds instead of flour, which makes it wonderfully moist. It's an excellent grown-up birthday cake, but if you wish to make this for children, fill it with whipped cream and raspberries instead.

FOR THE CAKE:
125g (4¹/₂oz) dark chocolate
4 eggs
150g (5oz) caster sugar
150g (5oz) ground almonds
Icing sugar, for dusting
FOR THE BRANDY CREAM:
100ml (3¹/₂fl oz) double cream
1–2 tbsp icing sugar
2 tbsp brandy (or another liqueur like rum or Cointreau)

Preheat the oven to 180°C (350°F), Gas mark 4. Prepare two 18cm (7in) cake tins by oiling the sides and lining the bases with discs of greaseproof paper. Melt the chocolate in a bowl by sitting it over a saucepan of gently simmering water.

While the chocolate is melting, place the eggs and sugar in a food mixer and whisk for about 5–8 minutes until light and frothy. When the chocolate has melted, allow to cool for a minute, then pour the egg and sugar mixture gradually onto the chocolate, stirring all the time, and mix until combined. Gently stir in the ground almonds.

Divide the mixture between the two prepared tins and place in the preheated oven. Cook for 17–22 minutes (in my oven they usually take 19 minutes) until the tops of the cakes feel firm in the centre. Allow to cool in the tins for about 10 minutes before carefully transferring to a cooling rack. As they cool, the tops and sides of the cakes will crisp up and crack a little.

Meanwhile make the brandy cream. Whip the cream until just stiff and fold in the sifted icing sugar and brandy. Spread the brandy cream on one cake. Sandwich the cakes together and dust with icing sugar.

Sponge Cake with Rhubarb Cream

SERVES 6-8 / VEGETARIAN

This is a classic Victoria sponge cake, made all the more gorgeous with the rhubarb cream filling. Also try filling it with raspberry jam and whipped cream, sliced strawberries and whipped cream, or with fresh, hand-picked blackberries and cream. This is perfect for Father's or Mother's Day (that's a hint, boys!) or, of course, as a birthday cake.

FOR THE CAKE:
125g (4½oz) butter, softened
175g (6oz) caster sugar
3 eggs
175g (6oz) plain flour
1 tsp baking powder
1 tbsp milk
Icing sugar or caster sugar, for dusting

FOR THE RHUBARB CREAM:
100g (4oz) rhubarb, trimmed and sliced
50g (2oz) sugar
4 tbsp water
75ml (2¾fl oz) double cream

Preheat the oven to 180°C (350°F), Gas mark 4. Grease and flour the sides of two 18cm (7in) cake tins, and line the bases with discs of greaseproof paper.

Cream the butter until soft, then gradually add the sugar, and beat until light and fluffy. Add the eggs one by one, beating well all the time. Sieve the flour and baking powder, and stir in gently, then stir in the milk until just combined.

Divide the mixture between the two tins, hollowing it slightly in the centre, so that it will be flat on top when cooked. Bake for 20-25 minutes, or until the centre of the cake springs back when you push it gently. Turn out onto a wire rack and allow it to cool. (Place the cake that will become the top layer on its base so that the top isn't marked by the cooling rack.)

Meanwhile, place the sliced rhubarb, sugar and water in a saucepan, cover and cook over a gentle heat for about 10 minutes, until the rhubarb is soft. Take off the lid and boil while stirring until it is thick. Pour into a bowl and allow to cool. Whip the cream until it forms soft peaks, then fold in the rhubarb. Sandwich the cakes with the rhubarb cream and sprinkle with sieved icing or caster sugar.

3 Picnics and Days Out

Why is it that food eaten outside just tastes so much better? Even a simple sandwich and a cup of tea tastes like the best meal you have ever had! But something you've made yourself is bound to be a lot more delicious than anything you might buy. I love preparing food to take on a picnic or to the beach, or to bring to the woods for a mid-walk snack (a good incentive to get the children out walking). You might only go as far as your own back garden, it doesn't matter. My children love the novelty of gathering up the picnic blanket, putting food in a basket and finding a nice spot to eat. I'm sure the fresh air makes them eat that bit more too, which is always good!

Muffleta

SERVES 6-8

This is made from a hollowed-out loaf of bread with the top cut off and saved to make the lid. It's filled with layers of different fillings, then pressed for a few hours and cut into wedges so that each slice has a bit of crust surrounding a wonderful layered filling. It looks so impressive, but could not be easier to make. Vary the ingredients according to your taste. It's best if made a day in advance, so it can be pressed overnight in the fridge.

4 red onions, peeled and cut into
    wedges
1 tbsp olive oil
Sea salt and freshly ground pepper
1 round loaf of bread about 20cm (8in)
    in diameter
2 tbsp Basil Pesto (see page 217), mixed
    with 1 tbsp olive oil
3 slices Parma or Serrano ham

4 preserved roasted peppers (see
    page 177)
250g (9oz) soft goats' cheese,
    cut into slices
1 tbsp Olive Paste (see page 102),
    mixed with 1 tbsp olive oil
6-8 thin slices of salami
1 large handful of rocket leaves

Preheat the oven to 200°C (400°F), Gas mark 6. Toss the red onion with the olive oil on a baking tray, season and roast in the oven for 10–15 minutes or until soft. Set aside.

Using a serrated bread knife, slice the top off the loaf of bread and set aside until later. Scoop out most of the bread from inside the loaf and put to one side.

Spread the pesto and olive oil around the inside of the loaf and the cut side of the lid. Place half the Parma or Serrano ham in the base of the loaf, if using, then half of the pieces of roast peppers, followed by half the goats' cheese. Then drizzle half the tapenade or olive paste over the cheese, followed by the slices of salami, if using, and then the roasted red onions and lastly the rocket leaves.

Season with sea salt and pepper and repeat with the second half of all the ingredients. You might need to press it down gently with the palms of your hands to fit everything in – it should be very full or it will fall apart when you try to slice it. When you have finished with all the ingredients, place the lid on top.

Wrap the loaf in cling film, put it on a plate then place a side plate or board with weights or even jars of jam or anything heavy on top and place in the fridge. This will weigh it down, which will make it easier to cut into slices. Leave for 3 hours to 1 day, unwrap and cut into wedges to serve.

RACHEL'S HANDY TIP
You can always whiz up the discarded bread to make breadcrumbs for the freezer.

Chest of Sandwiches
MAKES ABOUT 15 SANDWICHES

This was ingeniously created by my husband's grandmother, Myrtle Allen. It's similar to the muffleta on the previous page, but for this you open the top of a loaf of bread like a flap, cut out the inside, make little sandwiches out of what you've taken out and miraculously pop them all back into the hollow 'chest'. What could be better to take on a long walk or to the races? Talk about picnic envy!

900g (2lb) rectangular loaf of unsliced bread
Sandwich fillings, such as Cheddar cheese and chutney (see pages 178–81);
   cooked chicken mixed with Mayonnaise (see page 232); smoked salmon
   and Cucumber Pickle (see page 174)

Insert a bread knife into one long side of the loaf, just above the bottom crust. Push the knife through until it reaches, but does not go through, the crust on the far side. Without making the cut through which the knife was inserted any bigger, work the knife in a fan shape from side to side, then pull it out. The bread should now be cut away from the bottom crust inside but without a very noticeable mark on the exterior of the loaf. This takes some practice, so you may wish to have an extra loaf spare the first time.

Next, cut through the top of the loaf to make a lid, carefully leaving one long side uncut as a hinge. When you open it, if it looks in danger of falling off, keep it propped up from behind with a couple of jars or something similar.

Finally, with the lid open, cut the bread away from the sides just inside of the crust on all sides and down to 1cm (1/2in) of the bottom crust. Ease the bread out carefully – it should turn out in a solid brick, leaving an empty case behind.

Cut the brick into four long, horizontal slices (cut it in half lengthways first to make it easier if you like) and make two long sandwiches using the fillings of your choice. Cut each big sandwich into four or five small finger sandwiches, press them together firmly and put them back into the chest. Surprise your friends by presenting the loaf and letting them open it up to find the treasure inside!

Salad of Haricot Beans with Tomatoes and Tuna

SERVES 3-4 / VEGETARIAN

This is one of those great salads that can be put together in no time. It's fresh and delicious and is made from ingredients that you're likely to have in your kitchen at any time.

FOR THE DRESSING:
3 tbsp olive oil
2 tbsp lemon juice
Salt and freshly ground black pepper

FOR THE SALAD:
1 x 410g tin of cooked haricot beans, drained

1 x 200g tin of tuna, drained and broken into chunks
150g (5oz) cherry tomatoes, quartered
2 spring onions, trimmed and thinly sliced
1-2 tbsp chopped fresh marjoram or mint

In a small jug, mix together the olive oil, lemon juice and seasoning. Assemble the remaining ingredients in a bowl and then drizzle over the dressing and toss.

Rocket, Tomato and Sugar Snap Pea Salad

SERVES 4-6 / VEGETARIAN

This is also a lovely fresh, light summer salad.

FOR THE DRESSING:
2 tbsp olive oil
1 tbsp lemon juice or cider vinegar
1/2 tsp wholegrain mustard
Pinch of sugar
Salt and freshly ground black pepper

FOR THE SALAD:
175g (6oz) sugar snap peas, topped and tailed
150g (5oz) rocket
250g (9oz) cherry tomatoes, halved or quartered

Whisk the dressing ingredients together and season to taste. Bring a pan of salted water up to the boil and add the peas. Boil for 2–3 minutes, until they still have a bit of bite, then drain and refresh in cold water and pat dry. Mix the peas, rocket and cherry tomatoes in a bowl. Drizzle the dressing over the salad and toss.

Duck, Lentil and Red Cabbage Salad

SERVES 4-6

This is a really delicious and very portable salad, and can also be prepared in advance. Leftover roast chicken works well as a substitute for the duck breast.

200g (7oz) duck breast
Salt and freshly ground black pepper
50g (2oz) roasted hazelnuts
200g (7oz) lentils
4 tbsp olive oil
Juice of 1 lemon
1/2–1 red chilli, deseeded and finely chopped
1/4 red cabbage, about 300g (11oz), core removed and very thinly sliced
3 tbsp chopped fresh coriander

Preheat the oven to 200°C (400°F), Gas mark 6. Using the tip of a knife, make three or four shallow incisions through the skin of the duck breast. Season the fat side with salt and pepper and drizzle with a tiny bit of olive oil. Place fat-side-down in an unheated frying pan or grill pan. Turn the heat on low and cook the duck breast very slowly, until golden brown, allowing the fat to render out – this may take 15–20 minutes. Turn the duck breast over and continue to cook for another 5–10 minutes, until it is just cooked through, or pop it into the oven on a roasting tray for the final 5–10 minutes.

Meanwhile, roast the hazelnuts by tossing them in a dry frying pan over a medium heat until golden, or put them into the oven with the duck for 5–7 minutes – but on a separate roasting tray.

While the duck is cooking, put the lentils in a saucepan and cover with cold water, bring up to the boil and cook for 15–20 minutes until soft. Drain and toss with the olive oil, lemon juice and chopped chilli and season to taste. Add the sliced red cabbage and chopped coriander and stir to mix. Taste and add a little more olive oil if it is a bit dry or more lemon juice if it needs sharpening up.

When the duck is cooked and has cooled slightly, slice it very thinly and toss with the salad. Tip into a large bowl or pile onto salad plates and sprinkle with the chopped roasted hazelnuts.

Asparagus and Spring Onion Tart

SERVES 6-8 / VEGETARIAN

This is one of the very best savoury tarts and it is perfect in the late spring/early summer when asparagus is in season. It is light and delicate in flavour, and has a wonderful crisp shortcrust pastry base.

25cm (10in) Shortcrust Pastry case, baked blind (see page 236)
1 tbsp olive oil
200g (7oz) spring onions, trimmed and finely sliced or chopped
200g (7oz) asparagus spears, trimmed
Salt and freshly ground black pepper
4 eggs
350ml (12fl oz) double cream
25g (1oz) Parmesan cheese, finely grated

Preheat the oven to 180°C (350°F), Gas mark 4. To make the tart filling, heat the olive oil in a small saucepan, add the spring onions and cook over a low heat until soft. Cook the asparagus by dropping it into boiling water with a pinch of salt, cover and bring back up to the boil, then remove the lid and boil, uncovered, for 3–4 minutes until it is just cooked. Drain, and then slice the asparagus into lengths 3cm (1½in) long, at an angle.

Whisk the eggs in a bowl, add the cream and the cooked spring onions and season. Pour this filling into the cooked pastry shell, still in the tin. Drop the asparagus into the tart and sprinkle the grated Parmesan cheese over the top. Carefully place the tart into the preheated oven and cook for 20–30 minutes, or until the tart is just set in the centre. Remove from the oven, and serve out of the tin, hot or at room temperature.

Potato, Chorizo and Feta Frittata

SERVES 8

A frittata is the best thing to eat outdoors and is just as fantastic hot or cold. For a vegetarian option you can leave out the chorizo.

250g (9oz) potatoes, peeled and cubed into 1cm (½in) pieces
6 tbsp olive oil
1 onion, peeled and sliced
8 eggs
100ml (3½fl oz) single cream
1 tsp salt
1 tbsp chopped fresh marjoram
125g (4½oz) chorizo, sliced
125g (4½oz) feta cheese, crumbled

Preheat the oven to 180°C (350°F), Gas mark 4. Place the potatoes in a saucepan, cover with boiling water and boil for 5 minutes, or until just cooked. Do not over-cook or they will go mushy. Drain and set aside.

Heat a 25cm (10in) ovenproof frying pan, add 3 tablespoons of olive oil and the sliced onion, cover with a saucepan lid and sweat over a gentle heat until soft and slightly golden. Set aside.

Whisk the eggs in a bowl, add the cream, 1 teaspoon salt and the marjoram. Stir in the sliced chorizo, the cooked onions and potatoes.

Heat 3 tablespoons of olive oil in the frying pan. When it is hot, pour in the egg mixture and stir briefly to distribute the ingredients evenly. Top with the crumbled feta cheese. Place in the preheated oven and bake for 25–35 minutes or until set in the centre. Remove from the oven and allow to cool a little before sliding it onto a large serving plate or a large cake tin lined with baking parchment, if you want to transport it on a picnic. Serve warm or at room temperature.

VARIATION

BUTTERNUT SQUASH, CHORIZO AND FETA FRITTATA

Follow the recipe above but replace the potato with the same weight of butternut squash, peeled (with a knife), deseeded and cubed.

Ham and Egg Pie

SERVES 6-8

This is such a lovely, old-fashioned picnic pie.

200g (7oz) Shortcrust Pastry, made with 125g (4½oz) flour,
  75g (3oz) butter, pinch of salt and ½–1 egg, following
  the instructions on page 236
FOR THE FILLING:
15g (½oz) butter
1 onion, peeled and chopped
6 eggs
75ml (2¾fl oz) double cream
150g (5oz) cooked ham or cooked bacon rashers,
  sliced into 1 x 2cm (½ x ¾in) pieces
1 tbsp chopped parsley
Salt and freshly ground black pepper

Preheat the oven to 180°C (350°F), Gas mark 4. Roll out the pastry and line a 25cm (10in) ovenproof plate. Trim the pastry so that it is a bit bigger than the plate, and then fold up the edges slightly so that you have a slight lip all the way around. This will prevent the cream from running off the plate when you put it in the oven. Place the pastry on its plate in the fridge while you prepare the filling ingredients.

For the filling, melt the butter in a small saucepan, add the onions and cook over a gentle heat until soft. Whisk two of the eggs in a bowl, add the cream, the cooked onions, chopped ham and parsley. Season with salt and pepper to taste. Pour this into the pastry case. Carefully break the remaining eggs onto the tart, trying to keep the egg yolks intact.

Bake for 25–35 minutes in the preheated oven until the custard is set in the centre and the eggs on top are just cooked. Serve warm or allow to cool and pack for a picnic. Cut slices of the tart straight from the plate.

Maple Syrup and Pecan Muffins

MAKES 12 / VEGETARIAN

These are gorgeous muffins and are great for a picnic or children's lunch boxes. They will keep for 4–5 days and also freeze well.

FOR THE MUFFINS:

1 egg

50g (2oz) oats

75ml (2³/₄fl oz) maple syrup

225ml (7¹/₂fl oz) milk

75g (3oz) butter, softened not melted

75g (3oz) light brown sugar

225g (8oz) plain flour, sifted

3 tsp baking powder

¹/₂ tsp salt

75g (3oz) chopped pecans or walnuts

FOR THE GLAZE (OPTIONAL):

50g (2oz) butter, softened

50g (2oz) icing sugar, sifted

1 tbsp maple syrup

12 pecans

Preheat the oven to 200°C (400°F), Gas mark 6. Line a muffin tray with 12 paper muffin cases.

Whisk the egg in a bowl, add the oats, maple syrup and milk and whisk to combine. Set aside to soak while you prepare the other ingredients.

In a large bowl beat the butter, add the sugar, and mix to make a soft paste. Gradually add the milk mixture, stirring all the time, then stir in the sifted flour, baking powder, salt and chopped nuts, until just combined. Do not over-stir.

Spoon the mixture into the paper cases in the tin and bake in the preheated oven for 18–25 minutes until the tops are golden and feel firm to the touch in the centre. Take out of the tin and allow to cool on a wire rack.

Make the glaze, if using, by mixing together the butter, sugar and syrup. Using a knife, spread the glaze over the tops of the cooled muffins and top each muffin with a pecan.

Jam Tarts

MAKES 12 / VEGETARIAN

These are a great way to use up leftover sweet or savoury pastry; my children love making them for our picnics. There are few things more delicious on a picnic than a jam tart with a cup of tea, so don't forget to bring some in a flask!

150g (5oz) Sweet or Savoury Shortcrust Pastry (see page 220)
12 tsp summer fruit, apricot, raspberry or strawberry jam

Preheat the oven to 200°C (400°F), Gas mark 6. Roll out the pastry between two sheets of cling film to a thickness of about 3mm (1/8in). Using a 6cm (2¹/₂in) cutter, cut out 12 rounds (you may need to gather up the scraps and re-roll the pastry).

Press the rounds into a shallow patty tin (you can use paper cases if you wish) and drop a teaspoon of jam into each. Cook in the preheated oven for 8–12 minutes until the pastry is golden and the jam bubbling. Allow to cool slightly in the tin before carefully transferring to a wire rack (the jam will thicken as it cools).

4 Food for Children

People often ask me what I cook for my children and how I get them to eat good nutritious food. Well, in this chapter I have included many of my boys' favourite things to eat so that you can see for yourself there is no trick – it just tastes good! This is simple, foolproof, no-fuss food that is easy to prepare, which makes it ideal if your children want to help you in the kitchen. I have included great ideas for breakfast, lunch, supper and for yummy snacks as well.

Yoghurt with Oats and Honey

SERVES 1 / VEGETARIAN

This is more a simple combination than a recipe, and is a fantastic, healthy, and very quick breakfast. The oats, with their slow-releasing carbohydrates, will keep your little ones going until lunch. Add some fruit too, if you wish, such as raspberries, blueberries, sliced strawberries, peaches or pears.

4-6 tbsp really good yoghurt, natural or with fruit
1 small handful of porridge oats
1 tsp honey

Place the yoghurt in a bowl, sprinkle with oats, drizzle with honey and serve.

Scrambled Eggs on Toast

SERVES 2 / VEGETARIAN

There is nothing like a classic scrambled egg on toast for breakfast or brunch, or even supper! Made in about two minutes, it's a perfect quick meal for hungry kids.

3 free-range eggs, best quality possible
2 tbsp milk (a little single cream mixed with the milk is, of course, divine!)
Salt and freshly ground black pepper
2 slices wholemeal bread
15g (¹/₂oz butter)

Break the eggs into a bowl, add the milk and seasoning, and whisk for about 10 seconds. Pop the slices of bread in the toaster. Put the butter into a cold saucepan, add the egg mixture and stir continuously with a wooden spoon over a low heat until the mixture looks scrambled but still soft and creamy. Check the seasoning and serve, piled onto buttered toast.

Super Smoothies

EACH SERVES 4-6 / VEGETARIAN

Smoothies are a great way to get little ones to have some fruit, and my children love these combinations in particular. The Nectarine, Berry and Plum Smoothie has oats in it, which will keep children's energy topped up for a few hours as the oats contain slow-releasing carbohydrates. It's good for their concentration levels, too.

BANANA AND CINNAMON SMOOTHIE

4 bananas
500ml (18fl oz) natural yoghurt
2-4 tsp honey
1 tsp ground cinnamon

Whiz all the ingredients together in a blender or food processor and serve.

NECTARINE, BERRY AND PLUM SMOOTHIE

2 nectarines, stones removed
2 tbsp raspberries, blueberries or blackberries
2 plums, stones removed
400ml (14fl oz) natural yoghurt
2 tbsp oats
Juice of 1/2 lemon
1 tbsp honey
10 ice cubes (optional)

Whiz all the ingredients together in a blender or food processor, adding more honey or lemon juice if you prefer a sweeter or sharper flavour respectively.

Quesadillas

MAKES 8 WEDGES / VEGETARIAN

Quesadillas are essentially the Central American toasted cheese sandwich! We make many versions of it at home, depending on what is in the fridge. Our children love plain cheese quesadillas or quesadillas filled with chicken or a little spinach (very handy as you can sneak it in almost unnoticed to greens-wary little ones). These are perfect for a snack or TV supper, and they are great for grown-ups too. I quite often have guacamole and tomato salsa with mine, as they do in Mexico, or else for a very fast sauce try Crème Fraîche with Sweet Chilli (see page 139). Not all children like chilli, but one of our boys actually likes it, so I sometimes leave it in for him.

2 wheat flour tortillas
100g (4oz) cheese (I like a mixture of Cheddar,
    Gruyère and mozzarella), grated
1 spring onion, trimmed and sliced (optional)
1/2 green or red chilli, deseeded and chopped finely
    (optional – chillies can be very hot!)

Heat a frying pan slightly. Place one tortilla in the pan and sprinkle with all the grated cheese, the sliced spring onion and chilli, if using. Cover with the other tortilla and press down with a spatula or your hands. The cheese will have started melting at this stage and the tortilla on the bottom should be golden brown. When it is, carefully turn it over and then cook the other side for another couple of minutes, until it is golden and all the cheese has melted. Transfer to a board and cut into wedges. Serve immediately on its own or with Crème Fraîche with Sweet Chilli or Tomato and Cucumber Salsa (see page 139).

VARIATIONS

QUESADILLAS WITH CHICKEN
Make as for the basic quesadillas, but add 75g (3oz) shredded cooked chicken with the grated cheese.

QUESADILLAS WITH SPINACH
Make as for the basic quesadillas, but add one handful of baby spinach leaves (about 15g (1/2oz)) with the grated cheese.

Parmesan Chicken Goujons

SERVES 6-8

These are one of my boys' favourite foods. Use good-quality free-range chicken and you'll have a delicious and nutritious meal that little ones will adore. My children love dipping these goujons into homemade Tomato Ketchup (see page 80) or Mayonnaise (see page 232), or sometimes a mixture of the two!

600g (1lb 6oz) boneless and skinless
   chicken
50g (2oz) plain flour
Salt and freshly ground black pepper
2 eggs, beaten

100g (4oz) breadcrumbs
50g (2oz) Parmesan cheese,
   or something similar, such as
   Grana Padano, finely grated
3 tbsp sunflower oil

These can either be cooked on the hob or in the oven. If using the oven, preheat to 200°C (400°F), Gas mark 6 and place a baking tray in the oven to preheat.

Cut the chicken into goujons the size of a big finger (1 x 10cm (1/2 x 4in)). Place the flour in a mixing bowl or in a plastic bag with some salt and pepper. Place the beaten eggs in another bowl. Mix the breadcrumbs and finely grated cheese together and place in a bowl or bag as well.

Toss the goujons in the seasoned flour, making sure they do not stick together, then remove. Shake off the excess flour and dip them in the beaten egg. Remove from the egg, letting the excess drip off, and toss into the breadcrumb and cheese mix. Shake off the excess and lay the goujons on a plate.

To cook on the hob, heat the oil in a large frying pan over a medium to high heat. When the oil is hot, add the goujons in a single layer, cook on one side for about 3 minutes until golden, then turn down the heat and flip the pieces over. Cook on the other side for about 4 minutes, until cooked through and golden.

To cook the goujons in the oven, drizzle the base of the preheated baking tray with the oil and lay the floured and seasoned goujons in a single layer. Bake in the oven for about 12–18 minutes, turning the goujons over halfway through, or when golden on one side. When they are completely cooked, remove from the oven and serve.

PARMESAN FISH GOUJONS

Also known as fish fingers! Prepare as for chicken, but substitute skinned and filleted fish. Cut into finger size goujons as before. For this recipe I use firm fish, such as cod, hake or ling. Cooking time remains the same.

Tomato Ketchup

MAKES 400ML (14FL OZ) / VEGETARIAN

If your children regularly eat ketchup, then you might want to give them something a bit healthier and more delicious, like this real tomato ketchup. If you think they won't like this version, ease them into it by mixing some into their usual type and gradually adjust their taste. This is definitely best made in the summer with ripe red tomatoes.

2 tbsp olive oil
225g (8oz) onions, peeled and roughly chopped
600g (1lb 6oz) tomatoes, roughly chopped (no need to peel)
2 garlic cloves, peeled and crushed
75ml (2 3/4fl oz) white wine vinegar

75g (3oz) sugar
2 tsp Dijon mustard
1/2 tsp ground allspice
1/2 tsp ground cloves
1/2 tsp salt
1/2 tsp freshly ground black pepper

Heat the olive oil in a saucepan, add the onions and toss over a medium heat until cooked and a little golden. Add the rest of the ingredients and simmer with the lid on for about 30 minutes, until very soft.

Remove from the heat and whiz in a liquidiser or food processor. Pour through a sieve into a clean saucepan and simmer, uncovered and stirring regularly, for another 30 minutes, or until the mixture is thick.

Pour into sterilised jars or bottles (see page 177) and cover with lids.

Classic Spaghetti and Meatballs with Fresh Tomato Sauce

SERVES 6 (OR ABOUT 10 CHILDREN)

We used to have meatballs when we were little, and now our boys love them too. Children just love slurping up the spaghetti!

FOR THE MEATBALLS:
2 tbsp olive oil
1 onion, peeled and finely chopped
1 garlic clove, peeled and crushed
900g (2lb) freshly minced beef
2 tbsp chopped fresh herbs, such as marjoram, or a smaller quantity of rosemary
1 egg, beaten
Salt and freshly ground black pepper

FOR THE TOMATO SAUCE:
3 tbsp olive oil
100g (4oz) onion, peeled and sliced
1 garlic clove, peeled and crushed
2 x 410g tins chopped tomatoes (or use 900g (2lb) ripe, peeled (see page 178) and chopped tomatoes)
Salt, sugar and freshly ground black pepper

TO SERVE:
3 tbsp olive oil
150g (5oz) mozzarella, grated
450g (1lb) spaghetti

To make the meatballs, heat the olive oil in a heavy, stainless-steel saucepan over a gentle heat and add the onion and garlic. Cover and sweat for 4 minutes, until soft and a little golden, then allow to cool.

In a bowl, mix the minced beef with the cold sweated onion and garlic, then add the herbs and the beaten egg. Season the mixture to taste. Fry a tiny bit to check the seasoning and adjust if necessary. Divide the mixture into about 24 round balls and place in a dish. Cover the meatballs and refrigerate until required.

Meanwhile, make the tomato sauce. Heat the oil in a stainless-steel saucepan. Add the sliced onion and crushed garlic, toss until coated, cover and sweat over a gentle heat until soft and a tiny bit golden. Add the tomatoes, mix and season with salt, freshly ground pepper and a pinch of sugar. Gently simmer, uncovered, for approximately 30 minutes or until softened.

Heat up a frying pan over a medium heat with about 3 tablespoons of olive oil. Cook the meatballs for about 10 minutes. When they are done, transfer into a dish, add the tomato sauce and sprinkle the grated cheese on top. Place under a preheated grill to let the cheese melt.

Meanwhile, cook the spaghetti in a pan of boiling water. Drain and serve on individual plates with the meatballs piled on top.

Party Sausages with Mustard and Honey Dip
SERVES 10-12

This is really fast and easy and can be served with the Homemade Pork Sausages on page 196, or with store-bought cocktail sausages if you are in a hurry and have a lot of little mouths to feed. The dip is slightly sweet from the honey, which works very well with the sausages. The Dijon mustard is not very hot, although you can add more mustard if you prefer and are serving to adults.

FOR THE SAUSAGES:
1 quantity of Homemade Pork
    Sausages (see page 196) or 40
    cocktail sausages

FOR THE DIP:
250ml (8fl oz) crème fraîche
1 tbsp grainy mustard
½ tsp honey
1 tsp Dijon mustard

Cook the sausages in a frying pan, under the grill or in a hot oven.

In a serving bowl, mix together all of the dip ingredients to combine. When the sausages are cooked, place the bowl of dip in the centre of a large serving plate and arrange the sausages around.

Banana and Peanut Butter Muffins

MAKES 12 / VEGETARIAN

We all adore these muffins at home; they are sweet, delicious and nutty. They are also great for a snack or to take on a picnic. Put them in your kids' lunch boxes for a nice surprise!

275g (10oz) plain flour
50g (2oz) oats
1 tbsp baking power
2 eggs
150g (5oz) light brown sugar
2 bananas (200g (7oz)), peeled and mashed
125g (4¹/₂oz) crunchy peanut butter
50g (2oz) butter, melted
250ml (8fl oz) milk

Preheat the oven to 190°C (375°F), Gas mark 5. Line a muffin pan with 12 paper muffin cases.

Place the flour, oats and baking powder in a bowl, mix together and set aside. In another bowl, whisk the eggs, add the light brown sugar, mashed bananas, peanut butter and the melted butter. Stir to mix, then add the milk and stir to combine. Add the dry ingredients and fold in gently, do not over-mix.

Spoon the mixture into the prepared muffin cases and bake for 18–24 minutes, or until the tops spring back when gently touched. Allow to stand in the muffin pan for a minute before turning out to cool on a wire rack.

Drop Scones

MAKES 12 / VEGETARIAN

These little drop scones (or crumpets) are quite delicious and are very easy to make. They are fabulous for brunch or for a quick snack in the afternoon. My children love making these after school when they are always a bit peckish.

100g (4oz) self-raising flour
1 tsp baking powder
25g (1oz) caster sugar
Pinch of salt
1 egg
125ml (4fl oz) milk
Drop of sunflower oil, for greasing

Sift the flour and baking powder into a bowl, add the sugar and salt and stir to mix. Make a well in the centre, crack in the egg and whisk, gradually drawing in the flour from the edge. Add the milk gradually, whisking all the time, to form a smooth batter.

Lightly grease a frying pan and warm it over a moderate heat. Drop 3 tablespoons of the batter into the pan, keeping them well apart so they do not stick together. Cook for about 2 minutes or until bubbles appear on the surface and begin to burst and the drop scones are golden underneath, then flip them over and cook on the other side for a minute or until golden on this side as well.

Remove from the pan and serve warm with butter and jam, apple jelly, Lemon Curd (see page 186) or, if you are like my children, chocolate spread! (If you wish, wrap the drop scones in a clean tea towel to keep warm while you make the rest.)

Chewy Seedy Oat and Apricot Bars

MAKES ABOUT 18 BARS / VEGETARIAN

Pack these in lunch boxes, but always be sure to steal one for yourself to enjoy with a cup of coffee once the kids have gone to school!

300g (11oz) porridge oats
100g (4oz) pumpkin or sunflower
    seeds, or a mixture of the two
50g (2oz) desiccated coconut
50g (2oz) plain flour
200g (7oz) butter

200g (7oz) golden syrup
150g (5oz) soft brown sugar
150g (5oz) dried apricots, chopped
125g (4¹/₂oz) crunchy peanut butter
1 tsp vanilla extract

Preheat the oven to 160°C (325°F), Gas mark 3. Line an 18 x 28cm (7 x 11in) Swiss roll tin with non-stick baking parchment, leaving a little hanging over the edges for easy removal later.

Place the oats, seeds, coconut and flour in a large bowl and mix together. Melt the butter and golden syrup together in a saucepan, then mix in the sugar, chopped apricots, peanut butter and vanilla extract. Pour into the bowl of dry ingredients and mix until evenly combined.

Press the mixture into the prepared tin and bake in the oven for 20–25 minutes, or until golden and slightly firm. Allow to cool in the tin, then remove, still in the paper, and cut into 18 bars (or cut them depending on whatever size you want them to be). Store in an air-tight container for up to 1 week. These will also freeze well.

White Soda Scones

This has to be one of the fastest and most delicious scones you can make. The dough is just perfect for children to play around with, even if it does then get heavy from over-handling. You should see some of the creations that my sons make; dinosaurs are their favourites! This is the soda bread mixture we make at the Ballymaloe Cookery School, and there are countless variations you can experiment with from this basic recipe.

450g (1lb) plain white flour	**1 tsp bicarbonate of soda**
1 tsp salt	**400ml (14fl oz) buttermilk or sour milk**

Preheat the oven to 230°C (450°F), Gas mark 8. Sift the flour, salt and bicarbonate of soda into a large bowl, and rub the mixture in with your fingertips to incorporate some air. Make a well in the centre and pour in most of the buttermilk. Using one hand, with your fingers open and stiff, mix in a full circle, bringing the flour and liquid together, adding more liquid if necessary. The dough should be quite soft, but not too sticky.

Turn it out onto a floured surface, and do not knead it but gently bring it into one ball. Flatten it slightly to a height of about 3cm (1½in). Cut the dough into squares or whatever shape you like. Put the scones onto a baking tray and pop into the hot oven and cook for 10–15 minutes (depending on the size). Have a look at them after 10 minutes; if they are deep golden brown, then turn down the heat to 200°C (400°F), Gas mark 6 for the remainder of the time. When cooked they should sound hollow when tapped. Cool on a wire rack.

VARIATIONS

HERB SCONES
Add 1–2 tbsp of chopped thyme, rosemary, parsley, chives, marjoram, savoury or sage to the flour before you pour in the buttermilk. For even more flavour, you could sprinkle the tops with grated Cheddar cheese before they go into the oven.

PESTO SCONES
Add 1–2 tbsp basil pesto to the buttermilk before mixing with the flour. These are also delicious with chopped olives mixed in with the flour.

Add about 75g (3oz) crispy bacon, a good pinch of cayenne pepper and 50g (2oz) finely grated Parmesan cheese to the flour at the start, then brush the tops of the raw scones with beaten egg or leftover buttermilk and sprinkle with more grated Parmesan cheese.

SWEET SCONES

Add 25g (1oz) caster sugar to the dry ingredients. Also, put 1 egg into a measuring jug, lightly beat and make up to 400ml (14fl oz) with the buttermilk or sour milk. This makes the dough slightly richer. In addition, you could add any of the following ingredients to the flour at the start of the recipe: 100g (4oz) sultanas (or raisins or currants) and 1/2 teaspoon mixed spice; 100g (4oz) chopped chocolate; or 1 teaspoon ground cinnamon and an extra 25g (1oz) sugar. Then brush the tops with beaten egg and dip into 50g (2oz) granulated sugar mixed with 1/2 teaspoon ground cinnamon.

Jam Drops

MAKES ABOUT 30 / VEGETARIAN

These are quick little biscuits which makes them great to prepare with children since they won't lose their concentration halfway through. My boys love baking them!

200g (7oz) self-raising flour
100g (4oz) caster sugar
100g (4oz) slightly soft butter

1 small egg, beaten
Strawberry, raspberry or apricot jam

Preheat the oven to 190°C (375°F), Gas mark 5. In a food processor mix the self-raising flour, caster sugar and butter together. Add just enough egg to bring the mixture together to form a stiff dough. If you are not using a food processor, rub the butter into the flour and sugar, then add enough egg and with your hands work it until it forms a stiff dough.

Roll the mixture into balls the size of a walnut and place on a baking tray (no need to line). Flatten each ball slightly and make a small indentation in the middle of each biscuit with your thumb or the end of a wooden spoon. Drop half a teaspoon of jam in the centre. Bake for 10–15 minutes until just golden. Cool on a wire rack.

5 Extended Family

My extended family not only includes relatives (grandparents, in-laws, aunts, uncles and cousins), it also includes those close friends and neighbours we know so well that they may as well be family! The food in this chapter is for all those easy, casual occasions when the whole gang gets together.

Winter Vegetable Broth with Haricot Beans and Chorizo

SERVES 6

This soup is the best thing in winter time – comforting and nutritious. It's a meal in itself for lunch. And, even better, it's very easy to make.

2 tbsp olive oil
1 onion, peeled and chopped
1 large carrot, peeled and chopped
2 small leaks, trimmed and chopped
2 potatoes, peeled and chopped
2 large garlic cloves, peeled and
   crushed

150g (5oz) chorizo, sliced about 3mm
   (1/8in) thick
900ml (1¹/₂ pints) chicken stock
1 x 410g tin haricot beans, drained
2 tbsp chopped fresh coriander or
   parsley
Salt and freshly ground black pepper

Heat the olive oil in a large saucepan. Add the onion, carrot, leeks, potatoes, garlic and chorizo. Cover and sweat for 10 minutes over a low heat, stirring every now and then.

Add the chicken stock and drained haricot beans. Bring to the boil and simmer for 5 minutes until all the vegetables are cooked. Add the herbs, season to taste and serve.

Light Coconut Broth with Pak Choi and Basil
SERVES 8

I absolutely love this kind of recipe; you throw a few things in a pot, boil for a few minutes and end up with the most delicious result. I also adore these South-east Asian flavours.

2.4 litres (4 pints) vegetable (or light chicken) stock
2 x 410g tins coconut milk
2 red chillies, deseeded and finely sliced into rings
4 spring onions, trimmed and sliced thinly at an angle
2 garlic cloves, peeled and crushed
2 heaped tsp grated ginger
4 heads pak choi, stalk and leaves shredded
6 tbsp Thai fish sauce (nam pla)
Juice of 1 lime
4 tbsp sliced basil

Place the stock, coconut milk, chilli, spring onions, garlic and ginger in a saucepan and bring up to the boil. Add the pak choi and continue cooking for 1–2 minutes or until the pak choi is just cooked. Add the fish sauce, lime juice and basil. You probably won't need any additional salt since the fish sauce is already quite salty. Serve in warm bowls.

VARIATION

LIGHT COCONUT BROTH WITH PAK CHOI AND PRAWNS
Add 32 peeled tiger or or other large prawns into the broth with the shredded pak choi and cook as above. The prawns will cook in the same time as the pak choi.

Asparagus with Easy Hollandaise Sauce

SERVES 4 AS A MAIN COURSE OR 8 AS A STARTER / VEGETARIAN

I love it when the first asparagus appears in the shops in late spring. These bright green spears are so delicious cooked simply in a little salted boiling water. There are few things much better than a big feast of asparagus and a divine bowl of homemade hollandaise sauce, mopped up with toasted bread and washed down with a glass of wine!

32 spears fresh green asparagus
4–8 slices good-quality white bread
Soft butter, for the toast
FOR THE HOLLANDAISE SAUCE:
2 egg yolks
100g (4oz) butter, cubed
1–2 tsp lemon juice

To make the hollandaise sauce, place the egg yolks in a heatproof glass bowl. Heat the butter in a saucepan until foaming, then pour gradually onto the egg yolks, whisking all the time. Add the lemon juice to taste, then pour into a heatproof measuring jug. Half-fill a saucepan with hot water from the kettle and place the jug of hollandaise in the saucepan to keep warm. When the water cools, just put the saucepan on a gentle heat, but do not let the water boil too long or the sauce will scramble.

Keep the sauce warm while you are waiting to serve it; it will sit quite happily like this for a couple of hours.

Half-fill a saucepan with water, add a good pinch of salt and bring to the boil. While it is heating up, remove the woody ends from the asparagus spears by snapping off about 3–4cm (1¹/₄–1¹/₂in) of the bottom of the stalk. Discard the woody ends.

Cook the asparagus by dropping it into the boiling water, cover and bring back up to the boil. Remove the lid and boil, uncovered, for another 4–7 minutes until just cooked. While the asparagus is cooking, toast the bread and butter it. Remove the asparagus and place on the buttered toast. Drizzle with some of the hollandaise sauce and serve the rest in a jug on the table.

Pasta with Tomato and Ginger Salsa and Crème Fraîche

SERVES 4-6 / VEGETARIAN

The flavours in this sauce are lovely and very fresh. Ginger works surprisingly well with pasta, and the little bit of crème fraîche added at the end gives it a delicious creaminess.

400g (14oz) farfalle, penne or rigatoni, or something similar
15g (¹/₂oz) butter
2 spring onions, trimmed and sliced
10 ripe cherry tomatoes or 2 ripe tomatoes, roughly sliced
1 tsp finely grated ginger
Salt and freshly ground black pepper
Pinch of sugar
2-3 tbsp crème fraîche

Cook the pasta in boiling water according to the packet's instructions.

Meanwhile, heat the butter in a frying pan or wide saucepan, add the sliced spring onions and toss on the heat for a minutes until almost soft. Add the chopped tomatoes and the ginger, and season with salt and pepper and a good pinch of sugar. Toss in the pan on the heat for another couple of minutes until the tomatoes almost begin to soften. Then toss with the hot, drained pasta, add the crème fraîche, stir and serve.

Pie with Bacon and Peas

My husband, Isaac, is an amazing cook, and this is one of his best weekend lunch dishes. It is so good and children love it too.

FOR THE FILLING:
1 chicken, about 2.25kg (5lb)
2 carrots, peeled and halved
1 celery stick, halved
1 onion, peeled and halved
Sprig of fresh thyme and fresh parsley
1 litre (13/4 pints) water or light
   chicken stock
Salt and freshly ground black pepper
250ml (8fl oz) single cream
Roux (see page 231)
450g (1lb) button mushrooms,
   cut in half

25g (1oz) butter
400g (14oz) cooked ham, chopped
   into 2cm (3/4in) cubes
450g (1lb) peas
6 eggs, hard boiled for 10 minutes,
   peeled and chopped roughly
2 tbsp chopped fresh tarragon
FOR THE TOPPING:
400g (14oz) puff or flaky pastry,
   rolled to 5mm (1/4in) thick
1 egg, beaten, to glaze
Or
1.75kg (33/4lb) mashed potato

Remove any giblets from inside the chicken and discard. Place the whole chicken in a large saucepan or casserole pot, add the carrots, celery, onion, thyme and parsley and the water or light chicken stock. Season with salt and pepper, cover with a lid and simmer for about 11/4 hours (or pop into a moderate oven) until the chicken is cooked. You will know when it is cooked as the leg will feel quite loose when you pull it from the carcass and the juices run clear when pierced.

If you have a pastry topping, preheat the oven to 230°C (450°F), Gas mark 8. For mashed potato, preheat the oven to 180°C (350°F), Gas mark 4.

Take the chicken out of the pot and set aside to cool for a few minutes. Remove the vegetables and herbs from the liquid in the pot and pour in the cream. Bring up to the boil, then whisk in some roux (about 2–3 tablespoons, but start with 1 tablespoon) until it has thickened slightly. The liquid must keep boiling while you add the roux in order to thicken.

Heat the butter in a pan over a high heat and fry the mushrooms for 4 minutes or until soft.

Remove the meat from the chicken carcass, chop roughly and place in a large pie dish (about 25 x 35cm (10 x 14in)), then add the chopped ham, peas (these can be straight from the freezer), chopped hard-boiled eggs, browned mushrooms and the chopped tarragon. Season to taste. If you are making this in advance, don't add the topping until just before you're ready to cook.

For a puff or flaky pastry top: cut the pastry to the same size as the top of the pie dish and arrange on top, making a hole in the centre to allow steam to escape. Brush the pastry with the beaten egg to give it a nice glaze. Cook it in the oven for 10 minutes, then turn down the oven to 190°C (375°F), Gas mark 5 and cook for another 20 minutes or until the pastry is golden brown and the mixture is bubbling hot.

For a mashed potato top: arrange the mashed potato on top of the chicken mixture and lightly score the surface. Place in the oven and cook for 30–40 minutes or until golden brown on top and bubbling hot.

Roast Leg of Lamb with Garlic and Rosemary and Olive Paste

SERVES 8-10

I love it when Isaac makes this for Sunday lunch. You can also serve it with Mint Sauce or Redcurrant Jelly (see pages 232 and 233).

FOR THE LAMB:
1 leg of lamb, about 2.5-3.25kg
  (5¹/₂-7¹/₄lb)
2 tbsp olive oil
1 tsp cracked black pepper (best if it is
  still a little coarse)
1 generous tbsp chopped rosemary
1 big pinch of sea salt
8 garlic cloves, peeled and sliced

FOR THE OLIVE PASTE:
100g (4oz) pitted black olives
1 tbsp capers
1 tsp Dijon mustard
1 tsp freshly squeezed lemon juice
Freshly ground black pepper
4 tbsp olive oil

Preheat the oven to 230°C (450°F), Gas mark 8. Using a very sharp knife, make about ten shallow slashes in criss-cross patterns on the top side of the meat. Mix together the olive oil, pepper, rosemary, sea salt and garlic and spread all over the lamb, pushing it into the incisions. Place it in a roasting tray and put it into the preheated oven.

Cook for 20 minutes, then turn the heat down to 180°C (350°F), Gas mark 4 and cook for a further 45 minutes for pink lamb, 1 hour 10 minutes for medium, or 1 hour 25 minutes for well-done. This cooking time allows 20 minutes per 500g (1lb 2oz) at this temperature. I usually aim for medium since there will inevitably be some pink bits and some well-done so that everyone can have their favourite!

To make the olive paste, whiz up the olives with the capers, mustard, lemon juice and pepper in a food processor – you probably won't need any salt. Add the olive oil. It keeps for months in a sterilised jar (see page 177) in the fridge.

When the lamb is cooked, allow it to rest for 15 minutes, covered with foil, somewhere warm if possible, then carve into slices and serve with the olive paste, mint sauce or redcurrant jelly.

Beef Stew with Brandy, White Wine and Cream

SERVES 10-12

This is such a good main course for entertaining, everyone always loves it. I usually make this quantity, even if I am just feeding six people, as it's useful having left overs for the next day or two.

500g (1lb 2oz) mushrooms, sliced
3-4 tbsp olive oil
3kg (7lb) stewing beef, cut into 3cm (1½in) cubes
150ml (5fl oz) chicken or beef stock
3 very large onions, peeled and sliced

5 garlic cloves, peeled and crushed
150ml (5fl oz) white wine
100ml (3½fl oz) brandy
325ml (11fl oz) single cream
Salt and freshly ground black pepper
2-3 tsp Roux (see page 231)

Preheat the oven to 160°C (325°F), Gas mark 3. Heat a large frying pan and sauté the mushrooms in batches in the olive oil until pale golden in colour. Tip onto a plate and set aside. Brown the meat in the same pan in small batches. When all the meat has browned, pour a small amount of the stock into the frying pan and bring to the boil to deglaze the pan and conserve the flavour.

Meanwhile, place a large flameproof casserole on the hob over a medium heat and pour the stock from the frying pan into it. Add the mushrooms, meat, sliced onions, garlic, white wine, stock and brandy. Cover with the lid, transfer to the oven and simmer for about 1-1½ hours or until tender.

When the meat is cooked, strain the liquid into a saucepan. Add the cream and boil uncovered for a few minutes until it has a good flavour, then season with salt and pepper.

With the liquid still boiling, add 2-3 teaspoons of the roux and whisk in until the juices have thickened slightly, adding more roux if necessary. Pour over the meat, stir and keep warm until you are ready to serve. Serve with Pilaff Rice (see page 234) or mashed potatoes.

Spaghetti with Beef, Olives, Capers and Anchovies

SERVES 6-8

This is a really good and gutsy pasta dish adapted from the classic pasta puttanesca (whores' pasta!). Leave out the beef if you wish. The sauce can be made in advance.

3-4 tbsp olive oil
575g (1lb 5oz) rump steak, cut into thin strips
2 onions, peeled and sliced
4 garlic cloves, peeled and crushed
1 x 410g tin chopped tomatoes (or 450g (1lb) of fresh tomatoes, peeled (see page 178) and chopped, reserving the juice)

Salt and freshly ground black pepper
Good pinch of sugar
25g (1oz) pitted black olives, chopped
25g (1oz) whole capers, rinsed if salted
12 whole anchovy fillets, roughly chopped
2 tbsp chopped tarragon or basil
600g (1lb 6oz) spaghetti

Heat half the olive oil in a pan, toss the meat for 30 seconds until brown, then remove from the pan and set aside. Add the remaining oil to the pan, and sweat the onion and garlic until soft. Add the tomatoes and their juices, salt and pepper and sugar. Cover with the lid and cook over a low heat for 10 minutes. Return the beef back to the sauce and allow it to simmer for a further 10 minutes or so until the sauce has thickened. Add the olives, capers, anchovies and chopped herbs, stir and set aside.

Cook the pasta in a large pot of boiling salted water until it is al dente. Drain and toss with the warm sauce and serve.

Gratin of Fish with Cheese, Tomatoes and Herbs

SERVES 6

Another great recipe of Isaac's! It is a terrifically easy and convenient main course and – even better – it can be prepared in advance.

75g (3oz) Gruyère cheese, grated
75g (3oz) Emmental, grated (or a total of 150g (5oz) Gruyère instead)
3 generous tsp Dijon mustard
4–5 tbsp single cream
Salt and freshly ground black pepper
18 cherry tomatoes
1 generous tsp fresh thyme leaves or 1½ tbsp torn basil
750g (1lb 10oz) filleted and skinned flat-fish, such as plaice or lemon sole

Preheat the oven to 180°C (350°F), Gas mark 4. In a bowl, mix the grated cheese with the mustard and cream, add a twist of black pepper and set aside. Cut the cherry tomatoes in half, season with a little salt and sprinkle with the herbs.

Spread half the cheese mixture in a gratin dish (or individual ovenproof dishes). Lay half the fish on top, then add all the tomatoes and herbs. Add the second layer of fish, followed by the second layer of the cheese mixture. Place the dish in the fridge until you are ready to cook it.

Cook in the preheated oven for 20–30 minutes (or 15 minutes for single portions) until golden and bubbly. Serve with a big green salad and some boiled new potatoes if you wish.

VARIATION
This dish can also be made using round, fleshy fish, such as haddock, cod or ling. Use the same weight as the flat fish but place just one layer of fish in the dish.

Chocolate and Hazelnut Toffee Tart

SERVES 8-10 / VEGETARIAN

This is a really special and divinely rich tart, which is perfect served at the end of a meal with a cup of espresso or a glass of sweet dessert wine. It looks fantastic with its layers of sweet biscuity pastry underneath the hazelnut toffee, topped off with a rich and intense chocolate mousse.

1 x portion of Sweet Shortcrust Pastry (see page 236)

FOR THE HAZELNUT TOFFEE:
50g (2oz) butter
75ml (2¾fl oz) single cream
100g (4oz) soft light brown sugar
150g (5oz) hazelnuts, roasted, peeled and coarsely chopped

FOR THE CHOCOLATE MOUSSE:
200ml (7fl oz) single cream
200g (7oz) dark chocolate, broken into pieces

TO SERVE:
Cocoa powder (optional)
Softly whipped cream

Roll out the pastry to line a 25cm (10in) tart tin (see page 236 for instructions). Cover and chill for 20 minutes, then blind bake (see also page 236). The pastry will not go into the oven again, so it must be completely cooked.

For the hazelnut toffee layer, place the butter, cream and brown sugar in a saucepan, bring to the boil and simmer for 2–3 minutes until slightly thickened. Remove from the heat, add the hazelnuts and allow it to cool. Spread over the cooked tart shell.

For the chocolate mousse, place the cream in a saucepan and bring to the boil, remove from the heat and immediately add the chocolate, stirring until the chocolate has melted and mixed with the cream. It should be just tepid now. Pour over the hazelnut toffee in the pastry case.

Place the tart somewhere cool until the chocolate mousse has set. If you are keeping it in the fridge, let it come back up to room temperature before you serve. Dust the tart with cocoa (if using), slice and serve with softly whipped cream.

Crème Brûlée Au Café

FILLS 4–5 ESPRESSO CUPS, SHOT GLASSES OR SMALL RAMEKINS / VEGETARIAN

Not many recipes come into my head as I sleep (unfortunately), but I woke up one morning having dreamt that I had eaten this in Italy. So when I tried it out later that day, I was delighted with the result! It's an excellent pudding to round-off a dinner party. The flavour of the coffee-infused custard is perfect with the 'burnt' sugar topping: divine inspiration! For the caramel topping you can use caster, granulated, light brown or dark brown sugar, but I have recommended light brown because the rich flavour works very well with the coffee custard. Since it is so rich it's best served in small portions. The custard needs to be made at least 5 hours in advance for it to set and be able to support the caramelised sugar top.

FOR THE CUSTARD:
1 generous tbsp ground coffee
  (not instant)
250ml (8fl oz) double cream

2 egg yolks
1 tbsp light brown sugar

FOR THE CARAMELISED TOPPING:
100g (4oz) light brown sugar

Place the coffee in a saucepan with the cream, bring up to just under boiling, then take off the heat and set aside for 1 minute to allow the coffee flavour to infuse. Pour through a very fine sieve into a bowl and wash out the saucepan.

Place the egg yolks and sugar in a bowl and whisk. Still whisking, add the coffee cream and mix completely. Pour this back into the clean, cool saucepan and place over a low heat. Stirring all the time, cook very slowly (it must not boil, otherwise it may scramble) until it thickens and can coat the back of a spoon – this will take a few minutes. Pour it immediately into serving cups, glasses or bowls and allow to cool, then place in the fridge for at least 5 hours (or overnight). Be careful not to break the skin on top or the caramel may sink later.

To prepare the caramel topping, place the sugar in a small saucepan over a medium heat and allow the sugar to caramelise, stirring all the time with a wooden spoon. It will look very lumpy and strange at first, but it will suddenly appear smooth, liquid and glossy. Immediately drizzle this caramel over the top of the custards. I like the custards to be just partially covered with the caramel. Do not swirl the custards while the caramel is being drizzled over as the skin may break and cause the caramel to sink. If using this method, the caramel can be made and poured on top of the custards about 5 or 6 hours in advance. Keep it somewhere dry so the caramel will not soften.

RACHEL'S HANDY TIP
If you have a cook's blow torch, you can sprinkle the set custards with a layer of sugar, about 1/2–1 teaspoon per portion. Light your blow torch and caramelise the sugar by holding the blow torch just a few centimetres from the cups until the sugar melts and bubbles. Allow to sit for 1 minute before serving. These can be finished a couple of hours before serving.

Amaretti Cookie Ice Cream with Hot Mocha Sauce

SERVES 6 / VEGETARIAN

This is the perfect dessert for the person who doesn't like to make either pastry or cakes. It's also great if you're in a hurry and want to make something fabulous with minimum effort. I love the rich, intense chocolate sauce with a hint of coffee and, if you like, you can leave out the brandy. The sauce can be prepared in advance (it will keep pretty much indefinitely in the fridge), just heat gently to serve.

FOR THE ICE CREAM:
400ml tub vanilla ice cream
100g (4oz) amaretti cookies,
   broken into chunks

FOR THE HOT MOCHA SAUCE:
100g (4oz) chocolate
100ml (3½fl oz) good strong coffee
   (can be left over from that morning!)
1 tbsp brandy (optional)

Take the ice cream out of the freezer and allow it to soften slightly, then add the broken amaretti cookies and fold into the ice cream. Cover and put back in the freezer until you are ready to serve.

To make the hot mocha sauce, melt the chocolate in a heatproof bowl in a low oven or microwave, or in a bowl set over a pan of simmering water. Take off the heat and whisk in the coffee and the brandy. Place a scoop or two of ice cream in a bowl, glass or cup and drizzle generously with the hot mocha sauce.

Little Hot After-dinner Shots

MAKES 8 / VEGETARIAN

Merrilees Parker, who is a great cook, made something similar to these when I appeared with her on *Great Food Live*. These are like little Irish coffees, only without the coffee!

200ml (7fl oz) brandy or whiskey
200ml (7fl oz) Stock Syrup (see page 237)
8 tbsp softly whipped cream

Place the brandy or whiskey in a saucepan with the stock syrup and heat very gently; do not boil. Divide between eight little glasses. Dip a spoon into boiling water and spoon on the cream, allowing it to slide off the spoon and sit on top of the sweet brandy or whiskey. The cream should not sink. Serve immediately.

6 Dining Alfresco

I absolutely adore eating alfresco. You just can't beat gorgeous, lazy days out in the garden with friends and family, fun barbecues, a lunch under an umbrella for shade, enjoying breakfast while listening to the birds and smelling the roses, romantic candle-lit meals under the stars . . . how lovely! I eat outdoors whenever I get the chance, so that I can make the most of our fairly brief but warm summers.

Summer Omelette with Crispy Bacon, Tomato and Rocket Salad

SERVES 6

This is very much like an Italian frittata, with a gorgeous salad on top. It looks very pretty and dramatic on the table.

FOR THE OMELETTE:

4 tbsp olive oil

1 onion, peeled and chopped

Salt and freshly ground black pepper

8 eggs

100ml (3½fl oz) double cream

100ml (3½fl oz) milk

125g (4½oz) Gruyère or Parmesan cheese, grated

1-2 tbsp snipped fresh chives

FOR THE SALAD:

8 slices of streaky bacon, cooked in a pan until golden and crispy

6 ripe tomatoes, chopped into large chunks

1 tbsp olive oil

1-2 tsp lemon juice

Salt, freshly ground black pepper and sugar

50g (2oz) rocket leaves (2 big handfuls)

Make the omelette first. Heat a 28cm (11in) frying pan, add 2 tablespoons olive oil and the chopped onion, season and cook for 5-8 minutes, until almost soft and a little golden. Remove from the heat and allow to cool for a minute.

Whisk the eggs in a large bowl, add the cream, milk, the cooked onions, grated cheese and chopped chives; season to taste. Wipe out the frying pan, then heat it again and add another 2 tbsp olive oil, swirl it around, then pour in the egg mixture. Stir a couple of times, then cook over a low heat until it is golden and set underneath (about 10-15 minutes), then place under a hot grill to set the top (this may take another 4-5 minutes).

When cooked, flip or slide it out onto a large plate, and allow it to sit while you prepare the salad. It needs to cool slightly and to be eaten at room temperature.

To make the salad, slice the cooked bacon into 1cm (½in) pieces. Place in a bowl, add the tomatoes and drizzle with the olive oil and the lemon juice, season with salt, pepper and a pinch of sugar. When you are ready, toss the rocket leaves in very gently, then place on top of the omelette and serve.

This salad is also delicious made with smoked mackerel instead of the crispy bacon. Use 2-3 fillets of skinned smoked mackerel, cut into slices.

Asparagus Soldiers with Softly Boiled Eggs

SERVES 4 / VEGETARIAN

I love dipping spears of asparagus into softly boiled eggs, and they are great served up for an outdoor brunch. Do make sure you don't over-boil the eggs or it will be tricky to dip the asparagus into the yolk!

4 eggs
12 asparagus spears, woody ends snapped off

Hollandaise Sauce (see page 98)
Salt

Bring two saucepans of water up to the boil, one for the eggs and one for the asparagus. Boil the eggs in their shells for 4 minutes. While the eggs are boiling, cook the asparagus by dropping it into boiling water with a pinch of salt, cover and bring back up to the boil, then remove the lid and boil, uncovered, for 3–4 minutes until it is just cooked. Drain the eggs and the asparagus.

To eat, break open the 'lid' of your boiled egg, and dip the asparagus spears into the runny yolk.

Onion and Blue Cheese Tart

SERVES 6-8 / VEGETARIAN

Combined with a big green salad, this tart is perfect for an alfresco lunch in the garden. It is nice and easy to make, too, and there is no need to pre-cook the pastry.

FOR THE PASTRY:
250g (9oz) plain flour
125g (4¹/₂oz) butter
Pinch of salt
1 egg, beaten

FOR THE FILLING:
4 tbsp olive oil
3 very large onions, peeled and sliced
2 sprigs of fresh thyme or rosemary
Salt and freshly ground black pepper
100g (4oz) blue cheese, crumbled roughly into 1cm (¹/₂in) pieces

Make the pastry following the method on page 236 and allow it to rest in the fridge. Meanwhile, place the olive oil in a saucepan, add the sliced onions, herbs and salt and pepper. Stir, put on the lid and cook over a low heat for about 20 minutes, stirring regularly, until the onions are soft and tender. Discard the herb sprigs and pour out onto a plate to cool.

Roll out the chilled pastry between two sheets of cling film. When it is big enough to line a 20 x 30cm (8 x 12in) Swiss roll tin, remove the top layer of cling film and flip the pastry into the tin with the remaining sheet of cling film on top. Press it into the edges of the tin, remove the cling film and trim the edges. Using a fork, prick holes into the base of the pastry case. If you have time, it is best to allow the pastry to cool again before it goes into the oven to cook, so pop it into the freezer for 5 minutes if possible.

Preheat the oven to 180°C (350°F), Gas mark 4. Place a baking tray in the oven to heat up (this will help the base of the tart cook more evenly).

Pour the onions into the chilled pastry case, place on the hot baking tray in the oven and cook for 25–35 minutes until the pastry around the edge is crisp and golden. About 3 minutes before the end of the cooking time, sprinkle the tart with the crumbled blue cheese and pop back into the oven for another 3 minutes. The blue cheese will just begin to melt. Remove the tart from the oven and allow to cool slightly before sliding out onto a serving plate.

Nettle Soup

SERVES 6-8 / VEGETARIAN

People may not believe you when you say that you are making nettle soup, but it really is delicious. Even better, if your garden is anything like mine, the nettles are free and organic! Years ago, nettle soup was eaten to celebrate the arrival of spring, and this is the time to eat it as the young new shoots are the ones to pick. Just remember to wear your rubber gloves when picking them. To remove the formic acid (the part that gives them their sting), they do need to be cooked. This soup can also be served cold, like the Green Leaf and Pea Soup (see page 120), and with a little swirl of crème fraîche or thick natural yoghurt in the centre. If you don't have nettles to hand, you can use spinach, kale or watercress in their place.

25g (1oz) butter
1 potato, peeled and chopped
1 onion, peeled and chopped
Salt and freshly ground black pepper
600ml (1 pint) vegetable
   (or chicken) stock

600ml (1 pint) milk (add some single
   cream to this if you wish)
225g (8oz) nettle leaves,
   roughly chopped

Melt the butter in a saucepan, add the potatoes and onions, and season with salt and pepper. Cover and sweat on a gentle heat for 10 minutes, stirring every now and then. Take off the lid, add the stock and milk and bring to the boil. Cook until the potatoes are soft.

Add the nettles and boil, uncovered, over a high heat for just 2–3 minutes until the nettles have wilted. Do not overcook this soup or it will lose its fresh green colour and flavour. As soon as it is cooked, liquidise it. Taste and correct the seasoning and serve.

Green Leaf and Pea Soup

SERVES 6-8 / VEGETARIAN

My husband Isaac makes this in about 10 minutes flat. It can be served chilled as a nice starter on a hot day, or served hot for a cool summer's evening eating outside. Whether you are serving it cold or hot, it is also lovely to add a tiny blob of crème fraîche or a swirl of thick natural yoghurt in the centre.

1 litre (13/4 pints) vegetable (or chicken) stock
6 spring onions, trimmed and sliced
4 garlic cloves, peeled and crushed
Salt and freshly ground black pepper
450g (1lb) peas, fresh or frozen
250g (9oz) watercress, rocket or spinach, or a mixture of all three, roughly chopped and large stalks removed
200ml (7fl oz) single cream

Place the stock, spring onions and garlic in a saucepan, season with salt and pepper and bring to the boil. Boil for about 4 minutes, until the onions are soft, then add the peas and continue to boil over a high heat, removing the lid once the mixture comes to the boil.

After 1 minute, add the roughly chopped leaves and boil for a further 30 seconds–1 minute, until the peas and leaves are just tender. Add the cream and liquidise immediately. Then season to taste and serve.

Crab and Avocado Salad
SERVES 3-4

Not only is this a delicious salad, it is also great as a sandwich filling between two slices of really good brown or white bread.

200g (7oz) cooked crabmeat
1 tbsp Dijon mustard
1 tbsp Mayonnaise (see page 232)
2 tbsp chopped watercress

1 tbsp torn basil
1 ripe avocado, peeled,
    stoned and diced
Salt and freshly ground black pepper

Mix all the ingredients together and season to taste. Place on a lettuce leaf on a plate to serve for a starter or, if eating as a light main course, enjoy with some green salad and some bread on the side.

Avocado, Orange and Watercress Salad
SERVES 6 / VEGETARIAN

This salad has wonderful fresh flavours. It's great with spicy food, like South American Beef Steak with Chimichurri Salsa (see page 127). If you want to make this in advance, leave out the avocado and watercress until you are almost ready to serve.

50ml (2fl oz) olive oil
Juice of 1/2 lime
Sea salt and freshly ground
    black pepper
1 orange, peeled and chopped

2 avocados, halved, peeled, stoned
    and chopped roughly
125g (4 1/2oz) watercress sprigs
    (about 6 handfuls)

In a bowl mix the olive oil and lime juice and season with sea salt and freshly ground black pepper. Add the chopped orange and avocado. Then gently toss in the watercress sprigs and serve.

Warm Pasta Salad with Herbs, Garlic and Rocket Leaves

SERVES 4-6

This is perfect for alfresco eating; fresh and light and wonderful eaten either hot or just slightly warm. Leave out the chilli if you wish.

400g (14oz) pasta, like farfalle (pasta bows)
25g (1oz) butter
2 tbsp olive oil
4 cloves of crushed or grated garlic
1/2-1 red chilli, deseeded and finely chopped (optional)
2 generous tbsp chopped herbs (I use a mixture
   of parsley, chives, basil and thyme)
20 cherry tomatoes, quartered
2 big handfuls of rocket leaves, left whole
Sea salt and freshly ground black pepper
50g (2oz) grated Parmesan cheese

Bring a large saucepan of salted water to the boil, add the pasta, and cook until al dente.

While the pasta is cooking, heat the butter and olive oil in a saucepan, add the garlic and chilli, and cook for about 20 seconds. Be careful not to burn the garlic.

Remove from the heat and add the chopped herbs, the quartered cherry tomatoes and the rocket leaves (they will wilt a bit from the heat). Season to taste with sea salt and freshly ground black pepper. Toss with the grated Parmesan and serve hot, or allow to cool and serve at room temperature.

South American Beef Steak with Chimichurri Salsa

SERVES 6

The flavours in the salsa marry beautifully with the steak, which can be cooked on a barbecue, in a frying pan or grill pan on the hob. It is delicious served with the Avocado, Orange and Watercress salad (see page 123).

6 sirloin steaks, about 1cm (1/2in) thick

FOR THE MARINADE:

6 garlic cloves, peeled and finely chopped
1 red chilli, deseeded and finely chopped
Juice of 1 orange
Juice of 1 lemon
2 tbsp chopped fresh parsley
100ml (3 1/2fl oz) olive oil

FOR THE CHIMICHURRI SALSA:

1 garlic clove, peeled and finely chopped
1 tbsp finely chopped spring onion
1 tbsp white wine vinegar
1 pinch of dried chilli flakes
2 tbsp chopped fresh coriander
2 tbsp chopped fresh parsley
Juice of 1/2 lime
100ml (3 1/2fl oz) olive oil
Salt and freshly ground black pepper

Using a sharp knife score the steaks 1mm (1/16in) deep in a criss-cross pattern. Combine the ingredients for the marinade in a shallow glass or china dish or strong plastic bag, add the beef and toss in the marinade. Then place in the fridge for at least 1 hour (or up to about 8 hours).

To make the salsa, combine all the ingredients in a bowl and season to taste with salt and pepper.

Heat a grill pan, frying pan or your barbecue until very hot. Remove the beef from the marinade and cook for about 3-4 minutes on each side or longer, depending on your taste. Reserve the marinade and use it to brush over the steaks during cooking. Transfer to serving plates, spoon over the chimichurri salsa, with more in a bowl on the side, and serve.

Fruity Cocktails

MAKES 2-4 / VEGETARIAN

These are all really refreshing cocktails to have on a summer's evening with friends.

CAMPARI AND GRAPEFRUIT FIZZ

5 tbsp Stock Syrup (see page 237)
1 tbsp Campari
125ml (4fl oz) grapefruit juice
200ml (7fl oz) sparkling white wine

Place the syrup, Campari and grapefruit juice in a jug and stir. Add the sparkling wine and pour into chilled champagne or wine glasses.

COOL CAMPARI AND LIME GIN AND TONIC

75ml (2³/4fl oz) gin
25ml (1fl oz) Campari
Juice of 1 lime (or ¹/2 lemon)
200ml (7fl oz) crushed ice
100ml (3¹/2fl oz) tonic

Pour the gin, Campari and lime or lemon juice into a jug. Add the crushed ice, stir to mix, then add the tonic water. Serve in whiskey tumblers or strain into cocktail glasses.

STRAWBERRY OR RASPBERRY DAIQUIRI

150ml (5fl oz) white rum or vodka
250g (9oz) strawberries or raspberries (can be frozen)
75ml (2³/4fl oz) lime juice (approximately 3 limes)
100-125ml (3¹/2-4fl oz) Stock Syrup (see page 237), to taste
Crushed ice, to serve

Place the rum, strawberries (or raspberries), lime juice and 100ml (3¹/2fl oz) stock syrup in a blender and whiz until smooth. Taste and add more stock syrup if necessary. Pour into tumblers half-filled with crushed ice.

Summer Tiramisu

SERVES 10-12 / VEGETARIAN

This is such a great dessert to serve when you have lots of people over for a big get-together. My friend, Clare Pocock, made this gorgeous tiramisu and brought it along to a big extended family barbecue and everyone loved it.

150ml (5fl oz) water
200g (7oz) unbleached caster sugar
400g (14oz) mixed berries (fresh or frozen)
50ml (2fl oz) crème de cassis or crème de framboise
4 eggs, separated
250g tub mascarpone cheese
1 x 200g packet boudoir biscuits (sponge biscuits)
50g (2oz) flaked or slivered almonds

Make a syrup by dissolving half the sugar in the water, then boiling for 2 minutes. Add in the fruit. If using fresh fruit, turn off the heat and leave it to cool. If using frozen fruit, bring the syrup back to the boil and let it simmer very gently for 1-2 minutes, then leave to cool. Add the cassis or framboise to the syrup.

Beat the egg yolks in a bowl with the remaining sugar until pale and thick. Beat in the mascarpone cheese. In a separate bowl, whisk the egg whites until they form stiff peaks. Fold them lightly into the egg and mascarpone mixture.

Strain the fruit from the syrup. Place the syrup in a wide bowl. Dip half the biscuits in the cooled syrup and use them to line the base of a 28cm (11in) gratin dish. Spread half the mascarpone mixture over, followed by half the fruit. Cover the fruit with another layer of the biscuits dipped in the liquid. Spread over the remainder of the fruit, followed by the remaining mascarpone mixture. Cover and chill for a minimum of 6 hours, or ideally overnight, to allow the biscuits to absorb the juices and soften.

Meanwhile, toast the almonds by heating a dry frying pan, tossing in the nuts and frying for 2-3 minutes until golden. Set aside to cool. Use to sprinkle over the tiramisu just prior to serving.

Custard Tart

This is quite simply a tasty and light, old-fashioned tart.

1 x 25cm (10in) sweet pastry shell (see page 236),
  blind baked
475ml (16fl oz) milk
3 eggs
50g (2oz) caster sugar
1 tsp vanilla extract or essence
Pinch of ground nutmeg or cinnamon

Preheat the oven to 180°C (350°F), Gas mark 4. Place the blind baked pastry shell in its tin on a baking tray.

Heat the milk to just under boiling point. Whisk the eggs in a bowl, add the sugar and vanilla and whisk. Then whisk in the hot milk. To avoid spills, place the empty pastry shell on the oven shelf and very carefully pour in the custard. Close the oven door and cook for 10 minutes, then open the oven door and sprinkle the top of the tart with the ground nutmeg or cinnamon and bake for another 10 minutes, or until it is just set in the centre. Remove from the oven and allow to cool a little before removing from the tin. It will set a little more as it cools. Cut into slices and serve.

RACHEL'S HANDY TIP

To remove the tart from a loose-bottomed tin, make sure that the pastry is not stuck to sides of the tin, then place the tin on a small bowl or cup and the outer ring part should fall down. Then lift the tart slightly and remove the ring and the bowl. If you are feeling confident you can remove the base of the tin by sliding a palette knife or a fish slice between the pastry and the base of the tin, and sliding the tart onto your chosen plate. Alternatively, just leave the tart on the tin base.

Baked Meringue with Peaches

SERVES 6 / VEGETARIAN

A past student at the cookery school, Jo Jessop, who comes from South Highlands, Australia, gave me this recipe. It's wonderful served with vanilla ice cream; the hot baked meringue with the frozen ice cream works very well in that 'baked Alaska' kind of way. It is just as easy to make this for 26 as it is for six, provided you have a large enough gratin dish!

4 peaches or nectarines
25g (1oz) brown sugar
2 tbsp Marsala, sweet sherry or lemon juice
4 egg whites
250g (9oz) light brown sugar or caster sugar

Preheat the oven to 180°C (350°F), Gas mark 4. Cut the peaches in half (there's no need to peel them) and remove the stones. Slice the peaches about 5mm (1/4in) thick and lay in a 1.25 litre (2 1/4 pint) pie dish. Sprinkle with brown sugar and drizzle with the Marsala, sherry or lemon juice. If the peaches are not very ripe and juicy (although they should be ripe enough to eat), pop them into the oven for 5 minutes to cook, while you make the meringue. If they are very ripe and juicy there is no need to do this.

To make the meringue, whisk the egg whites in a bowl with an electric beater until stiff. Still beating, gradually add the light brown sugar and continue to beat until the meringue holds stiff peaks. Spoon the meringue on top of the peaches and cook in the preheated oven for 15–20 minutes, or until the meringue feels slightly firm in the centre and is a deep golden colour on top.

7 Home Cinema

Cooking for an evening of home cinema is such fun. It is the perfect excuse to indulge and eat sticky, gooey treats in front of the telly, all snuggled up under a blanket watching your favourite flicks. The only trick is to make sure you prepare food that can either be eaten with your hands, or food that is all on the one plate and not awkward to eat, or else you'll be forever picking bits off the sofa, your lap, or each other!

Baked Potatoes

SERVES AS MANY AS YOU LIKE / VEGETARIAN

A baked potato is the perfect food to eat while watching a good movie. Whether your favourite topping is baked beans or Manchego cheese with Serrano ham, there is always something in the fridge for everyone. Baked potatoes are good and wholesome because most of the goodness in a potato is stored just under the skin, which is retained when you bake it – none of it is lost in cooking water.

1 large potato per person in its skin, scrubbed clean

Preheat the oven to 230°C (450°F), Gas mark 8. Pierce a few holes in the potato with a skewer or a fork and put on a tray or rack into the preheated oven. Cook for 40–55 minutes, until the potato feels soft under the crispy skin. You can cook the potatoes with a metal skewer stuck through them to speed up the cooking process. When the potato is baked, remove it from the oven and cut a cross in it to open it out slightly. Serve with a topping of your choice – each of those given here (there are two more overleaf) makes enough for two potatoes.

SERRANO HAM AND MANCHEGO CHEESE WITH WALNUT DRESSING
2 slices Serrano ham (or Parma ham)
4 slices of Manchego cheese, or Parmesan cheese
FOR THE WALNUT DRESSING:
1 tbsp walnut oil
1 generous tsp white wine vinegar
1/4 tsp Dijon mustard
Salt and freshly ground black pepper

Shake all the dressing ingredients together in a jar with a screw-top lid. Drape a slice of Serrano ham and a couple of thin slices of Manchego cheese over the top of each opened potato. Drizzle with a teaspoon or two of the walnut dressing.

GRUYÈRE CHEESE AND CRISPY BACON
2 tbsp bacon lardons, 1 x 2cm ($^{1}/_{2}$ x $^{3}/_{4}$in) in size
15g ($^{1}/_{2}$oz) butter
4 tbsp grated Gruyère cheese
Freshly ground black pepper

Cook the lardons in a hot pan until crispy. Dot each potato with the butter, sprinkle with the crispy bacon, the grated cheese and a little black pepper, and pop it back into the hot oven for 3–4 minutes until the cheese is melted and bubbling.

SMOKED SALMON
50g (2oz) smoked salmon (for 2 people)
15g ($^{1}/_{2}$oz) capers, rinsed then dried in kitchen paper
10g ($^{1}/_{4}$oz) butter or $^{1}/_{2}$ tbsp olive oil
Freshly ground black pepper
Squeeze of lemon juice
2 tbsp crème fraîche
Handful of snipped fresh chives

Cut the salmon into little lardons and toss with the capers in the butter or olive oil in a hot pan. Add the pepper and a squeeze of lemon juice. Add a good tablespoon of crème fraîche onto the split cooked potatoes, sprinkle with the salmon and capers and decorate with chopped chives.

Yummy Dips

EACH DIP SERVES 4-6 PEOPLE / VEGETARIAN

I love having a selection of dips on a home-cinema night. Tortilla chips (bought, or homemade and baked) are great for dipping, as are roast potato wedges or even, dare I say, raw vegetable sticks (but only if I am feeling very good and virtuous). These dips can all be made in advance, and their individual flavours work well with each other.

HUMMUS

1 x 400g tin of chickpeas, drained, or 200g (7oz) dried chickpeas
Juice of 1/2-1 lemon
2 garlic cloves, peeled and crushed

3-4 tbsp olive oil
2 generous tbsp tahini paste (sesame seed paste)
Salt and freshly ground black pepper
2 tbsp natural yoghurt (optional)

If using dried chickpeas, soak them in water overnight, then drain and cook in fresh water for about 45 minutes, or until soft. Drain again and allow to cool. Put all the ingredients into a food processor and pulse until smooth. Check for seasoning, add more olive oil or some natural yoghurt if it is too thick. This keeps in the fridge for up to a week.

TOMATO AND CUCUMBER SALSA

16 cherry tomatoes, or 4 red ripe tomatoes, finely chopped
1/4 cucumber, deseeded and finely chopped
2 garlic cloves, peeled and crushed

1/2 small red onion, peeled and finely chopped
1-2 tbsp lemon or lime juice
1-2 tbsp chopped mint
Salt and freshly ground black pepper

Mix all the ingredients in a bowl and season to taste.

CRÈME FRAÎCHE WITH SWEET CHILLI

6 tbsp crème fraîche
2 tbsp sweet chilli sauce

Mix together the ingredients, adding more sweet chilli sauce if you like.

Toasted Ham and Gruyère Sandwich
MAKES 1 SANDWICH

This is a classic combination, and I think it makes the ultimate TV supper. This recipe makes enough for one sandwich, but you can easily make more for a crowd!

2 slices of white bread, ciabatta or sourdough bread
Softened butter
2 slices of ham or, even better, glazed bacon
2-3 slices of Gruyère cheese
1 tbsp wholegrain or Dijon mustard

Lay the slices of bread on a work top. Spread one slice with butter, add a layer of ham, then the Gruyère cheese. Spread the other slice of bread with the mustard and place on top of the ham, mustard-side-down. Spread some butter on the top of the sandwich.

Place a frying pan on the heat and straight away put the sandwich in the pan, butter-side-down. Place a saucepan lid on the pan and cook over a medium heat for about 3–4 minutes, until golden on the underside. Spread a tiny bit of butter on the top and flip over. Cover again, turn down the heat and cook for another 3–4 minutes until golden and the cheese is just melted. Remove from the pan and serve.

RACHEL'S HANDY TIP
To make a lot of these I would cook the sandwiches in a hot oven for 8–10 minutes, which is far more convenient than cooking them one by one in a frying pan.

Lamb Samosas

MAKES 20

I love it when Isaac makes these for a night in front of the flicks. Samosas are the ultimate finger food, which makes them the ultimate telly food! Use filo pastry as a faster alternative to the traditional samosa pastry. For a vegetarian version, replace the lamb with an equal quantity of boiled, skinned and chopped potato.

2 tbsp sunflower or olive oil
300g (11oz) finely chopped
   or minced lamb
1 onion, peeled and chopped
1 tsp ground cumin
1 tsp ground coriander
Salt and freshly ground black pepper

100g (4oz) peas (fresh or frozen)
1 tbsp chopped fresh coriander
5 sheets of filo pastry, measuring
   25 x 50cm (10 x 20in)
1 egg, beaten

Heat a frying pan, add the sunflower or olive oil, then toss in the lamb, onion and ground spices. Season and cook for about 10 minutes without a lid until the lamb is just cooked and the juices have evaporated. Add the peas and toss. Take off the heat and add the chopped coriander and season again to taste. Set aside for a minute to let the lamb cool.

Meanwhile, lay the filo pastry out on a board and cut into half lengthways, then into half widthways, so you have four rectangles from each whole sheet. Cover all the pieces of filo with a barely damp tea towel (to prevent them from drying out). Place one sheet lengthways in front of you and pile a dessertspoon of the lamb mixture at the end closest to you. Roll the pastry from the end closest to you, once, then fold in both the long sides and then roll over and over, away from you, into a little parcel. Brush the finishing edge with a little of the beaten egg to seal and then place on a baking tray. Brush the finished samosa with beaten egg and repeat with all the remaining pastry and meat.

These can be prepared earlier in the day up to this point and chilled in the fridge. To cook, place the baking tray into an oven preheated to 220°C (425°F), Gas mark 7 for 10-12 minutes until golden.

Creamy Tomatoes on Toast

SERVES 2 / VEGETARIAN

My mum used to make this for us when we came home from school and I still adore it. This is great, easy food to have in front of the television.

200ml (7fl oz) single cream
1 sprig of fresh rosemary or 2 sprigs of fresh thyme
1 garlic clove, peeled and chopped
4 ripe tomatoes, cut in half
Sea salt and freshly ground black pepper
2-4 slices of white yeast or soda bread
About 2 tbsp olive oil

Preheat the oven to 200°C (400°F), Gas mark 6. In a saucepan, simmer the cream with the herbs and garlic for 5 minutes until it has thickened slightly.

Place the tomatoes cut-side-up in a gratin or ovenproof dish and pour over the cream with garlic and herbs. Season with salt and pepper and then bake in the oven for 15–20 minutes or until the tomatoes are soft and blistered and the cream is thick and reduced.

Meanwhile, drizzle the bread with a little of the olive oil and pop into the oven for the last 5 minutes of the cooking time. When the toast and tomatoes are cooked, remove from the oven. Place the toast on warm plates and divide the tomato halves out between the toast, then spoon any cream left in the gratin dish over the top and serve.

Raclette

SERVES 4

Raclette is both the name of a semi-soft Savoyard cheese and a traditional dish in which slices of the cheese were put on the hearth near a glowing fire. Diners would gather around with plates, knives and forks in hand and a bowl of boiled potatoes. As the cheese melts, it is scraped off, spread across the potatoes and eaten with gusto! Today, most people use electric raclette machines at the table and each diner helps themselves to cheese to melt on their own little handled tray under the raclette grill, which they then enjoy with hot boiled potatoes, a selection of charcuterie, cornichons and tomatoes. Similar to a cheese fondue, it's great fun for a big casual supper party, or amazing to enjoy in front of a good movie – slide a low coffee table near to the sofa on which to stand the raclette machine.

8–12 floury potatoes
500g (1lb 2oz) Raclette cheese, cut into slices 5mm (¼in) thick
A selection of charcuterie
Ripe tomatoes
Cornichons, sliced
Cucumber Pickle (see page 174)
A chutney such as Spicy Tomato and Apple Chutney (see page 179) or Onion Marmalade (see page 181)
Sea salt and black pepper in a mill

Plug in the raclette machine and allow it to heat up. Boil the potatoes until soft.

Put the cheese, charcuterie, tomatoes, cornichons, cucumber pickle and relishes on plates or in bowls. When the potatoes have boiled, place them in a warm bowl on the table. Let each guest take a slice of cheese and place it under the grill on the raclette machine. While the cheese is melting, let everyone help themselves to all the other ingredients on the table. Split open a potato and when the cheese is melted and bubbling, scrape it onto the potato and enjoy.

Popcorn Paradise

SERVES 4 / VEGETARIAN

It is difficult to have a home-cinema night without popcorn, so why not try this recipe and all its variations? Serve the popcorn in a big bowl or in paper cornets for each person.

PLAIN POPCORN
3 tbsp sunflower oil
75g (3oz) popcorn
25g (1oz) butter
Pinch of salt

Heat the oil in a medium saucepan. Add the popcorn and swirl the pan to coat the popcorn in oil. Turn down the heat to low, cover, and the corn should start to pop in a couple of minutes. As soon as it stops popping (after 5–7 minutes), take the saucepan off the heat and add the butter and salt. Put the lid back on the pan and shake to mix. Pour out into bowls and leave to cool a little.

VARIATIONS

TOFFEE POPCORN

Cook the popcorn as for the plain popcorn recipe, but while the corn is popping, make the toffee coating by melting 25g (1oz) butter in a small saucepan. Then add 25g (1oz) brown sugar and 1 generous tablespoon golden syrup and stir over a high heat for 1/2–1 minute until thick. Pour the toffee over the popcorn, put the lid on the pan and shake to mix. Pour out into bowls and cool a little before serving.

SPICED POPCORN

Cook the popcorn as for the plain popcorn recipe as far as removing the pan from the heat. In a bowl, mix 11/2 teaspoons each of ground cumin and coriander seeds with 1/2 teaspoon each of medium-strength curry powder and ground paprika and 3/4 teaspoon ground cayenne pepper. Heat 2 teaspoons sunflower oil in a frying pan, add the spices and stir for about 30 seconds until lightly toasted. Throw in 25g (1oz) caster sugar and 3/4 teaspoon salt, stir, then add all of this into the popped popcorn in the saucepan, toss and empty into a big bowl.

8 Big Celebrations

From time to time we all find ourselves in a situation where we need to cook for lots of people – it could be for a big birthday or anniversary party, or maybe even an informal party after a wedding. On such occasions, the food needs to be something that can be prepared in advance, food that is easy to serve, and food with ingredients that everyone will like. To top it all, the food must also be just as easy to make for 26 as it is for 16 or even six! So hopefully you'll find lots of inspiration in this chapter.

Green Salad with Honey Mustard Dressing

SERVES ABOUT 20 PEOPLE / VEGETARIAN

There can be nothing easier to prepare for a large gathering than a bowl filled with a beautiful combination of your favourite salad ingredients. A green salad doesn't have to be bland and uninteresting. It all depends on the leaves that you use (a good selection will give a lovely range of colours and flavours – try edible flowers too!), and the oil in the dressing. Try to use as good an olive oil as you can afford and it will make all the difference.

FOR THE GREEN SALAD:

As large a selection as possible of edible leaves and herbs
Edible flowers, such as wild garlic, nasturtium, edible chrysanthemum and chive

FOR THE DRESSING:

3 tbsp olive oil (use your best extra-virgin for this)
1 tbsp white wine vinegar
1 tsp wholegrain mustard
1 tsp honey
1 large garlic clove, peeled and crushed
Sprig of parsley
A few chives, trimmed and chopped
Salt and freshly ground black pepper

Wash and dry the leaves and flowers and then tear them into bite-sized pieces. Put into a plastic bag or a covered bowl, which can be stored in the fridge for a couple of days if you need to get ahead. This is particularly good if you buy or pick all your leaves in one go or you have friends staying for the weekend. You can then just pick and choose whatever you need, whenever you need it.

To make the dressing, place all the ingredients in a jar with a lid and shake to mix. Taste for seasoning. Drizzle sparingly over a selection of your prepared salad ingredients in a bowl and toss to serve.

Chicken Pilaff

SERVES 6

This is a great main course for feeding lots of people and can be made in advance. It's a firm favourite of adults and children alike. For large gatherings, double or treble the quantities.

1 large chicken, about 2.5kg (5¹/₂lb)
1 carrot, peeled and halved
1 onion, peeled and halved
6 whole black peppercorns
Large sprig of parsley
Large sprig of thyme

750ml (1¹/₄ pints) chicken stock
250ml (8fl oz) white wine
Salt and freshly ground black pepper
250ml (8fl oz) single cream
2-3 tbsp Roux (see page 231)

Preheat the oven to 160°C (325°F), Gas mark 3. Remove any giblets from the chicken carcass and place the chicken in a large saucepan or casserole. Add the carrot, onion, peppercorns, herbs, stock and white wine and bring up to the boil. Season with salt and pepper, cover with the lid and place in the preheated oven to cook for 1¹/₂-2 hours or until the chicken is completely cooked. I test this by pulling the leg – if it feels as though it will come away from the carcass easily and the juices run clear when pierced, then it is ready. (For a larger chicken, cook for 20 minutes per 450g (1lb) plus 30 minutes.)

Remove the chicken from the stock and place it on a large plate. Remove all the meat from the carcass, discarding the skin and bones. Cut the chicken into strips approximately 1cm (¹/₂in) wide and 5cm (2in) long. Cover and keep warm.

Remove the vegetables, peppercorns and herbs from the liquid and discard. Add the cream, bring up to the boil and boil uncovered for a few minutes. If the flavour is a little weak, boil for longer, then season to taste. While still boiling, whisk in the roux – you need enough to thicken it so it just about coats the back of a spoon.

Place the chicken and any juices back in the casserole, once again correcting the seasoning, and keep warm until needed. Serve with Pilaff Rice (see page 234), mashed potatoes or boiled new potatoes and the Green Salad with Honey Mustard Dressing (see page 150).

Moroccan Lamb Tagine with Lemon and Pomegranate Couscous

SERVES 12-14

This is one of those great dishes that is perfect for small dinner parties and big celebrations alike. It's very straightforward to prepare and is so, so delicious!

4 tbsp olive oil
8 garlic cloves, peeled and crushed
4 onions, peeled and chopped
4 tsp grated ginger
1¹/₂ tbsp coriander seeds, crushed
3 tsp cumin seeds, crushed
3 tsp ground cinnamon
Salt and freshly ground black pepper
3kg (7lb) shoulder of lamb, boned,
    fat discarded and cut into 4cm
    (1¹/₂in) cubes
2 tbsp tomato paste

2kg (4¹/₂lb) ripe tomatoes or 4 x 400g
    tins tomatoes, coarsely chopped
4-5 tbsp honey
Wedges of lime and a bowl of Greek
    yoghurt, to serve

FOR THE COUSCOUS:
1 large or 2 small pomegranates
800g (1³/₄lb) couscous
6 tbsp olive oil
Juice of 2 lemons
1 litre (1³/₄ pints) boiling chicken stock
    or water
4 tbsp chopped fresh mint or coriander

Preheat the oven to 160°C/325°F/Gas mark 3. Heat a large flameproof casserole or heavy saucepan, add the olive oil, garlic, onions, ginger and spices. Season with salt and pepper, stir and cook on a low heat with the lid on for about 10 minutes, until the onions are soft.

Add the lamb, tomato paste, chopped tomatoes and honey. Stir it all together, bring to a simmer and place in the oven for 1¹/₂ hours, until the lamb is tender and cooked. Remove the lid halfway through cooking to let the liquid reduce and thicken. Season to taste. If it is still a bit thin, put the dish or saucepan on the hob on a medium heat and without the lid. Stir occasionally and let the liquid thicken.

Cut the pomegranate in half. Scoop out the seeds using a teaspoon and remove the white membrane. Place the couscous in a bowl and mix in the olive oil and lemon juice. Pour in the boiling stock or water and season. Allow to sit in a warm place for 5-10 minutes until the liquid is absorbed. To serve, stir in the chopped herbs and pomegranate seeds. Place the tagine on serving plates with couscous and a wedge of lime, and place a bowl of thick yoghurt in the middle of the table.

Thai Pork with Coconut Coriander Sauce

SERVES 10-12

This is a delicious recipe with mild South-east Asian flavours. The dish keeps very well if you make it in advance; just keep the cooked pork in a saucepan with the sauce, which will prevent the meat from drying out. Heat it up gently when you're ready to serve it.

2kg (4¹/₂lb) pork fillet (tenderloin), trimmed (about 4 fillets)

FOR THE MARINADE:

4 tbsp roughly chopped fresh coriander leaves and stalks

10 spring onions, trimmed

3cm (1¹/₄in) piece of fresh ginger, peeled and chopped

8 garlic cloves, peeled

Finely grated zest and juice of ¹/₂ lemon

1 red chilli, deseeded and roughly chopped

2 stalks of lemon grass, trimmed and outer leaves discarded

4 tbsp brown sugar

4 tbsp soy sauce

4 tbsp fish sauce (nam pla)

4 tbsp sesame oil

FOR THE SAUCE:

2 x 400ml tins coconut milk

2 tbsp fish sauce (nam pla)

2 tbsp lemon juice

1-2 tbsp chopped fresh coriander leaves and stalks

Salt and freshly ground black pepper

Cut the pork at an angle into slices 1cm (¹/₂in) thick, so that you have oval slices about 10cm (4in) long and 6cm (2¹/₂in) wide.

Make the marinade by placing the coriander, spring onions, ginger, garlic, lemon zest, chilli and lemon grass in a food processor and whiz until you have a fine paste. Put into a bowl and add the remainder of the marinade ingredients. (If whizzing in a liquidiser, simply whiz all the marinade ingredients together.) Add the slices of pork and toss in the marinade. Cover and place in the fridge until you are ready to cook the meat (for at least 30 minutes, or even overnight if you wish).

Heat a frying pan or grill pan until it is almost smoking, remove the pork from the marinade (reserving the marinade for the sauce) and cook the pork in a single layer over a high heat for 1-2 minutes or until golden underneath. Turn and continue to cook until the meat is cooked through. If you are cooking lots of meat, you can just toss for 1 minute on each side in the pan, then transfer it to a roasting tray and cook in a hot oven preheated to 220°C (425°F), Gas mark 7 for another 5 minutes or until it is cooked through.

While the pork is cooking, place the reserved marinade in a small saucepan. Add the coconut milk, bring up to the boil and boil uncovered for about 5 minutes until it has thickened a little. Add the fish sauce, lemon juice and chopped coriander and season to taste with more fish sauce or lemon juice if necessary. The fish sauce is quite salty so you might not need any additional salt.

Serve the pork on a bed of Thai Rice (see page 235) or Plain Boiled Rice (see page 234) with some sauce on top or in a bowl on the side.

RACHEL'S HANDY TIP

This main course also works very well as a canapé. Just cut the pork into small cubes about 2cm (3/4in) square and thread onto cocktail sticks (or small satay sticks) that have been soaking in water for 1 hour. Cook on a barbecue or in a frying pan for 6 minutes on each side and serve with a bowl of the coconut coriander sauce in the centre of the plate.

Thai Stir-fried Beef with Red Peppers and Pak Choy

SERVES 16

This is a great stir-fry that can be prepped in advance and then cooked when you are nearly ready to serve. I love to serve this with noodles or rice and some wedges of lime for each person to squeeze over their own plateful.

2.4kg (5¹/₄lb) rump or sirloin steak, trimmed and thinly sliced across the grain
8 tbsp fish sauce (nam pla)
8 tbsp oyster sauce
8 large garlic cloves, peeled and chopped
8 tbsp sunflower oil or vegetable oil
6 large red peppers, quartered, deseeded and finely sliced
8 heads pak choy, root end trimmed, then sliced across about 1cm (¹/₂in) thick
4-6 small chillies, deseeded and chopped
8 tbsp roughly chopped basil (only chop when you need it as it goes black if chopped in advance)
Lime wedges, to serve

Place the sliced beef in a bowl, add half the fish sauce, half the oyster sauce and half the chopped garlic. Stir to mix and leave to marinate in the fridge for 1–2 hours if possible, or even longer if you can.

Heat half the oil in a wok (or large frying pan), add the red pepper and toss over the heat for a couple of minutes, then add the pak choy. Keep tossing over the heat until just tender, then add the remaining garlic and the chillies. Cook for another 10 seconds, then remove from the heat and set aside.

Heat the remaining oil in the wok or pan, and when it is very hot, add the beef, drained from any marinade (reserve the marinade for later). Cook for 2 minutes, stirring all the time, or until cooked through.

Return the vegetables to the wok, add the remaining fish sauce, oyster sauce and marinade and toss over the heat for 30 seconds. Taste and add more fish sauce and oyster sauce if you wish. Remove from the heat and stir in the roughly chopped basil, and serve immediately with a wedge of lime on the side of each plate and with steamed rice or noodles.

Beef with Prunes and Peppers

This recipe of my friend, Iona Murray, is absolutely great for serving lots and lots of people. It is best made several hours in advance or even the day before, which makes it very handy for entertaining. The prunes seem to dissolve and give the sauce a sweet richness.

3.5kg (8lb) chuck/stewing beef, trimmed and cut into 2cm (3/4in) chunks
3–4 tbsp olive oil
Salt and freshly ground black pepper
3 large onions, peeled and chopped
6 fat garlic cloves, peeled
1 x 75cl bottle of red wine
8–10 red peppers, deseeded and chopped

Large bunch of thyme, tied together
3–4 fresh bay leaves
350g (12oz) pitted ready-to-eat prunes, cut in half
Zest of 1 large orange, pared and thinly sliced, and then juice the orange
4 red chillies, deseeded and chopped
4 tbsp tomato purée
1 cinnamon stick
Roux (see page 231) (optional)

Preheat the oven to 160°C (325°F), Gas mark 3. Trim the meat and put it in a large bowl. Pour over 1–2 tablespoons of the olive oil and season with salt and pepper.

Heat a frying pan over a high flame and brown all the meat in batches. Remove the meat from the pan and place in a large saucepan or casserole. Add some more olive oil to the pan and toss the onions and garlic on a high heat for a minute, then transfer to the casserole. With the frying pan still on the heat, pour some of the wine into it and stir around for a minute; this will deglaze the frying pan. Pour into the casserole.

Add the peppers, thyme, bay leaves, prunes, orange zest and juice, the chillies, the remaining wine, the tomato purée and the cinnamon stick, mix again and bring to the boil. Season and cover with a well-fitting lid and place in the oven. Cook for about 2 hours, until the meat is meltingly tender and you can cut it with a fork. If it is looking dry, add some water or light stock.

When it is done, remove from the oven and allow to cool. If the sauce is too runny, put a ladleful in a small saucepan, bring to the boil and whisk in some roux, return to the main dish and mix in. Or if the sauce is too dry, add a bit of stock or water to get the desired consistency. Serve with rice or mashed potatoes.

Roast Southeast Asian Salmon

SERVES 12-15

This is such a great main course for a big dinner party or family gathering.

2 fresh salmon fillets, each weighing
   1-1.25kg (2-2$\frac{1}{2}$lb)
Salt and freshly ground black pepper
FOR THE SAUCE:
150ml (5fl oz) fish sauce (nam pla)
150ml (5fl oz) white wine

2 garlic cloves, peeled and crushed
3 tsp finely grated ginger
2 tbsp brown sugar
Juice of 2 small limes
1 handful chopped fresh coriander

Preheat the oven to 200°C (400°F), Gas mark 6. Place the fish, skin-side-down, on an oiled piece of tin foil on a baking tray. Fold up the edges slightly to make a wall around the fish and season with salt and pepper.

Mix together the fish sauce, white wine, garlic, ginger and brown sugar in a saucepan and boil uncovered for about 5 minutes or until slightly thickened. Pour half of the sauce over the fish and cook in the oven for 20 minutes, or until the fish is cooked.

When the fish is cooked, transfer to a serving plate. Add the lime juice and chopped coriander to the remaining sauce and spoon over the hot salmon. Serve with noodles or rice. This dish is also delicious served at room temperature with salads.

Vietnamese Crab Salad with Rice Noodles

SERVES 8-10 AS A STARTER

This is a really gorgeous and substantial salad and I absolutely adore these sweet, salty Southeast Asian flavours.

FOR THE DRESSING:
100g (4oz) sugar, or more to taste
100ml (3½fl oz) fish sauce (nam pla)
100ml (3½fl oz) lemon or lime juice
   (juice of 2 lemons or about 3 limes)
2-3 small chillies, deseeded and
   sliced finely
4 garlic cloves, peeled and crushed
1 tbsp finely grated ginger

FOR THE SALAD:
250g (9oz) thin or medium rice noodles,
150g (5oz) peanuts
450g (1lb) cooked crab meat
1 large cucumber, chopped
300g (11oz) radishes, trimmed and
   sliced
4 tbsp roughly chopped fresh coriander
   leaves and stalks

To make the dressing, mix all the ingredients in a jug. Put the noodles in a bowl of boiling water for 5 minutes until they have softened. Drain and rinse. Meanwhile, toast the peanuts under a grill preheated to hot. Rub off the skins and roughly chop the nuts.

In a bowl, toss together the dressing with the noodles, then add the crabmeat, chopped cucumber and sliced radishes. Sprinkle over the toasted peanuts and the coriander and serve.

VARIATION

CRUNCHY VIETNAMESE SALAD WITH RICE NOODLES
Replace the crab with 100g (4oz) each of bean sprouts, cress and grated carrot.

Sicilian Pasta
SERVES 16-20 / VEGETARIAN

I first tasted this when a friend, James Folks, made it for a group of us, sitting outside on a hot summer's day drinking Prosecco, and it was absolutely divine. It is essential to make the marinade at least 2 hours in advance so that the vegetables almost soften and the flavours infuse.

FOR THE MARINADE:
4 large handfuls torn fresh basil
16 celery stalks, trimmed and finely chopped
16 garlic cloves, peeled and chopped
20 ripe tomatoes, chopped, or 40 cherry tomatoes, quartered
150ml (5fl oz) olive oil
600g (1lb 6oz) buffalo mozzarella, finely chopped
Sea salt and freshly ground black pepper

FOR THE PASTA:
1.8g (4lb) small pasta shapes, such as fusilli

Place all the marinade ingredients in a bowl and season to taste. Leave to sit for at least 2 hours or longer if possible; do not put it in the fridge.

Once the marinade is ready, cook the pasta in a large pot of salted water and drain. Immediately toss with the marinade ingredients – the mozzarella will just begin to melt. Tip into a large serving bowl and place in the middle of the table. This dish is best eaten just warm.

Pasta with Garlic, Anchovies and Breadcrumbs
SERVES 12-15

This very simple peasant pasta dish originates from Naples. It's quick and very delicious.

175g (6oz) breadcrumbs
250ml (9fl oz) olive oil
2 tsp dried chilli flakes
2 x 50g cans anchovy fillets, drained
   and roughly chopped

1 head garlic, separated into cloves,
   peeled and roughly chopped
2kg (4¼lb) spaghetti or tagliatelle
Juice of 1 lemon

Put the breadcrumbs in a dry frying pan and toss over a medium to high heat for a minute or two until they are golden, then set aside. Place the olive oil, chilli flakes, anchovies and garlic in the frying pan over a medium to high heat for about 30 seconds (just long enough for the garlic to lose its rawness). Take off the heat and throw in the breadcrumbs to stop it cooking any more, and set aside.

Cook the pasta in a pot of boiling salted water, until al dente, then drain, leaving a couple of tablespoons of the cooking water in with the pasta. Toss the pasta with the garlic, anchovies and breadcrumbs. Add lemon juice, to taste, toss and serve.

Peas with Leeks
SERVES 12-15

This is a great dish for lots of people as it is so quick to put together.

4 tbsp olive oil
3 leeks, finely sliced
6-8 rashers streaky bacon, finely
   chopped

900g (2lb) peas (can be frozen)
200ml (7fl oz) vegetable (or chicken)
   stock
Salt and freshly ground black pepper

Heat the oil, cook the leeks and streaky bacon over a high heat for 1-2 minutes. Add the peas, stock and seasoning. Bring up to the boil and simmer for 2-3 minutes or until the peas are cooked.

Garlic and Mustard Potatoes

SERVES 12-15 / VEGETARIAN

The flavour of the Dijon mustard goes beautifully with the garlic in this recipe and is the perfect potato dish for large parties.

25g (1oz) butter, softened, plus extra
    for greasing
1.8kg (4lb) peeled potatoes,
    sliced 5mm (¹/₄in) thick
Salt and freshly ground black pepper
¹/₂ tsp grated nutmeg

3-4 large garlic cloves, peeled
    and chopped
500ml (18fl oz) double cream
3 tbsp Dijon mustard
75g (3oz) Parmesan cheese,
    finely grated

Preheat the oven to 180°C (350°F), Gas mark 4. Using about 1 teaspoon of butter, butter an ovenproof gratin dish about 25cm (10in) square.

Divide the sliced potatoes into three piles. Place one-third of the potatoes on the base of the dish, season with a pinch of salt, pepper, nutmeg and half the chopped garlic, and dot with butter. Then add another layer of potatoes, season the same way, add the remaining garlic, then add a third layer of potatoes and season again.

Heat the cream in a saucepan, stir in the mustard, and pour over the potatoes; it should come just over halfway up the sides of the dish. Scatter with the finely grated Parmesan, cover with foil and place in the oven for 1¹/₄–1 ¹/₂ hours. Remove the foil after 30 minutes. The potatoes should be soft and the top should be golden, with the cream bubbling up the sides of the dish.

RACHEL'S HANDY TIP
If this needs to sit and keep warm in the oven for 30 minutes or so, cover it to prevent it drying out.

Rhubarb, Plum and Cardamom Crumble

SERVES 8-10 / VEGETARIAN

Another lovely recipe from my friend, Iona Murray. This rich, sweet and perfumed crumble is perfect for entertaining as it can be made in advance. It's also great for large parties as all you have to do is multiply the quantities by two or three.

FOR THE FILLING:
50g (2oz) butter
125g (4¹/₂oz) brown sugar
400g (14oz) rhubarb, washed and
   sliced into 1cm (¹/₂in) pieces
8-12 dark red plums, quartered,
   de-stoned and washed
1 tbsp runny honey
6-8 cardamom pods
1 cinnamon stick, broken in half

1 strip of lemon peel (using a potato
   peeler, peel one strip of the lemon
   zest from top to bottom)
FOR THE TOPPING:
300g (11oz) plain flour
75g (3oz) light brown sugar
2 tsp ground cinnamon
200g (7oz) butter, melted
Approx 1 tbsp sugar, for scattering
   on top

Preheat the oven to 180°C (350°F), Gas mark 4. Melt the butter for the filling in a saucepan and stir in the brown sugar. Then add the rhubarb and plums and a tablespoon of water. Mix, add the honey, cardamom, cinnamon and lemon peel, and cook for about 5 minutes, stirring regularly but gently.

Meanwhile, make the topping. Mix together the dry ingredients and add the melted butter, mixing quickly but lightly to form a crumbly texture. Set aside.

Remove the broken cinnamon stick and lemon peel from the fruit mixture and discard. Pour the mixture into a pie dish, then lightly scatter the crumble mixture on top. Do not press down or it will sink and form a mush. Scatter a tablespoon of sugar on top. Cook in the oven for 20-25 minutes or until the top is golden brown and the juices are bubbling up the side. Serve with softly whipped cream or vanilla ice cream.

VARIATION
The topping mixture is also delicious with a good handful of chopped toasted walnuts, hazelnuts or toasted almonds added.

Toffee, Apple and Almond Crumble

SERVES 12 / VEGETARIAN

This has to be one of my favourite desserts – it's completely divine. The toffee sauce keeps for months in the fridge – so handy for a quick sweet treat. It's great with ice cream and baked bananas too. I usually make twice this recipe, so that I have some left over to store in the fridge.

FOR THE TOFFEE SAUCE:
250g (9oz) golden syrup
250g (9oz) light brown sugar
100g (4oz) butter
200ml (7fl oz) single cream
2 tsp vanilla extract

FOR THE CRUMBLE:
350g (12oz) self-raising flour
Finely grated zest of 2 lemons
150g (5oz) butter, chopped or cubed

175g (6oz) light brown sugar
100g (4oz) ground almonds

FOR THE FILLING:
12 eating apples, peeled, quartered, cored and cut into 2cm (3/4in) chunks
50g (2oz) butter

TO SERVE:
Softly whipped cream, vanilla ice cream or Crème Anglaise (see page 237)

Preheat the oven to 180°C (350°F), Gas mark 4. Put all the ingredients for the toffee sauce into a saucepan over a medium heat and boil for 2–3 minutes, stirring regularly until smooth. Set aside.

Next, make the crumble topping. Place the flour and lemon zest in a bowl, rub in the 150g (5oz) of butter, leaving it a little rough and uneven. Stir in the sugar and ground almonds. Place the crumble in the fridge until you are ready to use it.

To make the filling, melt the 50g (2oz) of butter in a wide saucepan or frying pan, add the chopped apples and toss on the heat for a few minutes until the apples start to soften. Add 125ml (4fl oz) of the toffee sauce (about half; keep the rest for serving) and continue to simmer for a few minutes longer until the apples are just cooked.

Pour into two 1.25 litre (2¼ pint) pie dishes. Sprinkle the crumble over the top and place in the preheated oven for 20–30 minutes, or until the crumble is light golden and with toffee sauce juices bubbling up the sides. Serve warm with softly whipped cream and a jug of the remaining warm toffee sauce.

Lemon and Ginger Ice Cream

SERVES 12 / VEGETARIAN

This is such a delicious, light, one-step ice cream – and you don't need an ice-cream machine to make it. Leave out the ginger if you prefer.

400ml (14fl oz) cool Lemon Curd
  (see page 186)
600ml (20fl oz) natural yoghurt

600ml (20fl oz) crème fraîche
4 tbsp finely grated ginger

Fold together the lemon curd, yoghurt, crème fraîche and ginger and place in the freezer for a few hours until frozen.

VARIATION

LEMON AND GINGER PUDDING

This is a very quick and easy pudding to make. Make exactly as above, but do not freeze! Serve with Lemon Biscuits (see page 45).

9 Edible Gifts

There is something really lovely about giving and receiving gifts that have been made by hand, and all the better if you can eat them! They're a thoughtful alternative to the usual bottle of wine when going to someone's house for dinner, or as a thank-you present, or a Christmas gift. Jams, chutneys, preserves, biscuits, chocolates and fudge can all look so pretty when packaged nicely in lovely jars or bags tied up with ribbon. It's a friendly finishing touch to make your own labels, too – you can be as creative as you wish, and always be sure to include how best to store your gift, and how long it should keep.

Cucumber Pickle

MAKES ABOUT 4 X 400G (14OZ) JARS / VEGETARIAN

Mrs Allen started making this at Ballymaloe over 30 years ago and it is one of the handiest recipes to have in your repertoire. Not only is it good for burgers and all kinds of sandwiches, but it is wonderful with cold sliced meats and smoked fish, and it transforms a humble hard-boiled egg and a chunk of Cheddar into a meal. It is a true pickle, so even though it will lose its vibrant green colour, it will keep for weeks and weeks and weeks . . .

900g (2lb) unpeeled cucumber, thinly sliced
3 small onions, peeled and thinly sliced (optional)
350g (12oz) sugar
1 tbsp salt
225ml (7¹/₂fl oz) cider vinegar or white wine vinegar

Mix the cucumber and onion in a large bowl, add the sugar, salt and vinegar, and mix well to combine.

Make 1 hour ahead, if possible, and store in a jar or bowl in the fridge.

Preserved Roasted Peppers with Basil

MAKES 1 MEDIUM-SIZED JAR / VEGETARIAN

I adore having some good roast peppers in the fridge, ready to eat as part of a salad or a Market Plate (see page 230), to throw on top of some freshly cooked pasta, or in a sandwich, or whatever takes your fancy! These make a lovely gift potted into a pretty jar and topped up with olive oil.

4 peppers of various colours, left whole
Olive oil
Basil leaves

Preheat the oven to 230°C (450°F), Gas mark 8. Rub some olive oil over the peppers, then pop on a baking tray in the oven. Cook for about 40 minutes, or until very soft and a little blackened. Take them out of the oven, put into a bowl, cover with cling film and leave to cool.

Once the peppers are cool enough to handle, take them out of the bowl and use your fingers to peel off the skin and break the peppers into quarters. Do not rinse in water or you'll lose the flavour. Then, using a butter knife, scrape the seeds away, which should leave just the flesh. Layer in a sterilised jar (see below), adding basil leaves between the peppers, and fill up with olive oil.

RACHEL'S HANDY TIP
To sterilise jars, either put them through a cycle in your dishwasher, boil them for 5 minutes in a pan of water or place in an oven preheated to 150°C (300°F), Gas mark 2 for 10 minutes.

Tomato, Ginger and Chilli Jam

MAKES 2 X 400G (14OZ) JARS / VEGETARIAN

This is a gorgeous, sweet preserve and makes a great gift. It's really versatile – you can enjoy it with everything from cheese and sausages to roast chicken and cold meats.

50g (2oz) ginger, peeled and chopped
4 large garlic cloves, peeled
4 red chillies
25ml (1fl oz) fish sauce (nam pla)
750g (1¹/₂lb) tomatoes or cherry tomatoes, peeled (see below) and chopped
400g (14oz) sugar
150ml (5fl oz) red wine vinegar

Put the ginger, garlic, chillies and fish sauce into a blender and whiz to purée. Place the purée in a saucepan with the tomatoes, sugar and vinegar and bring to the boil. Stir and simmer, uncovered, for about 40 minutes, stirring regularly until thick and jammy. Pour into sterilised jars (see page 177), cover, and allow to cool.

RACHEL'S HANDY TIP

To peel tomatoes, cut a cross in the skin at the base of the tomato and cover with boiling water for 30 seconds. Remove carefully from the hot water and, holding the tomato in a clean tea towel, slip the skins off. If the skins do not come away easily, return to the hot water for another 30 seconds or so.

Spicy Tomato and Apple Chutney

MAKES ABOUT 4 X 400G (14OZ) JARS / VEGETARIAN

A beautiful little jar of this chutney makes a perfect gift. If possible, it is best left to mature for 1–2 weeks before eating.

1kg (2¹/₄lb) ripe tomatoes, peeled (see page 178) and chopped
2 onions, peeled and chopped
100g (4oz) raisins or sultanas
1 large cooking apple, peeled, cored and roughly chopped
300g (11oz) sugar
225ml (7¹/₂fl oz) white wine vinegar
2 tsp salt
¹/₂ tsp allspice
¹/₂ tsp ground ginger
¹/₂ tsp freshly ground black pepper
¹/₂ tsp cayenne pepper

Place all the ingredients in a stainless-steel saucepan and bring up to the boil, stirring. Continue to simmer over a low heat, uncovered, stirring regularly to make sure the bottom does not burn, for about 1 hour or until it is thick and pulpy. Pour into hot, sterilised jars (see page 177) and cover while the chutney is still hot.

Spiced Cranberry and Orange Relish

MAKES ABOUT 2 X 400G (14OZ) JARS / VEGETARIAN

A perfect Christmas gift! It will keep for weeks and weeks in a sterilised jar.

340g (11³/₄oz) cranberries, fresh or frozen
1 large pinch of ground cinnamon
1 large pinch of ground ginger
Finely grated zest and juice of 1 large orange
175g (6oz) light muscovado sugar

Place the cranberries (no need to defrost if they are frozen), cinnamon, ginger and the orange juice in a small saucepan and cook over a low heat, with the lid on, stirring regularly, for about 6–7 minutes, until the cranberries have burst. Take off the heat and stir in the grated orange zest and the sugar. Pour into sterilised jars (see page 177).

Onion Marmalade

MAKES 2-3 X 400G (14OZ) JARS / VEGETARIAN

This is a great preserve to give as a gift since it's so versatile. It goes beautifully with cheese, pâtés and cold meats and is perfect with lamb chops or in a steak sandwich too. The marmalade keeps well in a sterilised jar for months.

25g (1oz) butter
675g (1¹/₂lb) onions, peeled and thinly sliced
150g (5oz) caster sugar
1 tsp salt
1 tsp freshly ground black pepper
100ml (3¹/₂fl oz) sherry vinegar, or balsamic vinegar
250ml (8fl oz) full-bodied red wine (it doesn't matter if it has been sitting around for a few days)
2 tbsp crème de cassis (a blackcurrant liqueur)

Melt the butter in the saucepan and add the onions, sugar, salt and freshly ground pepper. Stir, then cover the saucepan and cook for 30 minutes over a gentle heat, stirring from time to time to prevent it from sticking to the bottom of the pan.

Remove the lid and add the vinegar, wine and crème de cassis and cook, uncovered, for another 30 minutes, stirring every now and then. It should be slightly thick by now. Pour into sterilised jars (see page 177) and cover while hot. It will thicken as it cools.

Summer Fruit Jam

MAKES 2 X 400G (14OZ) JARS / VEGETARIAN

People always think you are a genius if you make jam, but it really couldn't be easier. So, impress your friends with jammy gifts! If you are going to double this recipe, make sure you use a suitably large saucepan.

400g (14oz) sugar
400g (14oz) summer fruit – a mixture of strawberries, raspberries, redcurrants, blackcurrants, blackberries and blueberries (you can use frozen fruits out of season)
Juice of 1 lemon

Place the sugar in a heatproof bowl and pop in a moderate oven for 10 minutes to heat up. You can also place the jars into the oven to warm, to prevent them cracking when the hot jam is poured into them.

Put a saucer in the freezer for testing the jam later on.

Place the fruit (which can be frozen) in a saucepan with the lemon juice and heat up. Simmer for 3 minutes and crush most of the fruit with a potato masher. Add the warm sugar, stir to dissolve and bring up to the boil. Boil for 3–4 minutes over a high heat, stirring regularly.

To test to see if the jam is cooked, take a spoonful of the jam, place it on the frozen plate and allow it to sit for a few seconds. Then push your finger through the blob of jam – if the skin on top forms a wrinkle when pushed, it is cooked. Remove from the heat immediately and pour into sterilised jars (see page 177) or a bowl. A jam funnel is handy for this if you have one. Place the lids on top. The jam will set as it cools.

Orange, Lemon and Grapefruit Marmalade

MAKES ABOUT 2.5KG (5½LB) OR 7 JARS / VEGETARIAN

There are certain mornings when all I feel like having for breakfast is a nice cup of tea and toast with really good marmalade. This particular recipe is made in the same no-fuss way that my grandpa makes his.

2 oranges
2 grapefruit
2 lemons
Water to cover the fruit plus 1 litre (1¾ pints)
1.25kg (2½lb) sugar

Place all the fruit in a large saucepan, cover with water and boil for 1 hour until soft. The lemons may cook slightly faster, so check after 45 minutes and, if soft, remove them while the other fruit finishes cooking.

Take the pan off the heat, discard the cooking water and allow the fruit to cool for a few minutes. Cut the fruit into quarters, then use a spoon to scrape out the pulp, discarding the pips. Place the pulp in a food processor or liquidiser. If you don't want peel in your marmalade, add the peel to the liquidiser, too. Add 50ml (2fl oz) of the 1 litre (1¾ pints) of water and whiz until fine, then push through a sieve into a large saucepan. Add the remainder of the water. If you do want peel in your marmalade, cut the peel into fine slices (or more roughly if you want chunky marmalade) and add to the saucepan.

Bring up to the boil and boil rapidly, uncovered, for 10 minutes stirring every now and then. Add the sugar, stir until it dissolves, then boil over a high heat for 10 minutes.

Meanwhile, place a saucer in the fridge or freezer. When the marmalade has boiled for 10 minutes, place a blob of the marmalade on the chilled plate and then chill for 1 minute. Push your finger through the blob – if the skin on top forms a wrinkle when pushed, it is cooked. If it is not ready, continue boiling it until it is cooked – this may take up to another 10 minutes, depending on the pectin levels in the fruit. When it is cooked, remove from the heat and pour into sterilised jars (see page 177).

EDIBLE GIFTS

Rhubarb and Ginger Jam

MAKES 3–4 X 400G (14OZ) JARS / VEGETARIAN

I adore this jam – the subtle flavour of the ginger is great with the rhubarb, and it is very quick and easy to make.

900g (2lb) rhubarb, trimmed and sliced
900g (2lb) sugar
100ml (3½fl oz) water
3 tbsp finely grated ginger
75ml (2¾fl oz) lemon juice (juice of 2 large or 3 small lemons)

Place a saucer in the freezer. Place all the ingredients in a large saucepan over a medium heat and stir until the sugar dissolves. Turn up the heat, bring to the boil and boil rapidly for 15 minutes until cooked. To test to see if the jam is cooked, take the saucer from the freezer and pour a teaspoon of jam onto it. If a wrinkle forms on the top when you push your finger through the blob, the jam is cooked. Pour into sterilised jars (see page 177) and cover while still hot.

Lemon Curd

MAKES 1 X 400G (14OZ) JAR / VEGETARIAN

My aunt, Gay, gave me a lovely big jar full of the most delicious lemon curd for Christmas. It kept me going for weeks – spreading it on toast and drop scones, enjoying it with meringues and cream, and then finally making it into Lemon and Ginger Ice Cream (see page 171). Delicious!

2 eggs
1 egg yolk
100g (4oz) butter
175g (6oz) caster sugar
Finely grated zest and juice of 3 lemons

Beat the whole eggs and extra egg yolk together. Melt the butter in a saucepan over a very low heat. Add the caster sugar, grated zest and lemon juice and then the beaten eggs. Stir carefully over a very gentle heat until the mixture thickens. This may take about 10 minutes. If the heat is too high, the eggs will scramble.

When the mixture is thick enough to coat the back of a spoon and leave a clear mark when you push your finger through it, the curd is cooked ready.

Remove from the heat and pour into a sterilised jar (see page 177). Allow to cool, then place in the fridge for up to 2 weeks.

Dark Chocolate and Stem Ginger Biscuits

MAKES ABOUT 25 BISCUITS / VEGETARIAN

These are gorgeous, intensely flavoured little shortbread biscuits. Serve them with coffee or pop them into a bag and tie it up with a ribbon for a perfect present.

150g (5oz) plain flour
25g (1oz) rice flour (if you do not have rice flour, use 175g (6oz) plain flour, although the rice flour gives a lovely crumbly texture)
125g (4½oz) butter, softened
50g (2oz) light brown sugar
75g (3oz) crystallised ginger, finely chopped
75g (3oz) dark chocolate, chopped

Preheat the oven to 180°C (350°F), Gas mark 4. Place the flours, butter, sugar, and ginger in a food processor and whiz to combine – if you do not have a food processor, cream the butter and add in the other ingredients, mixing with a wooden spoon until they form a dough.

Roll the dough into balls the size of large cherry tomatoes and place on a baking tray (no need to grease or line). Using a wet fork, flatten each one slightly and cook in the preheated oven for 8–12 minutes, or until golden and firm. Remove carefully from the tray and cool on a wire rack.

Melt the chocolate gently in a warm oven, a microwave or in a bowl sitting over a saucepan of simmering water. Allow to cool slightly, then use a pastry brush or a butter knife to spread the cooked biscuits with the melted chocolate or dip the top of the biscuits into the melted chocolate and allow the chocolate to cool and set.

Chocolate Praline Truffles

MAKES ABOUT 40 / VEGETARIAN

These are rich and delicious after-dinner truffles that are well worth the effort of making. They are an impressive gift – who wouldn't love them? For these you need to make praline in which to roll the truffles, but you could always roll them in cocoa powder too. Praline is a lovely, indulgent staple to have on hand in the kitchen. Try sprinkling on top of the Toffee Sundae on page 31.

FOR THE PRALINE:
100g (4oz) caster sugar
100g (4oz) unpeeled almonds
FOR THE TRUFFLES:
150ml (5fl oz) single cream
225g (8oz) dark chocolate, chopped
1 tbsp whiskey or rum (optional)

First, make the praline. Put a sheet of greaseproof paper on a baking tray. Place the sugar and almonds in a saucepan or a non-stick frying pan over a medium heat. Allow the sugar to caramelise slowly; do not stir the mixture, but you can swirl the pan if it is browning unevenly. Cook until all the sugar has caramelised to a rich golden brown (the colour of whiskey). Pour the mixture onto the parchment paper and allow to cool completely; it will harden as it cools.

When it is cool, whiz it up in a food processor or place in a plastic bag and bash it with a rolling pin – you want it to become the texture of breadcrumbs. Store in a covered box or jar until you need it; it will keep for a month like this.

To make the truffles, place the cream in a saucepan and bring up to the boil, add the chocolate and the whiskey or rum, if using. Stir until the chocolate has melted and the mixture is smooth. Pour into a shallow pie dish and allow to cool and set. Then either roll into balls with wet hands (nice messy work!) or scoop up with a melon baller or teaspoon (keep dipping it into hot water for easier scooping). Drop into a bowl of praline and toss to cover the chocolates in the crunchy nutty coating. Serve with coffee after dinner.

Heavenly Fudge

MAKES ABOUT 60 PIECES / VEGETARIAN

I adore this fudge – it's sweet, a little bit crumbly and creamy, and oh so hard to resist. It only takes 20 minutes to make from start to finish. My sister, Simone, and I used to make fudge with Mum when we were little, and I still make it now.

1 x 375g tin of condensed milk
100g (4oz) butter
450g (1lb) caster or muscovado sugar

Place the condensed milk, butter and sugar in a saucepan. Stir and bring to the boil. Boil for about 10 minutes, stirring all the time (do not let it burn on the bottom) until it reaches the soft ball stage. To test for this, put a 1/2 teaspoon blob of the fudge into a bowl of cold water – it should be firm but malleable.

Remove from the heat and sit the bottom of the saucepan in a bowl of cold water that comes 2–3cm (3/4–1 1/4in) up the outside of the pan. Stir until the fudge cools down a bit – it will go from smooth, shiny and toffeeish, to looking matt in appearance, thick and grainy.

Scrape the contents of the saucepan into a square cake tin 20 x 20cm (8 x 8in) or to cover about two-thirds of a small Swiss roll tin or baking tray. The fudge should be 1–1.5cm (1/2–3/4in) thick. Let it cool, then cut into squares.

VARIATIONS

VANILLA FUDGE
Add 1 teaspoon of vanilla extract or essence to the ingredients at the start.

CHOCOLATE FUDGE
Add 75g (3oz) dark chocolate (with 70% cocoa solids if possible), chopped, to the fudge when you take it off the heat. Stir to melt the chocolate before placing in the bowl of cold water.

Sinful Butterscotch

My dentist would not approve of this, but I secretly love it! I'd be happy to receive this as a gift any time . . .

400g (14oz) sugar
200ml (7fl oz) water
100g (4oz) powdered glucose (available in chemists)
100g (4oz) butter
½ tsp salt

Line an 18 x 24cm (7 x 9½in) tin with greaseproof paper.

Combine the sugar, water and glucose in a saucepan. Stir over a low heat until the sugar is dissolved, bring to the boil and boil for about 15 minutes or until the mixture is light golden brown. Remove from the heat, immediately add the butter and salt, and stir until well blended. Pour into the prepared tin. Mark into squares while still hot. The butterscotch will harden as it cools. Break into pieces.

Vanilla Melting Moments

MAKES 20 / VEGETARIAN

These light, crumbly little biscuits literally do melt in your mouth and are absolutely divine.

FOR THE BISCUITS:
175g (6oz) self-raising flour
125g (4¹/₂oz) cornflour
50g (2oz) icing sugar
225g (8oz) butter, cut into pieces
1 tsp vanilla essence

FOR THE VANILLA BUTTER ICING:
50g (2oz) butter, softened
125g (4¹/₂oz) icing sugar, plus extra
  to dust
¹/₂ tsp vanilla essence

Preheat the oven to 160°C (325°F), Gas mark 3. Place the self-raising flour, cornflour and icing sugar in a food processor and whiz for a second. Add the butter and vanilla essence and mix until it comes together. Roll the mixture into small balls the size of a large marble, and place on a baking tray (no need to line) with a little space in between them. Dip a fork in cold water and press down on each one to flatten slightly and score.

Bake for 10–15 minutes until still very pale in colour but slightly firm. Remove carefully from the tray and allow to cool on a wire rack.

Meanwhile, make the butter icing. (I usually make this in the food processor bowl in which I have just mixed the biscuit dough.) Mix all the ingredients until they come together. Keep at room temperature to remain soft.

When the biscuits have cooled, place a butter knife in a cup of boiling water and use the warm, damp knife to spread the icing on one half (take care not to break the biscuits). Sandwich with another half. Dust with icing sugar.

RACHEL'S HANDY TIP
If you do not have a food processor, just rub the butter and vanilla into the dry ingredients in a bowl, then work with your hands until it comes together.

VARIATION
Make single biscuits and brush with approximately 75g (3oz) melted chocolate. Top with small pieces of chopped crystallised ginger.

10 Just Like Mum Used To Make

There are times when we all need something really comforting to eat; food that is warming, wholesome, old-fashioned and hearty, with a hint of nostalgia. Chunky soups, gooey cheese fondue, great bangers and mash, Mum's macaroni cheese, and a butterscotch pudding will all help to beat the blues on a cold winter's day. This kind of food should be fairly easy and straightforward to make, and will even transport well to the sofa for those times when all you want to do is curl up under a blanket.

Homemade Pork Sausages with Colcannon and Apple Sauce

SERVES 4 (MAKES ABOUT 12)

For me there is nothing quite so comforting as bangers and mash, and these homemade sausages are ever so tasty and easy to make. They have no casing so are made in a flash, and are great for children and adults, alike. Colcannon, which is a traditional Halloween-time Irish mashed potato with cabbage, is perfect winter food. I also love to serve this colcannon with Pork Chops with Caramelised Apples (see page 202).

FOR THE SAUSAGES:
450g (1lb) fatty minced pork
50g (2oz) breadcrumbs
1 egg, whisked
1 garlic clove, peeled and crushed
1 tbsp chopped fresh parsley
   or marjoram
3 tbsp olive or sunflower oil
Salt and freshly ground black pepper

FOR THE COLCANNON:
1.5kg (3lb) floury potatoes, scrubbed
100g (4oz) butter
500g (1lb 2oz) green cabbage, outer
   leaves removed
250ml (8fl oz) hot milk
2 tbsp chopped parsley
FOR THE APPLE SAUCE:
1 large cooking apple (350g (12oz)),
   peeled, cored and roughly chopped
1 tbsp water
25-50g (1-2oz) caster sugar

For the sausages, mix together all the ingredients, except the olive oil, and season with salt and pepper. Fry a tiny bit of the mixture in a pan with a little olive or sunflower oil to see if the seasoning is good.

Divide the mixture into 12 pieces and shape each one into a sausage. Place on a baking tray or plate and set aside until you want to cook them. (Chilling them for a day in the fridge is fine, or you can freeze them.)

To make the colcannon, cook the potatoes in boiling salted water until tender, draining three-quarters of the water after 5-10 minutes and continuing to cook over a low heat. Avoid stabbing the potatoes with a knife as this will make them break up. When cooked, drain all the remaining water, peel and mash with 50g

(2oz) of the butter while hot. I usually hold the potato on a fork and peel with a knife if they are hot.

Meanwhile, cook the cabbage. Cut the cabbage into quarters, then cut out the core. Slice the cabbage finely across the grain. Heat a saucepan, add the remaining butter, 2 tbsp water and the sliced cabbage. Toss over a medium heat for 5–7 minutes, until just cooked. Add to the potatoes, then add the hot milk and the parsley, keeping some of the milk back in case you do not need it all. Season to taste and beat until creamy and smooth, adding more milk if necessary. Serve piping hot with the remaining butter melting in the centre.

To make the apple sauce, place the apple in a small saucepan with the water. Put the lid on and cook over a gentle heat (stir every now and then) until the apple has broken down to a mush. Add sugar to taste. Serve warm or at room temperature.

To cook the sausages, heat a frying pan on a low to medium heat, add 2 tablespoons of olive or sunflower oil and gently fry the sausages for 12–15 minutes, until golden on all sides and cooked on the inside. Serve with the colcannon and apple sauce.

RACHEL'S HANDY TIP
To make breadcrumbs, just put a slice of slightly stale bread (with or without crusts) in a food processor or liquidiser and whiz.

VARIATIONS
The sausage mixture is also delicious shaped into little balls and used instead of the minced beef for Meatballs with Fresh Tomato Sauce (see page 82).

SPICY SAUSAGES WITH CORIANDER
Replace the herbs with 2 tablespoons chopped coriander, and add half a deseeded, chopped red chilli or a pinch of dried chilli flakes and serve with sweet chilli sauce or Tomato, Ginger and Chilli Jam (see page 178).

Baked Eggs and Soldiers

SERVES 6 / VEGETARIAN

These always remind me of when I was little, as we would often have them for an easy brunch or for a late supper.

6 eggs
6 tbsp single cream
Salt and freshly ground black pepper
15g (¹/₂oz) butter, divided into 6 knobs
Bread, for toasting

Preheat the oven to 160°C (325°F), Gas mark 3. Bring the kettle to the boil. Break each of the eggs into a ramekin dish, add 1 tablespoon of cream to each and then top with a knob of butter and a pinch of salt and pepper. Place the ramekins in a roasting tin, pour boiling water into the tray so that it comes about halfway up the sides of the dishes and place carefully into the preheated oven. Bake the eggs for 10 minutes or until the eggs are almost set.

Toast some bread until golden, butter it and cut into soldiers (fingers). Serve the baked eggs with hot buttered soldiers on the side.

RACHEL'S HANDY TIP
Try dipping cooked asparagus spears (see page 98) into baked eggs for a sophisticated supper treat.

Chunky Mediterranean Pasta Soup

SERVES 6

This is a gorgeously gutsy soup – definitely a meal in itself. It's the best thing (apart from a sunny beach holiday) for beating the winter blues!

2 tbsp olive oil
250g (9oz) chorizo, chopped into 1cm
  (1/2in) chunks
1 large onion, peeled and chopped
4 large garlic cloves, peeled and
  crushed
Salt and freshly ground black pepper
2 x 400g tins chopped tomatoes (or
  900g (2lb) fresh tomatoes, peeled
  (see page 178) and chopped)
900ml (1 1/2 pints) chicken stock

2 tbsp chopped herbs – I like to use
  a mixture of rosemary, thyme
  and parsley
Pinch of sugar (optional)
250g (9oz) dried pasta, such as orzo
  or fusilli
150g (5oz) shredded spinach or whole
  baby spinach leaves
TO SERVE:
Freshly grated Parmesan cheese
Small bowl of Classic Basil Pesto
  (see page 233)

Heat the olive oil in a large saucepan, add the chorizo and cook for 2 minutes. Add the chopped onion and garlic and season, then sweat over a gentle heat for 7–8 minutes, until soft. Add the tomatoes, stock and herbs, if necessary season again with salt, pepper and a good pinch of sugar, and simmer with the lid on for another 10 minutes or until the tomatoes are soft.

Add the pasta and continue to simmer for another 6–10 minutes, stirring regularly or until the pasta is cooked. When you are ready to serve, drop in the spinach and boil for just 1 minute or until the spinach is wilted. Taste for seasoning. To serve, ladle the chunky soup into large warm bowls and sprinkle with some finely grated Parmesan and a drizzle of pesto.

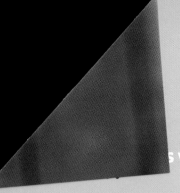

s with Caramelised Apples

I love this combination of flavours: pork and apples – and cooked like this, they make a perfect supper or big lunch.

2-3 small pork chops per person
Olive oil
Salt and freshly ground black pepper

FOR THE CARAMELISED APPLES:
25g (1oz) butter
3 eating apples, peeled, cored and
  cut into slices 5mm (¹/₄in) thick
25g (1oz) sugar
Juice of ¹/₂ lemon

Drizzle the chops with a little olive oil and black pepper. Leave to sit in the fridge until you need to cook them – all day is fine.

Preheat the oven to 190°C (375°F), Gas mark 5. Place a baking tray in the oven to heat up.

To prepare the caramelised apples, heat the butter in a frying pan. Add the apples and the sugar and toss on the heat for 4–5 minutes until cooked and golden. Squeeze in the lemon juice and keep warm.

Heat a frying pan until very hot, then cook the chops in batches, on both sides until golden. Sprinkle with salt, then pop them onto the hot baking tray in the oven and cook for another 5–10 minutes or until cooked through.

Serve the pork chops with the caramelised apples and some Garlic and Mustard Potatoes (see page 167) on the side.

Steak with Blue Cheese Butter and Walnut Salad

SERVES 2

This is serious comfort food and only takes 5 minutes to prepare, which is perfect for those times when you have just come home from work and need some real food fast!

FOR THE STEAKS:
2 sirloin or fillet steaks, excess fat removed
A drizzle of olive oil
Sea salt and freshly ground black pepper

FOR THE BLUE CHEESE BUTTER:
25g (1oz) blue cheese, rind removed
25g (1oz) butter
Freshly ground black pepper

FOR THE SALAD:
2 handfuls of a mixture of watercress, rocket and baby spinach
A drizzle of olive oil (about 1 tbsp)
A small squeeze of lemon juice (about 1/2–1 tsp)
Sea salt and freshly ground black pepper
25g (1oz) chopped walnuts, tossed over the heat in a dry pan until golden

Place the pan for the steaks on the heat. Drizzle the steaks with olive oil and sprinkle with black pepper, then allow to sit while the pan heats up.

To make the blue cheese butter, mash together the blue cheese and the butter in a bowl. Add some black pepper, then form into a log and wrap in cling film. Pop in the fridge to cool, or the freezer if you just have a few minutes.

When the pan is very hot, sprinkle the steaks with sea salt and place in the pan. Cook until one side turns a deep golden colour and is seared, then turn over and cook until they are how you like them, 1–2 minutes for rare, about 4 minutes for medium or 8–10 minutes on a lower heat (so they don't burn) for well done. The cooking times will vary depending on the thickness of the steaks and the heat of the pan. When the steaks are cooked, take them off the heat and allow to rest while you toss the salad leaves in the olive oil, lemon juice, sea salt and pepper. Put the steaks on warm plates and top with slices of blue cheese butter. Serve with the dressed leaves sprinkled with chopped walnuts.

Macaroni Cheese

SERVES 6-8 / VEGETARIAN

Macaroni cheese must be the ultimate cure-all for adults and children alike. You can also add small pieces of cooked ham or bacon to the sauce. Macaroni cheese can be made in advance and then reheated when you are ready to serve.

75g (3oz) butter
1 onion, peeled and chopped
75g (3oz) plain flour
900ml (1½ pints) boiling milk
1-2 tsp Dijon mustard
225g (8oz) cheese (Cheddar, or, even better, half Cheddar and half
  Gruyère), grated
Salt and freshly ground black pepper
300g (11oz) macaroni pasta

Melt the butter in a saucepan, add the chopped onions and cook gently until soft. Stir in the flour and cook for a minute, then gradually add the milk, whisking all the time, and the mustard. Whisk in three-quarters of the cheese and allow to melt into the sauce, then season to taste with salt and pepper.

Cook the pasta in a large pot of boiling water with a teaspoon of salt, until just soft. Drain, then toss into the cheese sauce and transfer into a gratin dish, about 25cm (10in) square. Sprinkle with the remaining cheese and pop under a hot grill for a few minutes to brown the cheese on top, or if you wish, put this aside for later. To reheat, put the dish into an oven preheated to 200°C (400°F), Gas mark 6 for about 25 minutes, or until golden and bubbling.

Oven-baked Risotto with Mushrooms and Thyme

SERVES 4-6 / VEGETARIAN

Risotto goes straight to the heart of both children and adults. You can always leave out the mushrooms if you wish.

Scant 25g (1oz) dried mushrooms, such as porcini or a mixture of types
400ml (14fl oz) boiling water
2 tbsp olive oil
1 small onion, peeled and chopped
2 garlic cloves, peeled and crushed
Salt and freshly ground black pepper

350g (12oz) risotto rice, such as carnaroli or arborio
1 tsp thyme leaves, chopped
750ml (1¼ pints) hot vegetable (or chicken) stock
125ml (4fl oz) white wine
75g (3oz) Parmesan cheese, grated
1 tsp fresh thyme leaves

Preheat the oven to 180°C (350°F), Gas mark 4. Place the dried mushrooms in a bowl, add the boiling water and leave to soak for 10 minutes. Meanwhile, heat the olive oil in a medium ovenproof saucepan or casserole and cook the onion and garlic for a few minutes until soft and a little golden. Season with salt and pepper.

Drain and chop the mushrooms, and reserve the liquid. Add the mushrooms to the garlic and onions with the rice, chopped thyme and the sieved, drained mushroom-soaking liquid. Pour in the stock and wine, bring to the boil and season to taste. Cover with the lid and place in the preheated oven and cook for 15–20 minutes, or until the rice is just cooked and all the liquid has been absorbed. Stir in 50g (2oz) of the grated Parmesan and check the seasoning. To serve, sprinkle with the remaining Parmesan and thyme leaves.

RACHEL'S HANDY TIP
The alcohol in the wine burns off during the cooking of the risotto and the flavour is lovely, but if you do not want to use it, just replace it with extra stock.

Fondue Savoyard

SERVES 4-6 / VEGETARIAN

There are not many cold-weather suppers (or lunches on the ski slopes) better than this: pieces of bread dipped into molten cheese. You can either invest in a fondue set (fun and handy for large numbers), or you can make a fondue for two in a saucepan on a very low flame on the hob and eat it right beside the cooker or even a camping stove! You need a good white bread for dipping, and, as with the Raclette (see page 145), charcuterie and gherkins are nice to have on the side; but not essential. Don't forget that if your piece of bread falls off your fork you have to kiss the person to your left, so it is important to position yourself very carefully!

1 garlic clove, peeled and cut in half
300ml (10fl oz) light dry white wine
650g (1lb 7oz) Gruyère, Beaufort or
   Raclette cheese, or a mixture of all
   three, grated

Pinch of grated nutmeg
Freshly ground black pepper
25ml (1fl oz) kirsch (optional)
1 loaf of good white or sourdough
   bread, cut into 2cm (3/4in) cubes

Rub the inside of a medium-sized saucepan with the garlic, then discard the garlic. Add the wine to the pan and bring to the boil over a high heat (this will get rid of the alcohol in the wine). Reduce the heat to medium and gradually add the cheese, stirring constantly with a wooden spoon to melt it – do not allow it to boil. Continue to cook for a few more minutes, add the nutmeg, pepper and kirsch and transfer to a fondue pot (if using).

Serve the cubed bread in a basket on the table. Using fondue forks (or just plain forks), dip pieces of bread into the cheese. Keep a wooden spoon in the fondue and stir it every now and then. Place it back on the heat for a few seconds if it cools down too much.

Bill Granger's Banana Butterscotch Pudding

SERVES 4-6 / VEGETARIAN

I absolutely adore this pudding from Bill's book, *Simply Bill*. He made this when I appeared with him on *Great Food Live*, and as soon as I tasted it I was hooked. I have adapted the recipe slightly to fit the pie dish that I have. To make this for 12 people, double this recipe and cook in a 25cm (10in) square gratin dish for 55 minutes.

FOR THE PUDDING:
125g (4¹/₂oz) plain flour
3 level tsp baking powder
125g (4¹/₄oz) caster sugar
1 egg, beaten
1 banana, mashed
250ml (8fl oz) milk
1 tsp vanilla extract
85g (3¹/₄oz) butter, melted

FOR THE TOPPING:
100g (4oz) soft brown sugar
2 tbsp golden syrup
150ml (5fl oz) boiling water
TO SERVE:
Softly whipped cream or vanilla
    ice cream

Preheat the oven 180°C (350°F), Gas mark 4. Sift the flour and baking powder into a bowl. Add the caster sugar. Mix together the beaten egg, the mashed banana, milk, vanilla extract and melted butter. Pour into the dry ingredients and stir to mix until combined. Pour this wet dough into a 1.25 litre (2¹/₄ pint) pie dish and place the dish on a baking tray.

To make the topping, put the brown sugar, golden syrup and boiling water into a saucepan. Bring to the boil and then drizzle it all over the pudding. Bake in the preheated oven for 30-40 minutes, or until it feels slightly firm in the centre. Serve with vanilla ice cream or softly whipped cream. If you're not going to serve the pudding immediately, keep it somewhere warm until you are ready – it sits quite happily.

Chocolate Comfort in a Cup

SERVES 2 / VEGETARIAN

Also known as hot chocolate! It always takes me right back to when I was little and on holiday staying with my grandparents in Canada. They always made us hot chocolate with lots of mini marshmallows on top, which slowly melt as you drink it. Heaven!

400ml (14fl oz) milk
150g (5oz) milk chocolate

2 tsp cocoa
2 tbsp mini marshmallows

Put the milk, chocolate and cocoa into a saucepan. Stirring all the time, warm over a low heat until the chocolate has melted, the cocoa dissolved and the mixture has almost come to the boil. Take off the heat and pour into two cups. Sprinkle with mini marshmallows and serve.

Vin Chaud

SERVES 4-6 / VEGETARIAN

Each café and restaurant on the slopes in the Alps has their own secret recipe for vin chaud – hot wine with spices. Sipping this at home on a wintry, drizzly night in Ireland makes me dream of skiing holidays.

1 bottle dry, fruity red wine
50ml (2fl oz) crème de cassis or brandy
100g (4oz) caster sugar
Finely grated zest of ¹/₂ lemon and
    ¹/₂ orange

Good pinch of grated nutmeg
2 cinnamon sticks
6 whole cardamom pods
6 cloves
Orange slices, to serve

Place all the ingredients in a saucepan and very gently simmer (do not boil) for about 5–10 minutes to let the flavours of the spices infuse. Serve in warmed glasses, with a slice of orange in each one.

11 A Few More Faves

Here's another handful of simple
and tasty recipes to suit any occasion.
Most of the ingredients are easy to
grab on your way home from work,
or may already be sitting in your fridge
or cupboard ready for you to conjure
up a quick meal or snack.

The Weekend Breakfast Bap
with Quick Hollandaise Sauce
SERVES 4

This is a great way to start a lazy Sunday when it's raining outside and you crave some comfort food!

4 flat mushrooms
15g (¹/₂oz) butter, cut into 4 pieces
Salt and freshly ground black pepper
2 tsp chopped fresh parsley
12 small rashers of good-quality
    streaky bacon
4 baps (flattish yeast rolls, like burger
    buns)

EASY HOLLANDAISE SAUCE
1 large egg yolk
50g (2oz) butter, cut into cubes
Splash of lemon juice

Preheat the oven to 200°C (400°F), Gas mark 6.

Remove the stalks from the mushrooms and discard. Place the mushrooms, stalk side up, on a baking tray, place the butter in the centre of each mushroom, season with salt and pepper and sprinkle with the chopped parsley. Place in the oven and cook for 10 minutes.

While the mushrooms are cooking, grill the streaky bacon until crisp and golden. Keep warm.

To make the Hollandaise sauce, place the egg yolk in a heatproof glass bowl. Heat the butter in a saucepan until foaming, then pour gradually onto the yolk, whisking all the time. Add the lemon juice, then pour into a heatproof measuring jug. Half-fill a saucepan with hot water from the kettle and place the jug of hollandaise in the saucepan to keep warm. When the water cools, place the saucepan on a gentle heat but do not let the water boil for too long or the sauce will scramble. Keep the sauce warm while you are waiting to serve.

Split the baps in half and toast lightly. To assemble, place the bottom of each bap on a warm plate and place a warm cooked mushroom on top, then add 3 rashers of streaky bacon before drizzling with warm hollandaise sauce. Top with the remaining bap half and serve.

Prawns with Lemon Mayonnaise

SERVES 4

One of the best ways to enjoy freshly cooked prawns is to serve them with a homemade mayonnaise and some crusty bread.

FOR THE LEMON MAYONNAISE:
2 egg yolks
A pinch of salt
½ tsp Dijon mustard
1 tbsp lemon juice
225ml (8fl oz) oil (I like to use 200ml
    sunflower oil and 25ml olive oil)
1-2 tsp chopped tarragon and chives

TO SERVE:
Crusty white or brown bread

FOR THE PRAWNS:
About 28 large prawns
Dash olive oil

First make the lemon mayonnaise. Put the egg yolks in a non-metallic bowl, add the salt, mustard and lemon juice and mix well.

Add the oil gradually, just a drop at a time, whisking continuously.

You should start to see the mixture thickening, keep adding the oil as you whisk.

Add the chopped herbs, stir and season to taste. Refrigerate until ready to serve.

To cook the prawns, pre-heat the olive oil in a large frying pan on a high heat.

Add the prawns and toss them in the olive oil for 2-3 minutes until cooked through to the centre. When they are cooked they will be firm and white. Very large ones may take 30 seconds to 1 minute more.

Serve with the mayonnaise drizzled on top and the fresh bread on the side.

heat Loaf with Oats and Seeds

I love this healthy, nutty brown bread, it keeps very nice and fresh for a couple of days, then after that it's delicious toasted.

200g (7oz) wholewheat flour
75g (3oz) plain flour
75g (3oz) mixture of sesame, poppy and sunflower
    seeds, plus 2 tbsp for scattering over the top
50g (2oz) oats
25g (1oz) bran
1 tsp salt
350-400ml (12-14fl oz) warm water
1 tbsp honey (or treacle or molasses)
15g (1/2oz) fresh yeast or 1 x 7g (1/4oz) sachet dried yeast
1 tbsp sunflower oil

Preheat the oven to 200°C (400°F), Gas mark 6. Line or grease a 900g (2lb) loaf tin.

In a large bowl, mix the flours, seeds (except those reserved for scattering), oats, bran and salt. Place 100ml (3½fl oz) of the water in a measuring jug, stir in the honey, then sprinkle in the yeast. Leave for about 5 minutes until frothy (fresh yeast will be more frothy than dried yeast). Add all of the remaining water except for 60ml (2fl oz) and sunflower oil and mix.

Pour into the dry ingredients and mix well. The mixture should be wet and sloppy, but if it's not, add the remaining 60ml (2fl oz) of warm water. Turn into the loaf tin and sprinkle over the reserved seeds. Cover with a light tea towel or napkin and leave in a warm place until risen to the top of the tin. Remove the tea towel and bake in the oven for 1 hour.

When you think it's cooked, remove the bread from the tin and check to see if it is – if it sounds hollow when you tap it on the bottom of the loaf then it's cooked. If it's not cooked, put it back in the oven without the tin for another 5–10 minutes. Cool on a wire rack.

Chicken and Avocado Salad with Anchovy Mayonnaise

SERVES 4-6

I love this salad, the dressing is very similar to a Caesar Salad dressing and the anchovies add a tasty kick. This is a great main course for lunch or for summer alfresco dining.

FOR THE SALAD:

1 head of cos (romaine) lettuce
1 large or 2 small chicken breasts
A drizzle of olive oil
Sea salt and pepper
3 slices of white bread, crusts removed,
    cut into 2cm cubes
3 tbsp olive oil

TO SERVE:

1 avocado, peeled, stone removed,
    and sliced or chopped
25g (1 oz) coarsely grated Parmesan cheese

FOR THE DRESSING:

1 small egg yolk
8 anchovies, finely chopped
1 small clove of crushed
    or finely grated garlic
$1/4$ tsp English mustard
1 tbsp lemon juice
1 tsp Worcestershire sauce
$1/2$ - 1 tsp Tabasco sauce
25ml (1fl oz) olive oil
50ml (13/4fl oz) sunflower oil
2 tbsp water

Preheat the oven to 220°C (425°F) Gas Mark 7. Wash the lettuce and place in a bowl in the fridge until ready for use (cover with a damp piece of kitchen paper).

Drizzle the chicken with a little olive oil, and sprinkle with salt and pepper. Place on a baking tray and cook in the oven for 15–20 minutes, until cooked through.

While the chicken is cooking toss the cubes of bread with the 3 tbsp olive oil, and place in a single layer on an ovenproof plate next to the chicken, cook for 4 or 5 minutes until golden, then place the croûtons on kitchen paper to drain.

Next, make the dressing. Place all the ingredients except the oils and water in a bowl or small food processor. Whisk everything together, then add the olive and sunflower oils very slowly whisking all the time, until all the oil is added and the mixture is emulsified. Whisk in the water to thin it slightly. Season to taste.

When the chicken has cooled slightly, cut it into slices at an angle. Take the lettuce leaves out of the fridge, add the croûtons, chicken and avocado. Add enough dressing to coat the leaves lightly, sprinkle with the grated parmesan cheese, and serve.

Chicken Casserole with Chorizo, Tomatoes and Beans
SERVES 6-8

This warming casserole is perfect for the winter weather, and the healthy ingredients are a welcome contrast to all that heavy seasonal food!

1 large chicken, approximately 2.5kg (5¹/₂lb) – 3.3kg (7¹/₄lb)
   cut into pieces
2tb sp olive oil
125g (5oz) chorizo, cut into 8mm (3/8 in) slices
2 x 400g tins of chopped tomatoes
5 cloves of garlic, peeled and left whole
Salt, freshly ground black pepper and sugar
200g (7oz) dried haricot beans (or 2 x 400g tins of pre-cooked
   beans, drained)
Squeeze of lemon juice

If using dried beans, soak them in cold water for at least 6 hours. Then drain, cover with fresh cold water and cook. Place the drained beans in a saucepan and cover generously with cold water. Don't add any salt as this will toughen the skins. Bring to the boil and simmer for 30–45 minutes. Remember to keep testing them – when they are cooked they will be soft all the way through.

Brown the chicken in a flameproof casserole with the 2tb sp of olive oil. Add the slices of chorizo, tomatoes and garlic. Season with salt, pepper and 1 or 2 good pinches of sugar. Bring up to the boil, cover with a lid and cook (on top of hob or in an oven pre-heated to 180°C/350°F), Gas mark 4, for 30 minutes until the chicken is cooked.

Remove from the oven and add the drained beans (freshly cooked or tinned) and simmer for another 5 minutes. Season to taste, adding a squeeze of lemon juice if necessary. Serve with orzo (a type of barley), boiled rice or pilaff rice.

Beef and Rocket Wraps
SERVES 4

I often find myself craving one of these wraps. Great for picnics and barbeques!

350g (12oz) sirloin of beef,
   cut into strips 5mm (¼in) thick
Freshly ground black pepper
4 tbsp mayonnaise
1 generous tbsp chopped fresh tarragon
1 level tbsp Dijon mustard
A drizzle of olive oil
4 wheat flour tortillas
4 handfuls of rocket
4 tbsp finely grated Parmesan cheese
2 tbsp chopped black olives

Heat up a frying pan. While the pan is heating, sprinkle the beef with pepper and mix the mayonnaise with the chopped tarragon and the Dijon mustard.

Place the beef on the hot pan with a drizzle of olive oil and cook on both sides for a minute or two, slightly longer if you want it well cooked.

When the beef is cooked, turn off the heat and allow it to sit and rest for a minute.

Spread 1 tbsp tarragon mayonnaise on each torilla, then scatter with the rocket. Arrange the beef over the rocket and sprinkle with the Parmesan and olives.
Roll up and eat straight away.

Carrageen Moss Pudding with Poached Rhubarb

SERVES 4-6

This delicate, summery dessert is a Ballymaloe favourite. Serve with poached fruit such as rhubarb, apricots or gooseberries.

7g (¹/₄oz or 1 fistful carrageen - don't use too much
   or it will be too set and strong in flavour)
900ml (1¹/₂ pints) milk
50g (2oz) caster sugar
1 egg, separated
1 tsp vanilla extract

FOR THE POACHED RHUBARB
100ml (3¹/₂fl oz) water
225g (8oz) sugar
450g (1lb) rhubarb, cut into 2cm (3/4in) chunks
   (discard the base and top of the stalk

Soak the carrageen in tepid water for 10 minutes, then drain and place in a saucepan with the milk. Bring to the boil, then simmer over a very low heat for 20 minutes.

Pour the milk through a sieve into a bowl. The carrageen will now be swollen and resembling a jellyfish, so push the jelly through the sieve into the milk. Discard the carrageen. Whisk in the sugar, egg yolk and vanilla extract.

Whisk the egg white until stiff and gently stir it into the milk – it will rise to give the pudding a light, fluffy top. Pour into one large bowl or into individual cups or glasses. Cover and place in the fridge for 1-2 hours to set.

To poach the rhubarb, place the water and sugar in a saucepan, stir and bring to the boil. Add the rhubarb, cover, bring to the boil and simmer for exactly 1 minute. Turn off the heat and allow the rhubarb to continue cooking in the covered saucepan until almost cool. Transfer to a bowl to finish cooling.

Serve the rhubarb on top of or with the carrageen moss pudding.

Irish Apple Cake

SERVES 4-6

This wonderful cake is a delicious way to make the most of the autumn apples. My husband's grandmother, Myrtle Allen, has been making this for many years, and it is still made today at Ballymaloe.

225g (8oz) plain white flour
1/2 tsp baking powder
100g (4oz) butter
100g (4oz) sugar, plus 2 tbsp
1 egg, beaten
100ml (31/2fl oz) milk (approximately)
1 large cooking apple, about 300g (11oz) in weight
1 level tsp cinnamon

TO SERVE
Softly whipped cream

Preheat the oven to 180°C (350°F), Gas Mark 4.

Mix the flour with the baking powder. Rub in the butter with your fingertips until the texture resembles breadcrumbs. Add the sugar, beaten egg and enough milk to form a soft dough. Pat out one half of the dough onto a greased 25cm (10in) ovenproof plate (don't worry – it is supposed to be very wet).

Peel, core and chop up the apple into 2cm (3/4in) squared pieces, place on the dough and sprinkle with 1 tbsp sugar and the tsp of cinnamon. Gently spoon out the remaining dough on top of the apples to cover them completely. Sprinkle with the remaining sugar and cut a slit through the middle of the lid.

Bake for 40–50 minutes until golden and crunchy on the outside (the apples should be soft on the inside). Serve with softly whipped cream.

RACHEL'S HANDY TIP:
If the butter is cold (i.e. taken from the fridge), grate it into the flour and it will rub in within a couple of seconds.

Useful Extras

The recipes in this section are either classic kitchen staples that form the backbone of so many wonderful dishes, or are timeless accompaniments. I use all of them on a regular basis, and many are called for in the recipes throughout this book.

Market Plate

Ironically enough (as it involves hardly any actual cooking) this is one of my favourite meals. We are very fortunate now to have so many excellent farmers' markets close to us, with stallholders selling everything from fabulous local potatoes to the most delicious locally made salamis and cheeses. What a delight it is to be able to go to a market and come back laden down with a basketful of the most amazing food, ready to go straight on the table – now that's what I call convenience food!

Of course, not all markets will have everything I list on this page, nor might you want it all, but this is a guide to inspire more than to tell you what to do. You will know what combinations you want on your table. And you can serve as many or as few of these selections as you like. It makes a great meal for a casual dinner party or for a lunch (alfresco or not), and it also travels incredibly well to make a delicious picnic.

BREAD: **white, wholemeal, baguette, sourdough, foccacia – many farmers' markets sell wonderful artisan breads baked that morning**

SELECTION OF CHARCUTERIE: **salamis (venison, pork and garlic, chorizo, etc.), cured meats such as Parma and Serrano ham**

CHEESE: **try your local and imported cheeses, aiming for a good selection, such as a goats' cheese, a Brie, a hard cheese, a semi-soft, a blue and a local Cheddar**

SMOKED FISH: **try smoked salmon, even hot-smoked salmon, or smoked mackerel, eel, mussels or trout**

SMOKED MEAT: **smoked chicken and duck are really delicious**

Buy, or make, some Cucumber Pickle (see page 174) – this is great with smoked fish, charcuterie and cheese. Pick up or make some Mayonnaise (see page 232), also delicious with smoked fish. Make your own or buy some chutneys and relishes, like Tomato, Ginger and Chilli Jam (see page 178), Spicy Tomato and Apple Chutney (see page 179) or Onion Marmalade (see page 181). Buy or make Preserved Roast Red and Yellow Peppers (see page 177), Olive Paste (see page 102) and Classic Basil Pesto (see page 233).

Always have to hand a gorgeous bottle of olive oil to drizzle over your bread (or truffle oil for a special treat), some dolmades (stuffed vine leaves), capers and anchovies.

Roux
VEGETARIAN

Roux is a basic and simple sauce thickener made with equal quantities of butter and flour so if you find yourself using quite a lot, you can easily increase the quantities. It is handy to have in the fridge and it keeps for 2–3 weeks.

100g (4oz) butter   **100g (4oz) plain flour**

Heat a saucepan over a medium heat and melt the butter, then add the flour, continuing to stir on the heat. Allow it to cook for 2 minutes. Pour into a bowl and use straight away, or allow to cool and put in the fridge.

Stock

Making stock is incredibly easy – it's just a state of mind! It takes only 5 minutes to throw everything into the pot, let it cook for a while and then you are halfway to creating a really wholesome, nutritious soup. Stock keeps in the fridge for 2–3 days and freezes very well. To defrost, reheat in a saucepan.

Chicken carcass, raw or cooked   **1 celery stick**
  (optional)   **1 small bay leaf**
1–2 carrots   **1 sprig of parsley**
1 onion or leek   **1 sprig of thyme**

Put all the ingredients into a large saucepan and then fill up the pot with cold water, and bring to the boil. Turn down the heat and let it simmer for 1–2 hours. Season to taste and then strain the stock and discard the bits. Skim the fat off the stock as it cools.

Mayonnaise

MAKES 300ML (10FL OZ) / VEGETARIAN

Homemade mayonnaise is so delicious. It can bring the simplest sandwich or salad to life and is great to have on hand for those last-minute snacks. Keep it covered in the fridge and it will keep for at least a week.

2 egg yolks
Pinch of salt
1 tsp Dijon mustard
2 tsp white wine vinegar

225ml (8fl oz) oil – I like to use 200ml (7fl oz) sunflower oil and 25ml (1fl oz) olive oil
A good pinch of salt

Put the egg yolks into a glass mixing bowl, add the salt, mustard and vinegar. Whisk together. Very gradually, add all the oil drop by drop, whisking all the time (I often use an electric hand blender). When you have whisked in all the oil, it should look thick and creamy. Add salt to taste.

VARIATION

Basic mayonnaise works incredibly well with many other flavours. Try varying your recipe by adding ground spices, chopped herbs or olives, or even chopped sun-dried tomatoes for unique flavours.

Mint Sauce

MAKES 60ML (2FL OZ) / VEGETARIAN

The classic sauce to serve with good old Roast Lamb (see page 102). It's made in minutes.

3 tbsp chopped fresh mint
25g (1oz) caster or light brown sugar
50ml (2fl oz) boiling water

1 tbsp lemon juice or white wine vinegar

Place the mint and sugar in a bowl and add the boiling water. Stir until the sugar is dissolved. Add the lemon juice or vinegar and let it cool for about 10 minutes before serving.

Classic Basil Pesto

MAKES 1 X 400G (14OZ) JAR / VEGETARIAN

Serve this versatile pesto with pasta, roasted or chargrilled vegetables, barbecued or grilled meats, as part of a salad, or on a simple crostini or bruschetta with roasted peppers and cheese. Try making variations by replacing the basil with parsley or rocket or wild garlic leaves – the possibilities are endless! It freezes very well, too.

50g (2oz) basil leaves
25g (1oz) Parmesan cheese,
    freshly grated
25g (1oz) pine kernels

1 garlic clove, peeled and crushed
75ml (23/4fl oz) olive oil
Salt

Put all the ingredients except the olive oil and salt into a food processor and whiz up. Add the oil and a pinch of salt and taste. Pour into a sterilised jar (see page 177), cover with a 1cm (1/2in) layer of oil and store in the fridge.

Redcurrant Jelly

MAKES 2 X 400G (14OZ) JARS / VEGETARIAN

This simple redcurrant jelly is another fine addition to Roast Lamb (see page 102).

500g (1lb 2oz) fresh or frozen
    redcurrants, destalked

500g (1lb 2oz) sugar

Put the redcurrants and sugar into a saucepan on a medium heat and stir until the sugar dissolves and the mixture begins to boil. Turn up the heat and boil rapidly for 6 minutes, stirring occasionally to prevent it sticking. Spoon off any froth that accumulates on top and pour the mixture into a sieve (not aluminium) and allow it to drip through into a bowl. Do not be tempted to push it through or the jelly will become cloudy. If you want to keep this for later use, pour the jelly into clean, sterilised jam jars (see page 177) immediately. After it has cooled and set a little, it will be ready to eat, else store it in the fridge. It will keep for months.

Rice

SERVES 6-8 / VEGETARIAN

A big bowl of rice is just what you need to serve with a big stew or curry, and is so convenient to cook for large numbers of people.

PLAIN BOILED RICE

400g (1lb) white rice, such as Basmati
1 tsp salt

15g (1/2oz) butter (optional)

Preheat the oven to 140°C (275°F), Gas mark 1. Bring a large saucepan of water to the boil. Add the rice and salt, give it a stir, cover and boil rapidly for 4–5 minutes, or until the rice is nearly cooked but still has a tiny bite. Strain the rice and place in a serving dish. Stir in the butter, if using, cover and put in the oven for at least 15 minutes. If you want to get the rice into the oven 30 minutes before you eat, just preheat it to 100°C (200°F), the lowest gas.

When ready to eat, fluff up the rice and serve. Sometimes I add whole spices to the water, such as a small cinnamon stick or two or three star anise and a few green cardamom pods, and serve them on top of of the rice.

PILAFF RICE

25g (1oz) butter
1 small onion, peeled and chopped
300g (11oz) Basmati rice

750ml (1¼ pints) vegetable
  (or chicken) stock
Salt and freshly ground black pepper

Melt the butter in a saucepan large enough to contain all the rice. Add the chopped onion, put on the lid and cook over a low heat for about 10 minutes until the onion is soft. Add the rice and stir on the heat for about 2 minutes. Add the stock and some salt and pepper, bring to the boil, then turn the heat right down to minimum and simmer on top of the stove for about 10 minutes until the rice is just cooked and all the liquid absorbed. Alternatively, cook in an oven at 160°C (325°F), Gas mark 3. Cover and keep warm if you need to.

THAI RICE

400g (14oz) Thai fragrant rice   **Approximately 400ml (14fl oz) water**

Place the rice and water in a medium-sized saucepan. There are a few ways of gauging the correct amount of water to put in, as it depends on the size of saucepan used. The method I use is to put my index finger into the water, pointing down, and just touching the rice. The water should come up to the first knuckle.

Bring to the boil, stir once, then cover with a lid (or a heatproof glass plate is quite handy as you can see inside). Turn the heat down to the lowest possible level. Continue to cook for 11–15 minutes, then have a quick look. The rice should be cooked and have absorbed all the liquid. Remove from the heat, keep covered and allow to sit for 5 minutes before serving. The rice will stay warm for a while like this if necessary.

Savoury Shortcrust Pastry

MAKES 450G (1LB) PASTRY / VEGETARIAN

This makes enough to line one 28cm (11in) square or one 25cm (10in) square tin (with a little left over), or two 20cm (8in) square tins, (it is best if they have removable bases). Uncooked pastry freezes perfectly, so it is handy to have some in the freezer. It will also keep in the fridge for a couple of days.

250g (9oz) plain flour $^1/_2$–1 egg, beaten
125g (4$^1/_2$oz) butter, diced and softened

Place the flour and butter in a food processor. Whiz for a few seconds, then add half the beaten egg and continue whizzing. You might need to add a little more egg, but don't add too much – the pastry should just come together. (If making by hand, rub the butter into the flour, then use your hands to bring it together with the egg.) Flatten out the ball of dough to a thickness of about 3cm (1$^1/_4$in), wrap or cover with cling film, and place in the fridge for at least 30 minutes.

When you are ready to roll the pastry, remove from the fridge. Place the pastry between two sheets of cling film, which should be bigger than your tart tin. Using a rolling pin, roll it out until it is no thicker than 3mm ($^1/_8$in). Make sure to keep it round, if the tin is round, and large enough to line the base and sides of the tin.

Removing the top layer of cling film, place the pastry upside-down (cling film side facing up) in the tart tin. Press into the edges, cling film still attached and, using your thumb, 'cut' the pastry on the edge of the tin to give a neat finish. Remove the cling film and pop the pastry in the freezer for at least 10 minutes.

BLIND BAKING
Blind baking is a way of partially cooking a pastry case before adding its filling. Preheat the oven to 180°C (350°F), Gas mark 4. Line the pastry with greaseproof paper when cold (leaving plenty to come up the sides), fill with baking beans or dried pulses (you can use these over and over), and bake for 15–20 minutes, until the pastry feels dry. Remove the paper and beans, brush with a little leftover beaten egg and return to the oven for 2 minutes. Take out of the oven and put to one side while you prepare the filling. This can be easily made a day in advance.

VARIATION

SWEET PASTRY

Use the recipe for savoury pastry but add 25g (1oz) icing sugar to the flour
and butter in the food processor at the start of the method.

Stock Syrup

MAKES 150ML (5FL OZ) / VEGETARIAN

This is the basic stock syrup recipe used for things such as cocktails and poaching fruit.
It keeps indefinitely and it is very handy to have some to hand.

200g (7oz) caster sugar   **200ml (7fl oz) water**

Place the ingredients in a saucepan and bring slowly to the boil, stirring to dissolve
the sugar. When the sugar has dissolved, boil for 2 minutes and allow to cool.

Crème Anglaise

MAKES 500ML (18FL OZ) / VEGETARIAN

This is a classic custard sauce that is delicious poured over a crumble or an apple pie.

500ml (18fl oz) milk   **5 egg yolks**
1 vanilla pod   **100g (4oz) caster sugar**

Bring the milk to the boil with the vanilla pod. In a large bowl, beat the egg
yolks and sugar until pale and thick. Gradually whisk in the hot milk and add the
mixture back into the saucepan. Cook over a very low heat, stirring all the time
with a wooden spoon until the mixture thickens slightly; it should just coat the
back of a spoon. Pour into a jug and serve warm. If you are reheating this, do so
very carefully on a low heat.

Index

ACKNOWLEDGEMENTS

I would like to thank all my lovely family and friends for their undying support.

A huge thank you goes to my amazing agents at Limelight Management, Fiona Lindsay and Linda Shanks, and also to Mary Bekhait.

At Collins, Jenny Heller and Emma Callery got me through months of writing, with constant encouraging and cajoling (not to mention bringing a whole new meaning to the word 'patience').

A big thanks, too, for the gorgeous photography to Peter Cassidy and Cristian Barnett, assisted by Claire Davies; to Felicity Barnum-Bobb for her glorious food styling; to Jim, Emma, Katrin, Saskia and Alex at Smith & Gilmour for their beautiful book design; and to Emma Ewbank for designing the lovely cover. Thank you also to Alastair Laing, Kerenza Swift, Iona Murray and make-up artist Liz McCarthy.

Enormous gratitude also to David Hare, Brian Walsh, Billy Keady, Ray de Brún, Anna Ní Mhaonaigh, Emma Brennan, Sally Walker, Neil McLaughlan, Kevin Lavelle, Shermin Mustafa and Caragh Thompson, without whom the filming of the series would not have happened. A very big thanks as well to Beth and Gerry Cuddigan for letting us live in their lovely house while our own home was turned into a film studio!

Finally, thank you to our lovely friends who came and happily drank and ate with us for the book photos: Lucy, Jasper, Helena, Francesca and Max Wight and Thomas Smiddy.